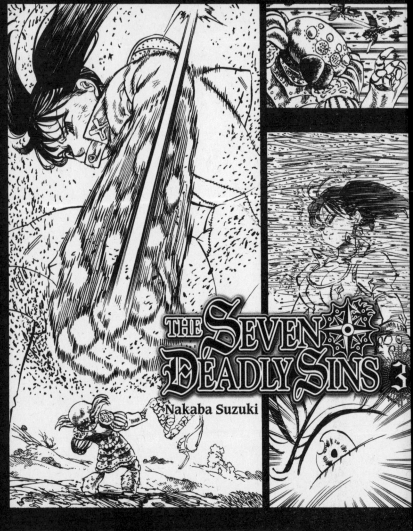

THE SEVEN DEADLY SINS 3

Nakaba Suzuki

BOOM

nakaba suzuki presents

CONTENTS

BOAR HAT

The Seven Deadly Sins

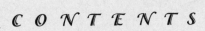

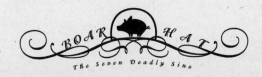

THE SEVEN DEADLY SINS

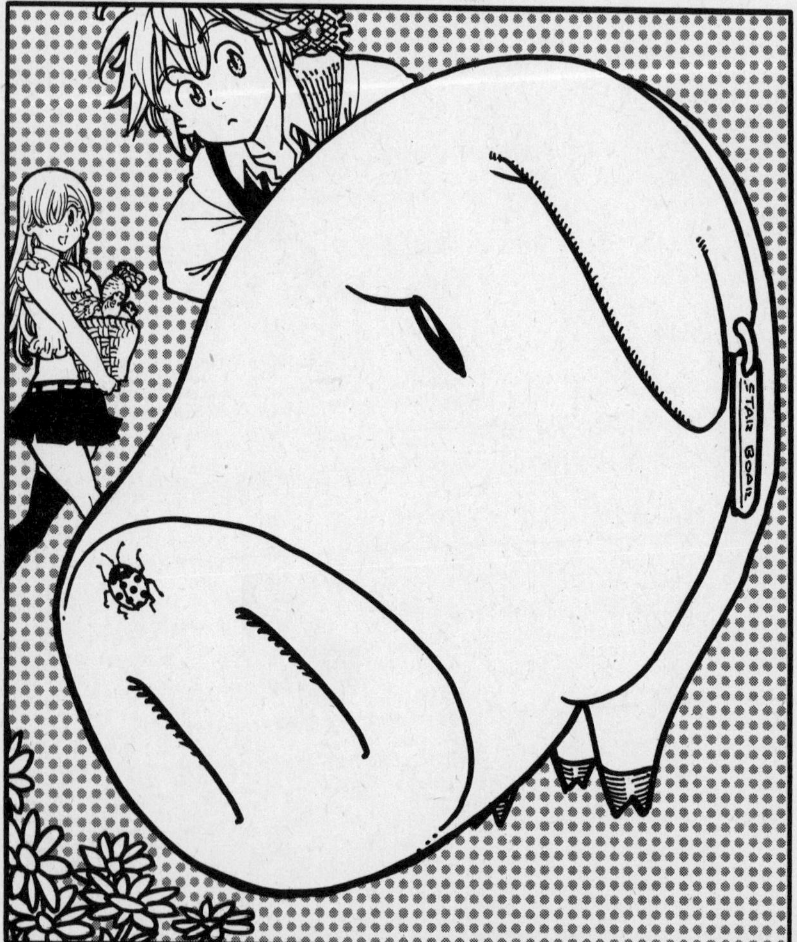
STAR BOAR

Chapter 15 - Caught In the Reunion

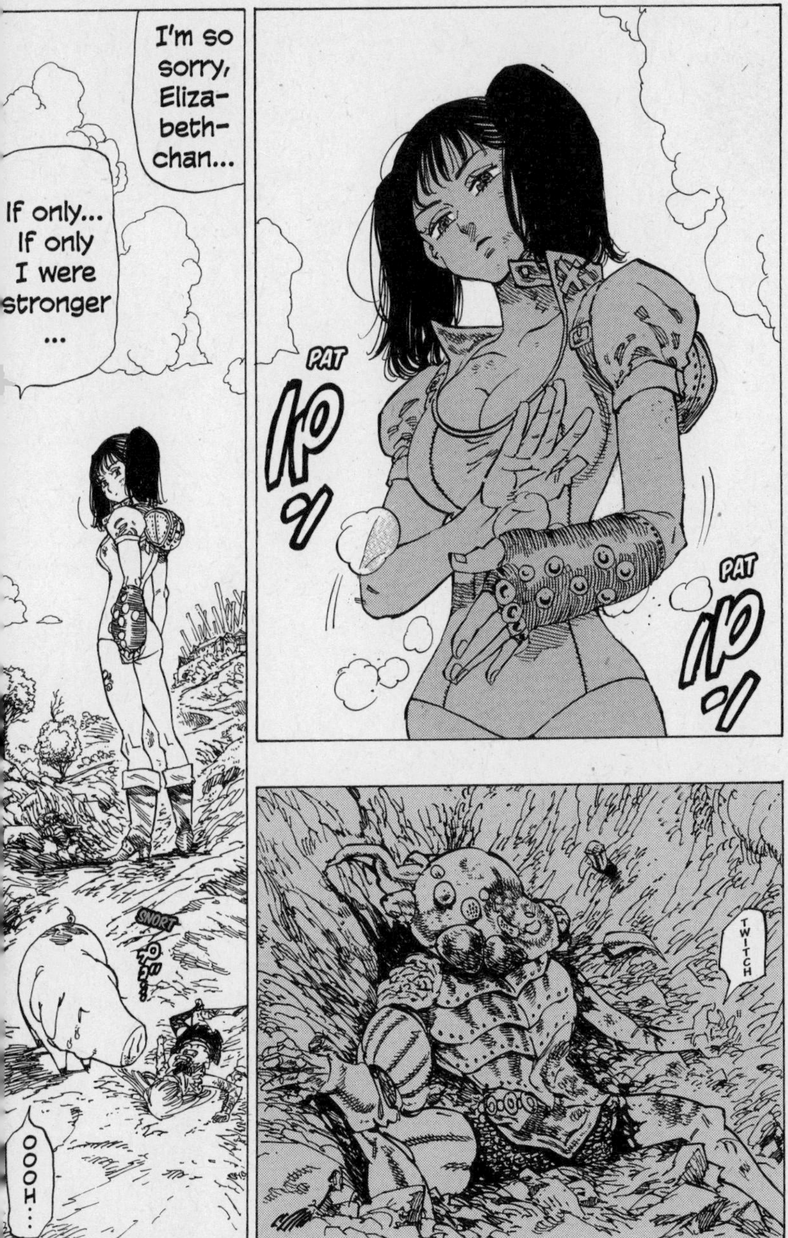
PAT
PAT
TWITCH
I'm so sorry, Eliza-beth-chan...
If only... If only I were stronger ...
SNORT
OOOH...

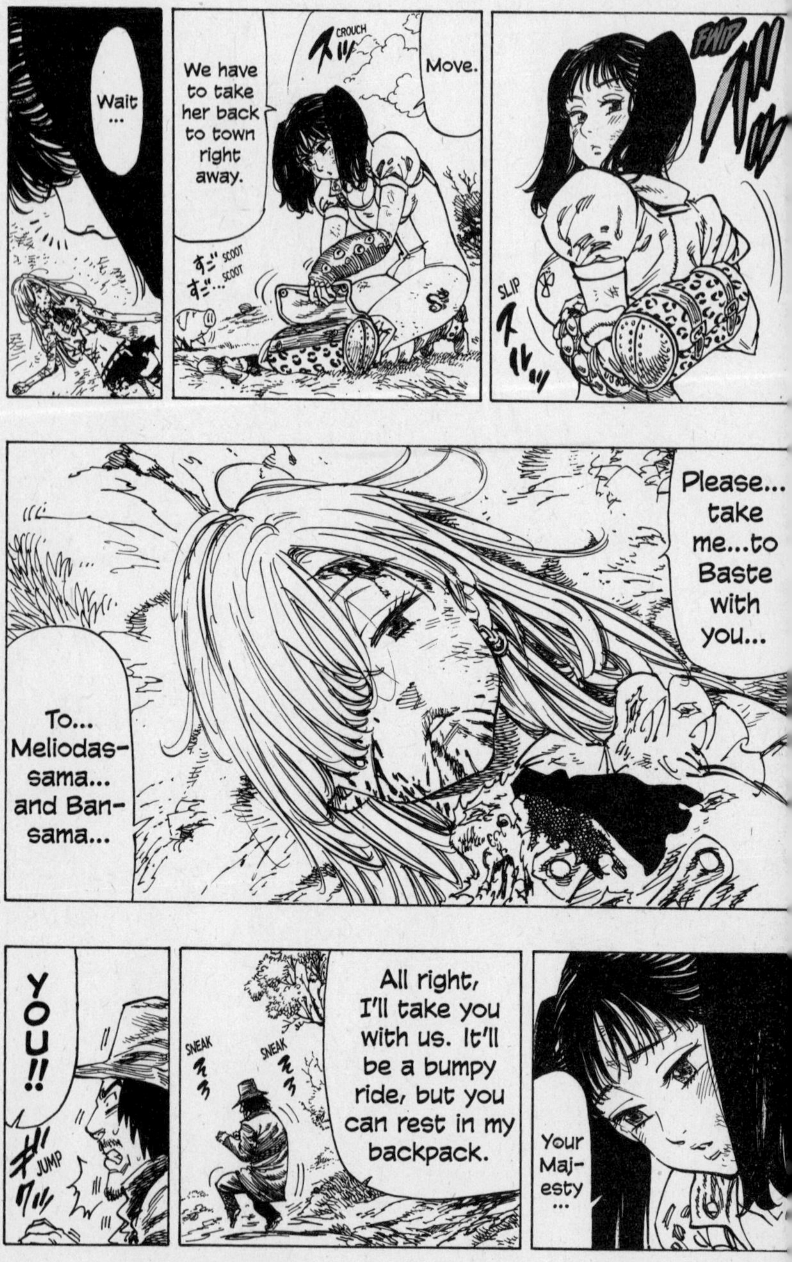
FWIP
SLIP
Move.
CROUCH
We have to take her back to town right away.
SCOOT
SCOOT
Wait ...
Please... take me...to Baste with you...
To... Meliodas-sama... and Ban-sama...
Your Maj-esty ...
All right, I'll take you with us. It'll be a bumpy ride, but you can rest in my backpack.
SNEAK
SNEAK
YOU!!
JUMP

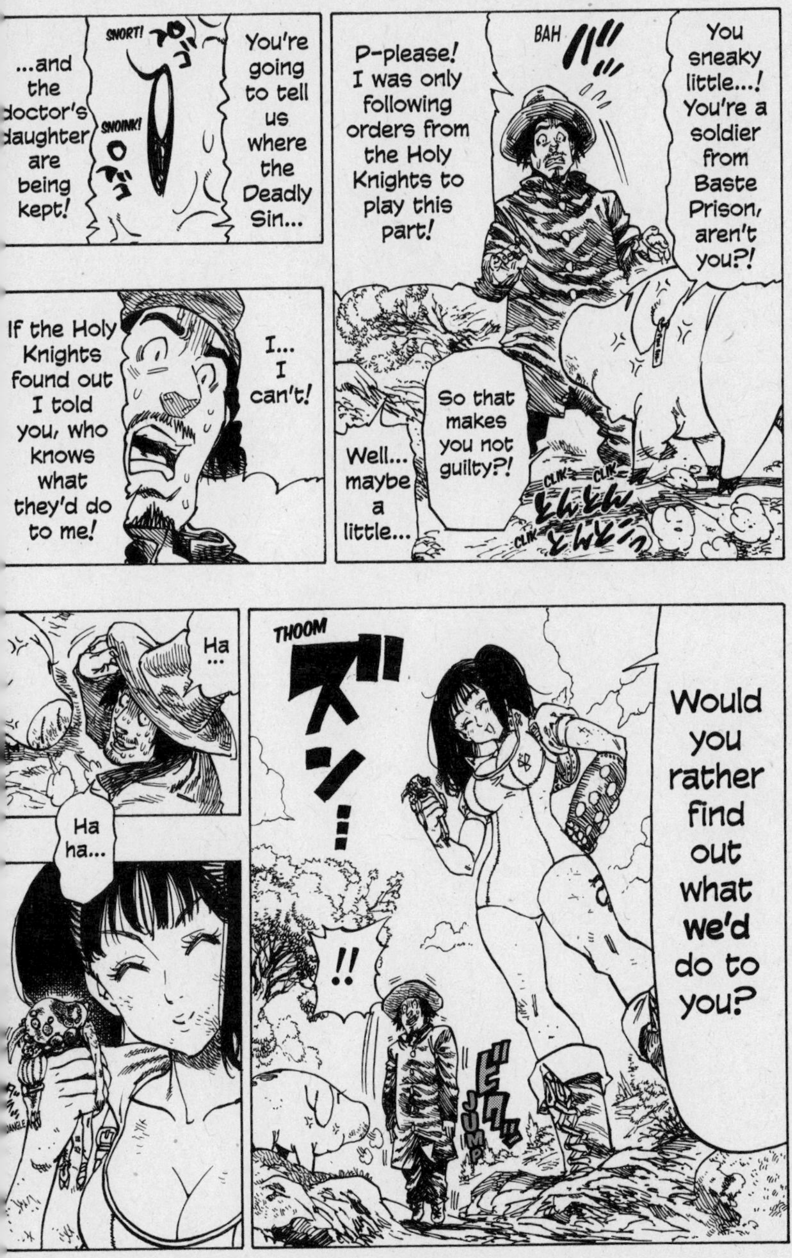

You sneaky little...! You're a soldier from Baste Prison, aren't you?!
BAH
P-please! I was only following orders from the Holy Knights to play this part!
So that makes you not guilty?!
Well... maybe a little...
CLIK CLIK
CLIK
You're going to tell us where the Deadly Sin...
SNORT!
SNOINK!
...and the doctor's daughter are being kept!
I... I can't!
If the Holy Knights found out I told you, who knows what they'd do to me!
Would you rather find out what we'd do to you?
THOOM
!!
JUMP
Ha...
Ha ha...
DANGLE

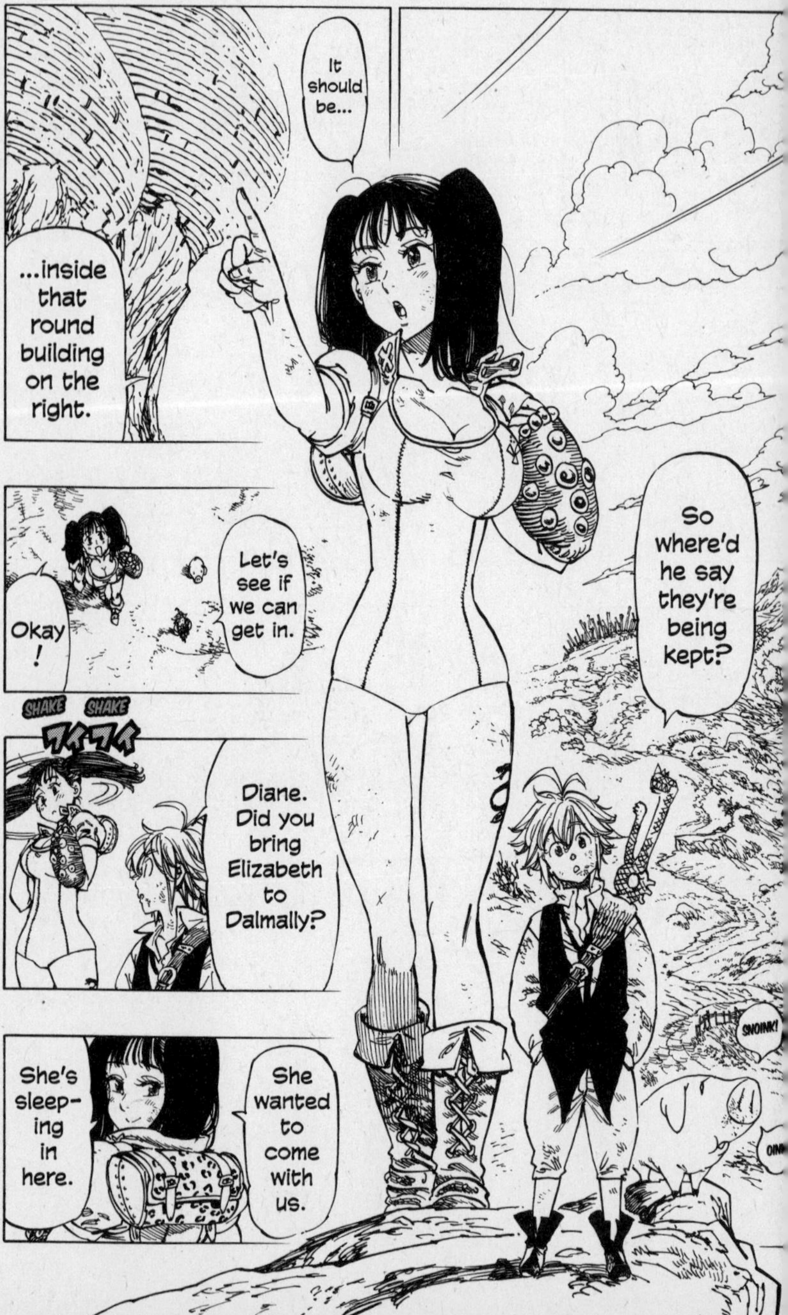

So where'd he say they're being kept?
SNOINK!
It should be...
...inside that round building on the right.
Let's see if we can get in.
Okay!
SHAKE SHAKE
Diane. Did you bring Elizabeth to Dalmally?
She wanted to come with us.
She's sleeping in here.

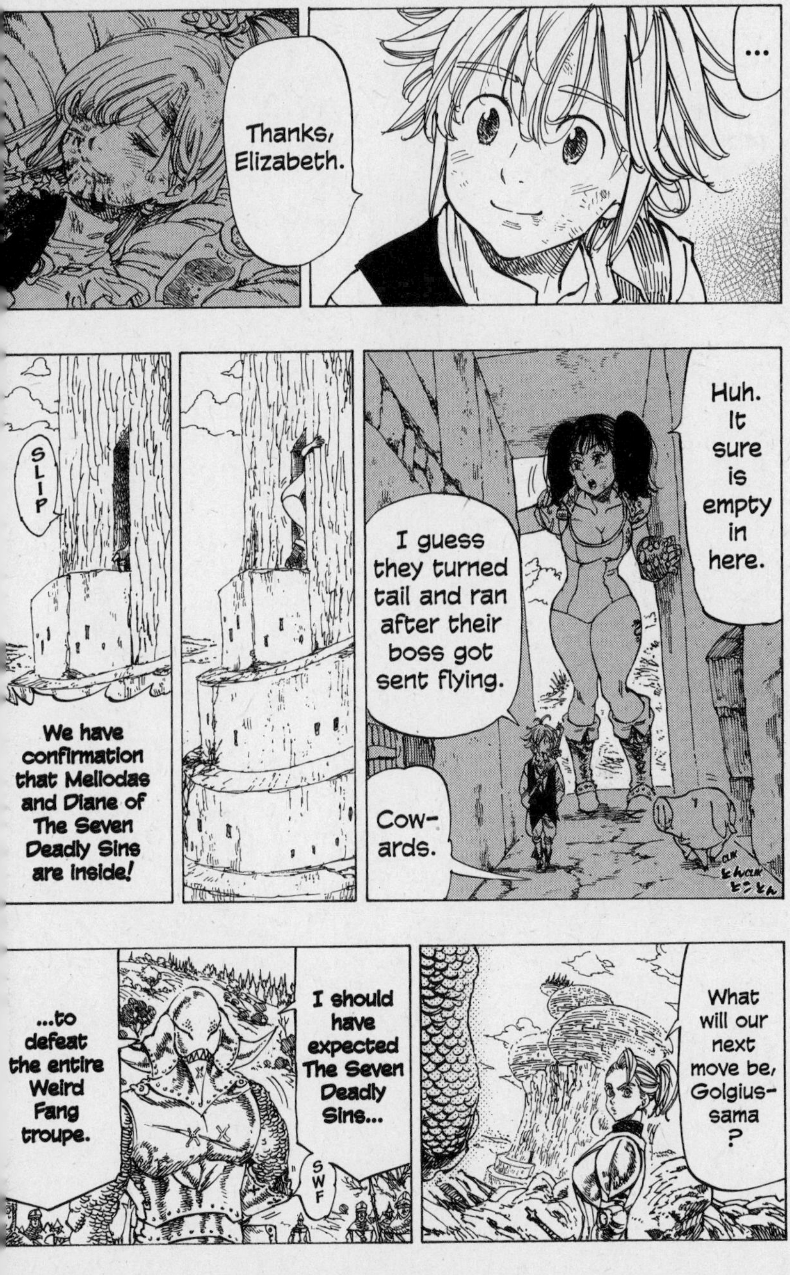
...
Thanks, Elizabeth.
Huh. It sure is empty in here.
I guess they turned tail and ran after their boss got sent flying.
Cow-ards.
SLIP
We have confirmation that Meliodas and Diane of The Seven Deadly Sins are inside!
What will our next move be, Golgius-sama?
I should have expected The Seven Deadly Sins...
...to defeat the entire Weird Fang troupe.
SWF

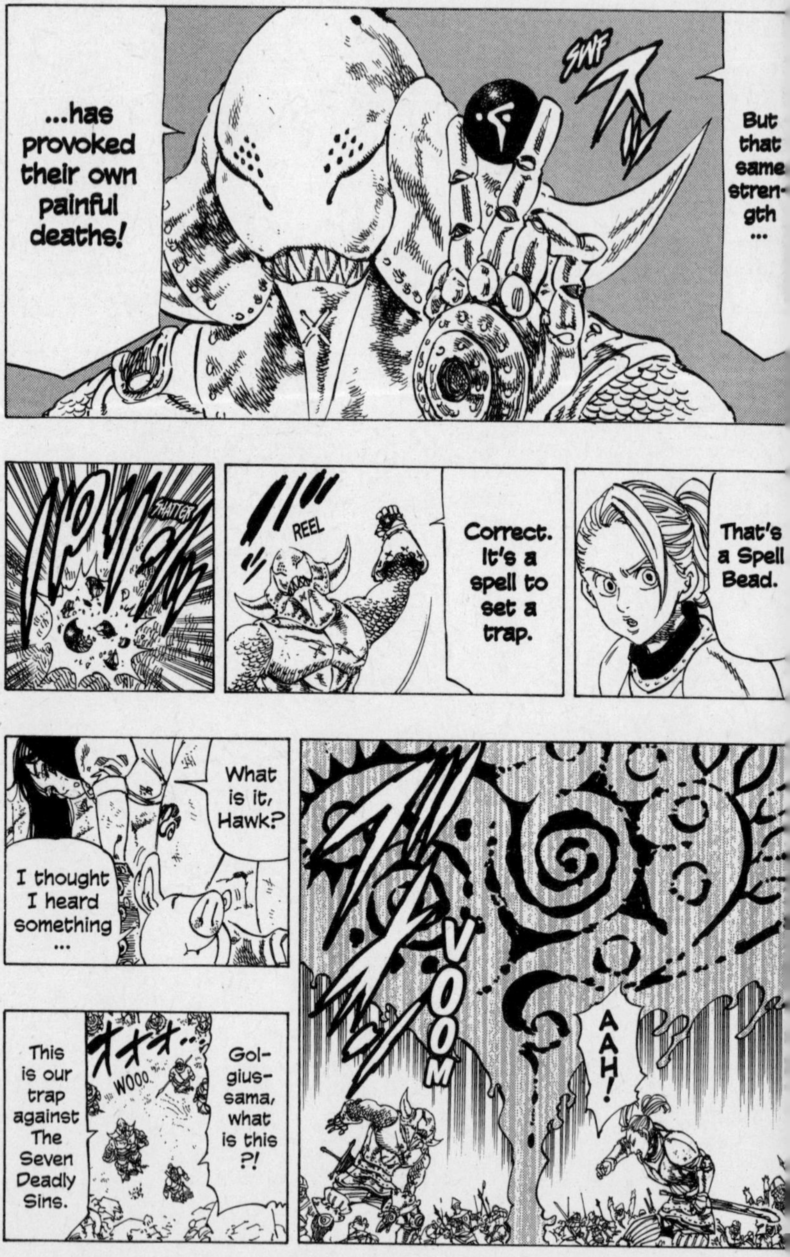

But that same strength ...
SWF
...has provoked their own painful deaths!
That's a Spell Bead.
Correct. It's a spell to set a trap.
REEL
SHATTER
VOOM
AAH!
What is it, Hawk?
I thought I heard something ...
Golgius-sama, what is this?!
WOOO
オオオ…
This is our trap against The Seven Deadly Sins.

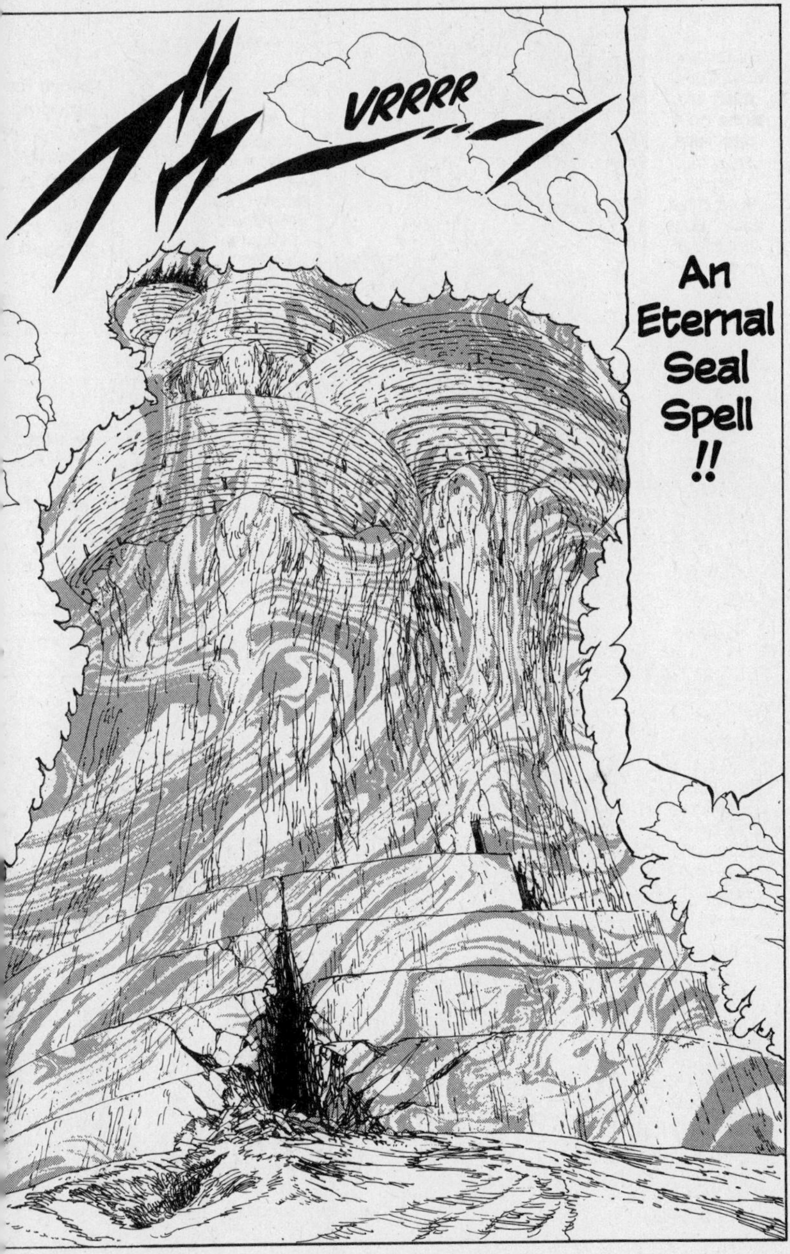
An Eternal Seal Spell !!
VRRRR

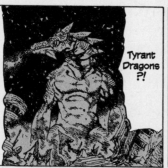

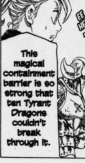

A last resort for stopping The Seven Deadly Sins in case they got through.
EE HEE!
This magical containment barrier is so strong that ten Tyrant Dragons couldn't break through it.
Tyrant Dragons?!
Beasts so violent that even one alone could decimate an entire village... And this could withstand ten of those?!
In other words, the one path left for our sorry friends in there...
...is to die an agonizing death as they rot away within their cage!
It's too small for me to go any farther.
S... save me!!
?!
What's a girl doing in here?
TMP
TMP
I... I'm the daughter of Dalmally's doctor and I've been taken here against my will!
Who?
Oh! Then you're...
TMP
TMP
B-but first! There's a legendary criminal in there who just killed a Holy Knight!

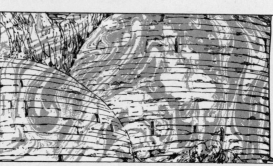

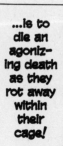

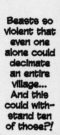

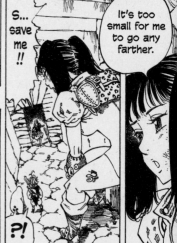

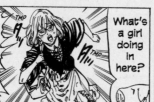

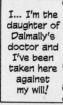

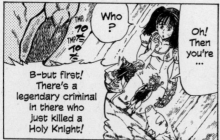

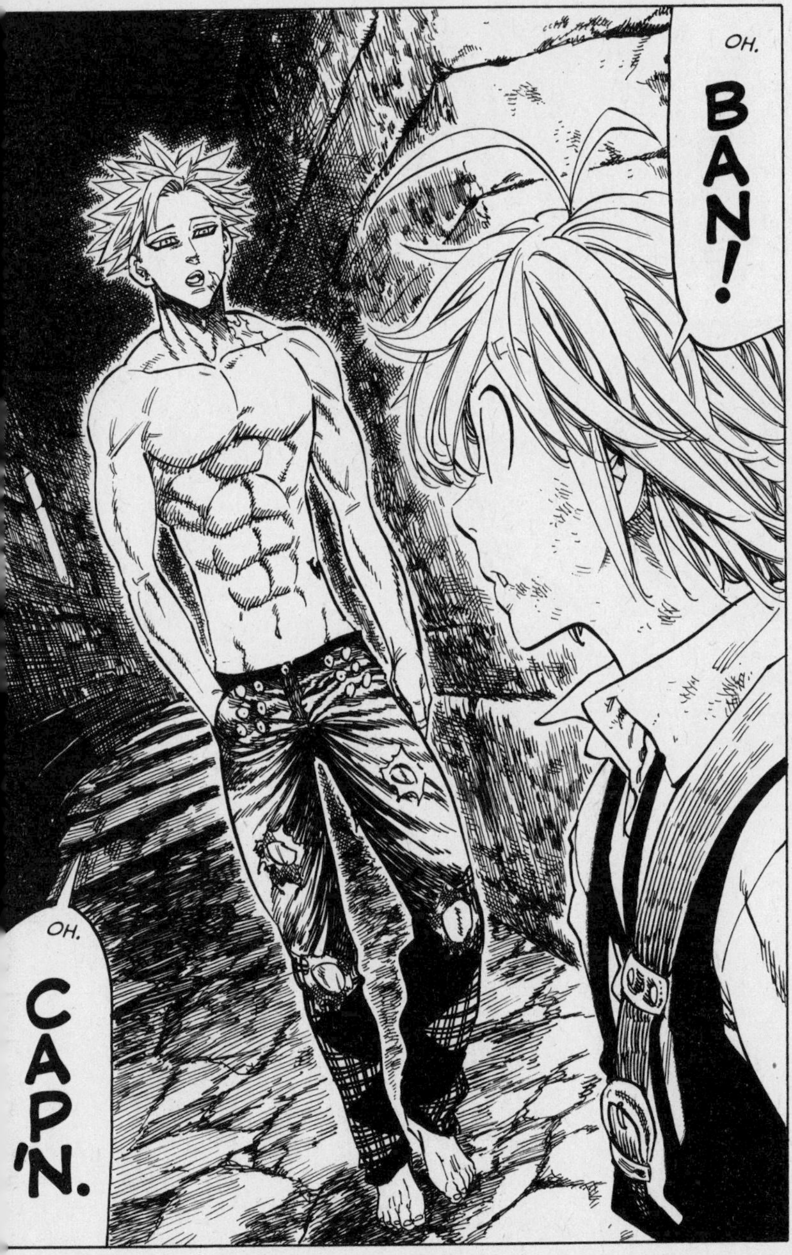
OH. BAN!
OH. CAP'N.

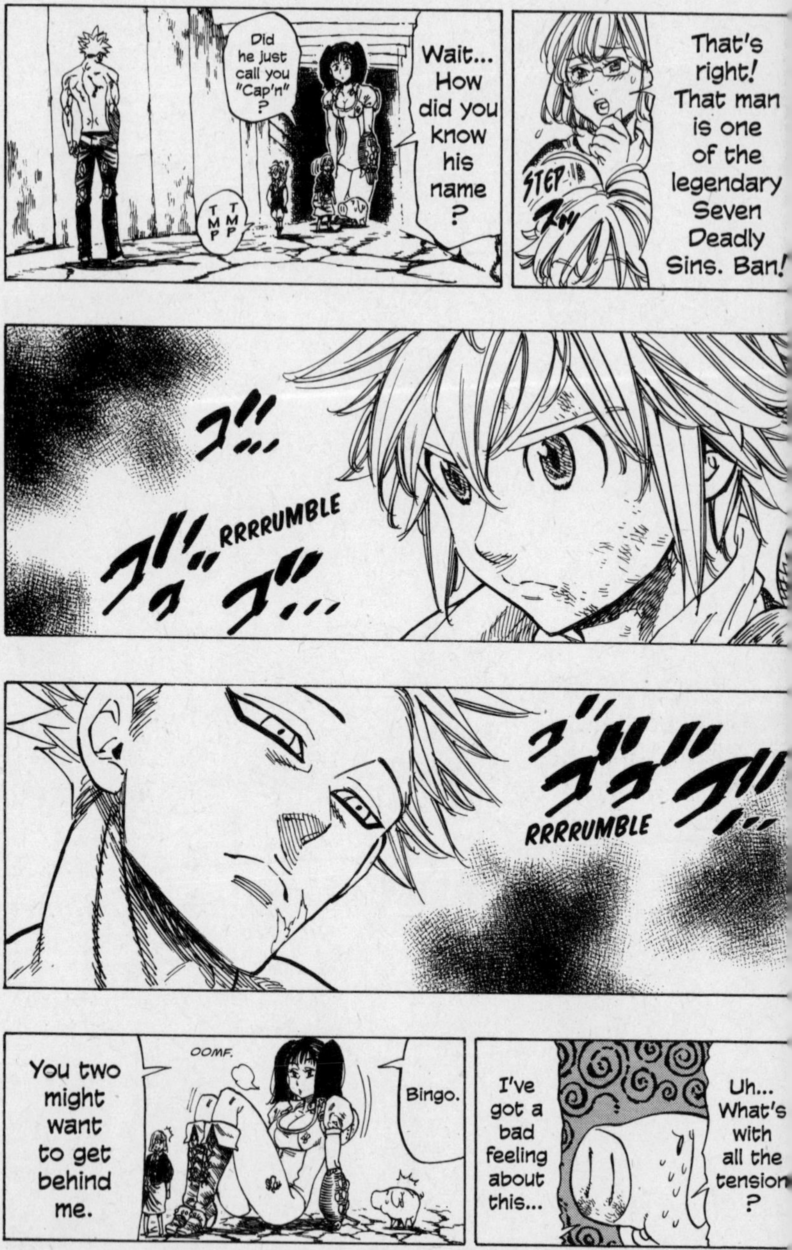
That's right! That man is one of the legendary Seven Deadly Sins. Ban!
STEP
Wait... How did you know his name?
Did he just call you "Cap'n"?
TMP TMP
RRRRUMBLE
RRRRUMBLE
Uh... What's with all the tension?
I've got a bad feeling about this...
Bingo.
OOMF.
You two might want to get behind me.

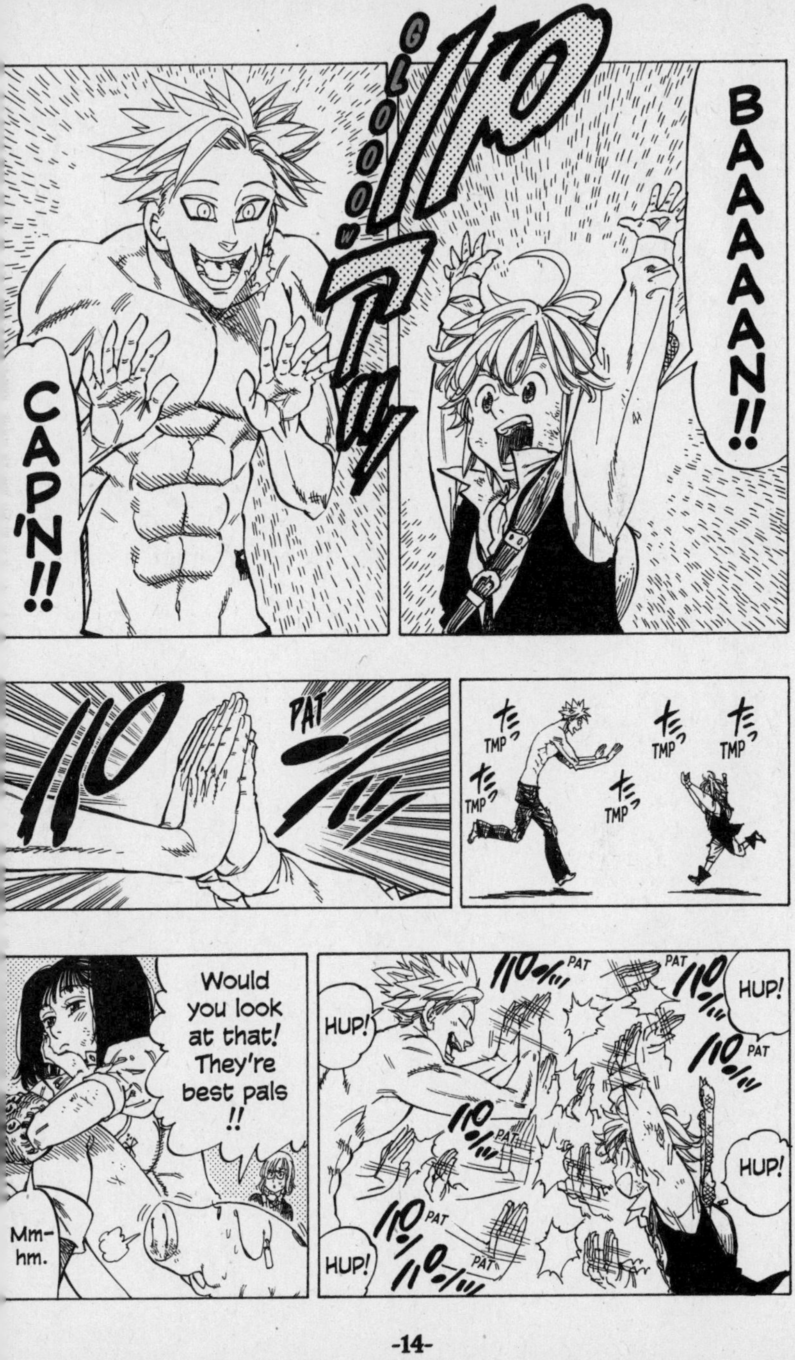
BAAAAAN!!
GLOOOW
CAP'N!!
TMP
TMP
TMP
TMP
TMP
PAT
HUP!
PAT
PAT
HUP!
HUP!
PAT
PAT
PAT
HUP!
HUP!
Would you look at that! They're best pals!!
Mm-hm.

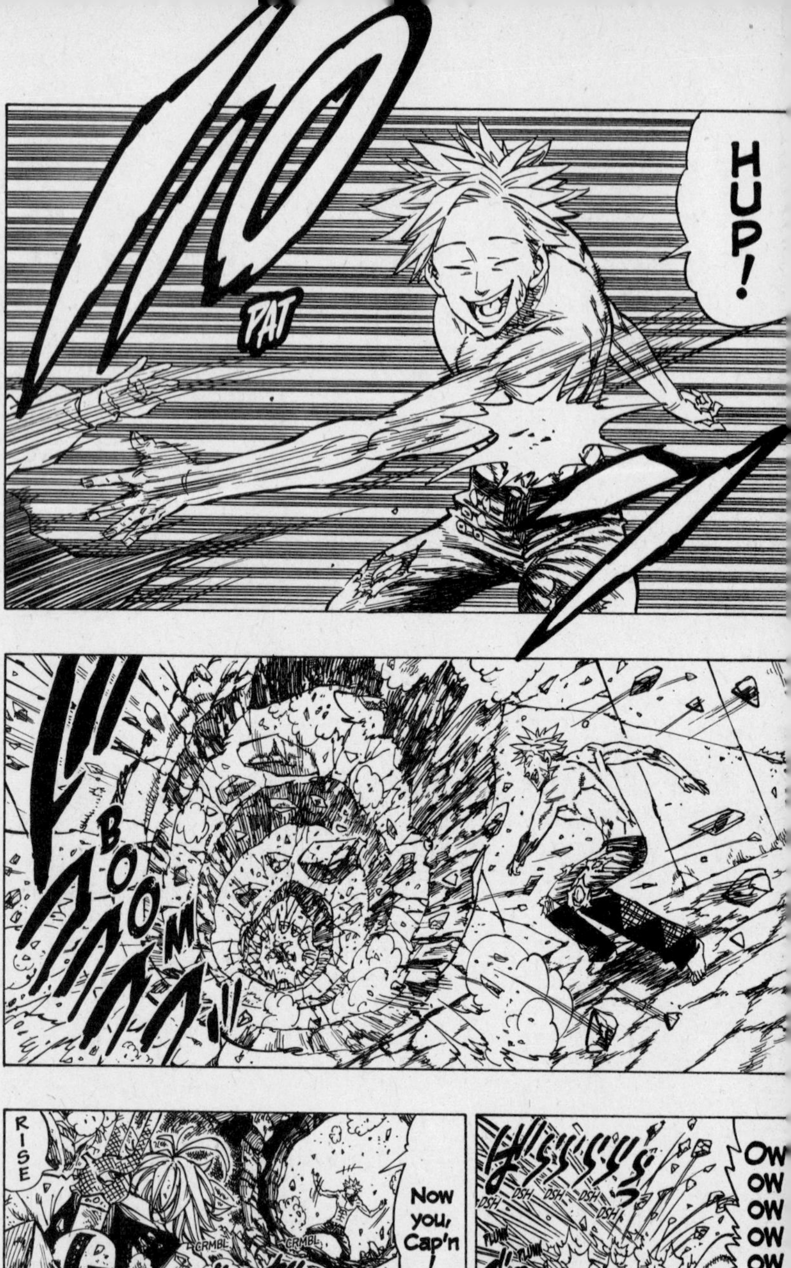
HUP!
PAT
BOOM!!
OWOWOWOWOWOW!
DSH DSH DSH DSH DSH
FLUNK FLUNK
Now you, Cap'n!
CRMBL CRMBL
RISE

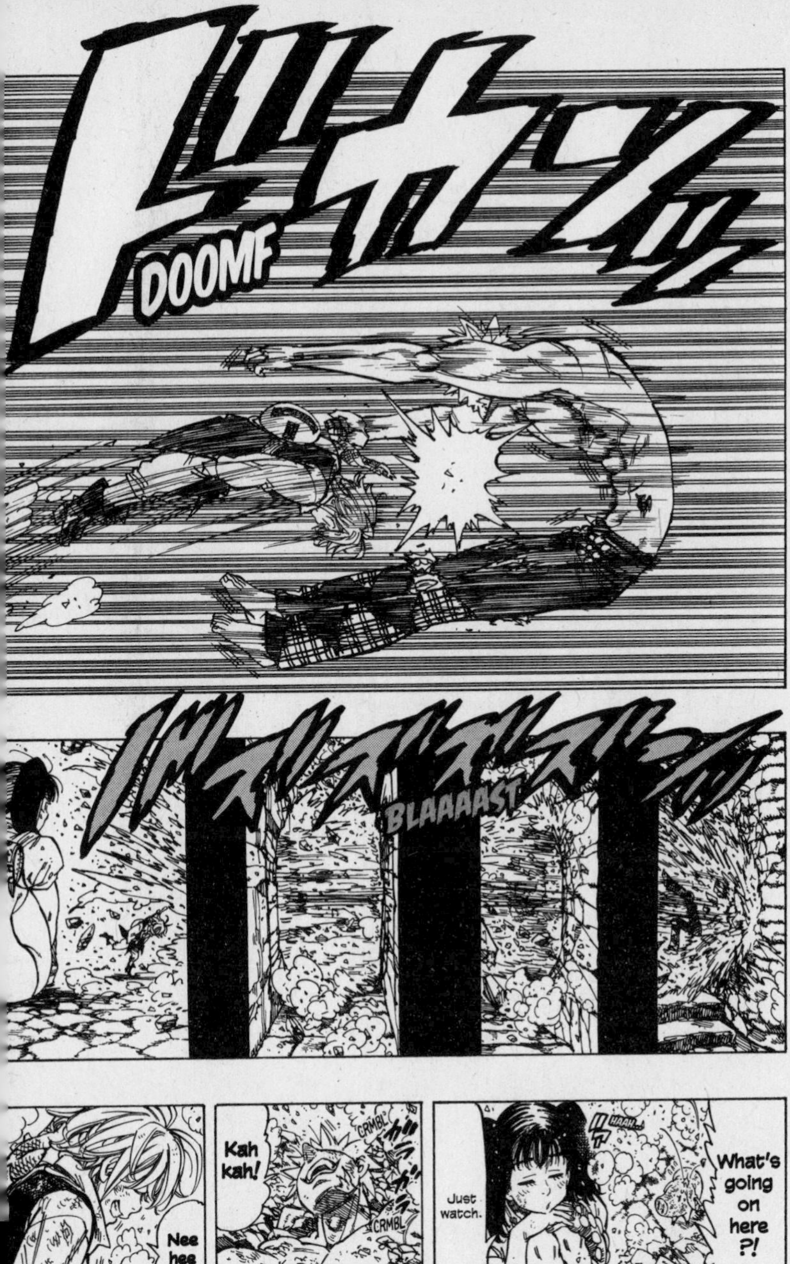
DOOMF
BLAAAAST
HAAH...
What's going on here ?!
Just watch.
CRMBL
Kah kah!
CRMBL
Nee hee hee.

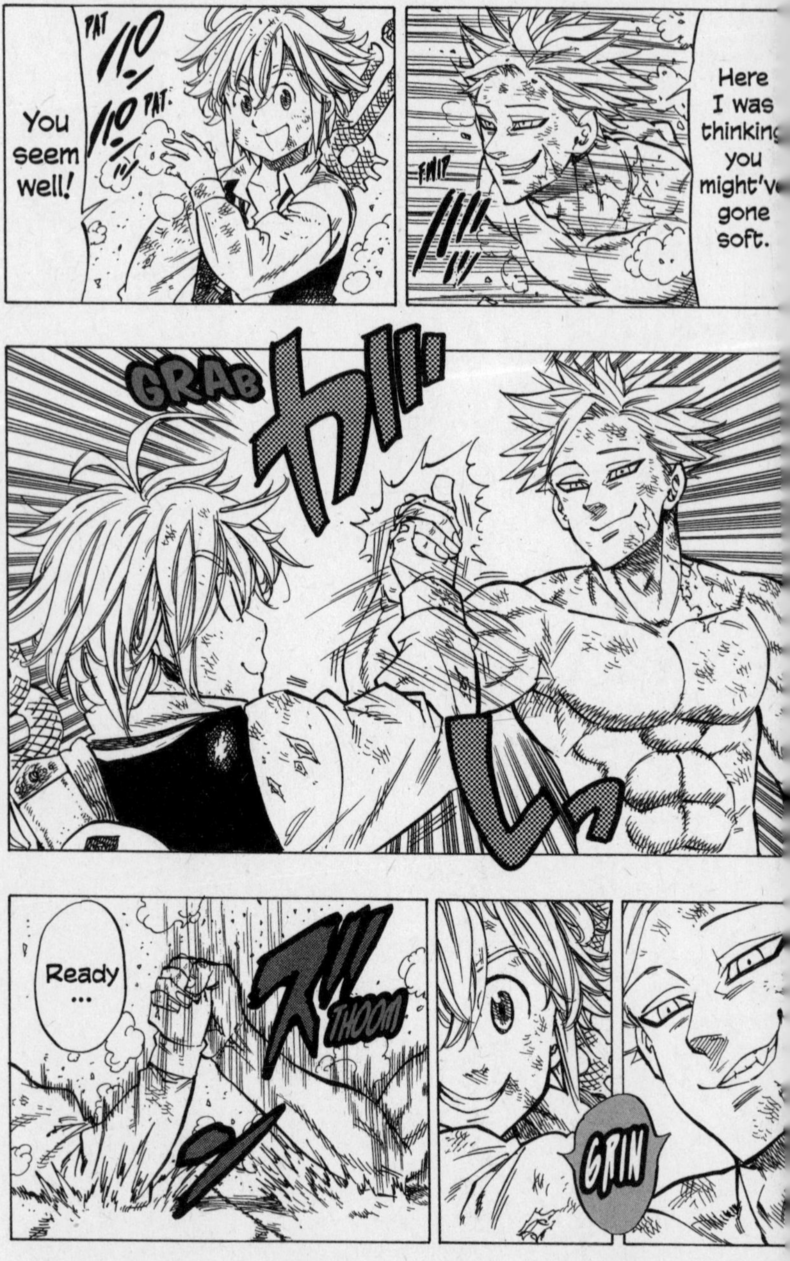
FWIP
Here I was thinking you might've gone soft.
PAT
PAT
You seem well!
GRAB
Ready...
THOOM
GRIN

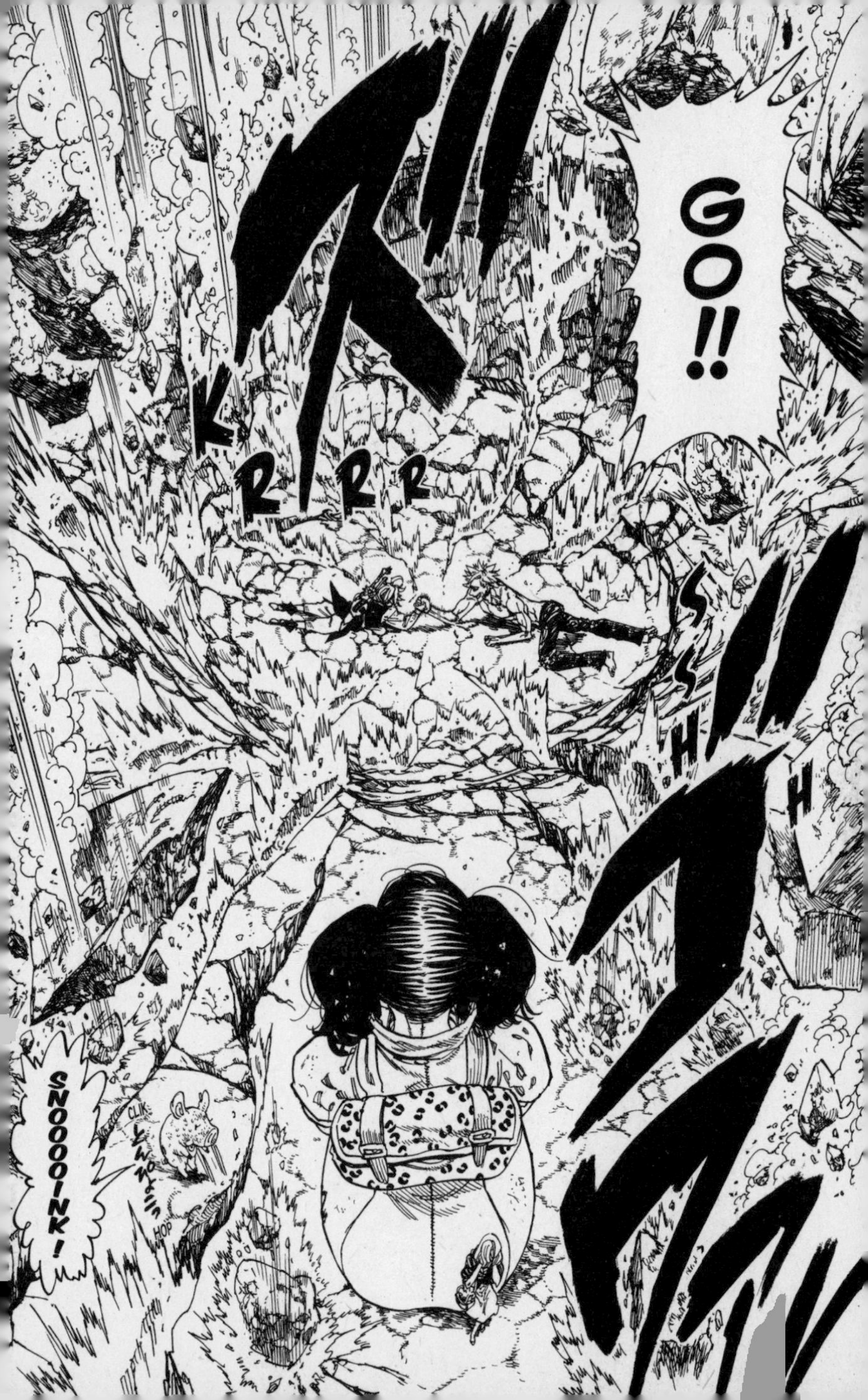
GO!!
KRRRR
SSHH
SNOOOOINK!
CLIK
YAWN
HOP

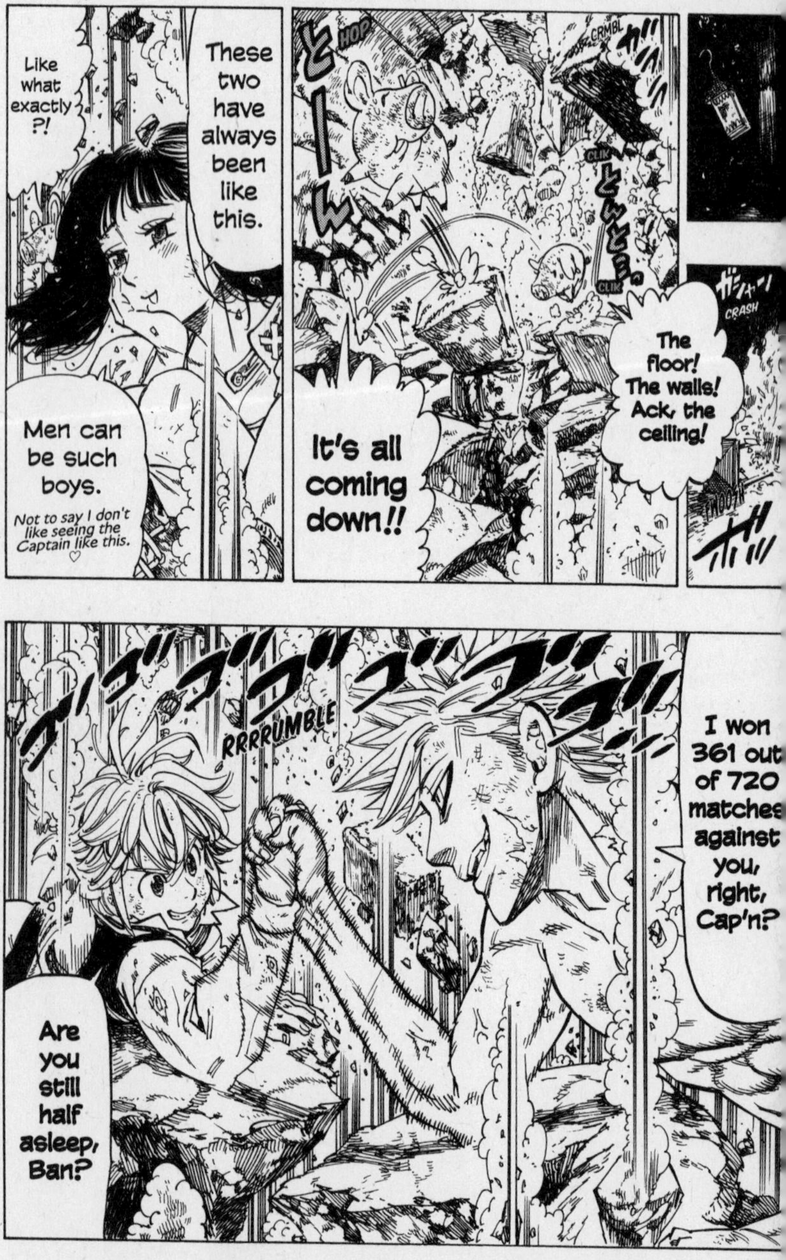
CRASH
The floor! The walls! Ack, the ceiling!
CRMBL
HOP
CLIK
CLIK
It's all coming down!!
These two have always been like this.
Like what exactly?!
Men can be such boys.
Not to say I don't like seeing the Captain like this. ♡
I won 361 out of 720 matches against you, right, Cap'n?
RRRUMBLE
Are you still half asleep, Ban?

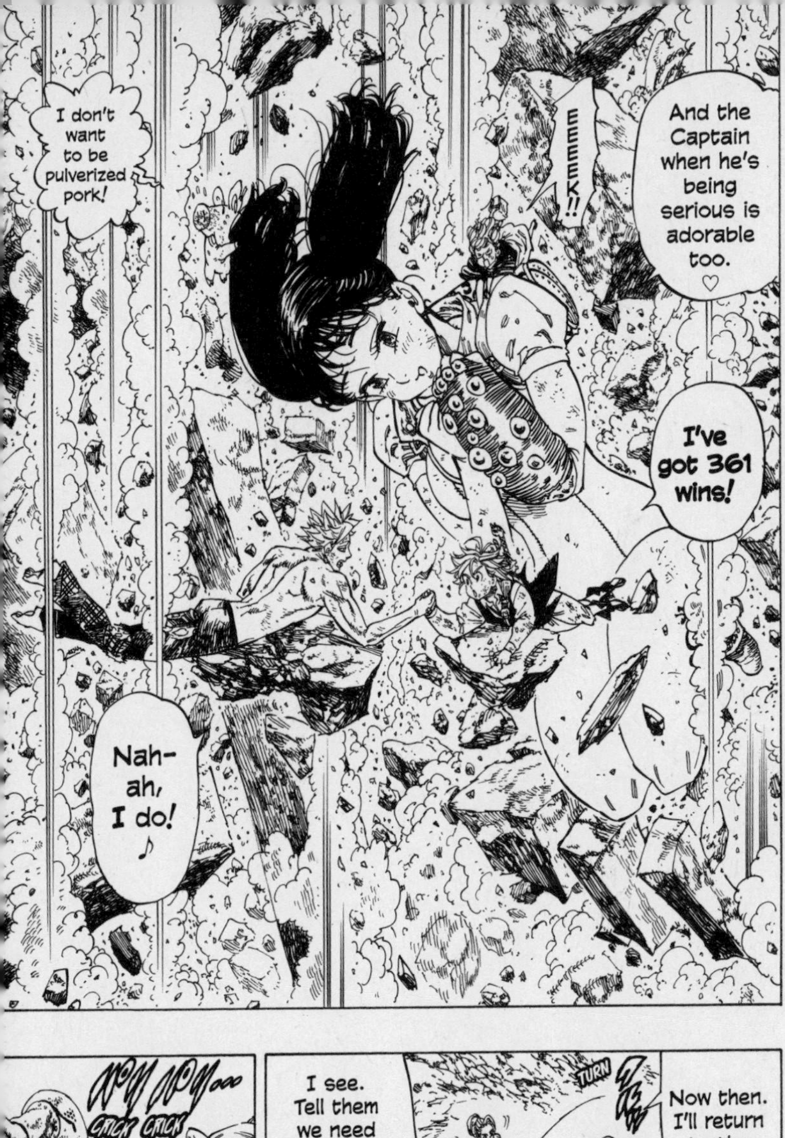
And the Captain when he's being serious is adorable too. ♡
EEEEK!!
I don't want to be pulverized pork!
I've got 361 wins!
Nah-ah, I do! ♪
TURN
Now then. I'll return to the kingdom to report to the higher-ups.
CLANG
I see. Tell them we need no longer fear The Seven Deadly Sins reuniting again!
CRICK CRICK
?

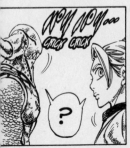

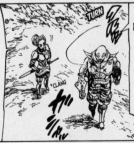

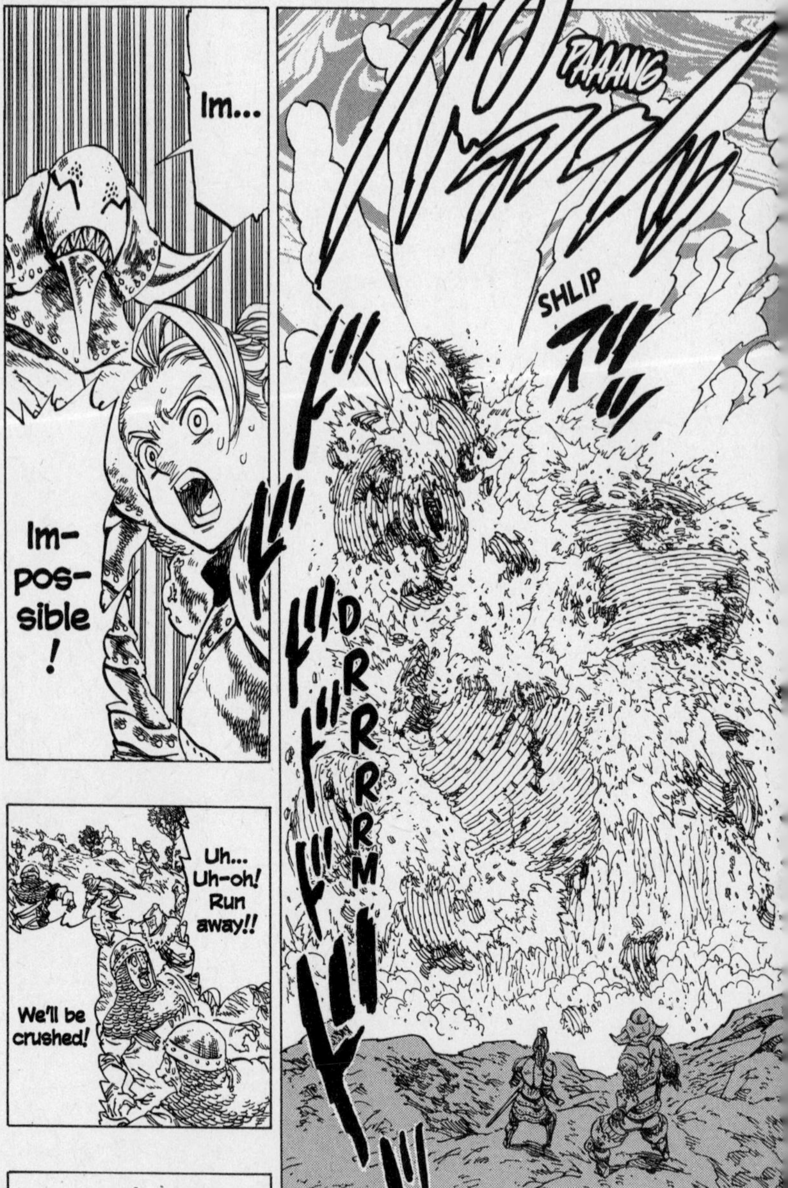
PAAANG
SHLIP
DRRRRM
Im...
Im-pos-sible!
Uh... Uh-oh! Run away!!
We'll be crushed!
. . . .

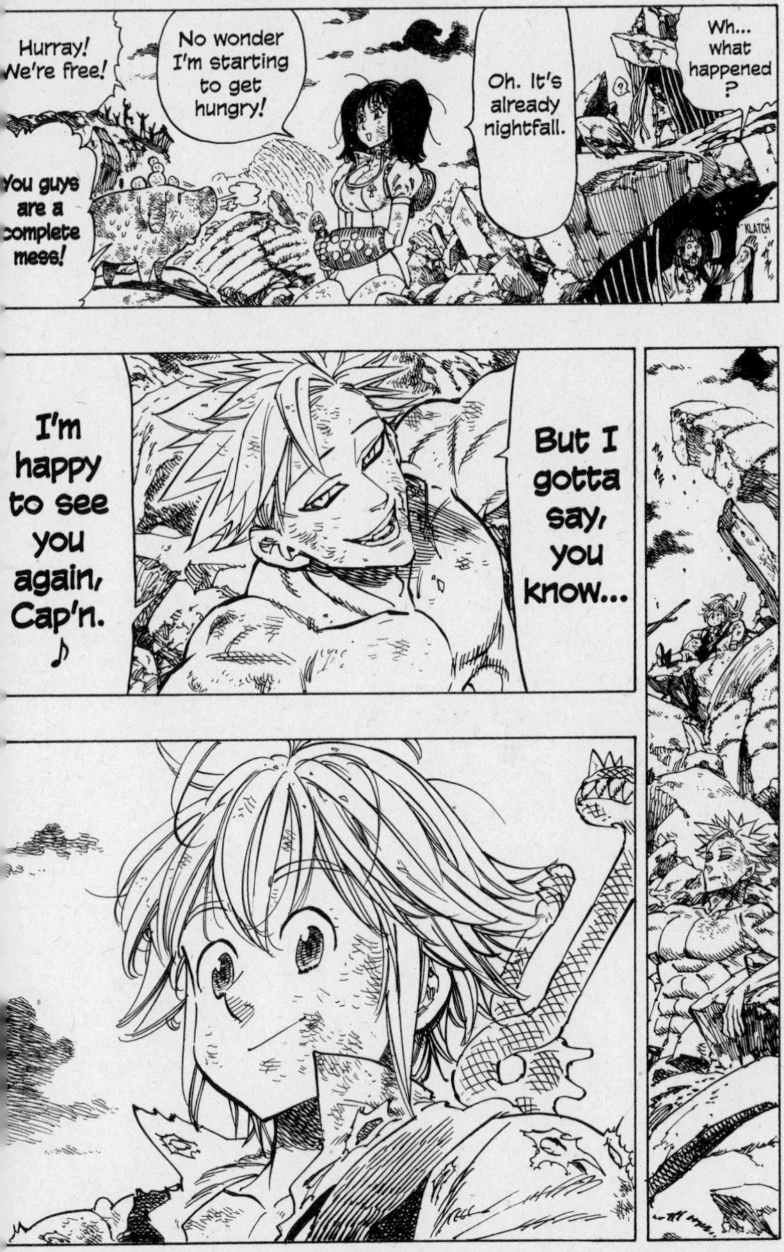
Wh... what happened ?
KLATCH
Oh. It's already nightfall.
No wonder I'm starting to get hungry!
Hurray! We're free!
You guys are a complete mess!
But I gotta say, you know...
I'm happy to see you again, Cap'n. ♪

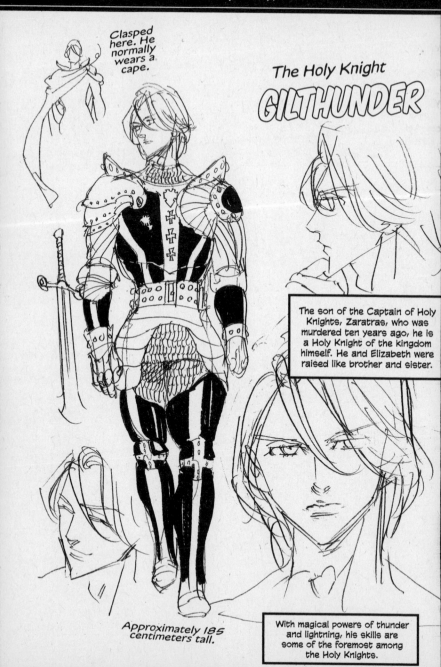

Clasped here. He normally wears a cape.

The Holy Knight
GILTHUNDER

The son of the Captain of Holy Knights, Zaratras, who was murdered ten years ago, he is a Holy Knight of the kingdom himself. He and Elizabeth were raised like brother and sister.

Approximately 185 centimeters tall.

With magical powers of thunder and lightning, his skills are some of the foremost among the Holy Knights.

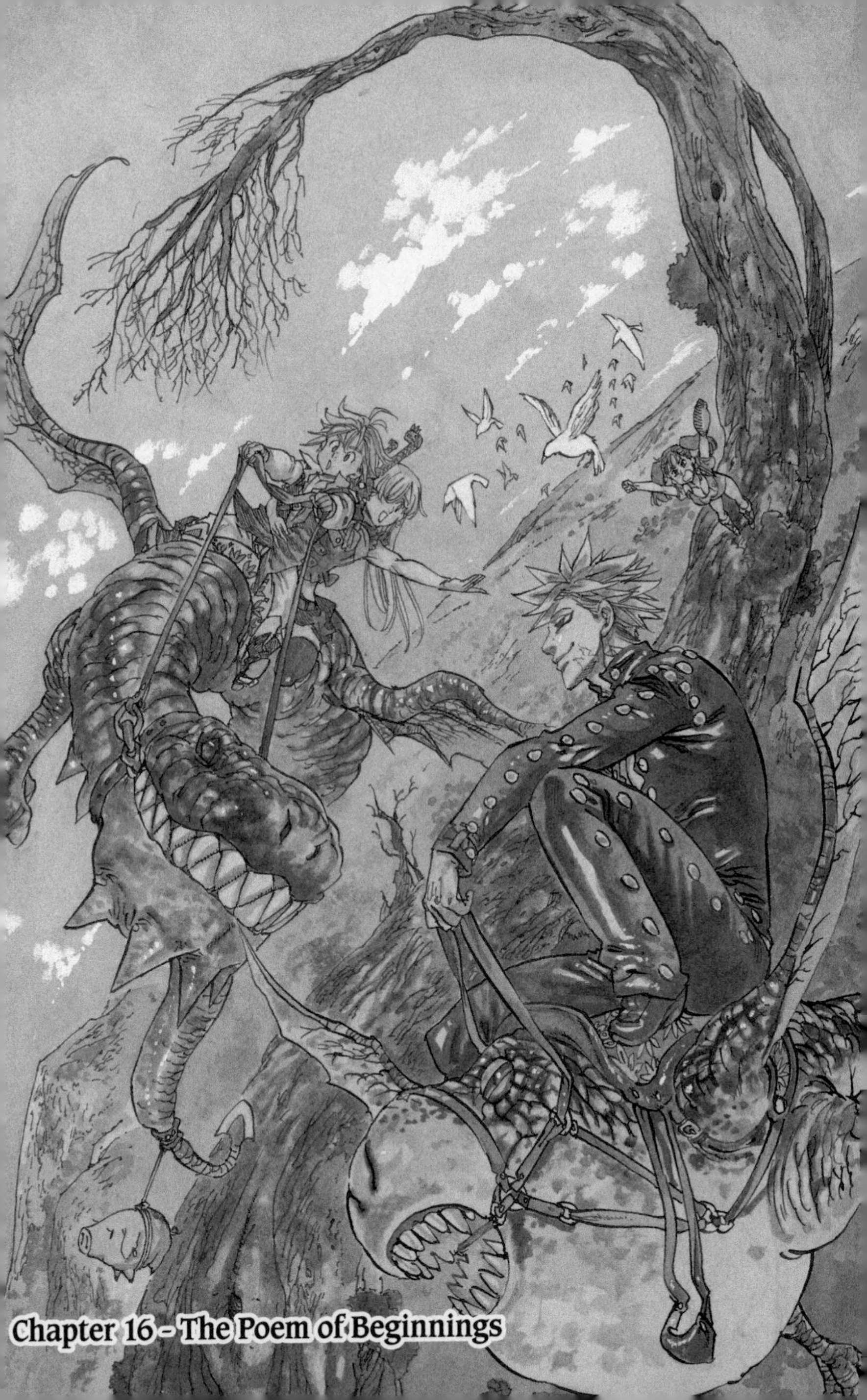

Chapter 16 - The Poem of Beginnings

Baste Prison is no more!

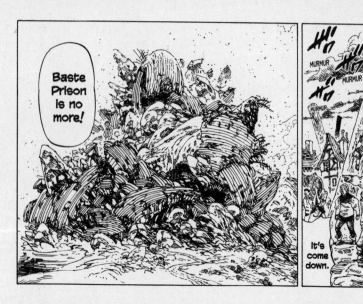

N... No way!

MURMUR
MURMUR
MURMUR
MURMUR

It's come down.

WAAAAH!

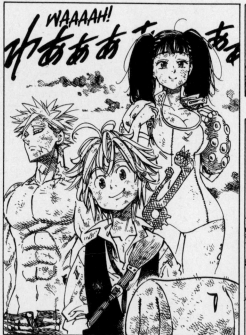

Is that...

Some people are coming this way!

And here come our men who were locked up for resisting the Holy Knights!

...Sennett?!

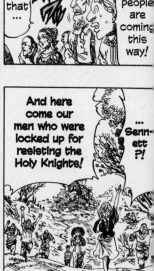

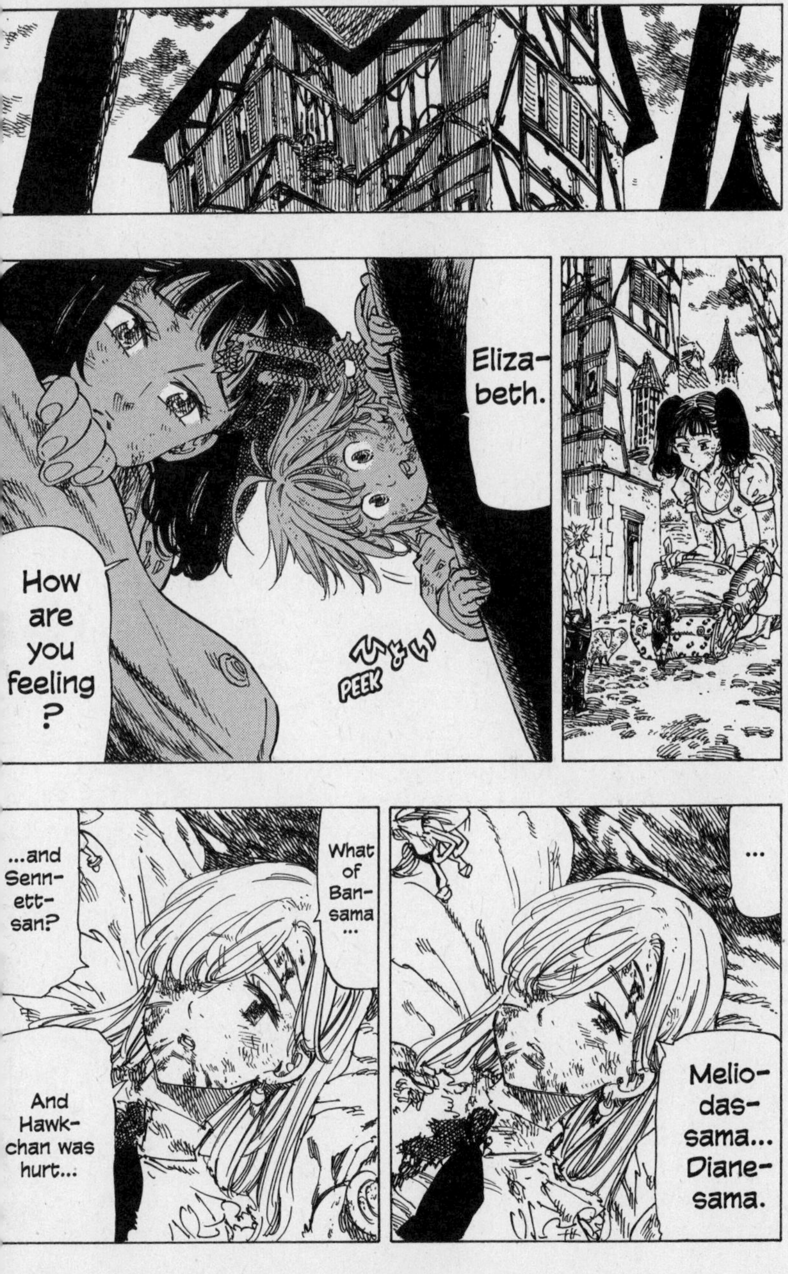
Eliza-beth.
ひょい
PEEK
How are you feeling?
...
Melio-das-sama... Diane-sama.
What of Ban-sama...
...and Senn-ett-san?
And Hawk-chan was hurt...

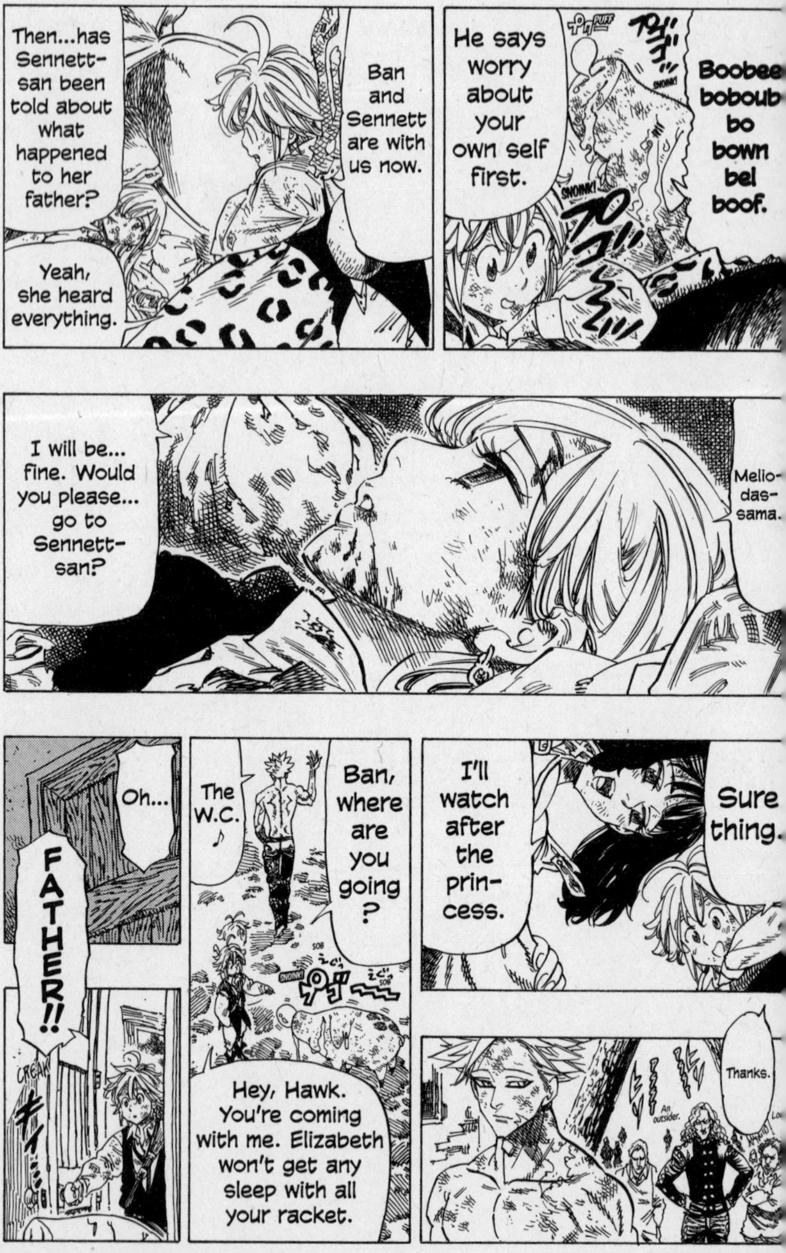
PUFF
SNOINK!
Boobee boboub bo bown bel boof.
SNOINK!
He says worry about your own self first.
Ban and Sennett are with us now.
Then...has Sennett-san been told about what happened to her father?
Yeah, she heard everything.
Melio-das-sama.
I will be... fine. Would you please... go to Sennett-san?
Sure thing.
I'll watch after the prin-cess.
Thanks.
An outsider.
Ban, where are you going?
The W.C. ♪
SOB
SNOINK!
SOB
Hey, Hawk. You're coming with me. Elizabeth won't get any sleep with all your racket.
Oh...
FATHER!!
CREAK

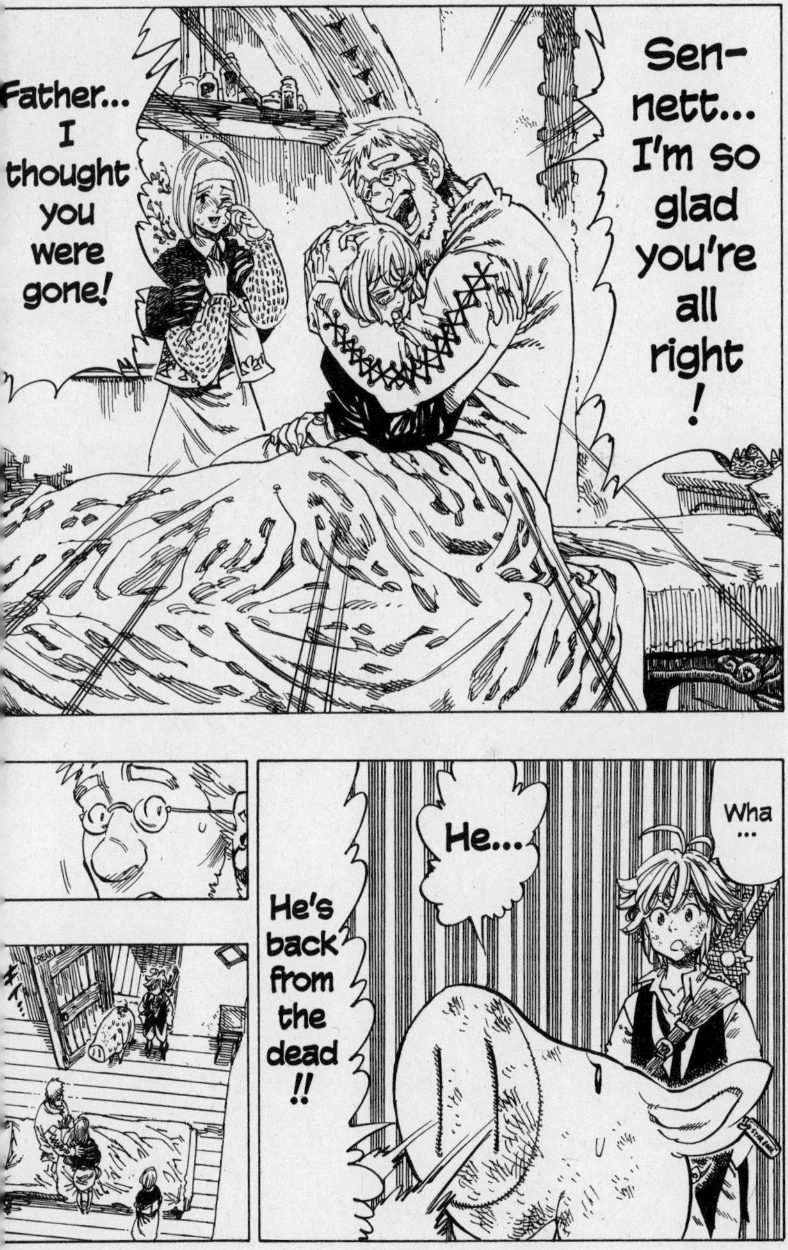
Sen-nett... I'm so glad you're all right!
Father... I thought you were gone!
Wha...
He...
He's back from the dead!!
CREAK

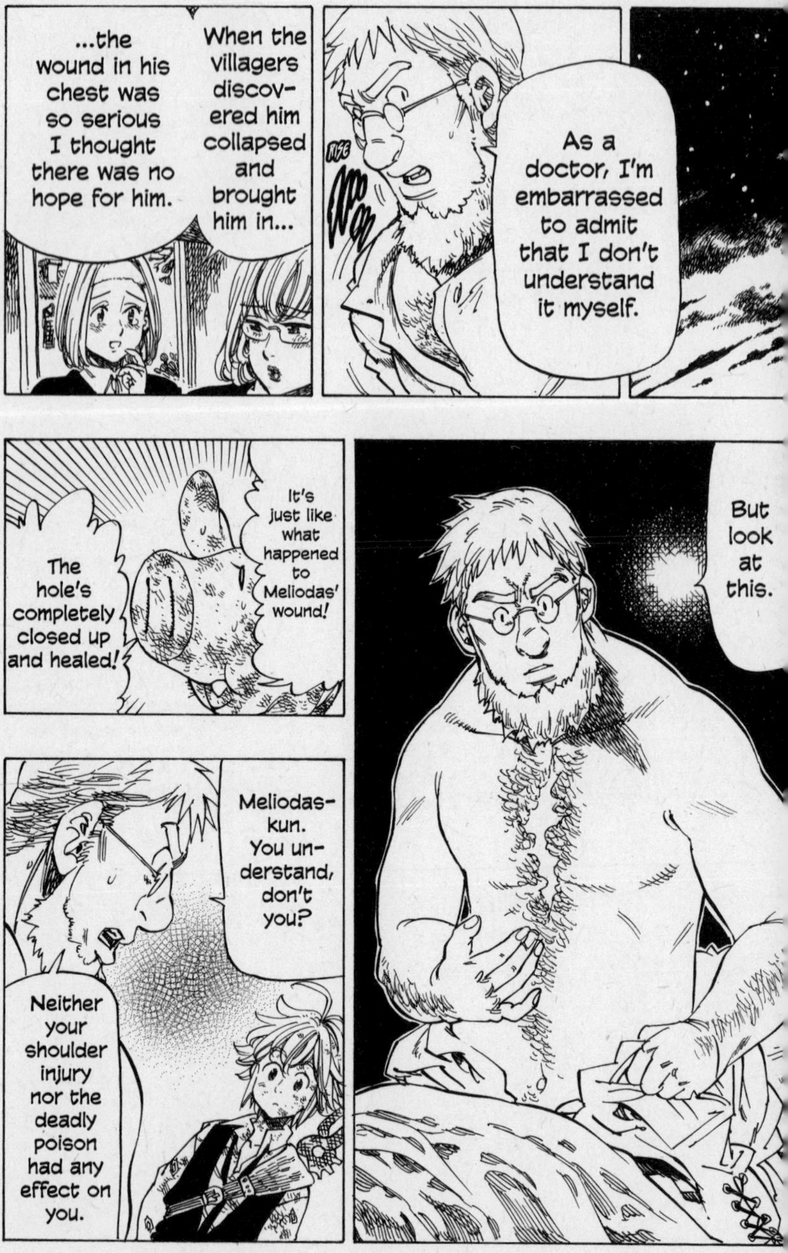
As a doctor, I'm embarrassed to admit that I don't understand it myself.
When the villagers discovered him collapsed and brought him in...
...the wound in his chest was so serious I thought there was no hope for him.
But look at this.
It's just like what happened to Meliodas' wound!
The hole's completely closed up and healed!
Meliodas-kun. You understand, don't you?
Neither your shoulder injury nor the deadly poison had any effect on you.

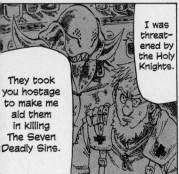

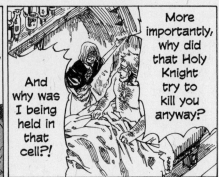

More importantly, why did that Holy Knight try to kill you anyway?
And why was I being held in that cell?!
I was threatened by the Holy Knights.
They took you hostage to make me aid them in killing The Seven Deadly Sins.
It may have been to save you, but I still tried to kill a young man.
That... That wasn't your fault, Father!
This is all their fault!
SCRATCH SCRATCH
The Seven Deadly Sins are known far and wide for being wanted criminals!
Listen to me!
He didn't blame me for what I did and still went out to rescue you.
How many people are there in this kingdom who would face off against a Holy Knight?

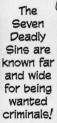

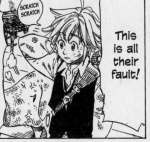

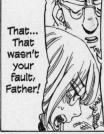

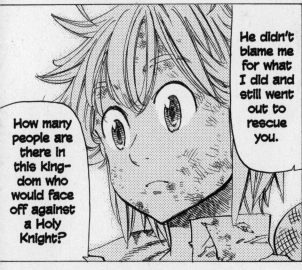

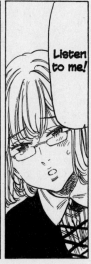

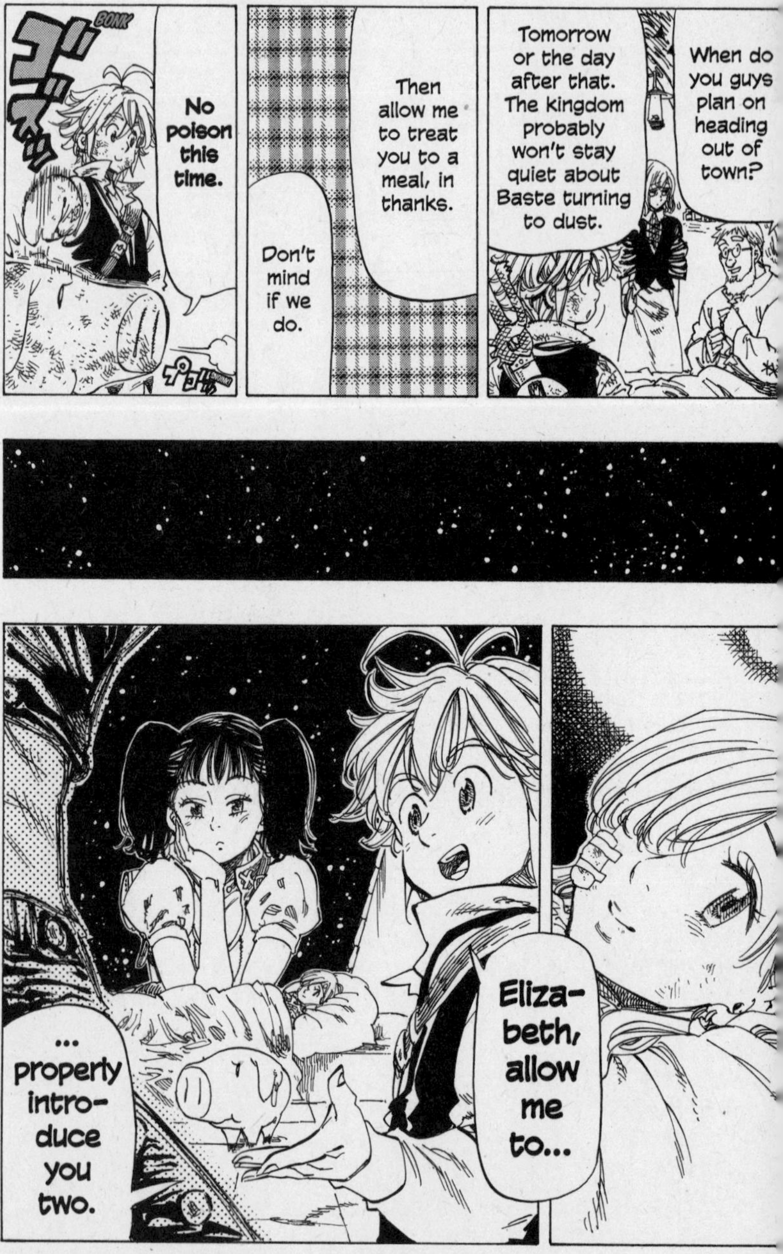
When do you guys plan on heading out of town?
Tomorrow or the day after that. The kingdom probably won't stay quiet about Baste turning to dust.
Then allow me to treat you to a meal, in thanks.
Don't mind if we do.
No poison this time.
BONK
Eliza-beth, allow me to...
... properly intro-duce you two.

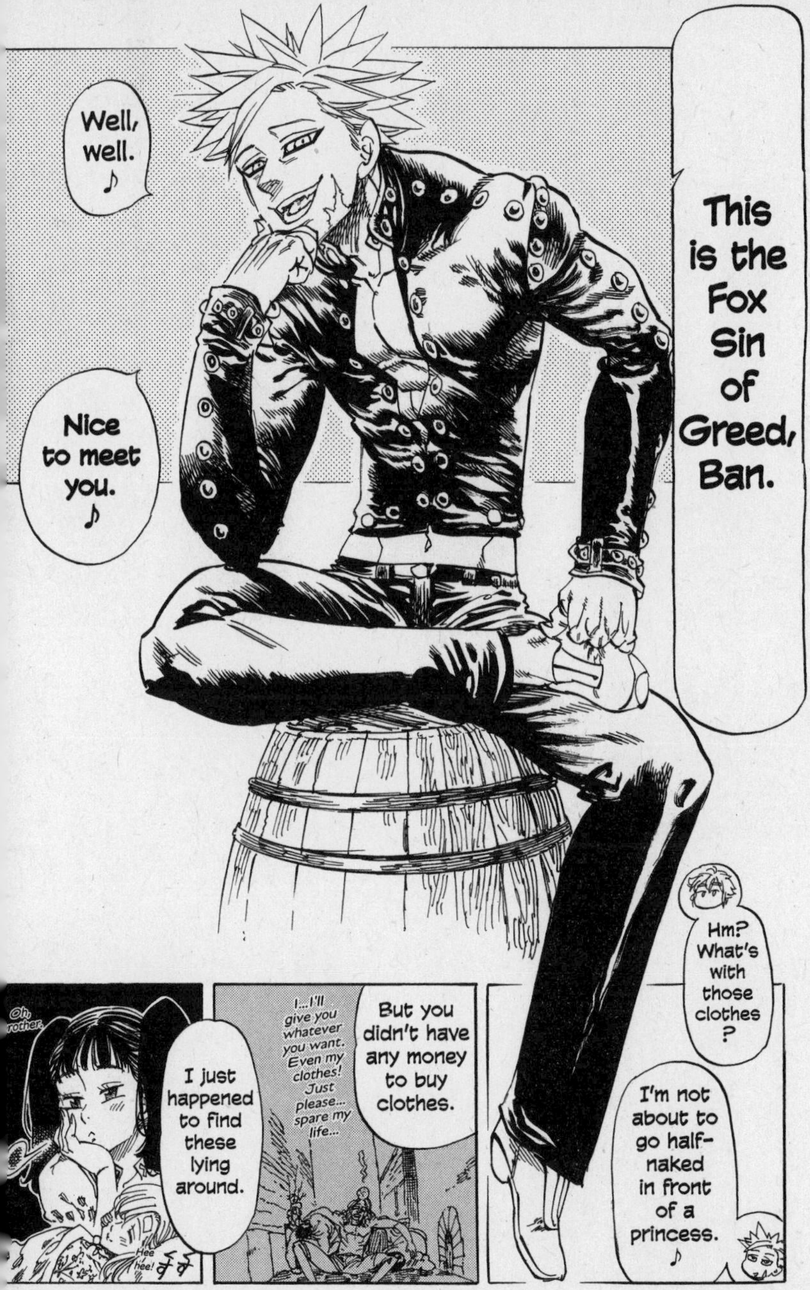
This is the Fox Sin of Greed, Ban.
Well, well. ♪
Nice to meet you. ♪
Hm? What's with those clothes?
I'm not about to go half-naked in front of a princess. ♪
But you didn't have any money to buy clothes.
I...I'll give you whatever you want. Even my clothes! Just please... spare my life...
Oh, rother.
I just happened to find these lying around.
Hee hee!

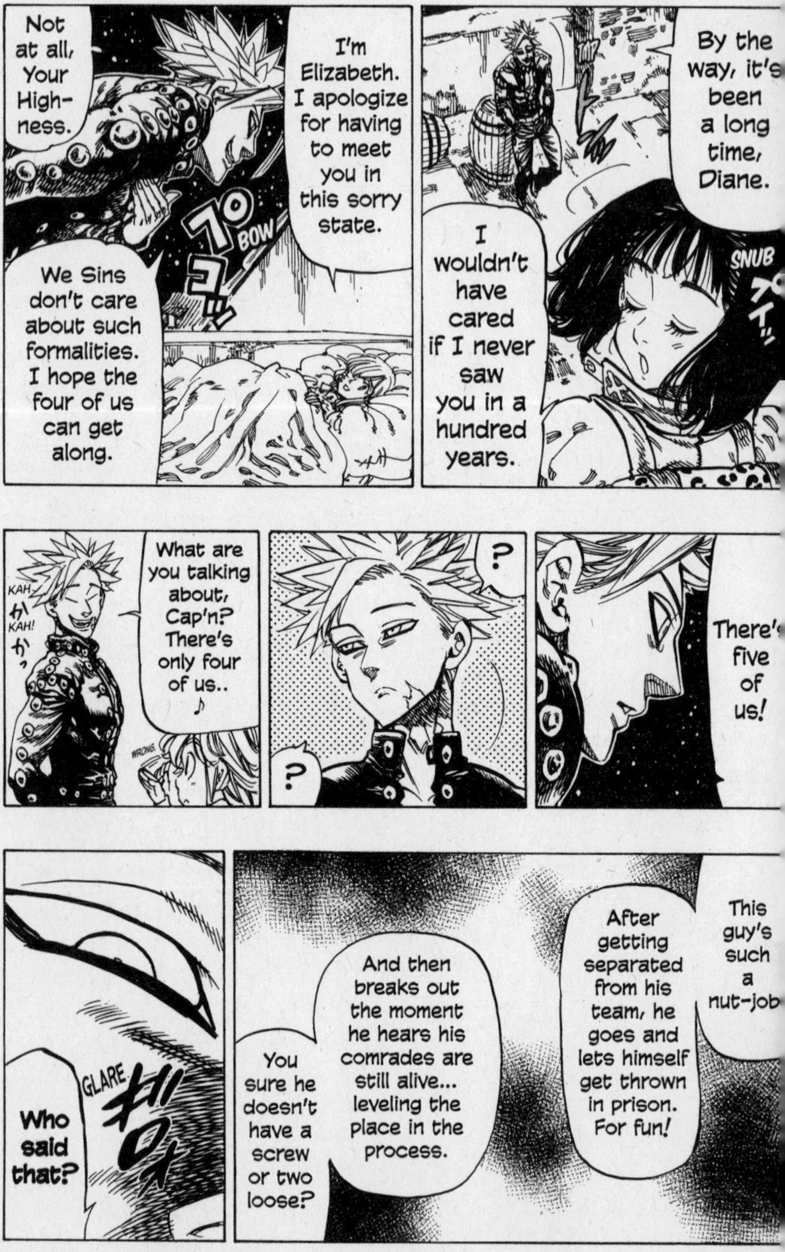
By the way, it's been a long time, Diane.
SNUB
I wouldn't have cared if I never saw you in a hundred years.
I'm Elizabeth. I apologize for having to meet you in this sorry state.
Not at all, Your Highness.
BOW
We Sins don't care about such formalities. I hope the four of us can get along.
There's five of us!
?
?
What are you talking about, Cap'n? There's only four of us.. ♪
KAH
KAH!
WRONG.
This guy's such a nut-job
After getting separated from his team, he goes and lets himself get thrown in prison. For fun!
And then breaks out the moment he hears his comrades are still alive... leveling the place in the process.
You sure he doesn't have a screw or two loose?
GLARE
Who said that?

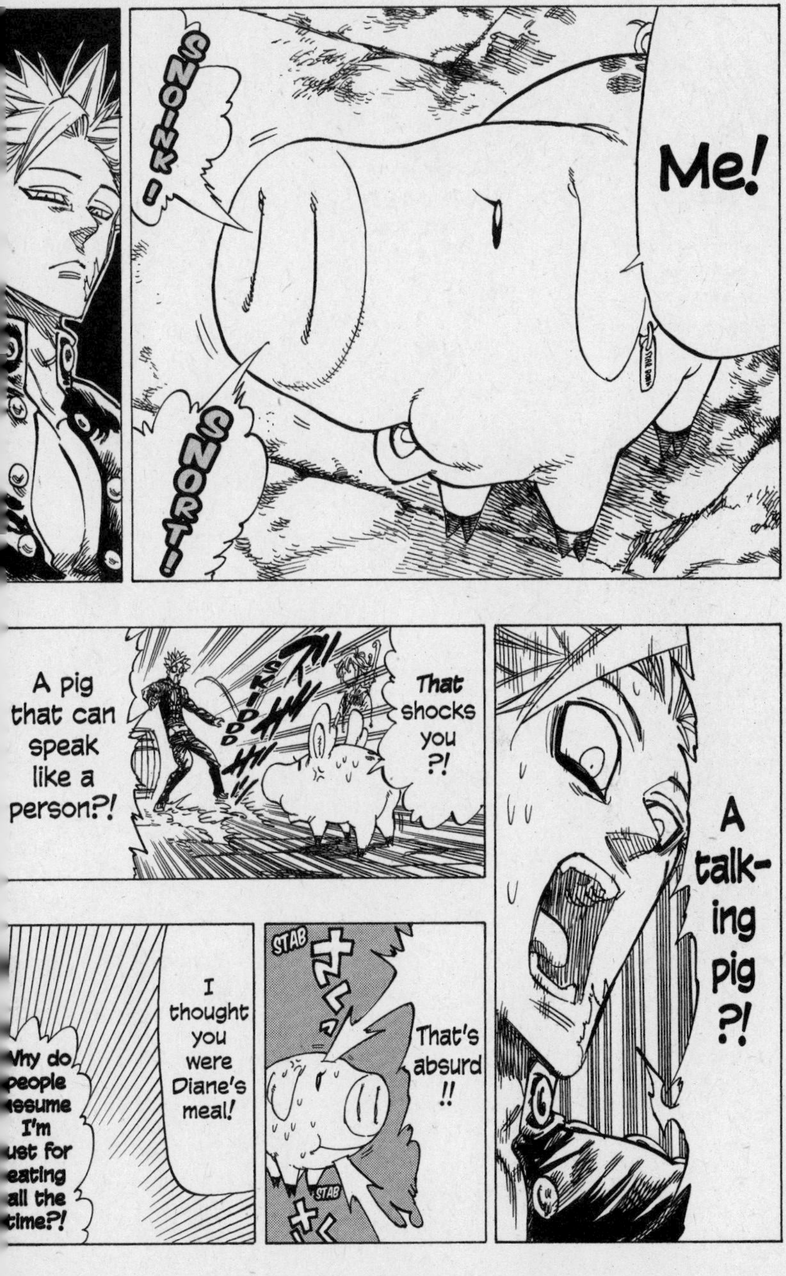
Me!
SNOINK!
SNORT!
A talking-ing pig?!
That shocks you?!
SKIDDD
A pig that can speak like a person?!
STAB
That's absurd!!
STAB
I thought you were Diane's meal!
Why do people assume I'm just for eating all the time?!

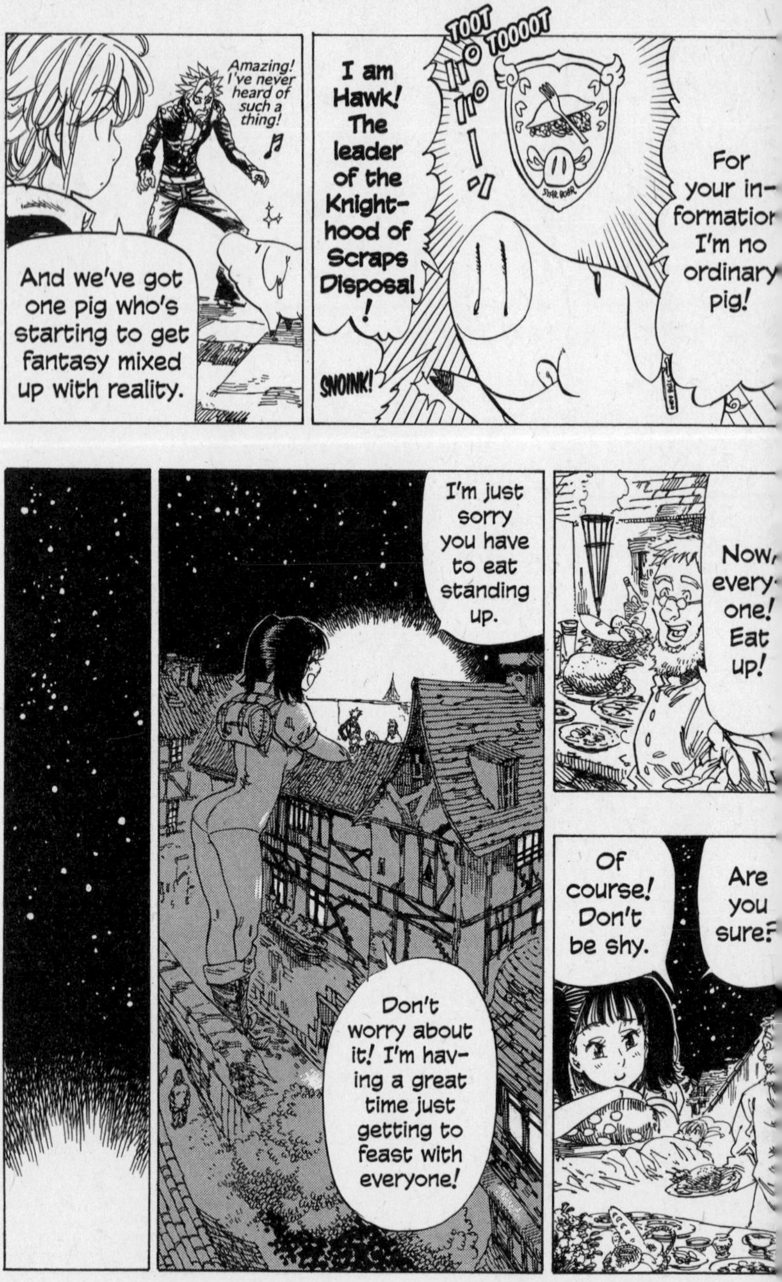
For your in-formatio I'm no ordinary pig!
TOOT TOOOOT
I am Hawk! The leader of the Knight-hood of Scraps Disposal!
SNOINK!
Amazing! I've never heard of such a thing!
And we've got one pig who's starting to get fantasy mixed up with reality.
Now, every-one! Eat up!
Are you sure?
Of course! Don't be shy.
I'm just sorry you have to eat standing up.
Don't worry about it! I'm hav-ing a great time just getting to feast with everyone!

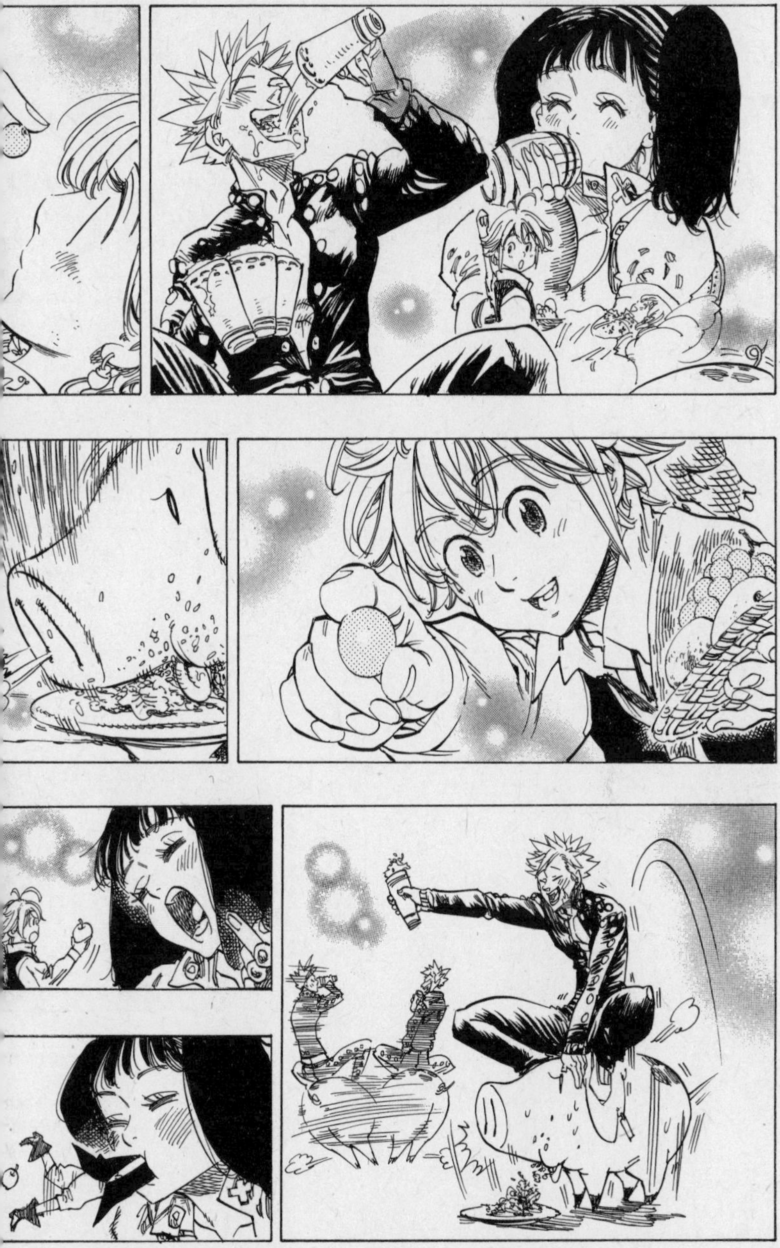

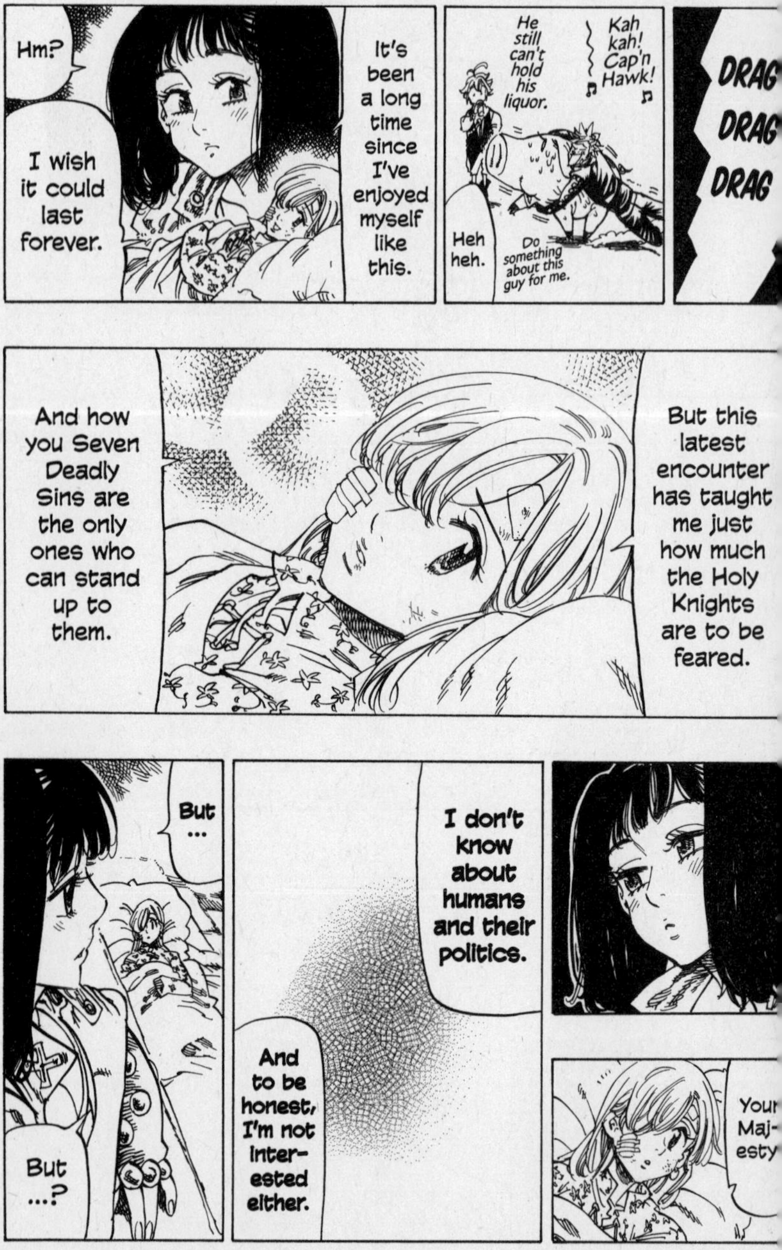
DRAG
DRAG
DRAG
Kah kah! Cap'n Hawk!
He still can't hold his liquor.
Heh heh.
Do something about this guy for me.
It's been a long time since I've enjoyed myself like this.
Hm?
I wish it could last forever.
But this latest encounter has taught me just how much the Holy Knights are to be feared.
And how you Seven Deadly Sins are the only ones who can stand up to them.
Your Majesty
I don't know about humans and their politics.
And to be honest, I'm not interested either.
But ...
But ...?

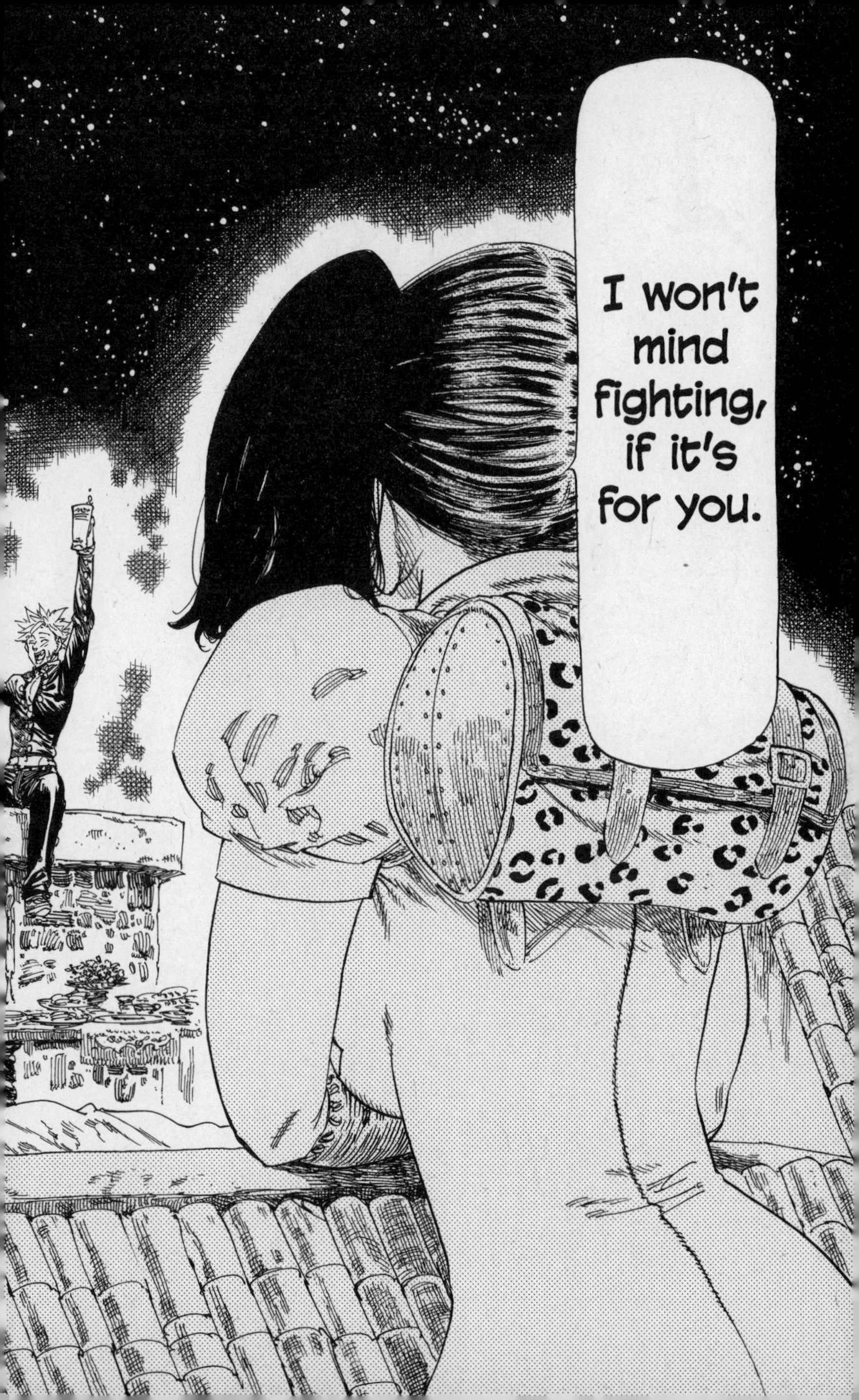
I won't mind fighting, if it's for you.

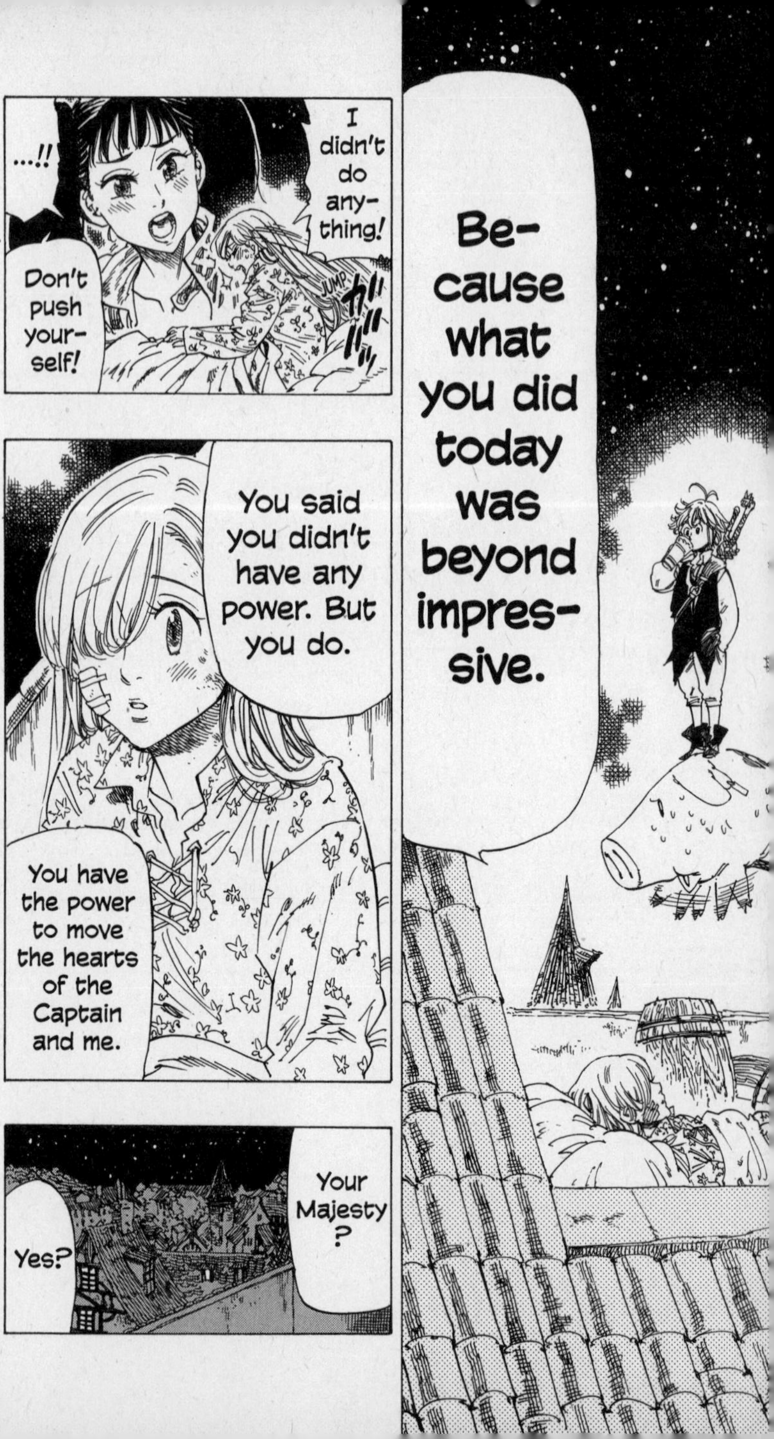
Be-cause what you did today was beyond impres-sive.
I didn't do any-thing!
...!!
JUMP
Don't push your-self!
You said you didn't have any power. But you do.
You have the power to move the hearts of the Captain and me.
Your Majesty?
Yes?

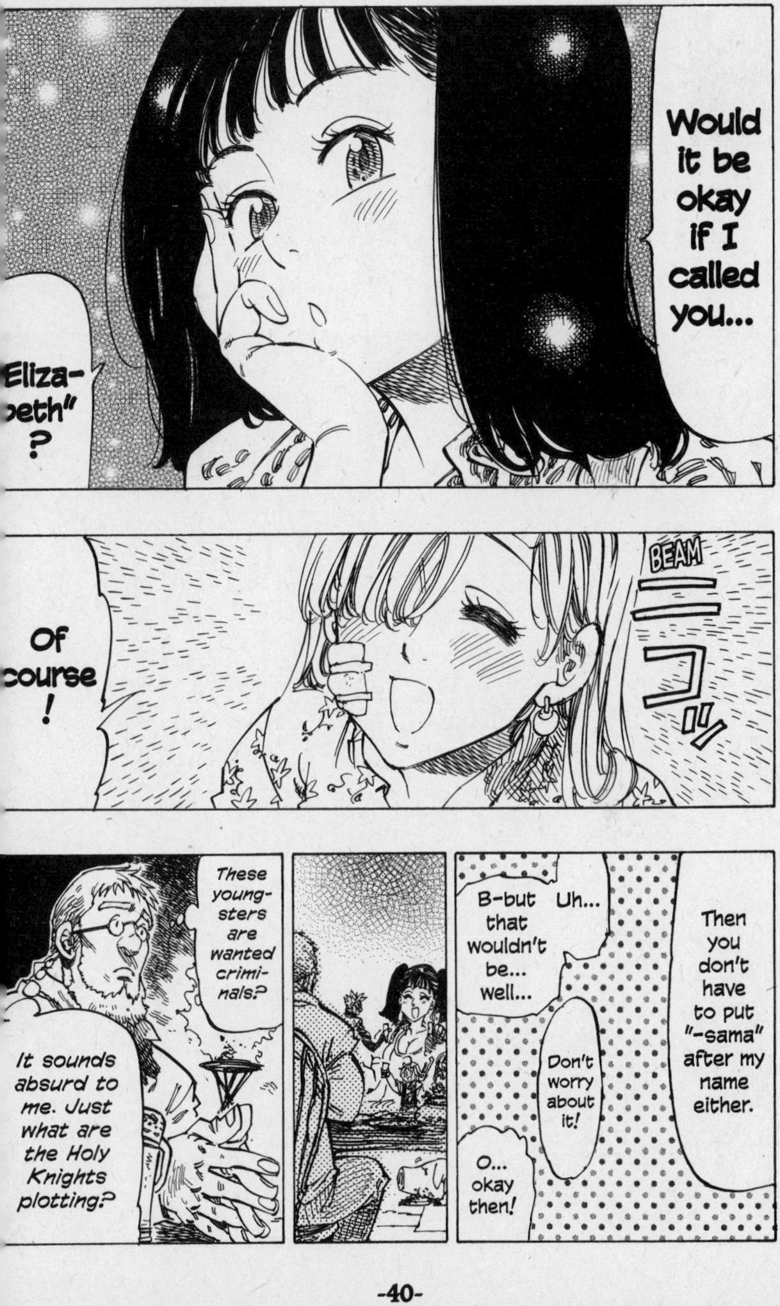
Would it be okay if I called you...
"Eliza-beth"?
BEAM
ニコッ
Of course!
Then you don't have to put "-sama" after my name either.
Uh...
B-but that wouldn't be... well...
Don't worry about it!
O... okay then!
These youngsters are wanted criminals?
It sounds absurd to me. Just what are the Holy Knights plotting?

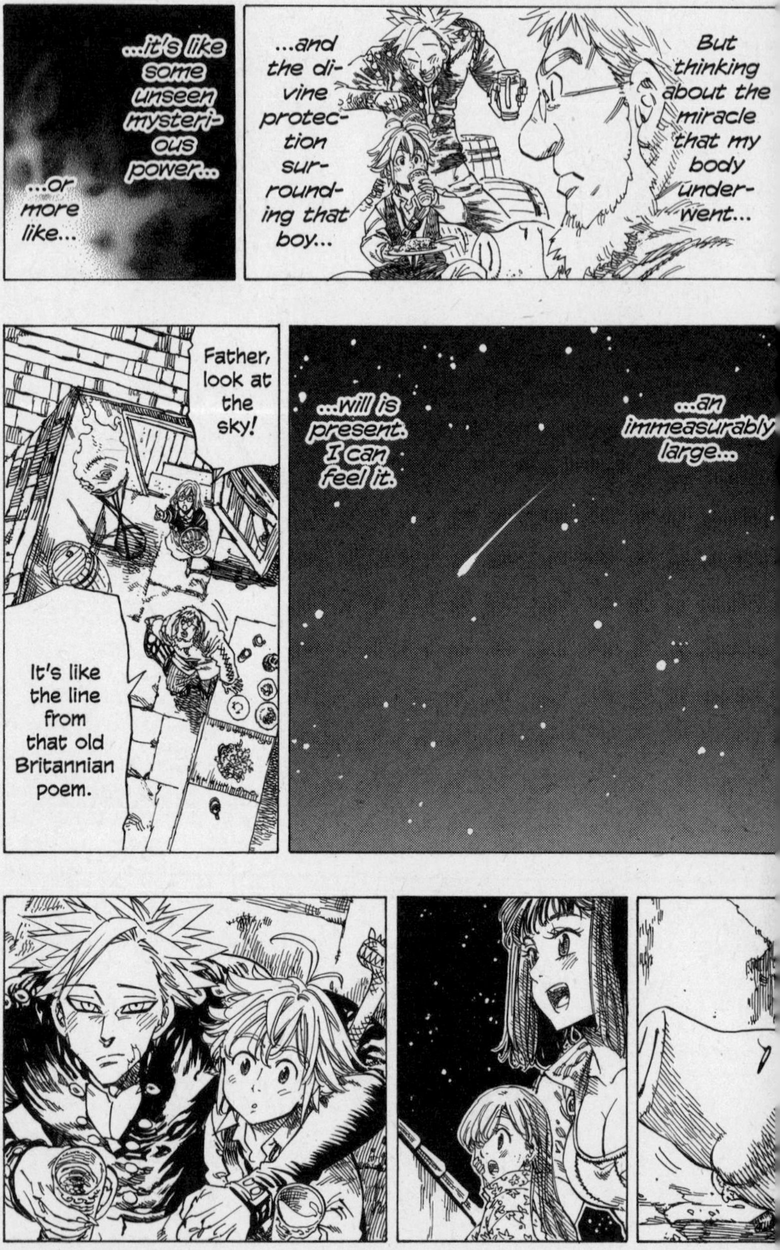
But thinking about the miracle that my body underwent...
...and the divine protection surrounding that boy...
...it's like some unseen mysterious power...
...or more like...
...an immeasurably large...
...will is present. I can feel it.
Father, look at the sky!
It's like the line from that old Britannian poem.

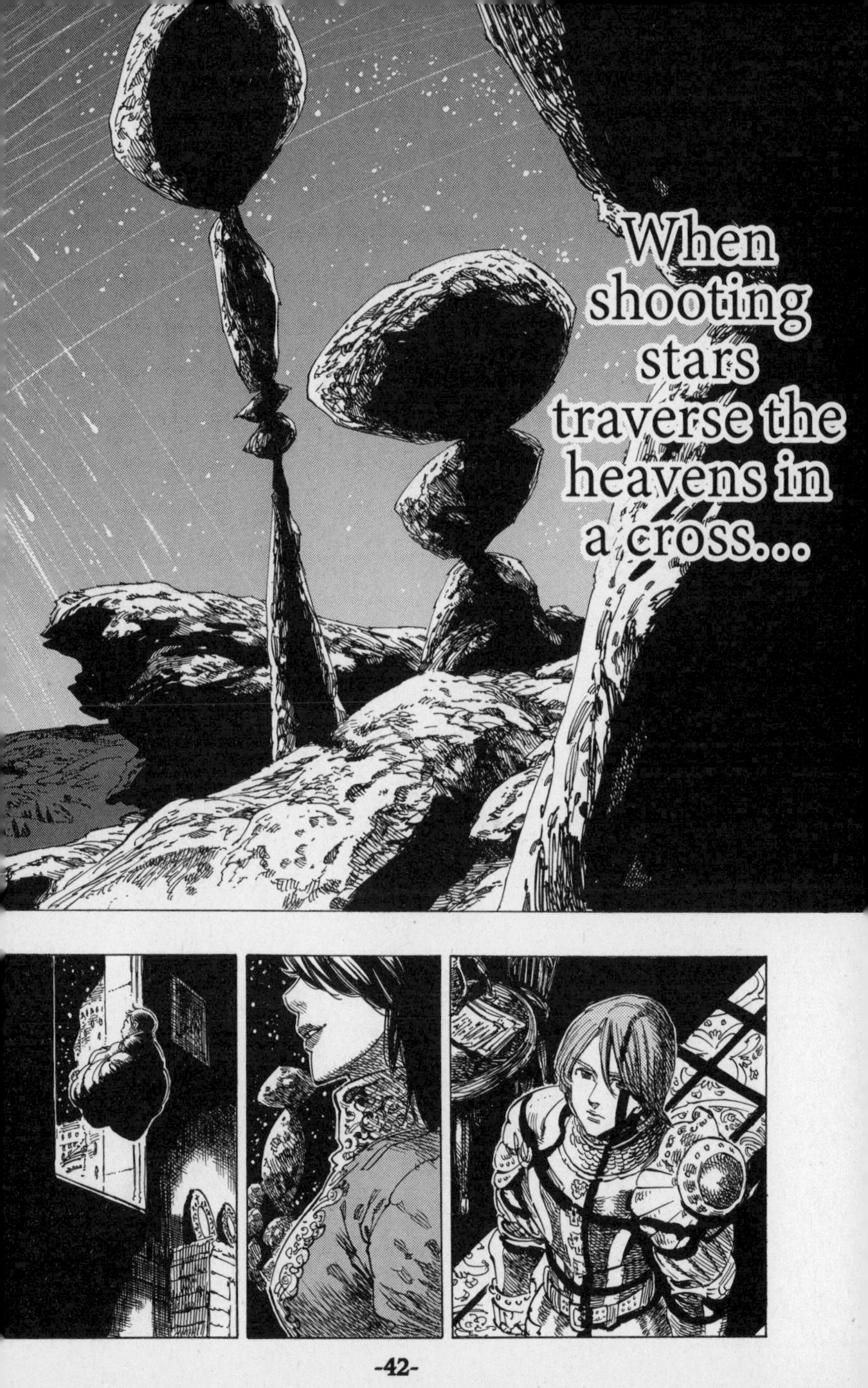
When shooting stars traverse the heavens in a cross...

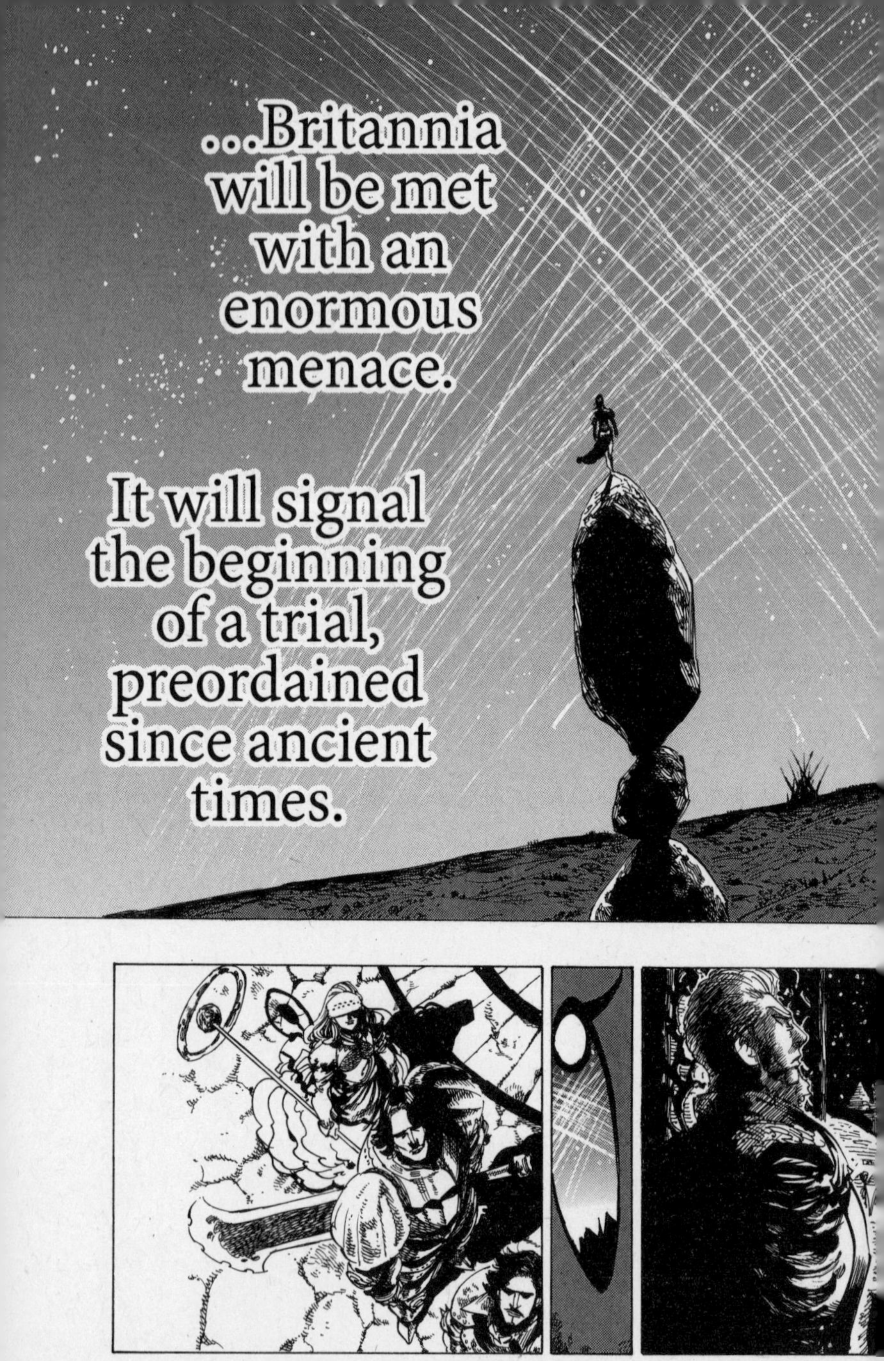
...Britannia will be met with an enormous menace.
It will signal the beginning of a trial, preordained since ancient times.

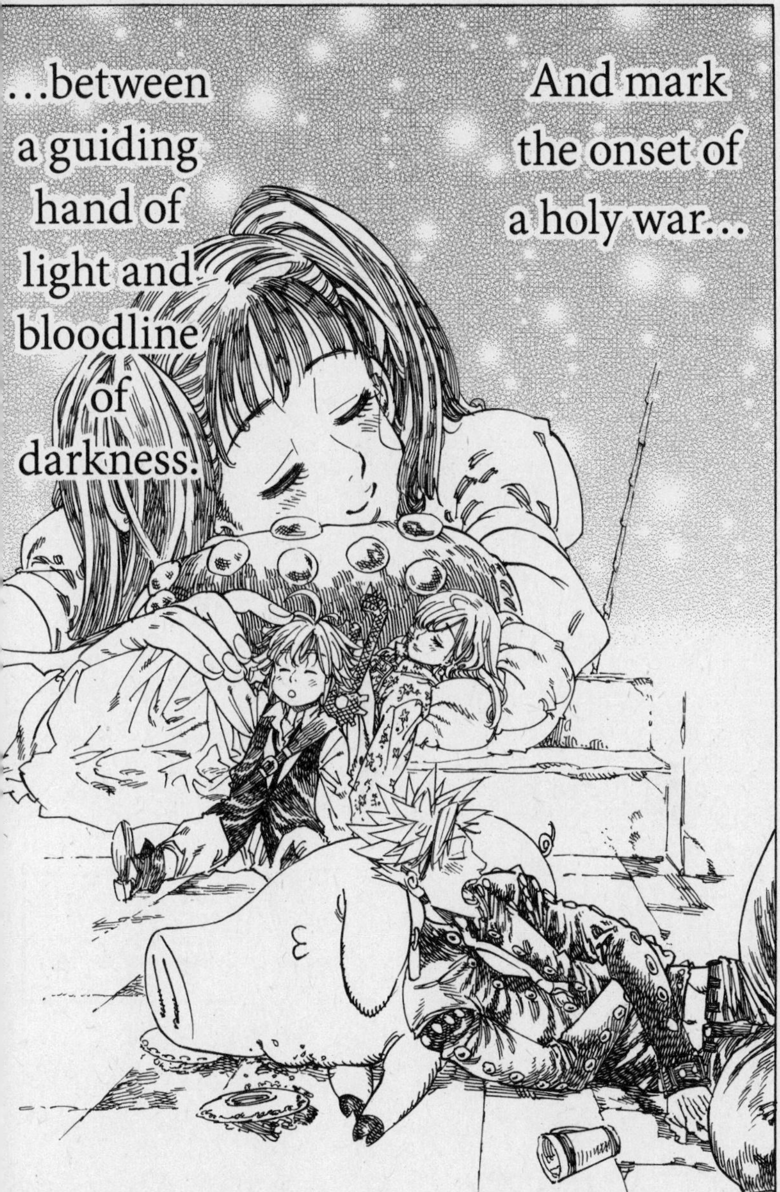
And mark the onset of a holy war...
...between a guiding hand of light and bloodline of darkness.

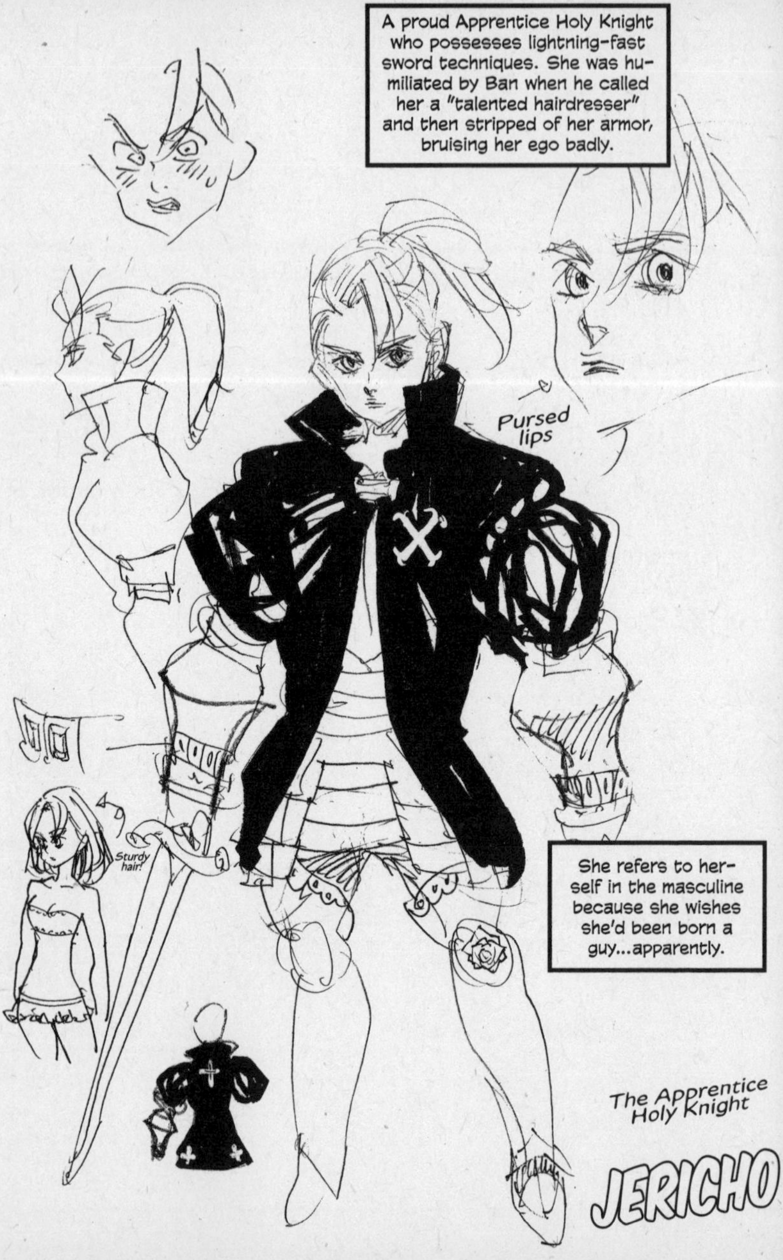
A proud Apprentice Holy Knight who possesses lightning-fast sword techniques. She was humiliated by Ban when he called her a "talented hairdresser" and then stripped of her armor, bruising her ego badly.
Pursed lips
Sturdy hair!
She refers to herself in the masculine because she wishes she'd been born a guy...apparently.
The Apprentice Holy Knight
JERICHO

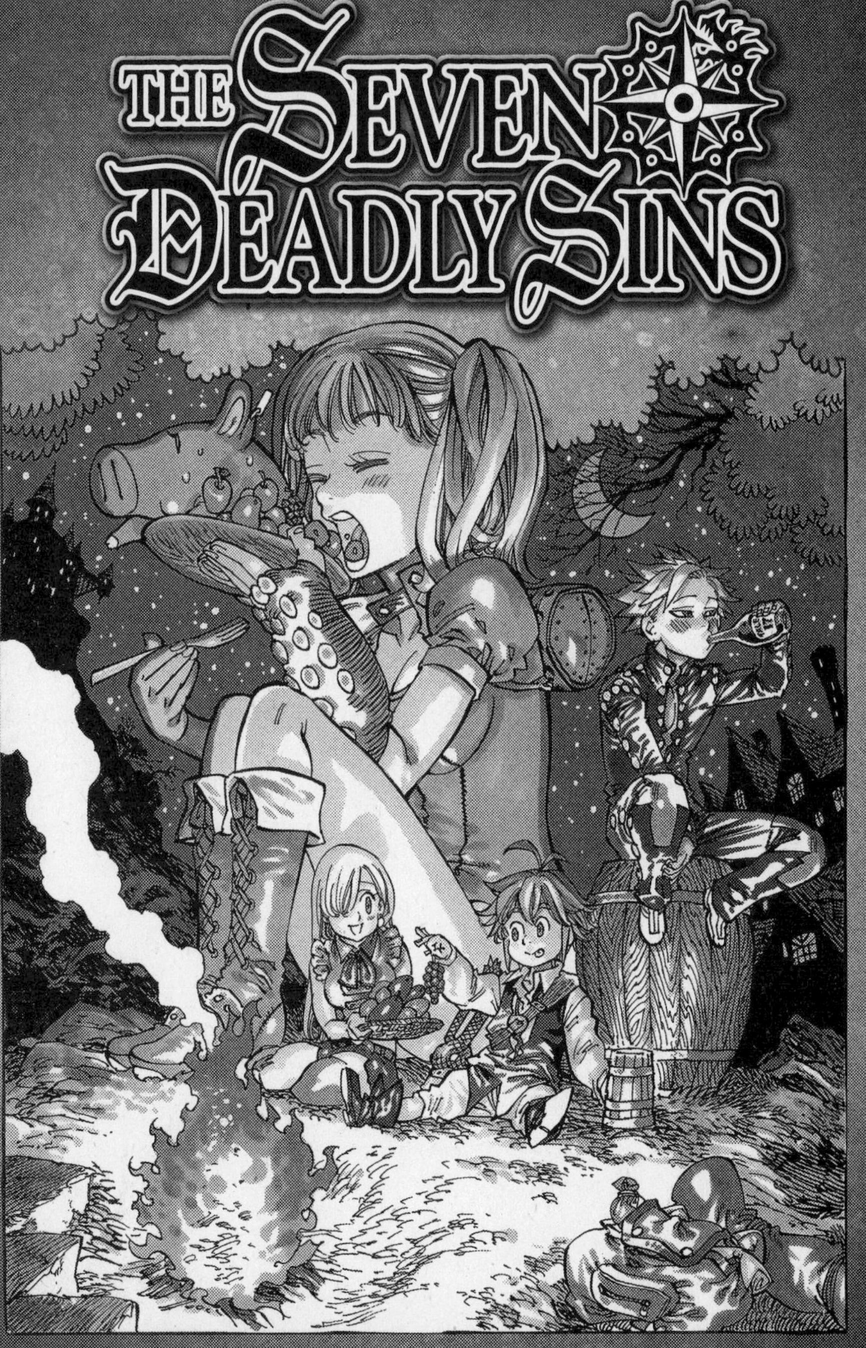
THE SEVEN DEADLY SINS

Chapter 17 - Storm's Brewing

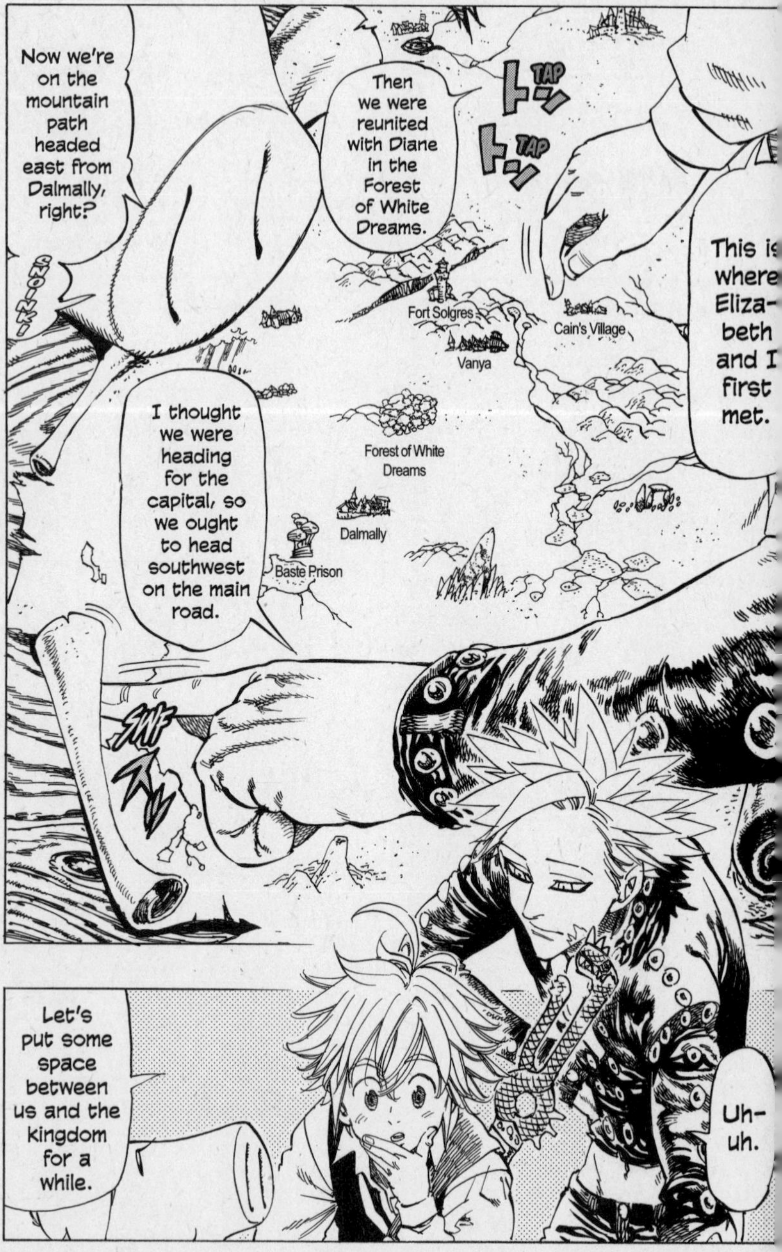
This is where Elizabeth and I first met.
TAP
TAP
Then we were reunited with Diane in the Forest of White Dreams.
Now we're on the mountain path headed east from Dalmally, right?
SNOINK
Fort Solgres
Cain's Village
Vanya
Forest of White Dreams
Dalmally
Baste Prison
I thought we were heading for the capital, so we ought to head southwest on the main road.
SWF
Uh-uh.
Let's put some space between us and the kingdom for a while.

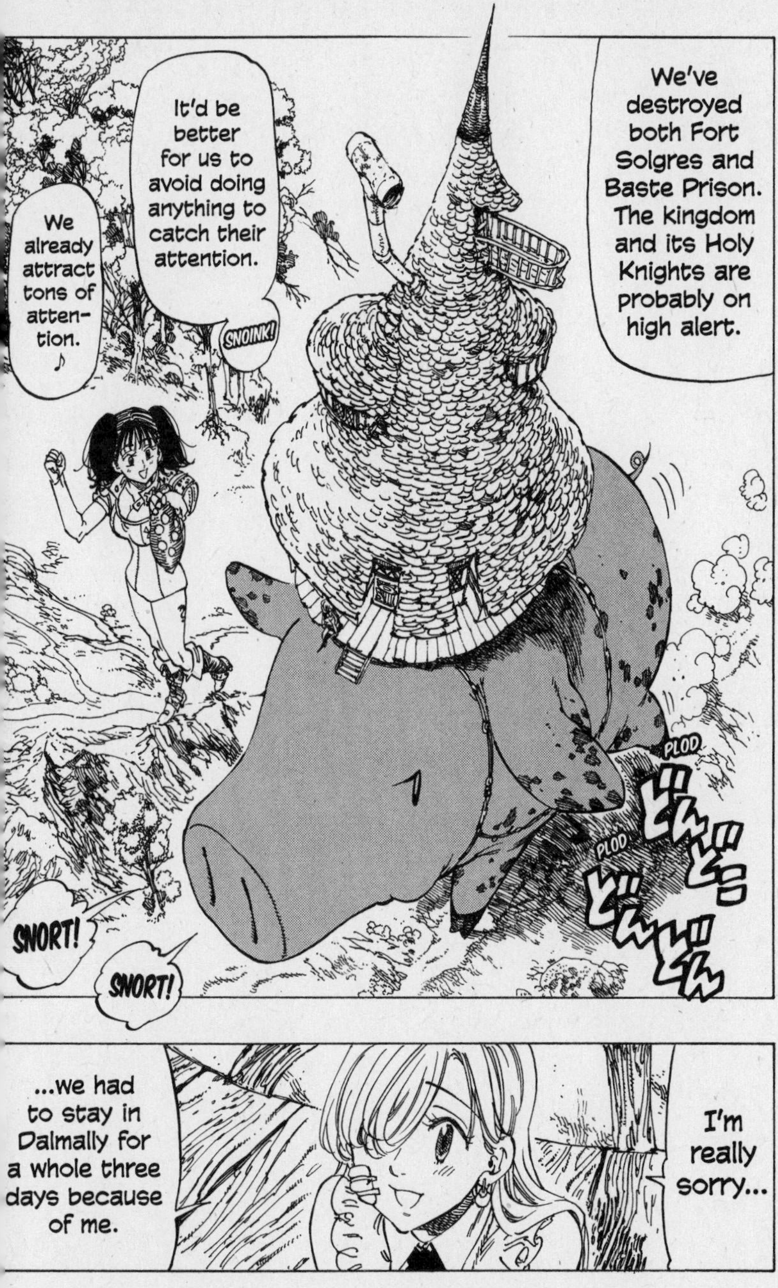
We've destroyed both Fort Solgres and Baste Prison. The kingdom and its Holy Knights are probably on high alert.
It'd be better for us to avoid doing anything to catch their attention.
SNOINK!
We already attract tons of atten-tion. ♪
PLOD
PLOD
SNORT!
SNORT!
I'm really sorry...
...we had to stay in Dalmally for a whole three days because of me.

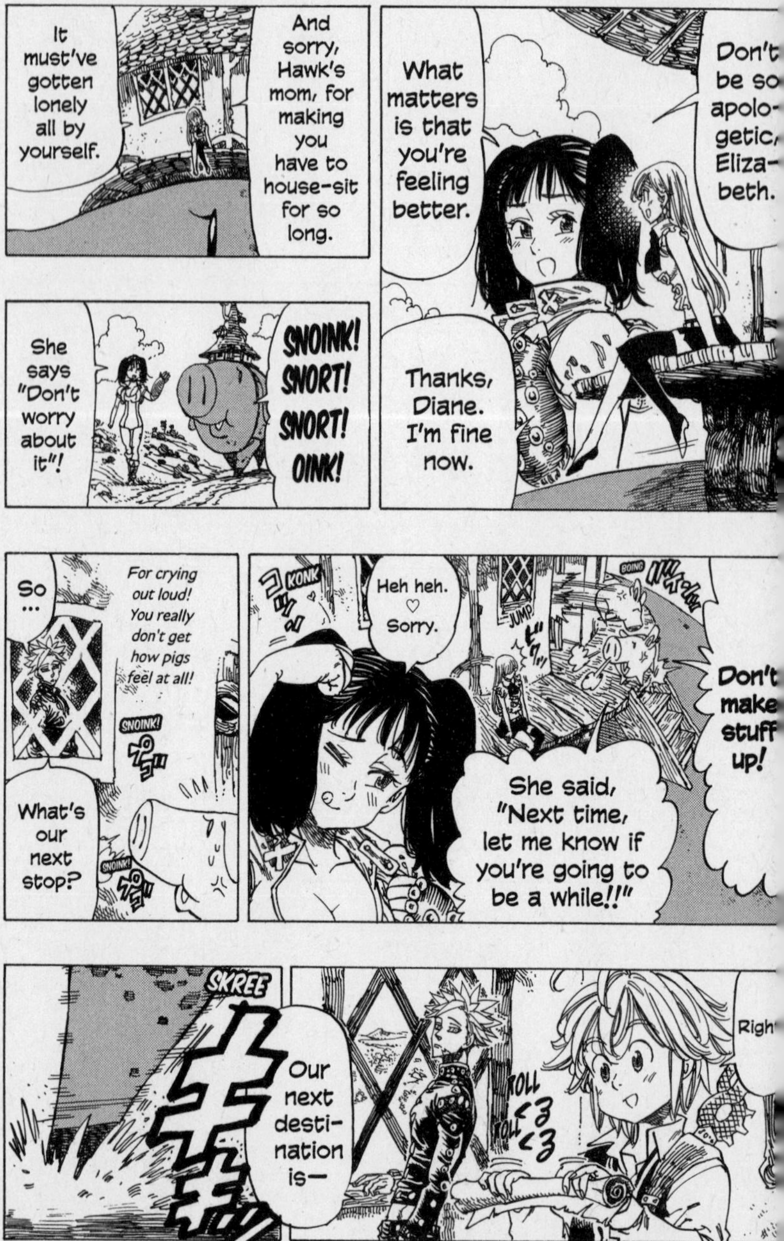
Don't be so apolo-getic, Eliza-beth.
What matters is that you're feeling better.
Thanks, Diane. I'm fine now.
And sorry, Hawk's mom, for making you have to house-sit for so long.
It must've gotten lonely all by yourself.
SNOINK! SNORT! SNORT! OINK!
She says "Don't worry about it"!
BOING
Don't make stuff up!
JUMP
Heh heh. ♡ Sorry.
KONK
She said, "Next time, let me know if you're going to be a while!!"
For crying out loud! You really don't get how pigs feel at all!
So ...
SNOINK!
What's our next stop?
SNOINK!
Righ
ROLL ROLL
SKREE
Our next desti-nation is—

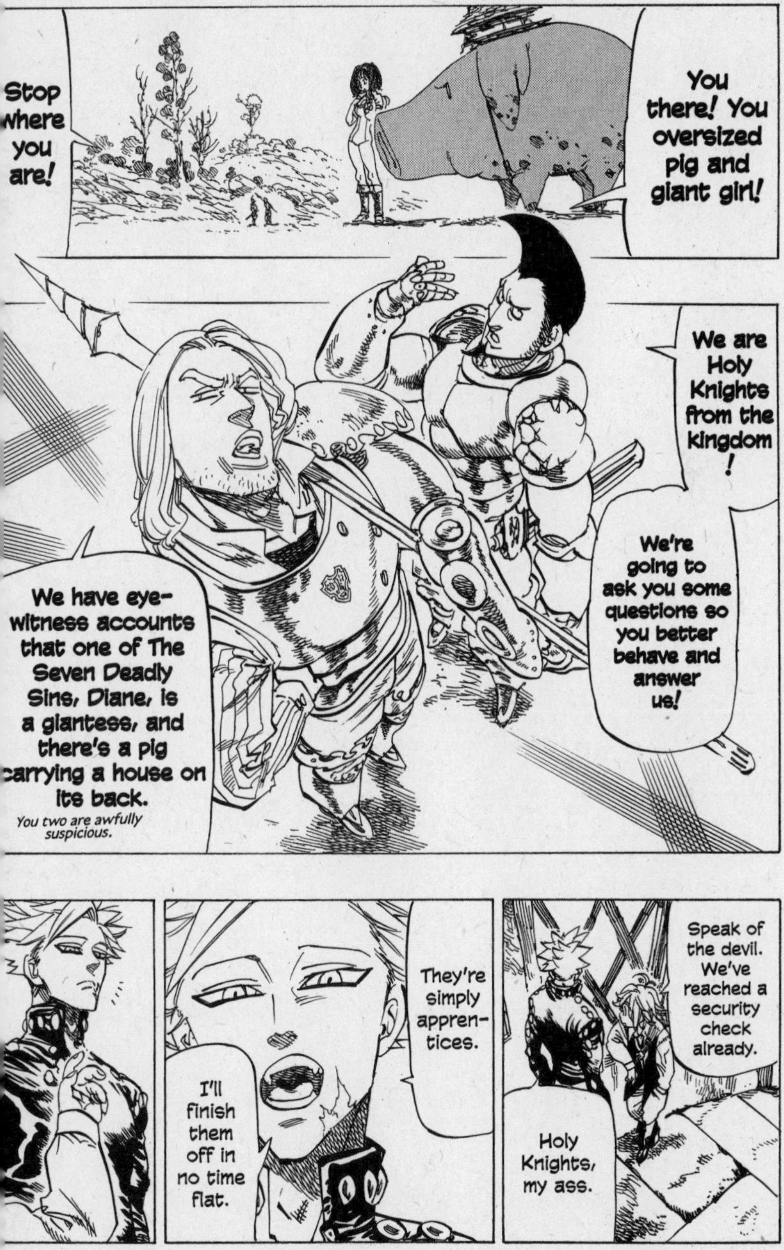
You there! You oversized pig and giant girl!
Stop where you are!
We are Holy Knights from the kingdom!
We're going to ask you some questions so you better behave and answer us!
We have eye-witness accounts that one of The Seven Deadly Sins, Diane, is a giantess, and there's a pig carrying a house on its back.
You two are awfully suspicious.
Speak of the devil. We've reached a security check already.
Holy Knights, my ass.
They're simply appren-tices.
I'll finish them off in no time flat.

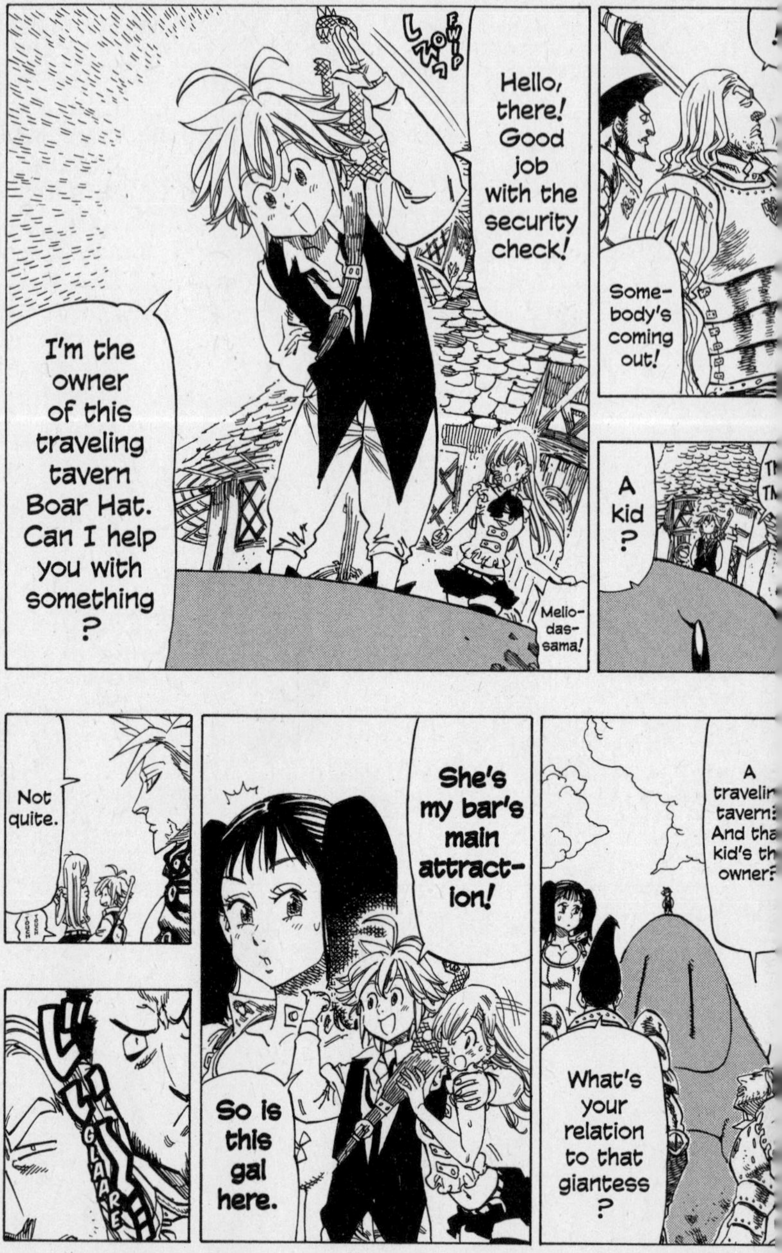

Somebody's coming out!
A kid?
FWIP
Hello, there! Good job with the security check!
I'm the owner of this traveling tavern Boar Hat. Can I help you with something?
Meliodas-sama!
What's your relation to that giantess?
She's my bar's main attraction!
So is this gal here.
Not quite.
GLAARE

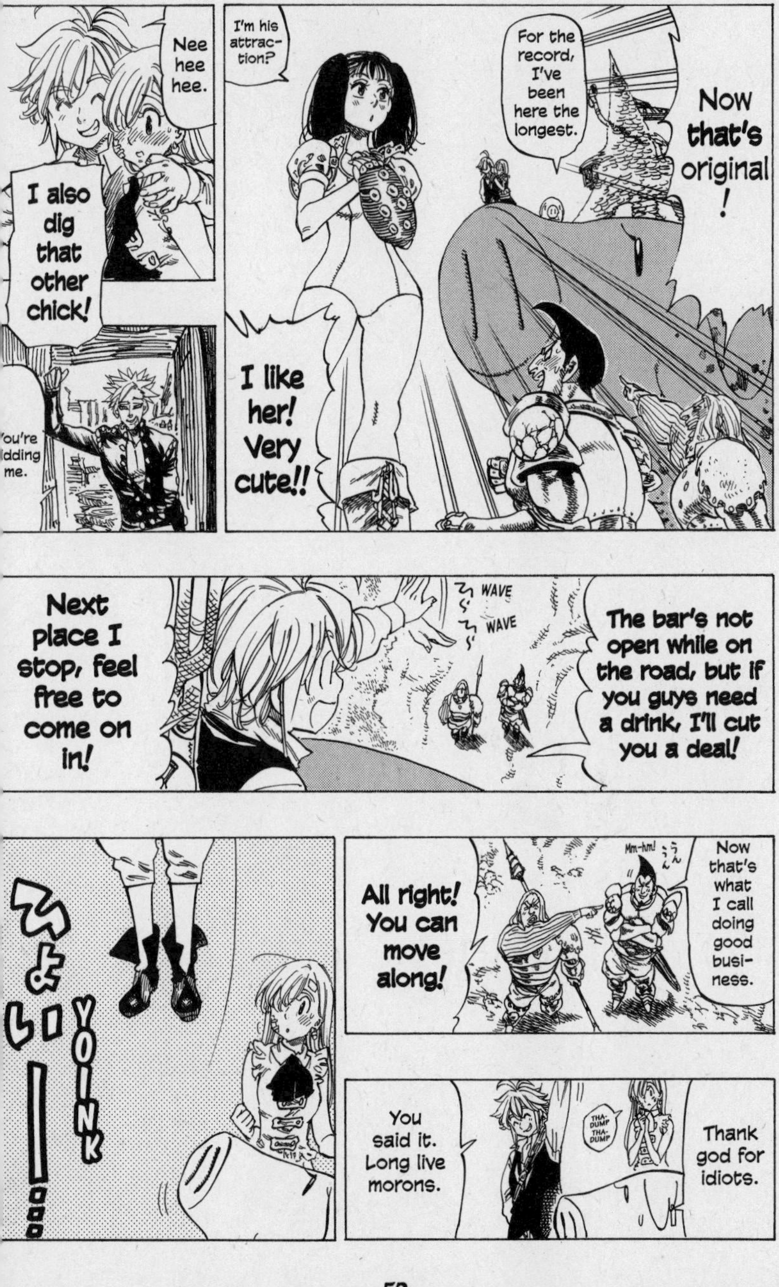
Now that's original!
For the record, I've been here the longest.
I'm his attrac-tion?
I like her! Very cute!!
Nee hee hee.
I also dig that other chick!
ou're idding me.
The bar's not open while on the road, but if you guys need a drink, I'll cut you a deal!
WAVE WAVE
Next place I stop, feel free to come on in!
Now that's what I call doing good busi-ness.
Mm-hm! うんうん
All right! You can move along!
Thank god for idiots.
THA-DUMP THA-DUMP
You said it. Long live morons.
ひょい—
YOINK

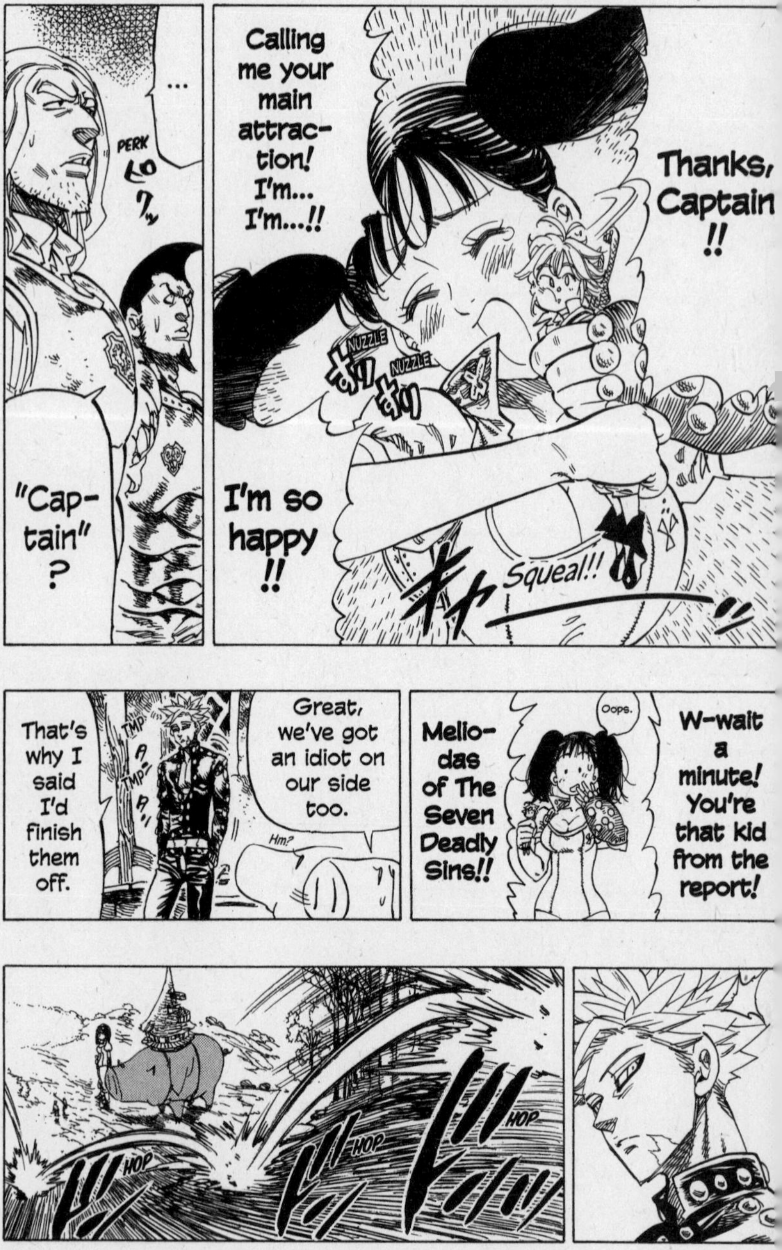
Thanks, Captain!!
Calling me your main attraction! I'm... I'm...!!
NUZZLE
NUZZLE
I'm so happy!!
Squeal!!
...
PERK
"Captain"?
W-wait a minute! You're that kid from the report!
Oops.
Melio-das of The Seven Deadly Sins!!
Great, we've got an idiot on our side too.
Hm?
TMP
TMP
That's why I said I'd finish them off.
HOP
HOP
HOP

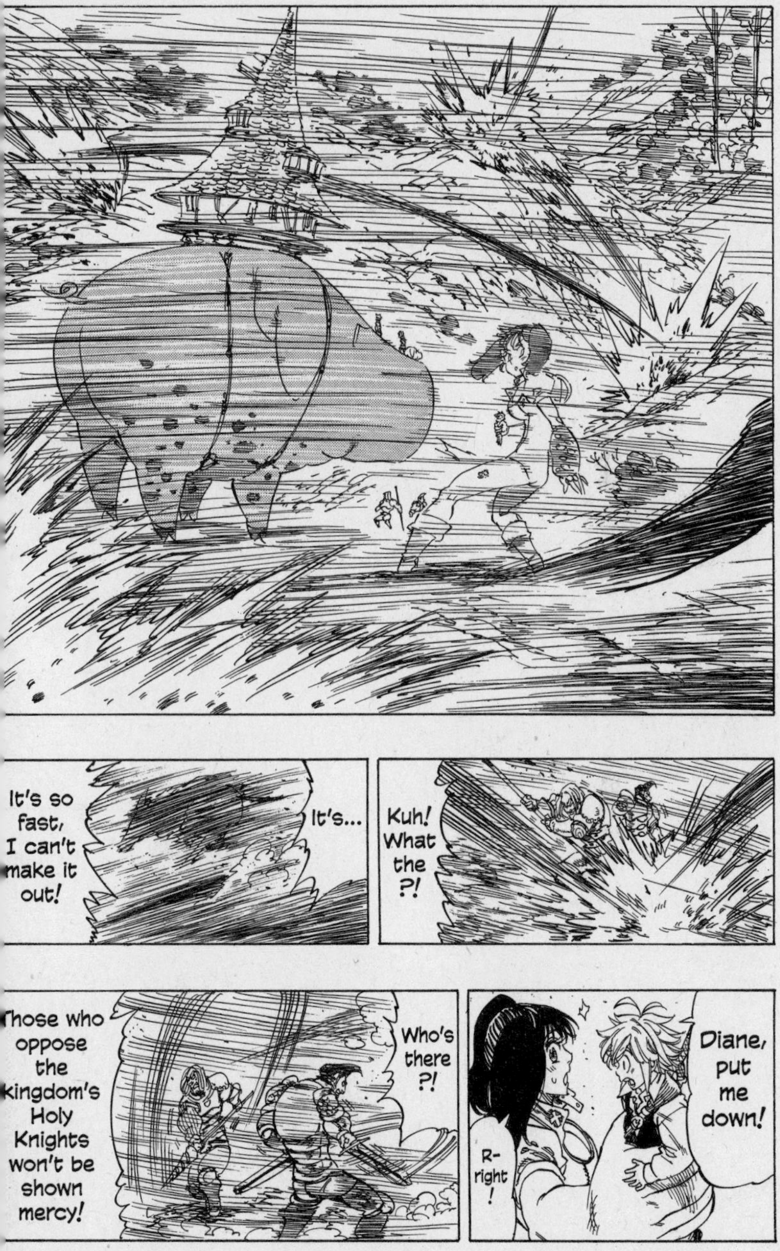
Kuh! What the ?!
It's...
It's so fast, I can't make it out!
Diane, put me down!
R-right!
Who's there ?!
Those who oppose the kingdom's Holy Knights won't be shown mercy!

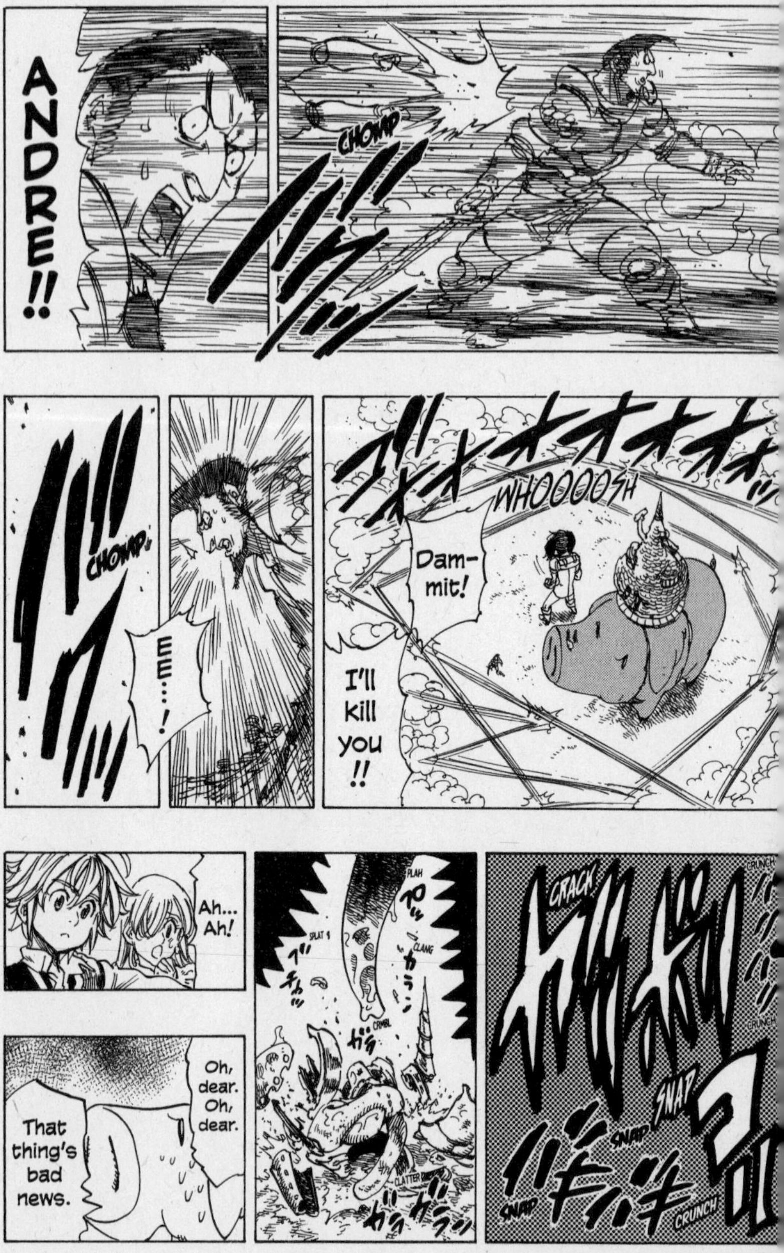
CHOMP
ANDRE!!
WHOOOOSH
Dam-mit!
I'll kill you!!
EE...!
CHOMP
CRACK
CRUNCH
SNAP
SNAP
SNAP
CRUNCH
CRUNCH
PLAH
CLANG
SPLAT
CRMBL
CLATTER
Ah... Ah!
Oh, dear. Oh, dear.
That thing's bad news.

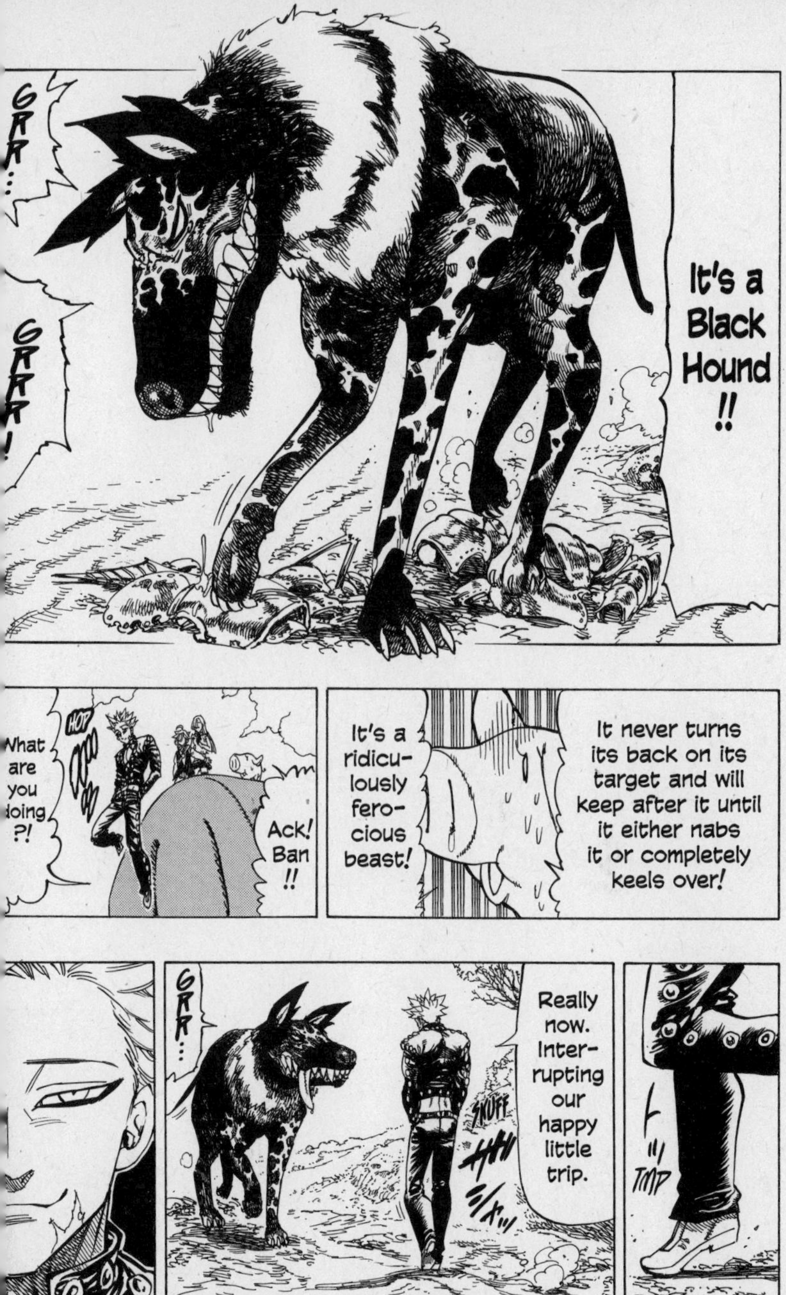
It's a Black Hound !!
GRR...
GRRR!
It never turns its back on its target and will keep after it until it either nabs it or completely keels over!
It's a ridiculously ferocious beast!
Ack! Ban !!
HOP
What are you doing ?!
TMP
Really now. Interrupting our happy little trip.
SNUFF
GRR...

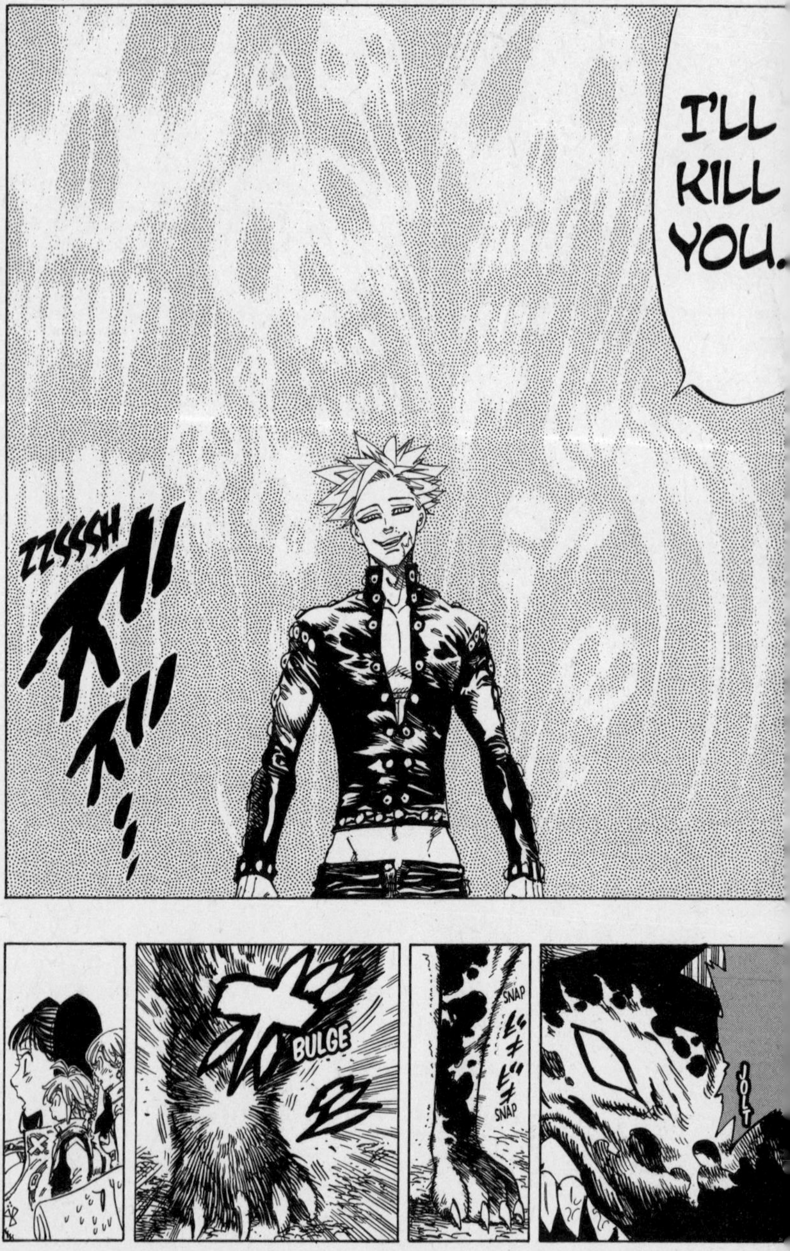
I'LL KILL YOU.
ZZSSSH
JOLT
SNAP
SNAP
BULGE

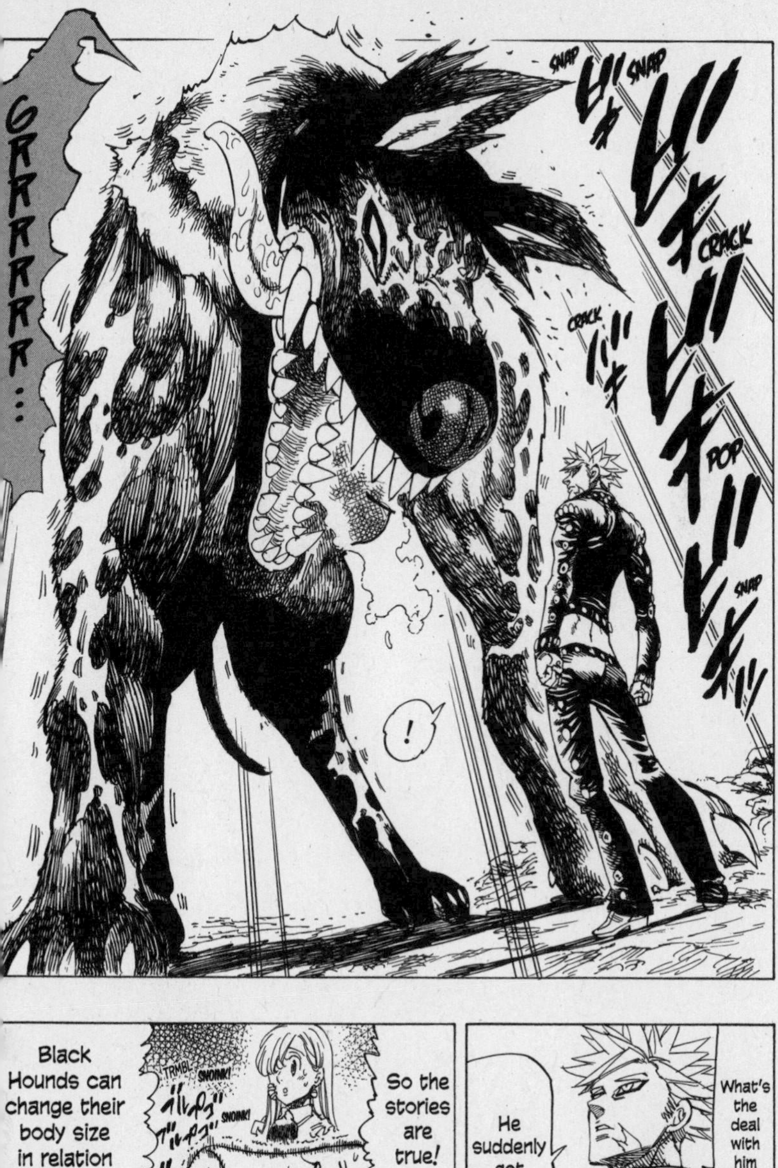
SNAP
SNAP
CRACK
CRACK
POP
SNAP
GRRRRRRR...
!
What's the deal with him?
He suddenly got bigger.
So the stories are true!
TRMBL
SNOINK!
SNOINK!
TRMBL
Black Hounds can change their body size in relation to how threatened they feel!

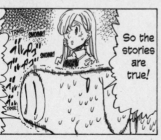

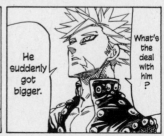

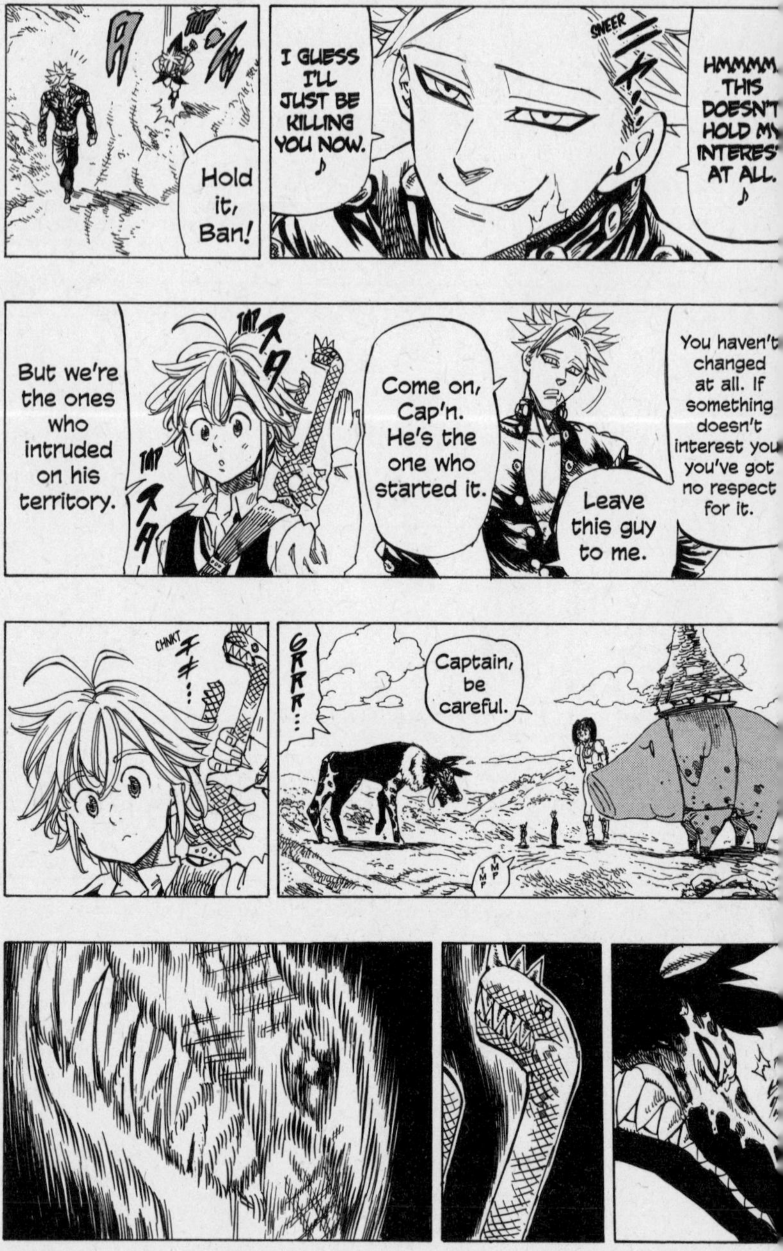
SNEER
HMMMM. THIS DOESN'T HOLD MY INTERES AT ALL. ♪
I GUESS I'LL JUST BE KILLING YOU NOW. ♪
TMP
Hold it, Ban!
You haven't changed at all. If something doesn't interest you you've got no respect for it.
Leave this guy to me.
Come on, Cap'n. He's the one who started it.
TMP
TMP
But we're the ones who intruded on his territory.
GRRR...
Captain, be careful.
TMP TMP
CHNKT

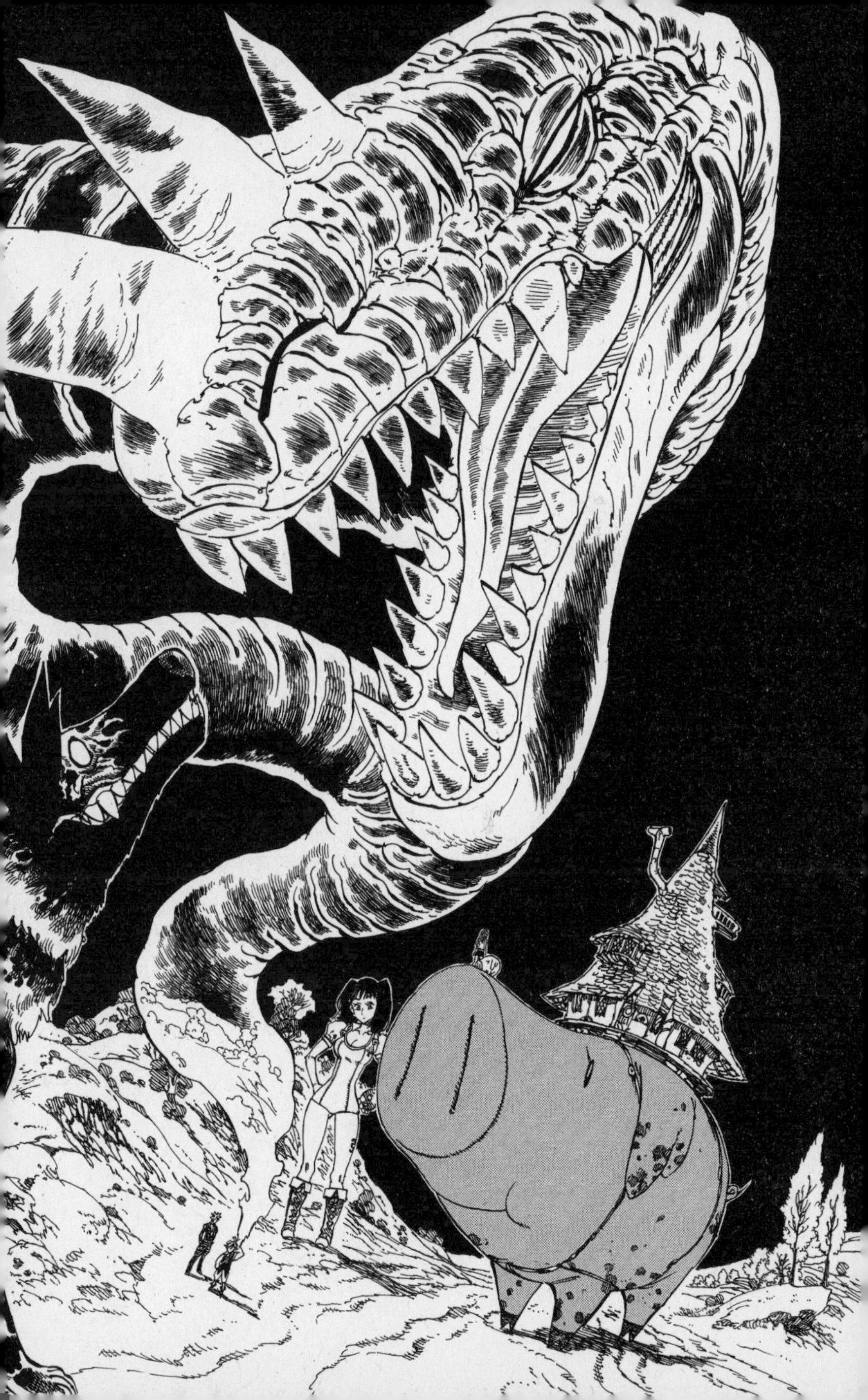

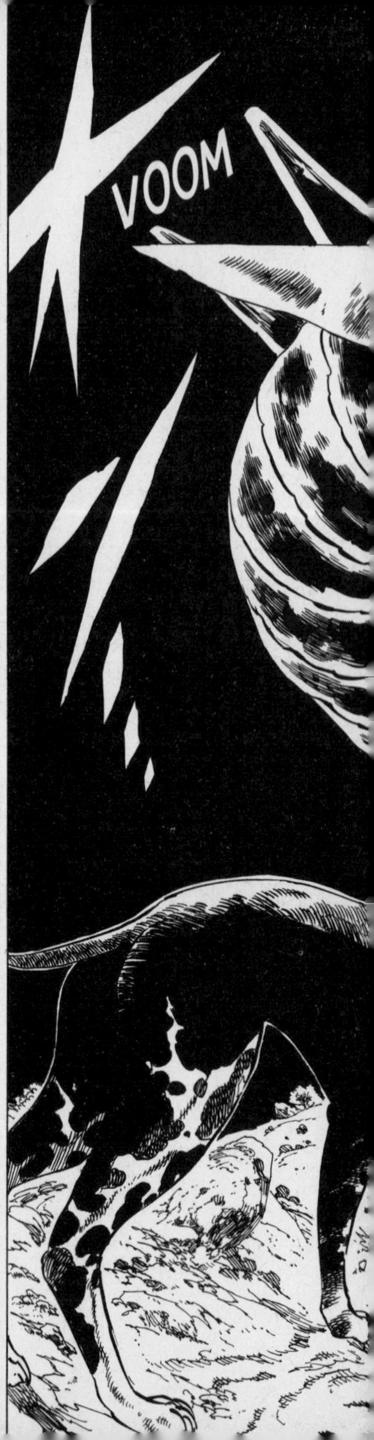
VOOM

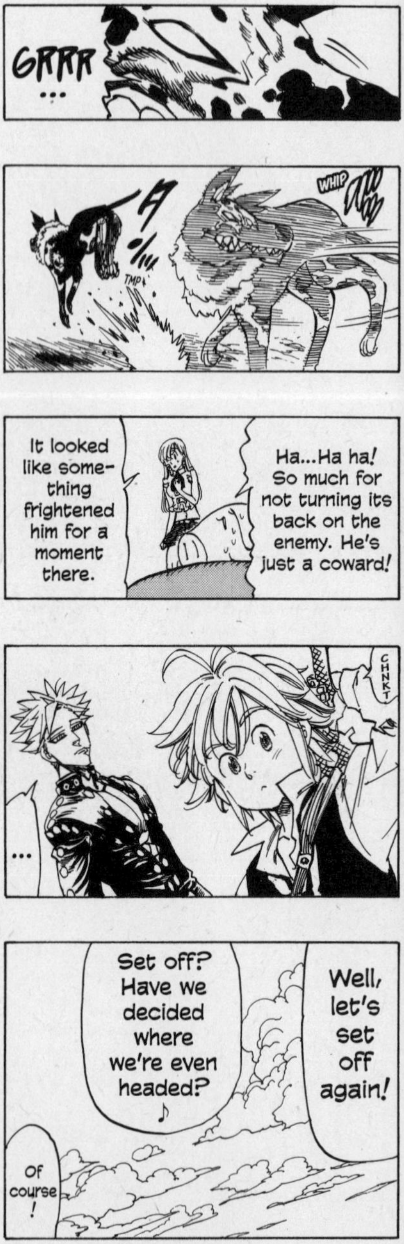
GRRR
...
WHIP
TMP
Ha...Ha ha! So much for not turning its back on the enemy. He's just a coward!
It looked like some-thing frightened him for a moment there.
CHNKT
...
Well, let's set off again!
Set off? Have we decided where we're even headed? ♪
Of course!

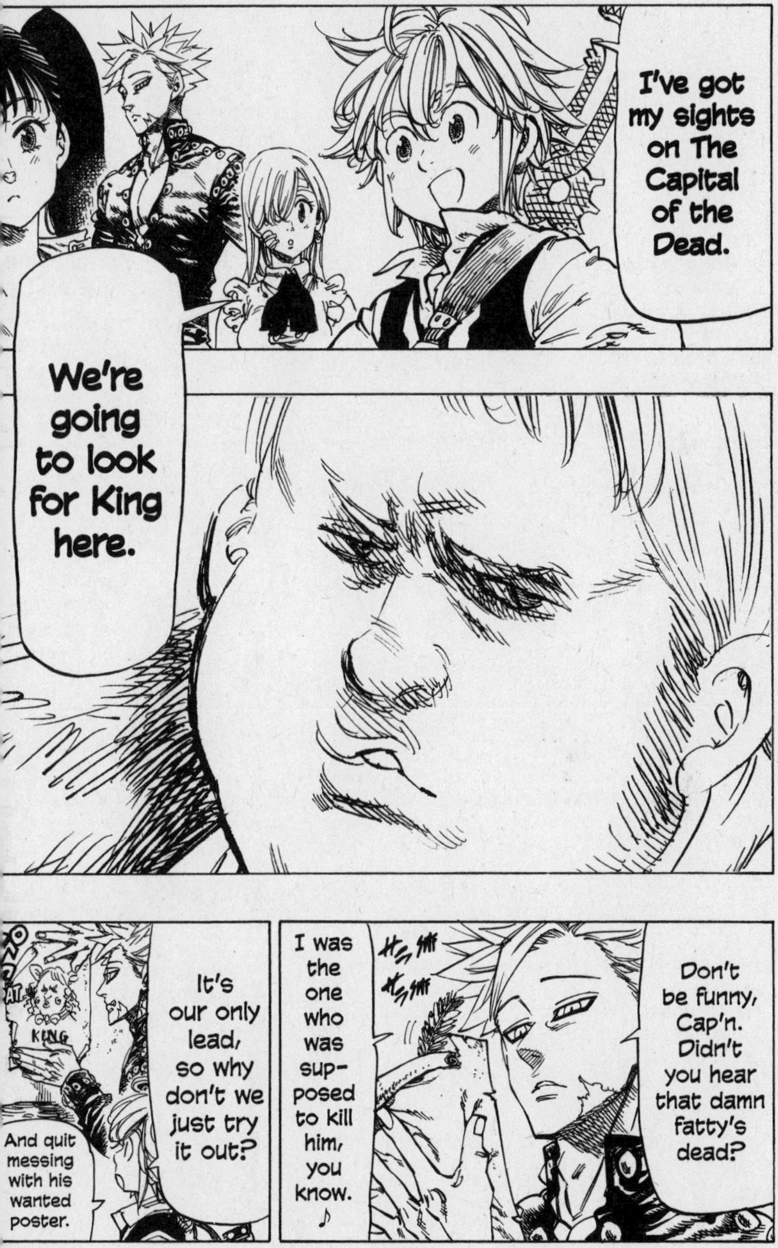
I've got my sights on The Capital of the Dead.
We're going to look for King here.
Don't be funny, Cap'n. Didn't you hear that damn fatty's dead?
I was the one who was sup-posed to kill him, you know. ♪
It's our only lead, so why don't we just try it out?
KING
And quit messing with his wanted poster.

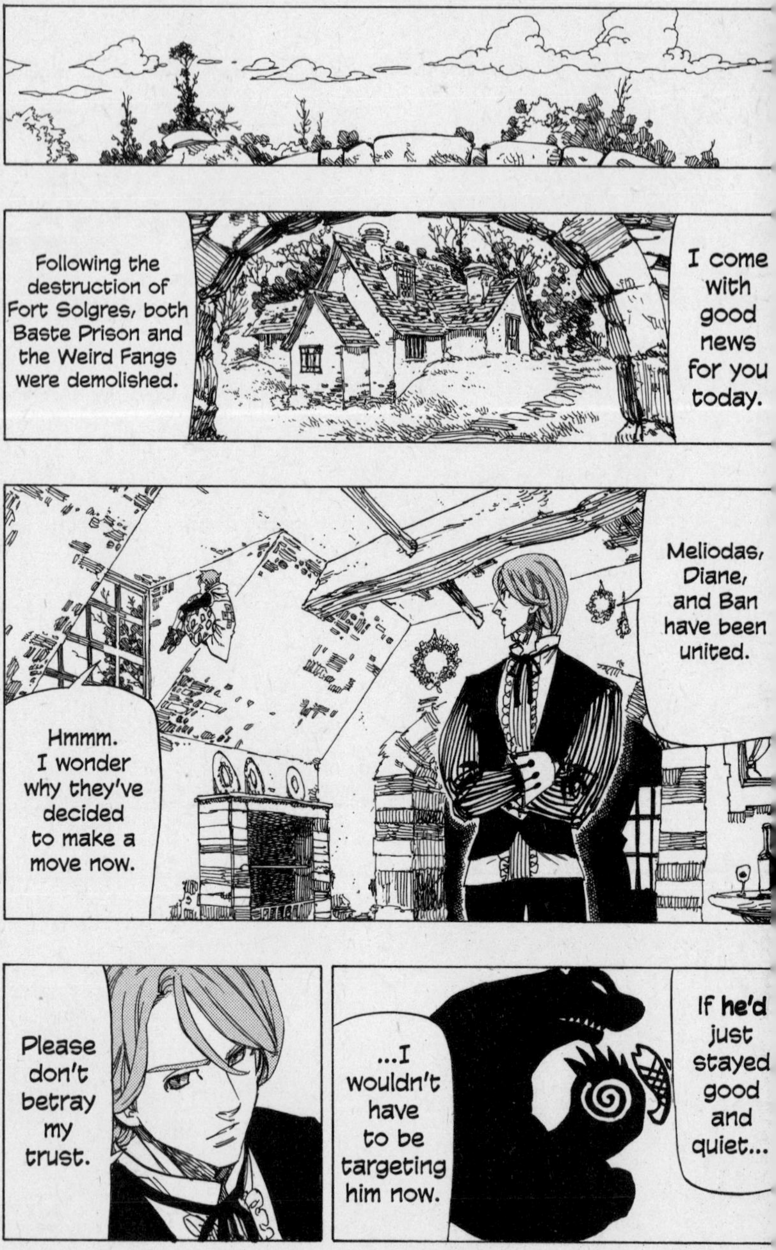
I come with good news for you today.
Following the destruction of Fort Solgres, both Baste Prison and the Weird Fangs were demolished.
Meliodas, Diane, and Ban have been united.
Hmmm. I wonder why they've decided to make a move now.
If he'd just stayed good and quiet...
...I wouldn't have to be targeting him now.
Please don't betray my trust.

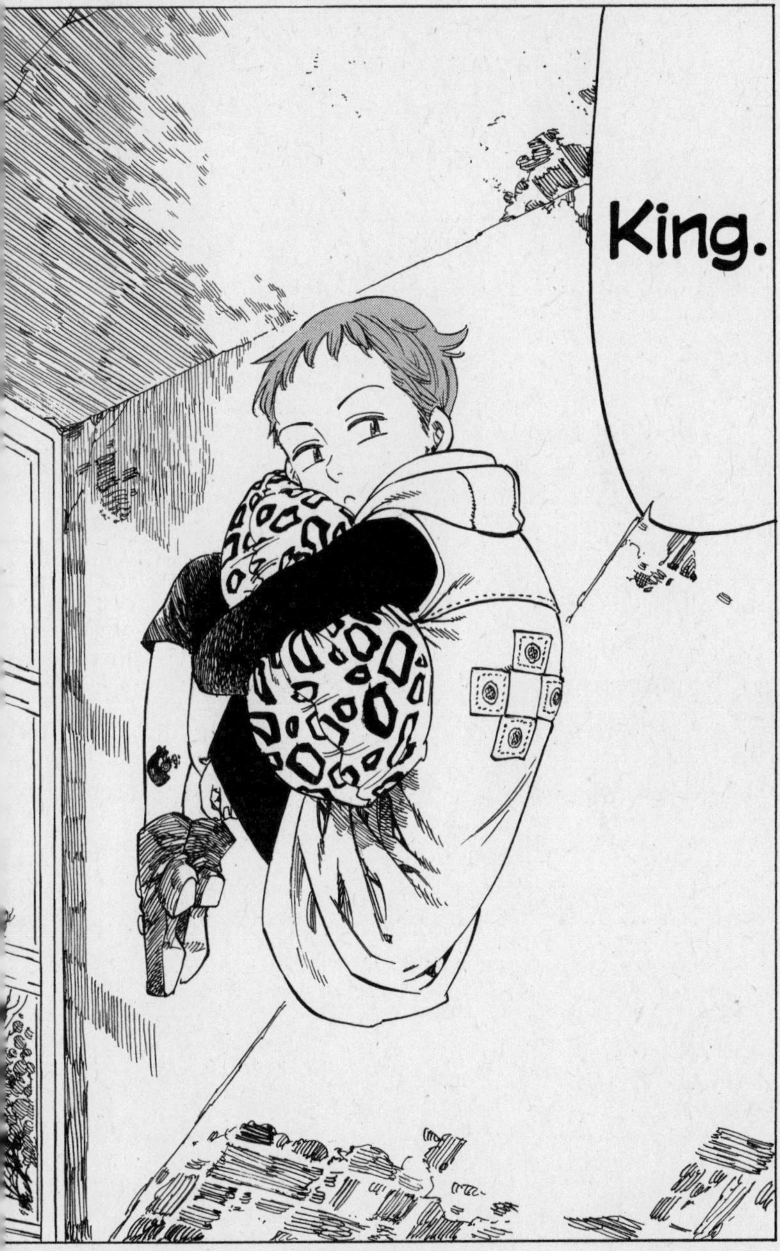
King.

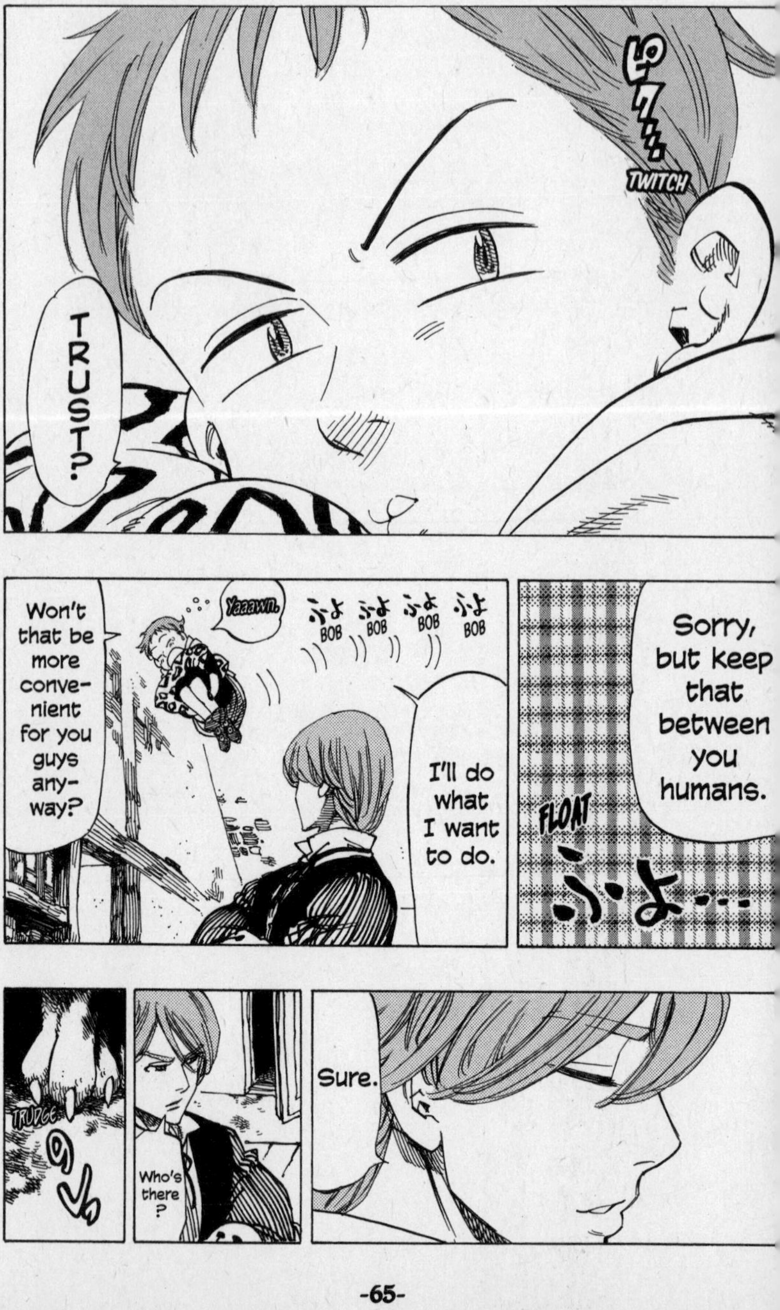
TWITCH
TRUST?
Sorry, but keep that between you humans.
FLOAT
ふよ...
ふよ BOB ふよ BOB ふよ BOB ふよ BOB
Yaaawn.
Won't that be more convenient for you guys anyway?
I'll do what I want to do.
Sure.
Who's there?
TRUDGE

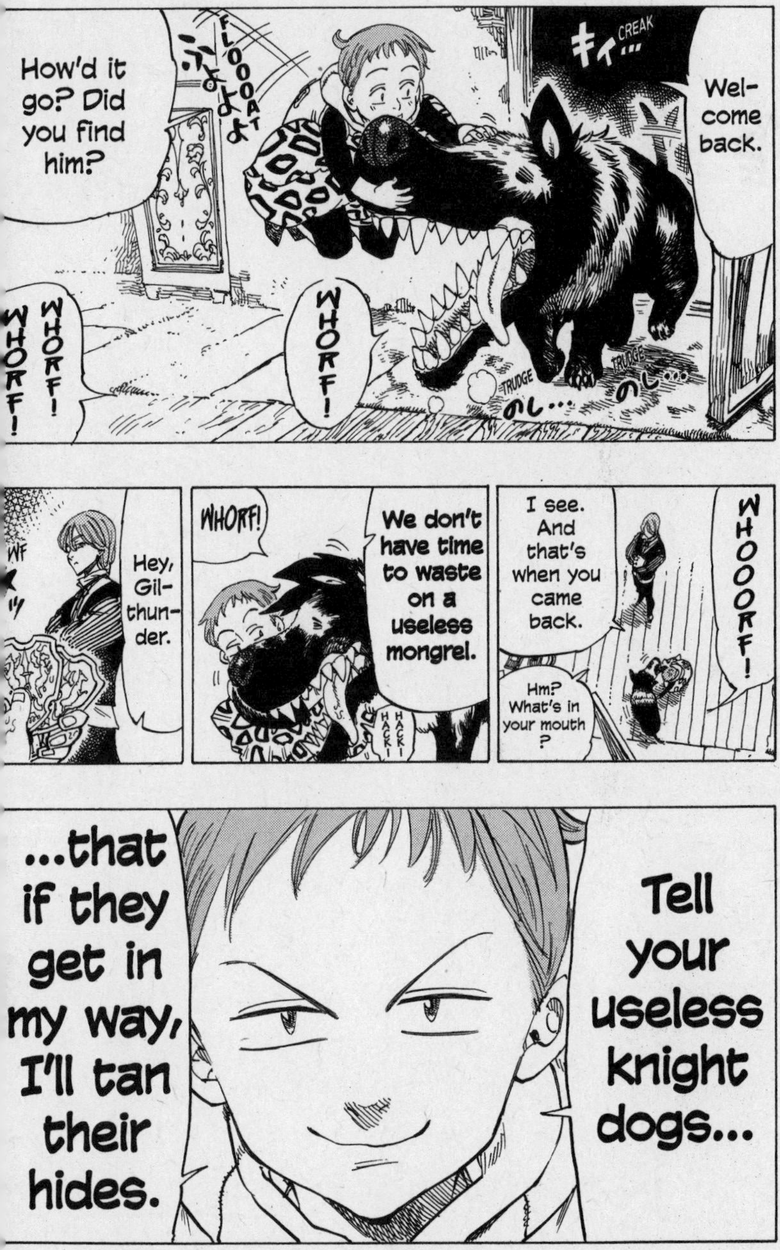
キィ
CREAK
Wel-come back.
ふよよ
FLOOOOAT
How'd it go? Did you find him?
WHORF!
WHORF!
WHORF!
のし…
TRUDGE
のし…
TRUDGE
WHOOOORF!
I see. And that's when you came back.
Hm? What's in your mouth?
We don't have time to waste on a useless mongrel.
WHORF!
HACK HACK
Hey, Gil-thunder.
Tell your useless knight dogs...
...that if they get in my way, I'll tan their hides.

Chapter 18 - A Touching Reunion

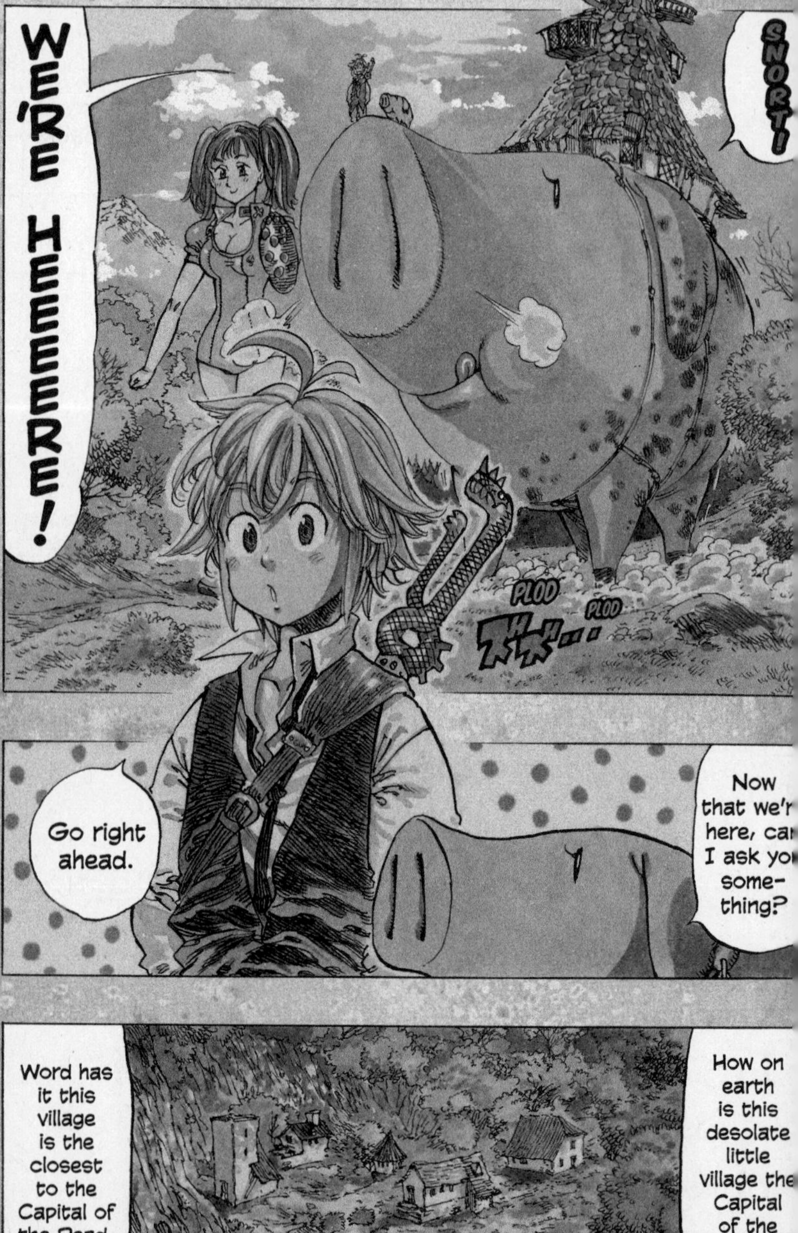
SNORT!
WE'RE HEEEEERE!
PLOD
PLOD
Now that we'r here, ca I ask yo some-thing?
Go right ahead.
How on earth is this desolate little village the Capital of the Dead?!
Word has it this village is the closest to the Capital of the Dead.

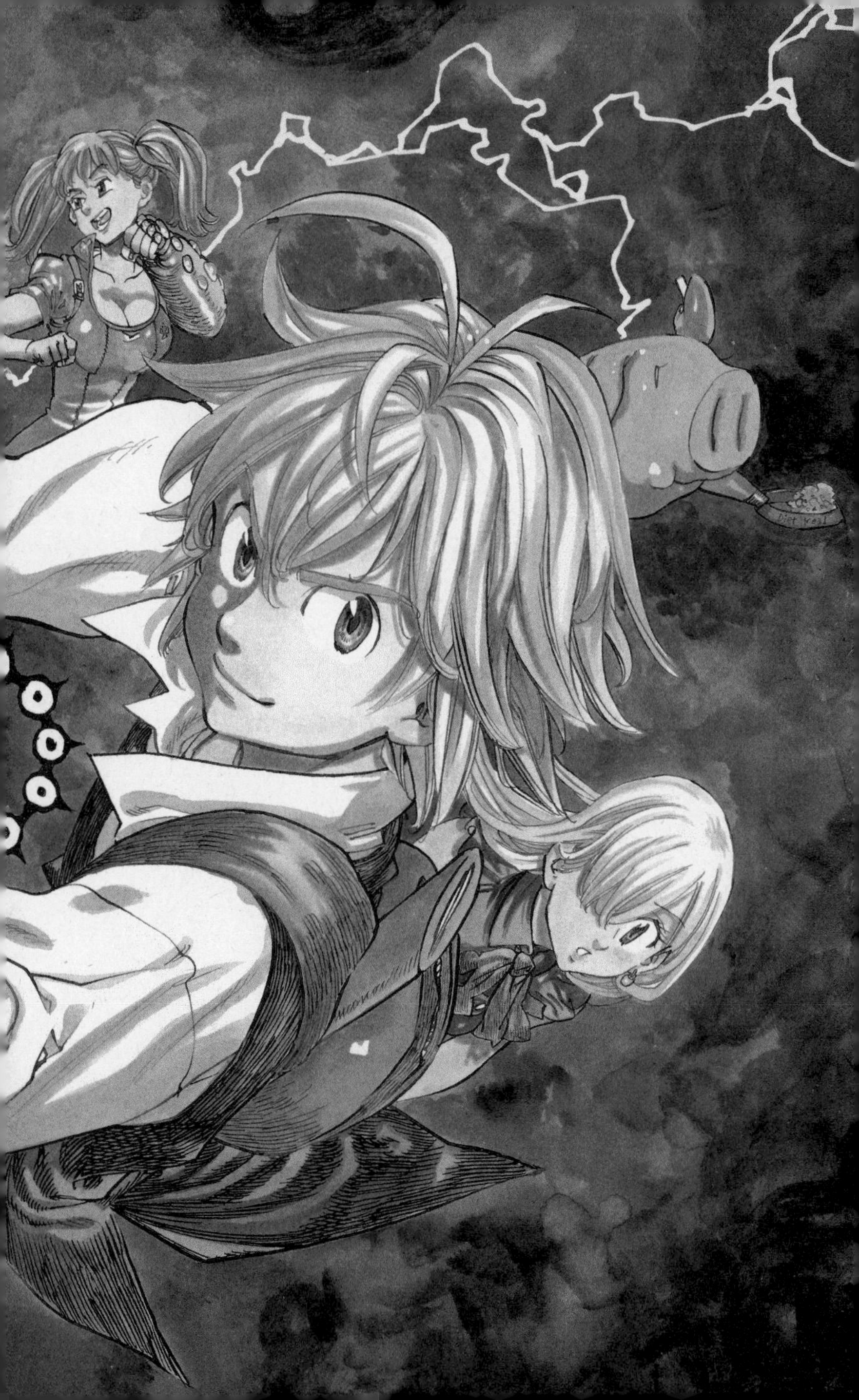

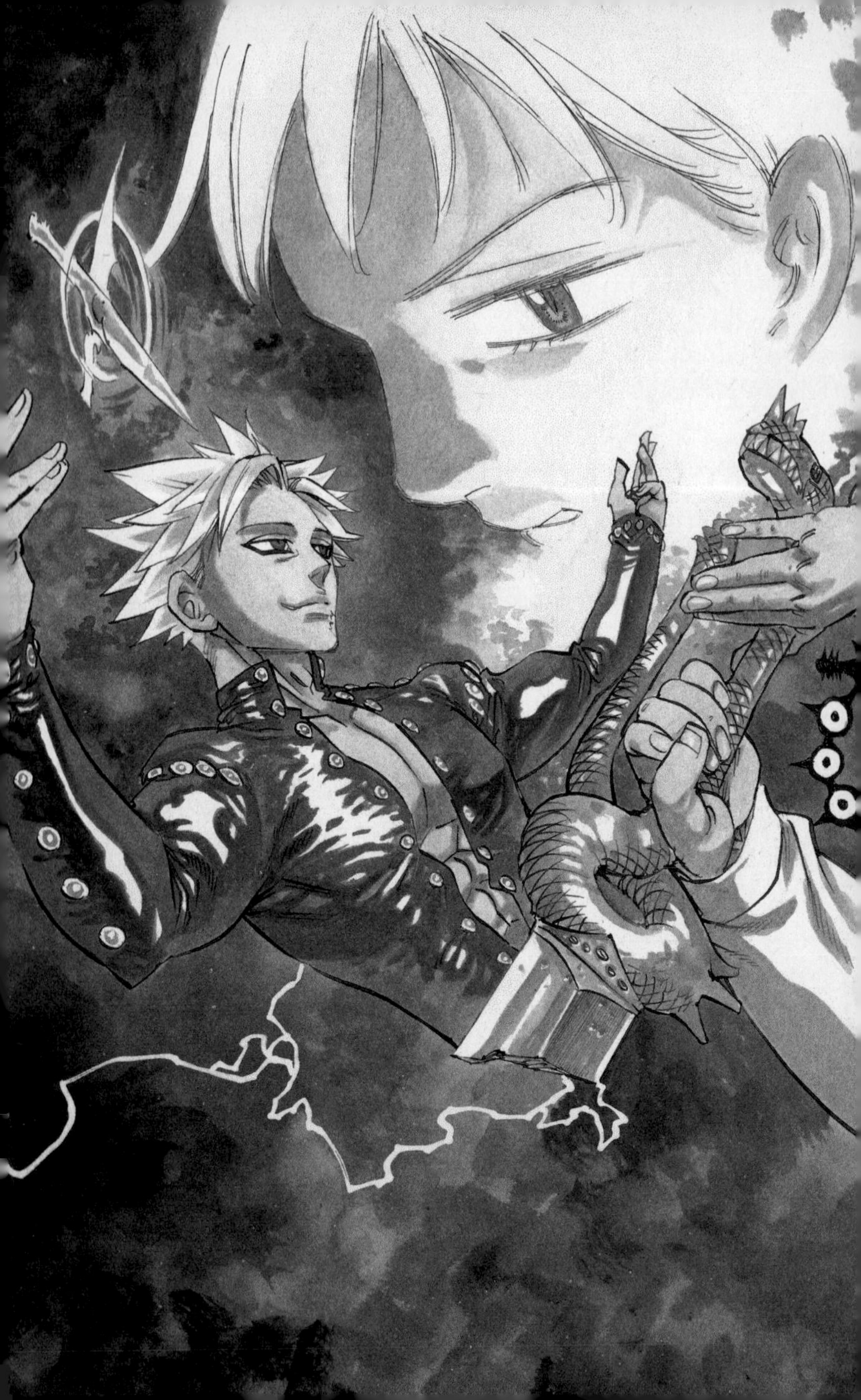

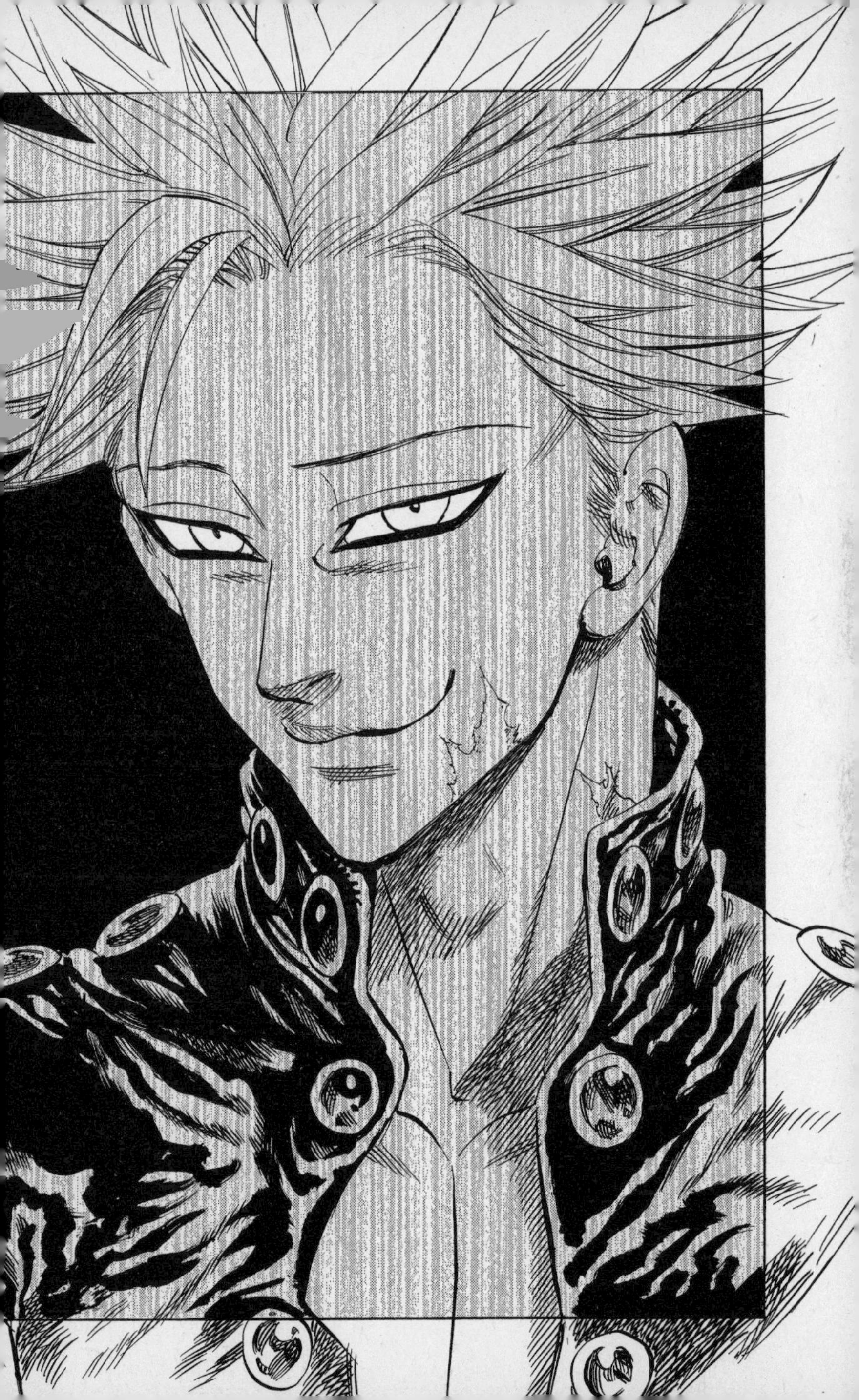

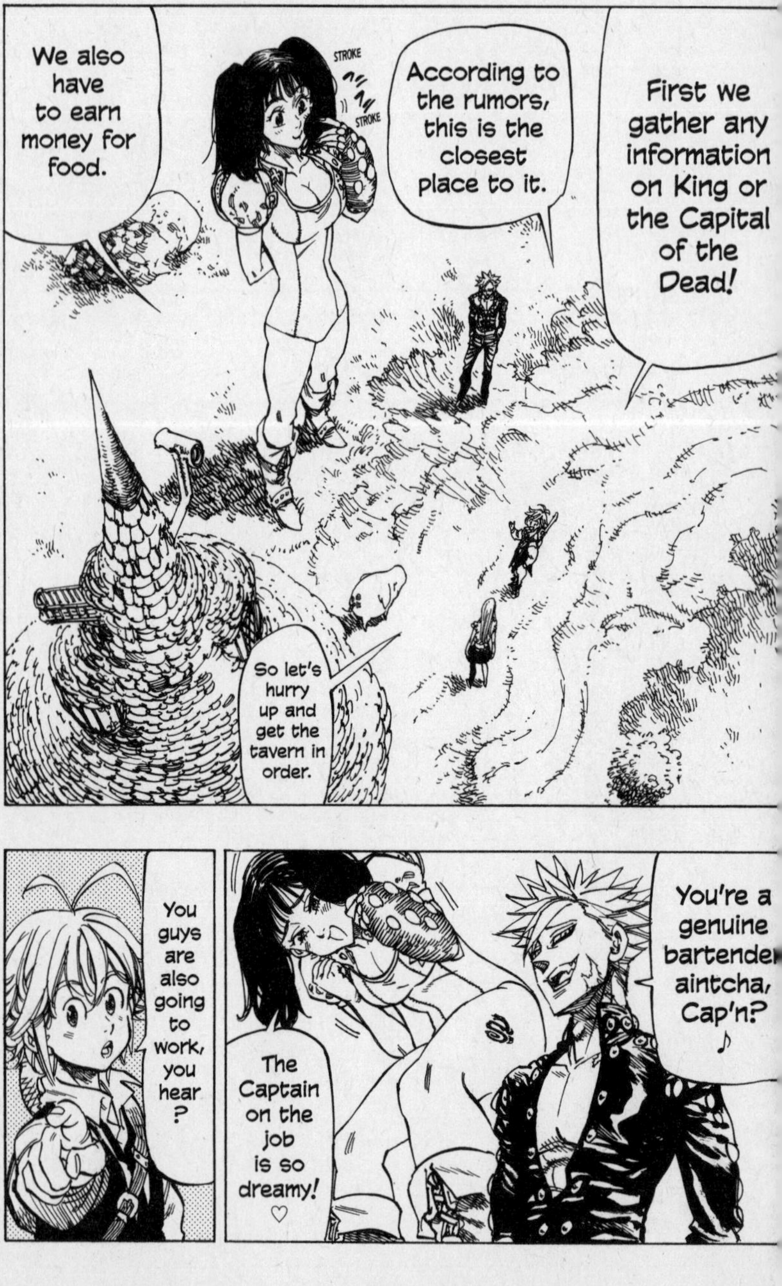
First we gather any information on King or the Capital of the Dead!
According to the rumors, this is the closest place to it.
STROKE
STROKE
We also have to earn money for food.
So let's hurry up and get the tavern in order.
You're a genuine bartende aintcha, Cap'n? ♪
The Captain on the job is so dreamy! ♡
You guys are also going to work, you hear?

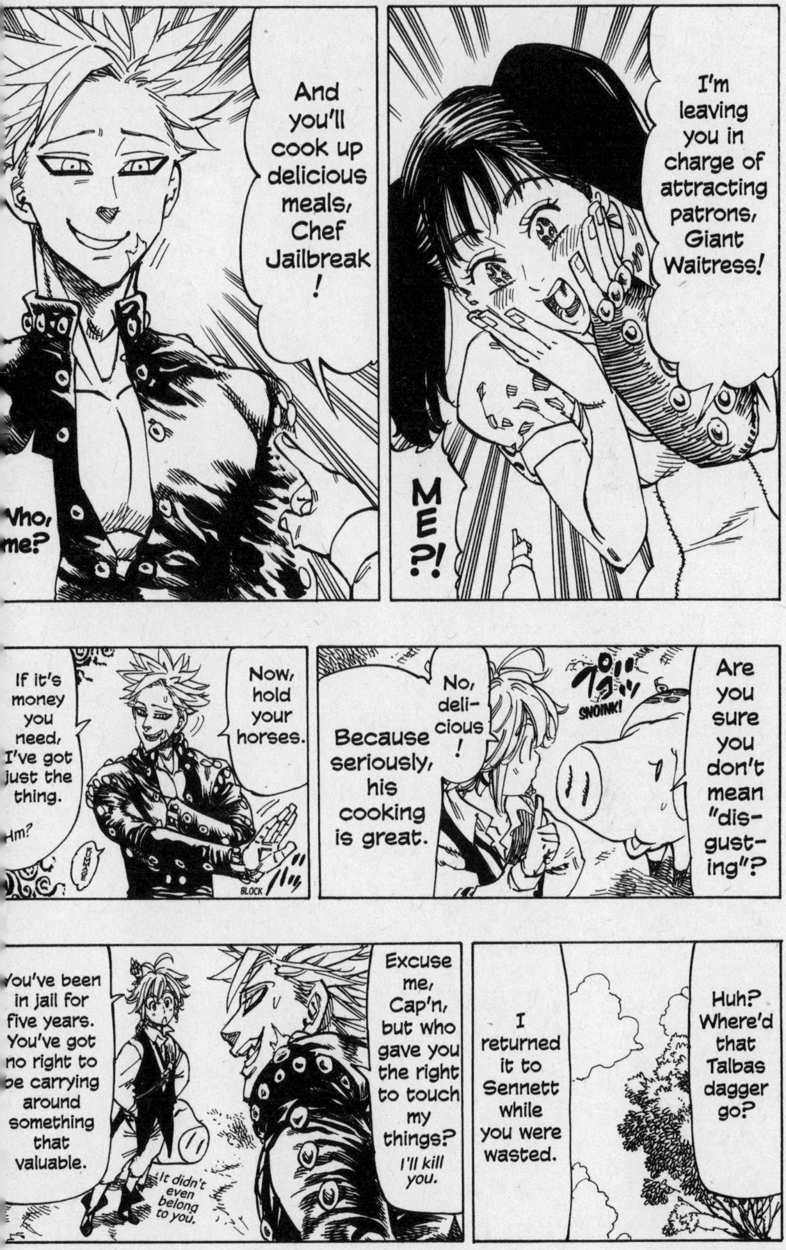
I'm leaving you in charge of attracting patrons, Giant Waitress!
ME?!
And you'll cook up delicious meals, Chef Jailbreak!
Who, me?
Are you sure you don't mean "dis-gust-ing"?
SNOINK!
No, deli-cious!
Because seriously, his cooking is great.
Now, hold your horses.
If it's money you need, I've got just the thing.
Hm?
BLOCK
Huh? Where'd that Talbas dagger go?
I returned it to Sennett while you were wasted.
Excuse me, Cap'n, but who gave you the right to touch my things?
I'll kill you.
You've been in jail for five years. You've got no right to be carrying around something that valuable.
It didn't even belong to you.

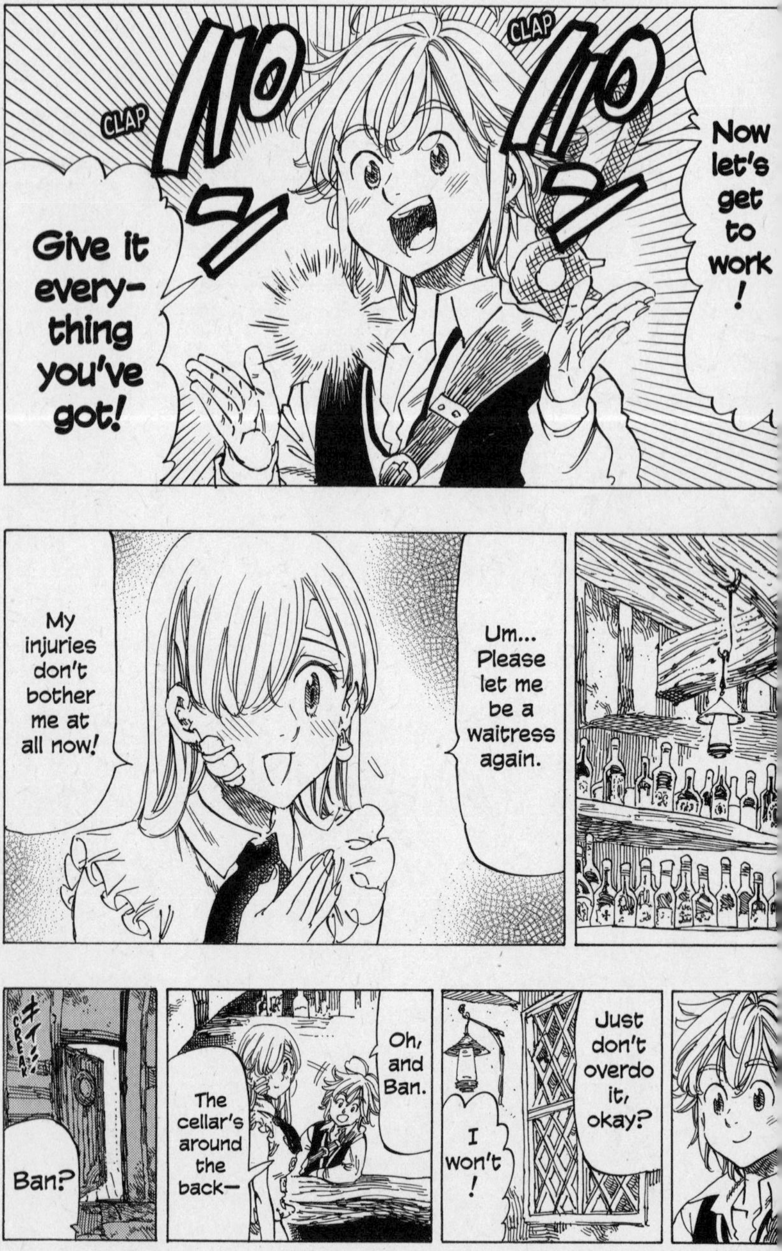
CLAP
Now let's get to work!
CLAP
Give it everything you've got!
Um... Please let me be a waitress again.
My injuries don't bother me at all now!
Just don't overdo it, okay?
I won't!
Oh, and Ban.
The cellar's around the back—
CREAK
Ban?

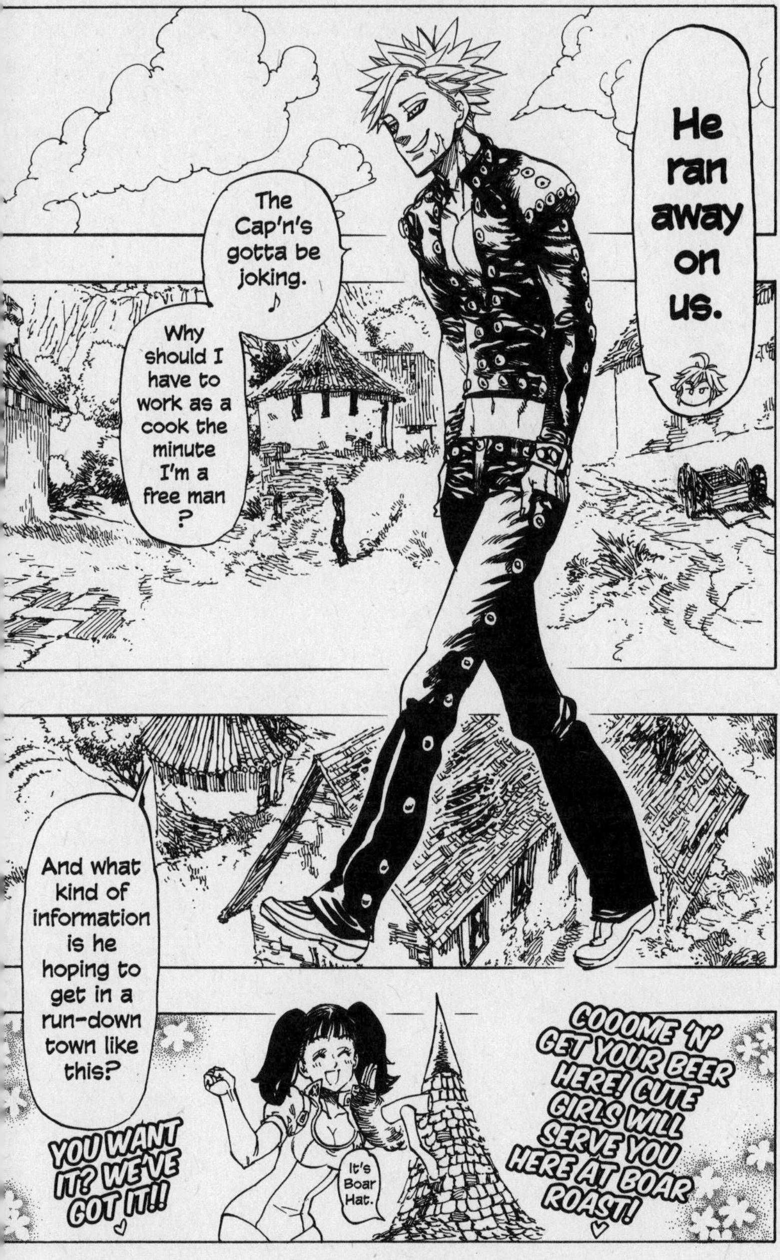
He ran away on us.
The Cap'n's gotta be joking. ♪
Why should I have to work as a cook the minute I'm a free man?
And what kind of information is he hoping to get in a run-down town like this?
COOOME 'N' GET YOUR BEER HERE! CUTE GIRLS WILL SERVE YOU HERE AT BOAR ROAST! ♡
It's Boar Hat.
YOU WANT IT? WE'VE GOT IT!! ♡

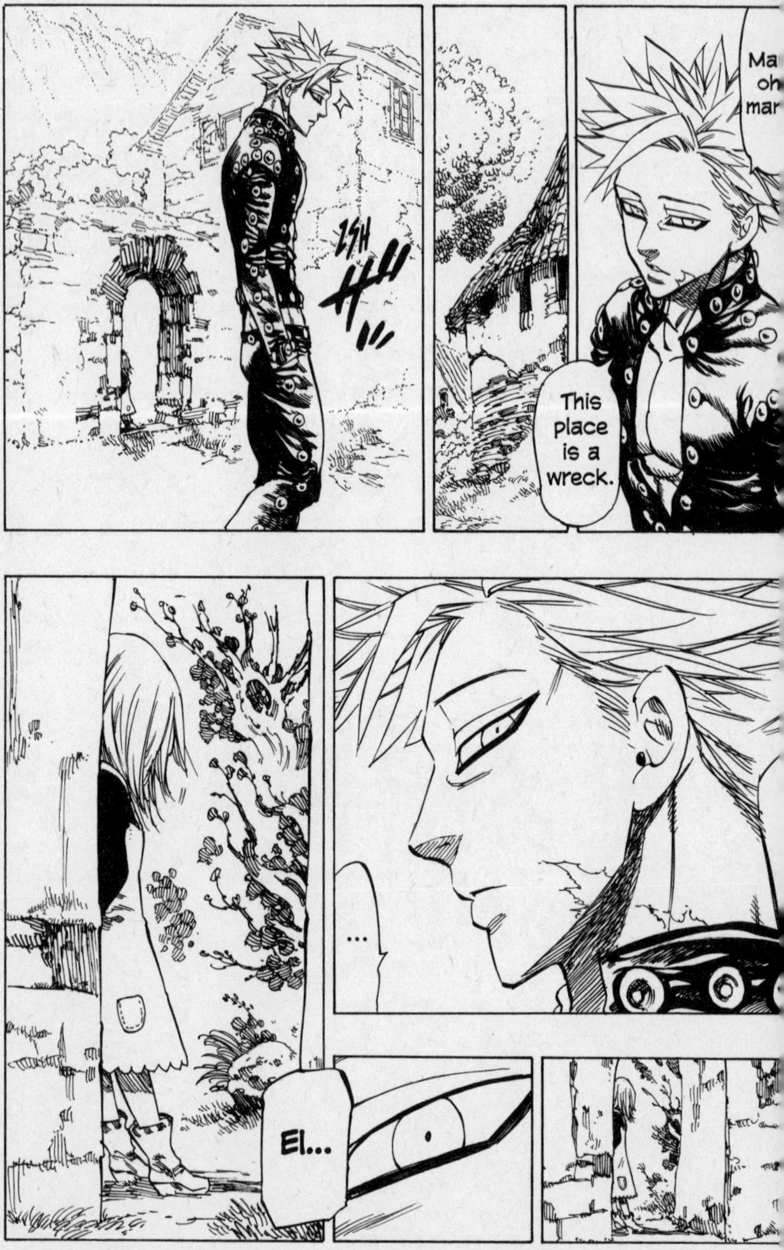
This place is a wreck.
ZSH
...
El...

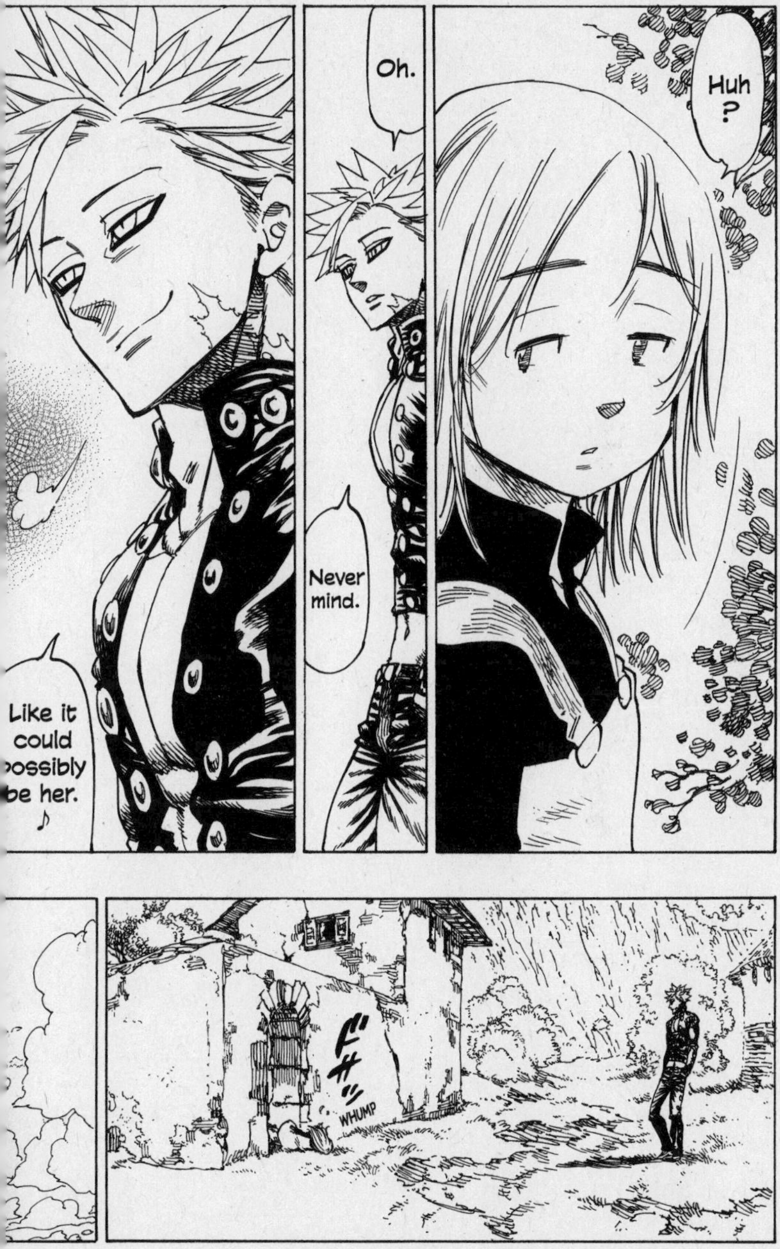
Huh?
Oh.
Never mind.
Like it could possibly be her. ♪
ドサッ
WHUMP

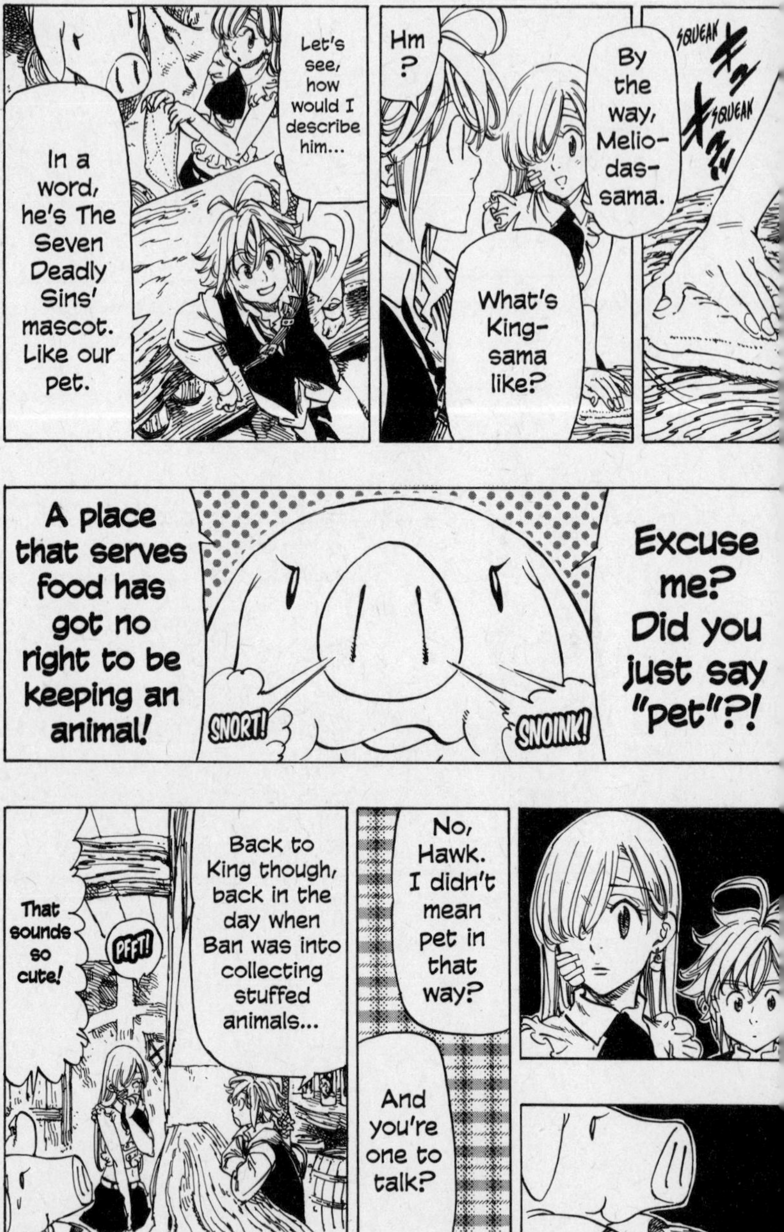
SQUEAK
SQUEAK
By the way, Melio-das-sama.
Hm?
What's King-sama like?
Let's see, how would I describe him...
In a word, he's The Seven Deadly Sins' mascot. Like our pet.
Excuse me? Did you just say "pet"?!
SNOINK!
SNORT!
A place that serves food has got no right to be keeping an animal!
No, Hawk. I didn't mean pet in that way?
And you're one to talk?
Back to King though, back in the day when Ban was into collecting stuffed animals...
PFFT!
That sounds so cute!

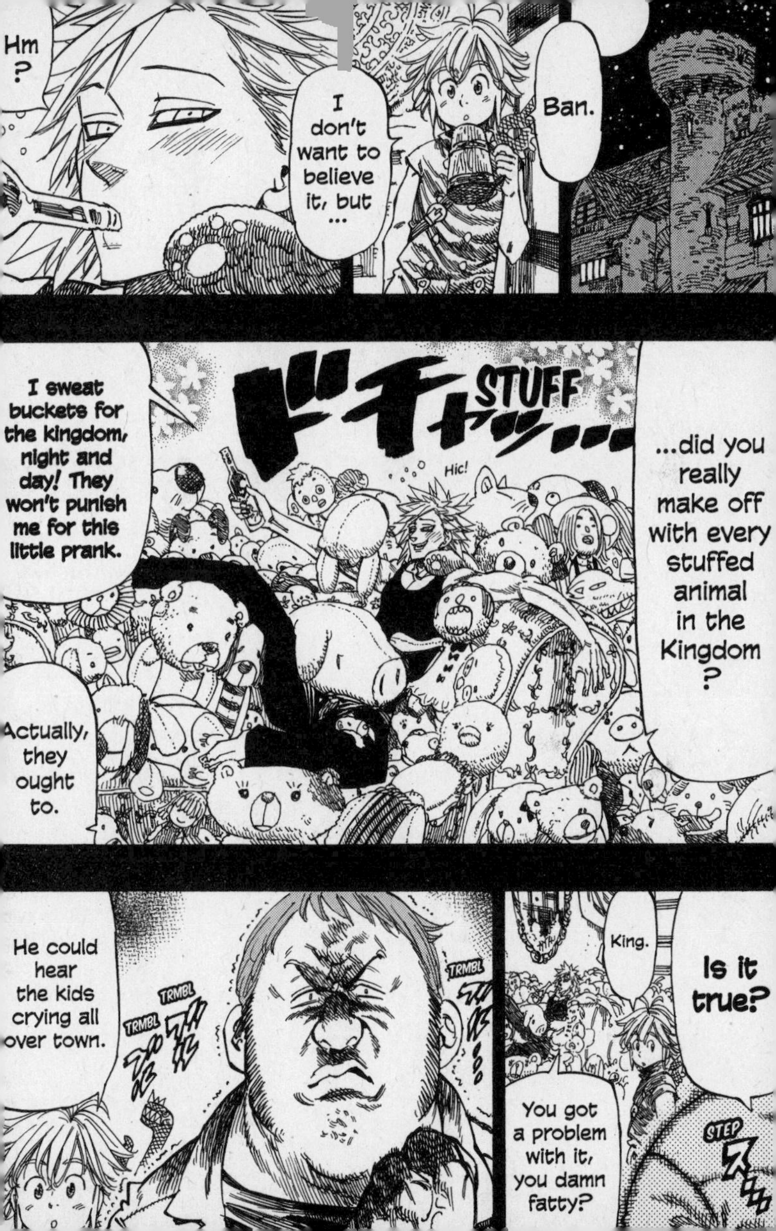
Ban.
I don't want to believe it, but ...
Hm?
...did you really make off with every stuffed animal in the Kingdom?
STUFF
Hic!
I sweat buckets for the kingdom, night and day! They won't punish me for this little prank.
Actually, they ought to.
King.
Is it true?
STEP
You got a problem with it, you damn fatty?
TRMBL
TRMBL
TRMBL
He could hear the kids crying all over town.

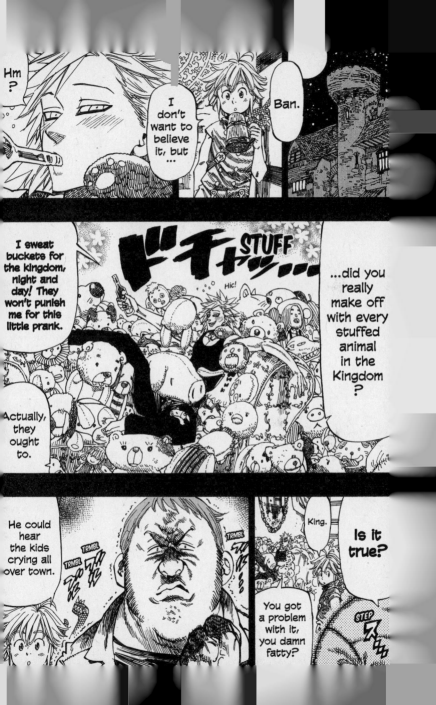

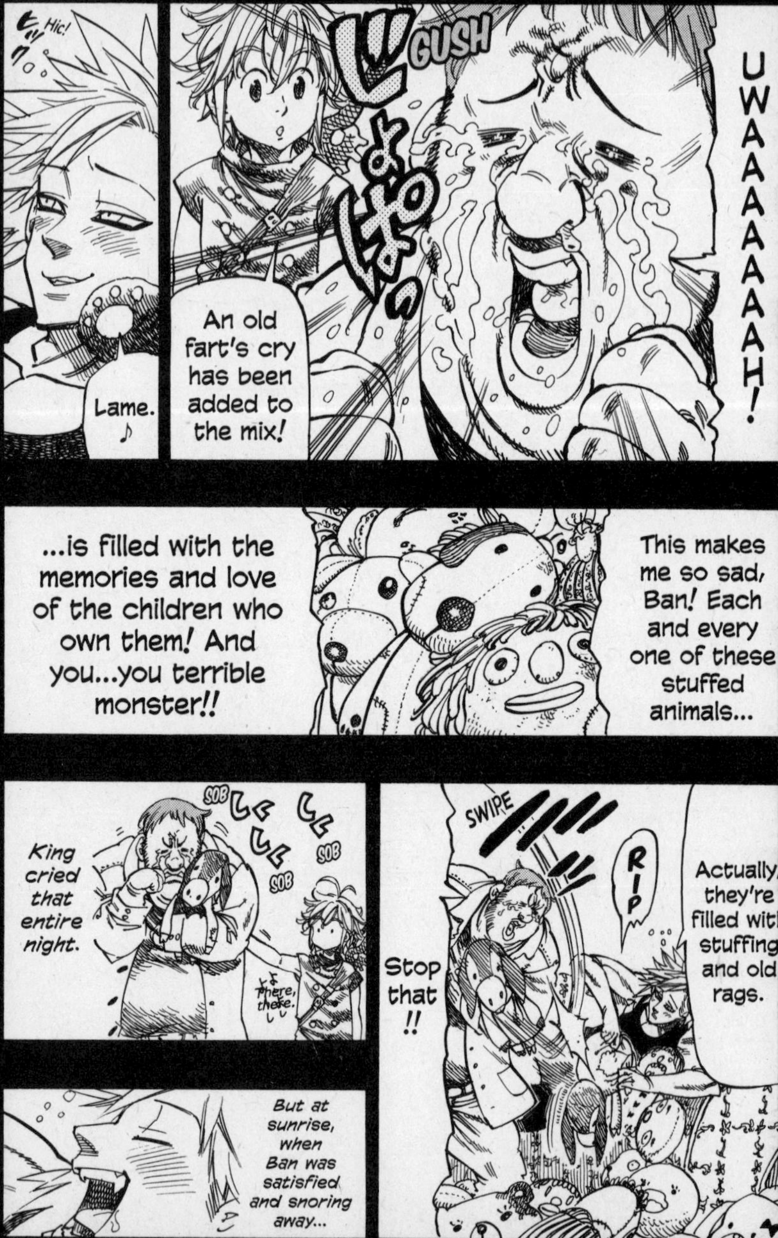

UWAAAAAAAAH!
GUSH
An old fart's cry has been added to the mix!
Hic!
Lame. ♪
This makes me so sad, Ban! Each and every one of these stuffed animals...
...is filled with the memories and love of the children who own them! And you...you terrible monster!!
Actually, they're filled with stuffing and old rags.
RIP
SWIPE
Stop that!!
SOB
SOB
SOB
King cried that entire night.
There, there.
But at sunrise, when Ban was satisfied and snoring away...

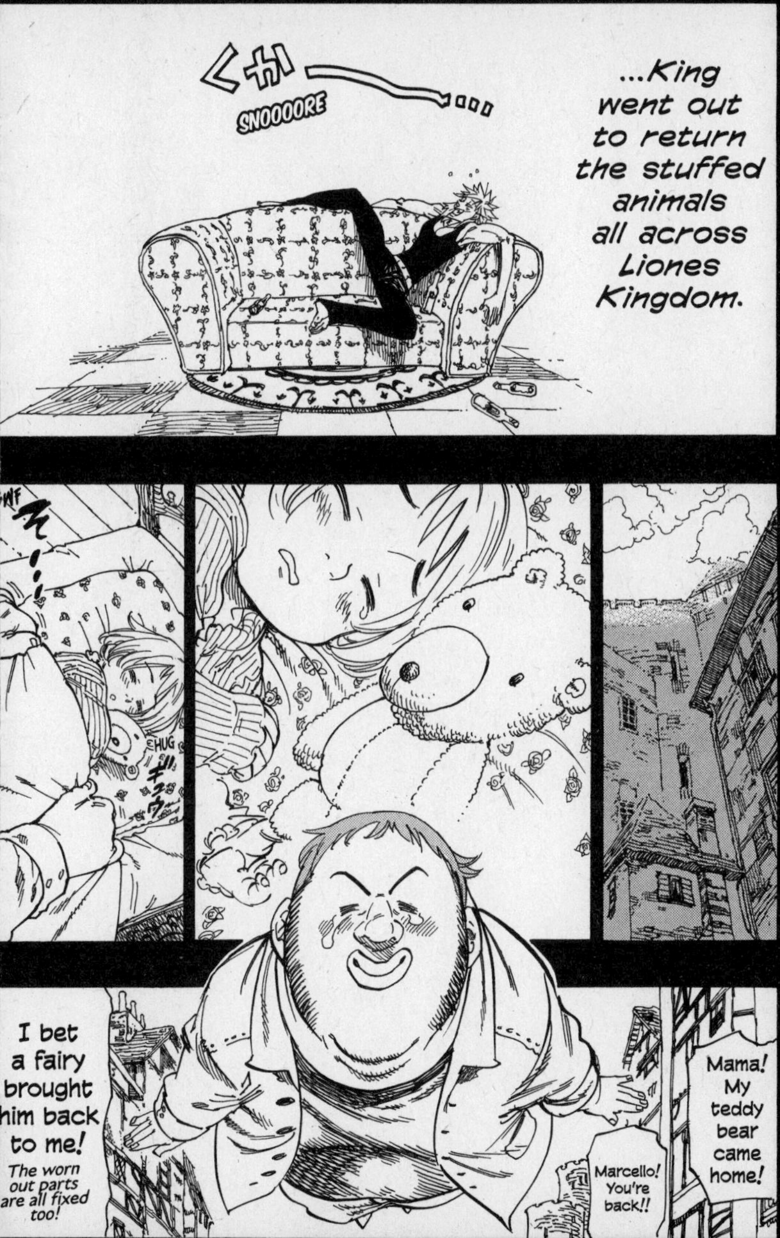
...King went out to return the stuffed animals all across Liones Kingdom.
SNOOOORE
HUG
Mama! My teddy bear came home!
Marcello! You're back!!
I bet a fairy brought him back to me!
The worn out parts are all fixed too!

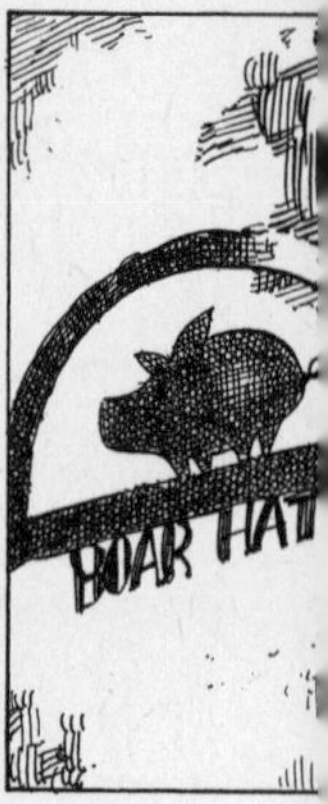
BOAR HAT

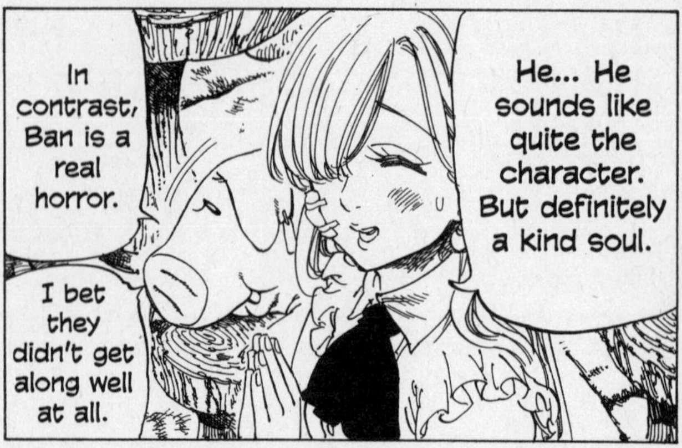
He... He sounds like quite the character. But definitely a kind soul.
In contrast, Ban is a real horror.
I bet they didn't get along well at all.

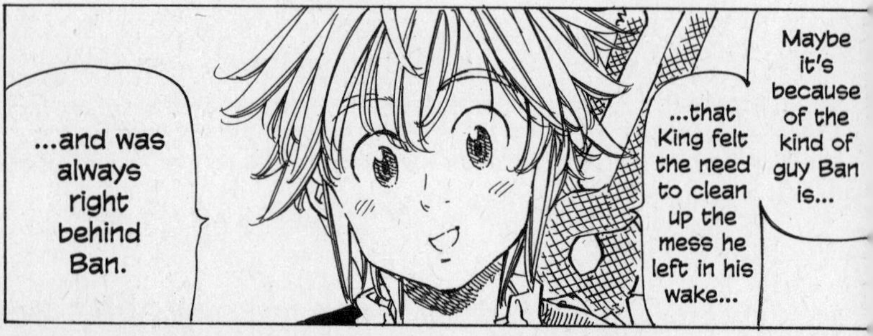
Maybe it's because of the kind of guy Ban is...
...that King felt the need to clean up the mess he left in his wake...
...and was always right behind Ban.

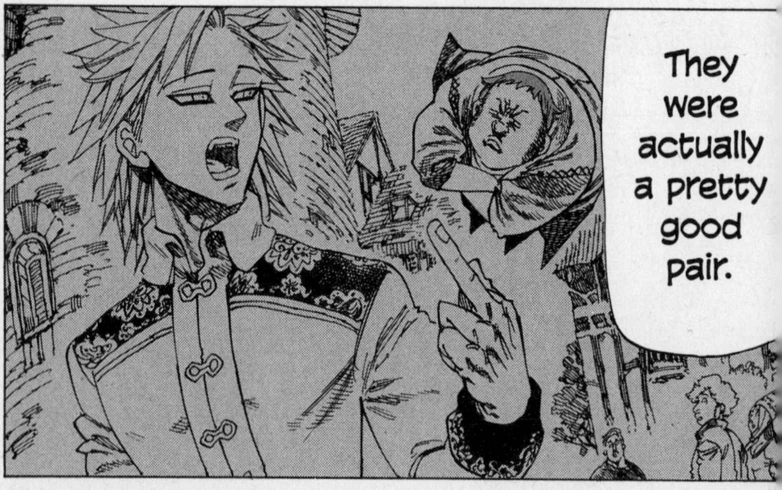
They were actually a pretty good pair.

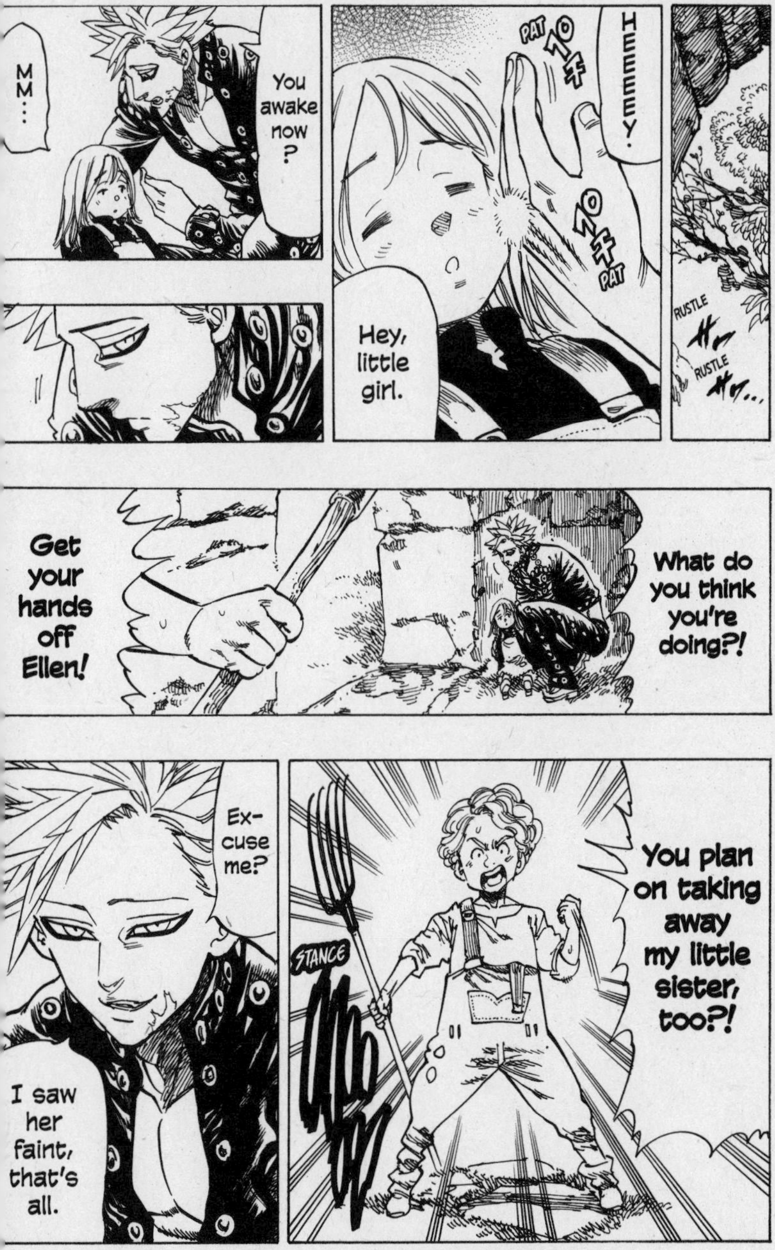
RUSTLE
RUSTLE
HEEEEY.
PAT
PAT
Hey, little girl.
You awake now?
MM...
What do you think you're doing?!
Get your hands off Ellen!
STANCE
You plan on taking away my little sister, too?!
Ex-cuse me?
I saw her faint, that's all.

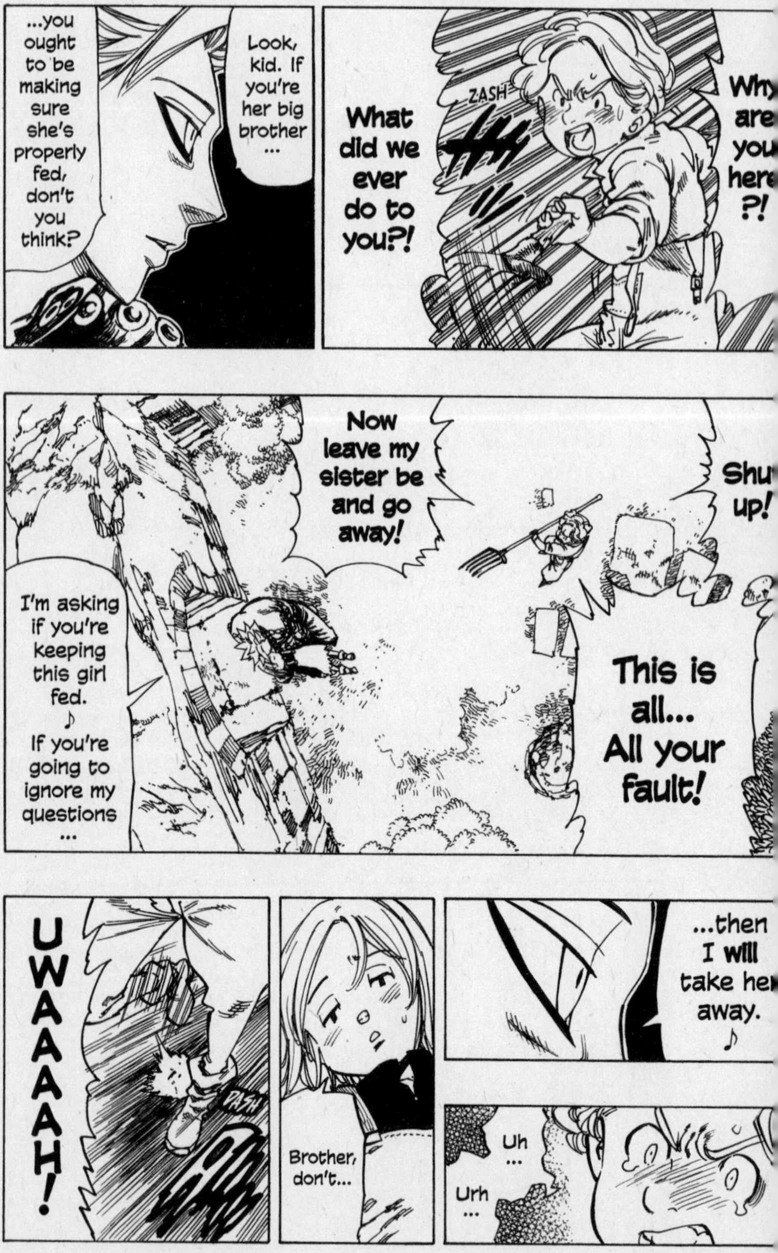
Why are you here?!
ZASH
What did we ever do to you?!
Look, kid. If you're her big brother ...
...you ought to be making sure she's properly fed, don't you think?
Shu up!
This is all... All your fault!
Now leave my sister be and go away!
I'm asking if you're keeping this girl fed. ♪ If you're going to ignore my questions ...
...then I will take he away. ♪
Uh ...
Urh ...
Brother, don't...
UWAAAAAH!

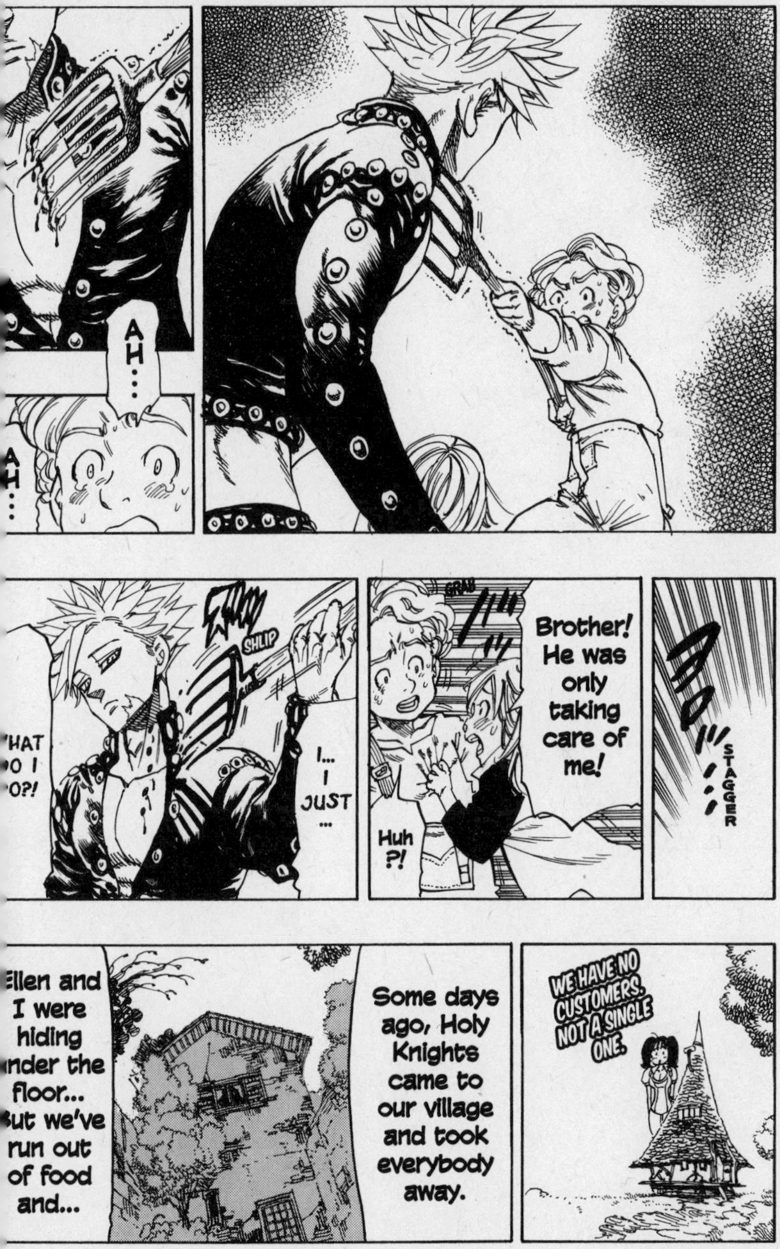
AH...
AH...
STAGGER
GRAB
Brother! He was only taking care of me!
Huh?!
SHLIP
I... I JUST ...
HAT O I O?!
WE HAVE NO CUSTOMERS, NOT A SINGLE ONE.
Some days ago, Holy Knights came to our village and took everybody away.
llen and I were hiding nder the floor... ut we've run out of food and...

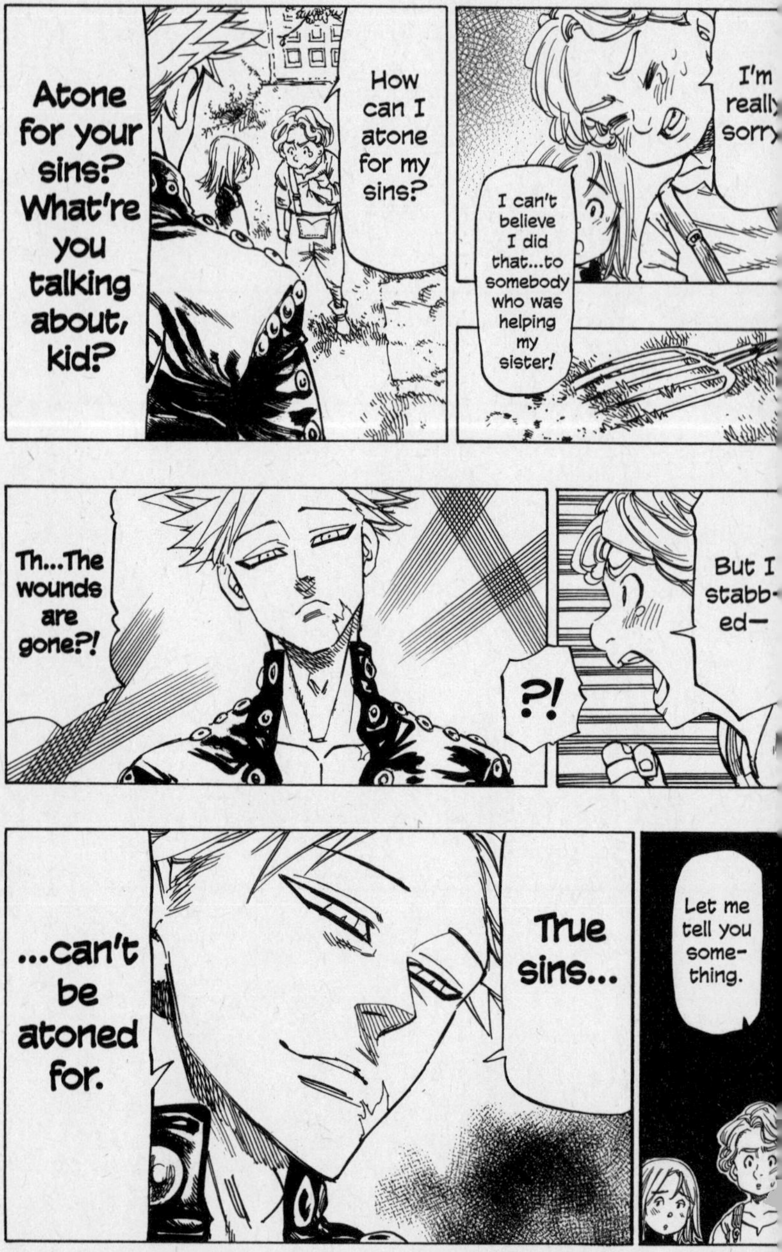

I'm really sorr
I can't believe I did that...to somebody who was helping my sister!
How can I atone for my sins?
Atone for your sins? What're you talking about, kid?
But I stabb-ed—
?!
Th...The wounds are gone?!
Let me tell you some-thing.
True sins...
...can't be atoned for.

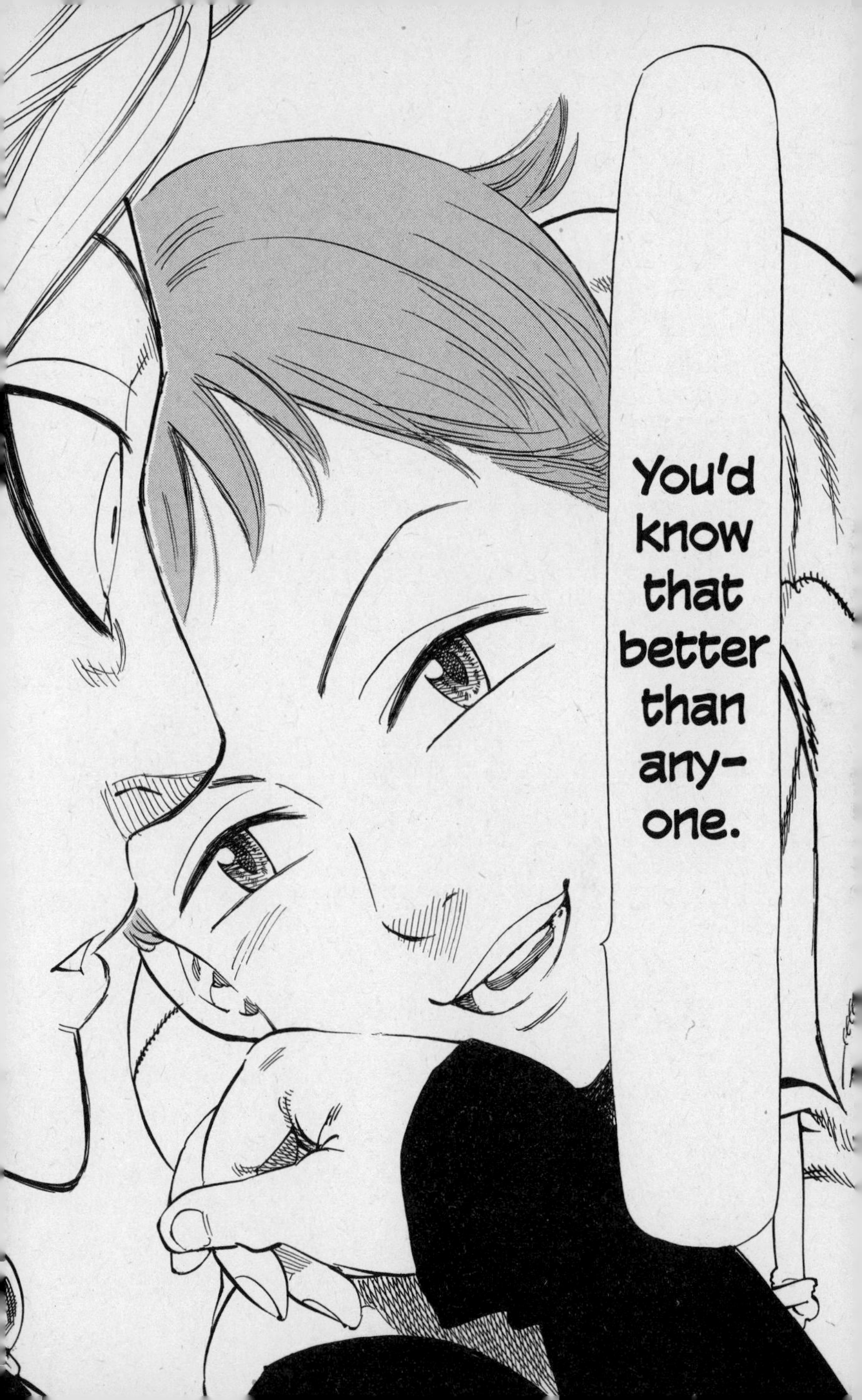
You'd know that better than any-one.

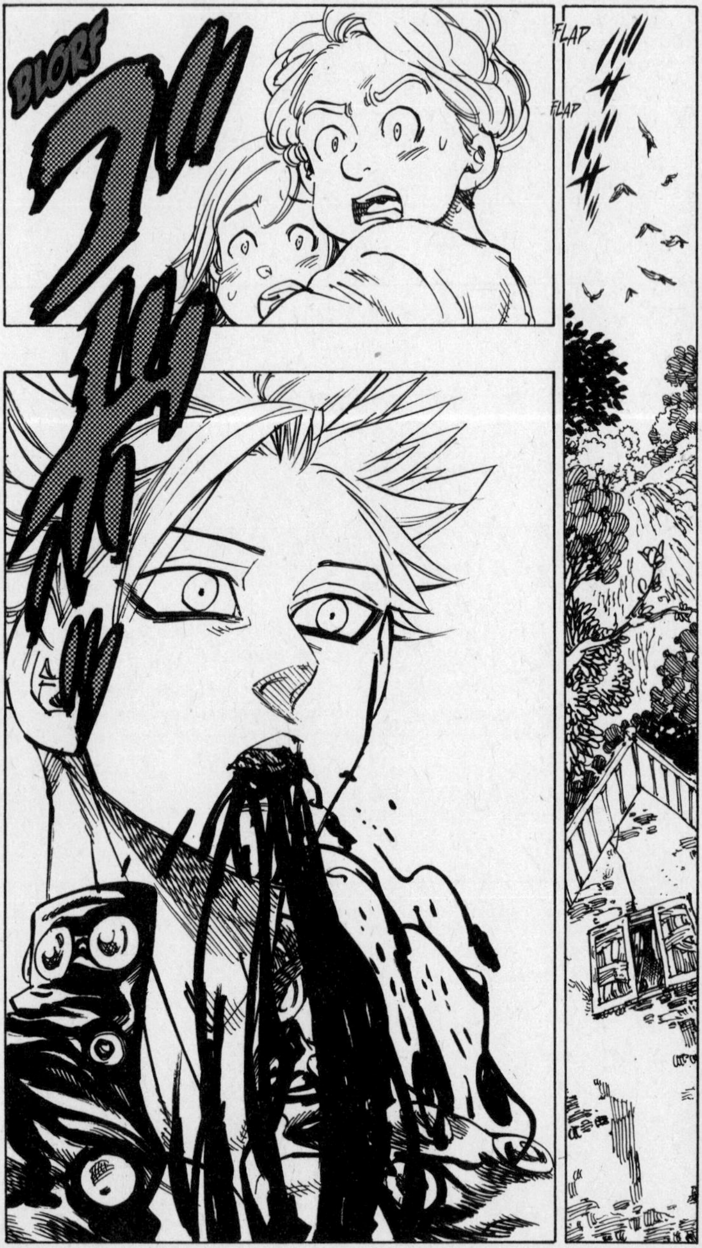
FLAP
FLAP
BLORF

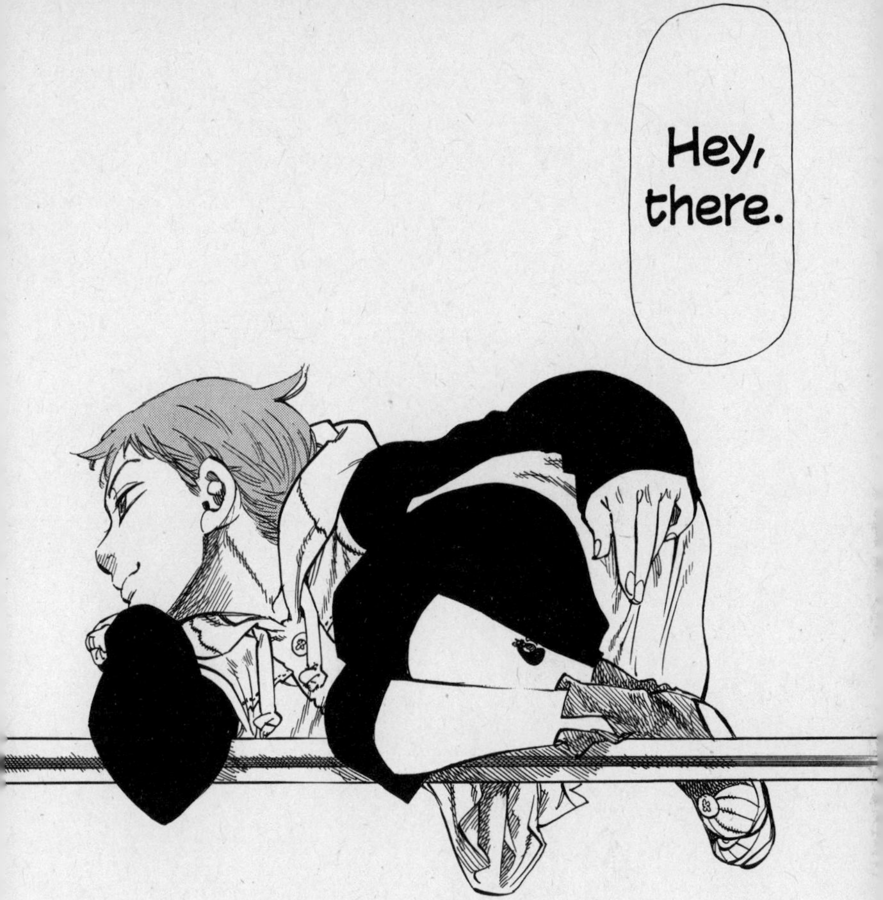
Hey, there.

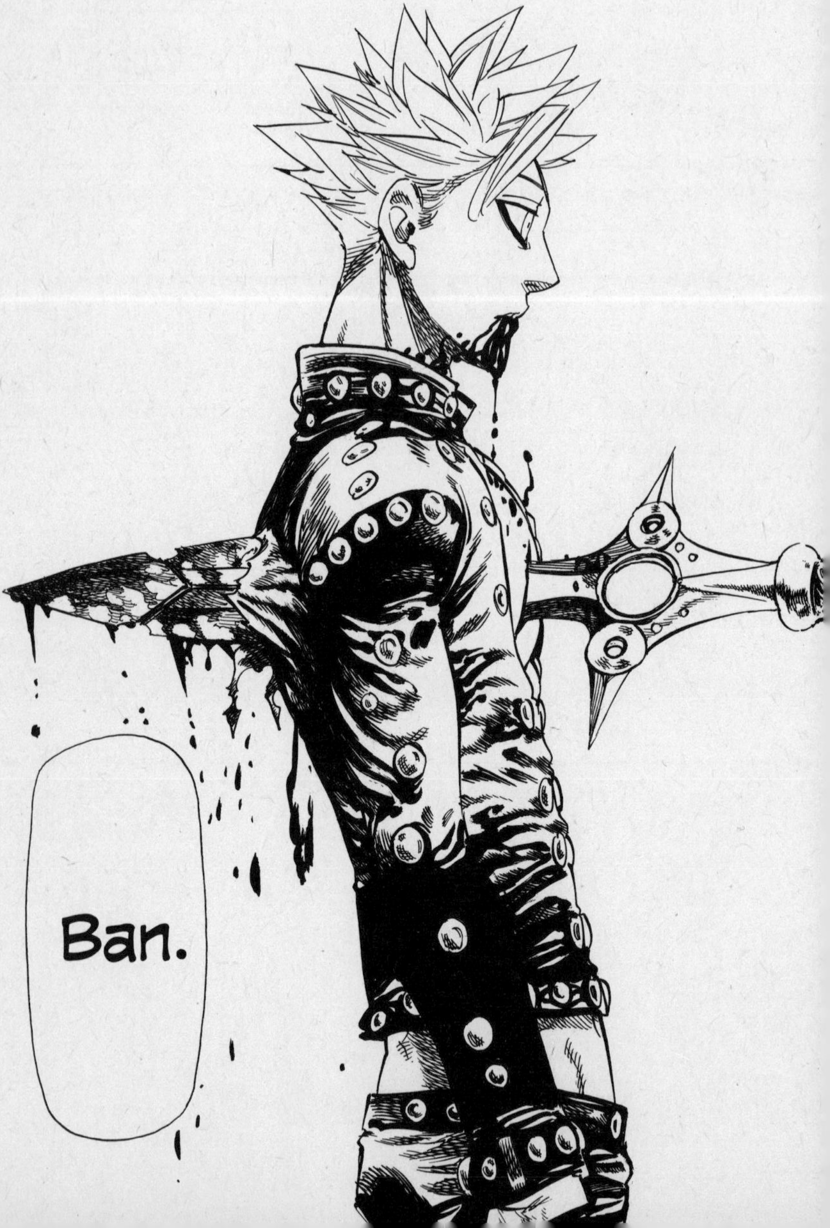
Ban.

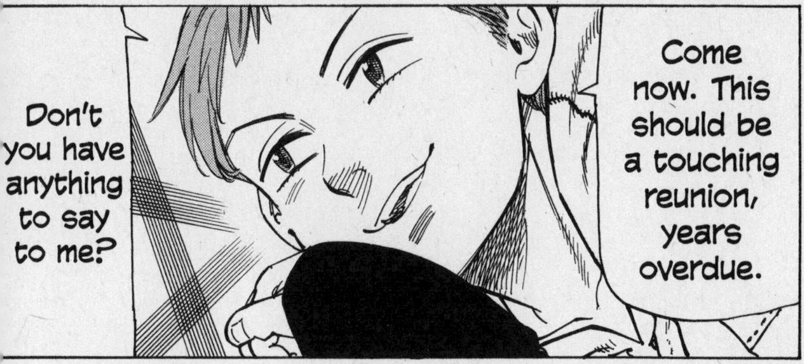
Come now. This should be a touching reunion, years overdue.
Don't you have anything to say to me?

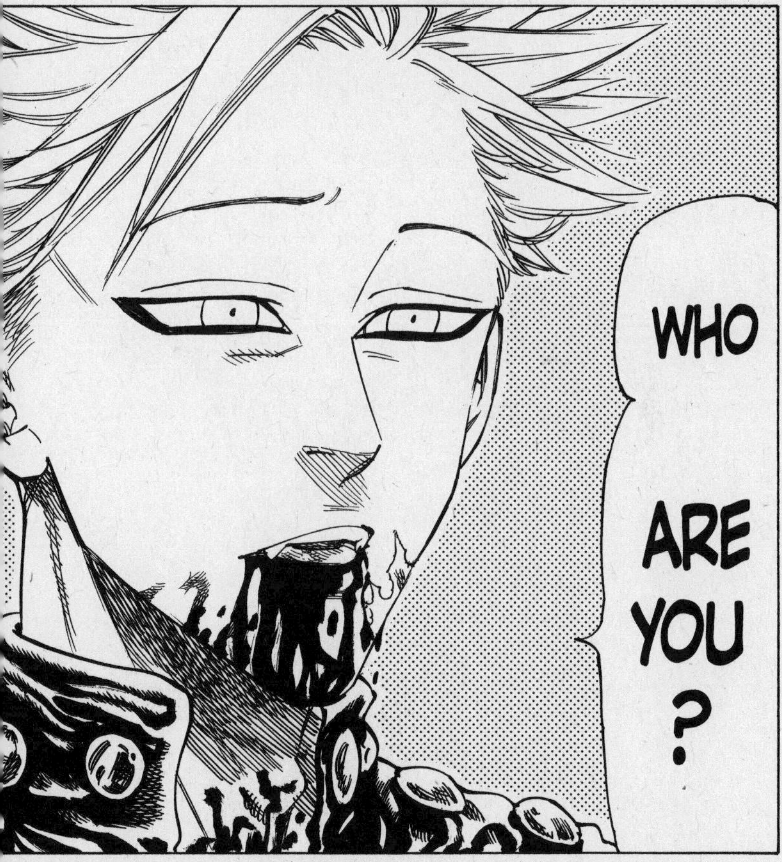
WHO ARE YOU?

Chapter 19 - The Sin of Greed

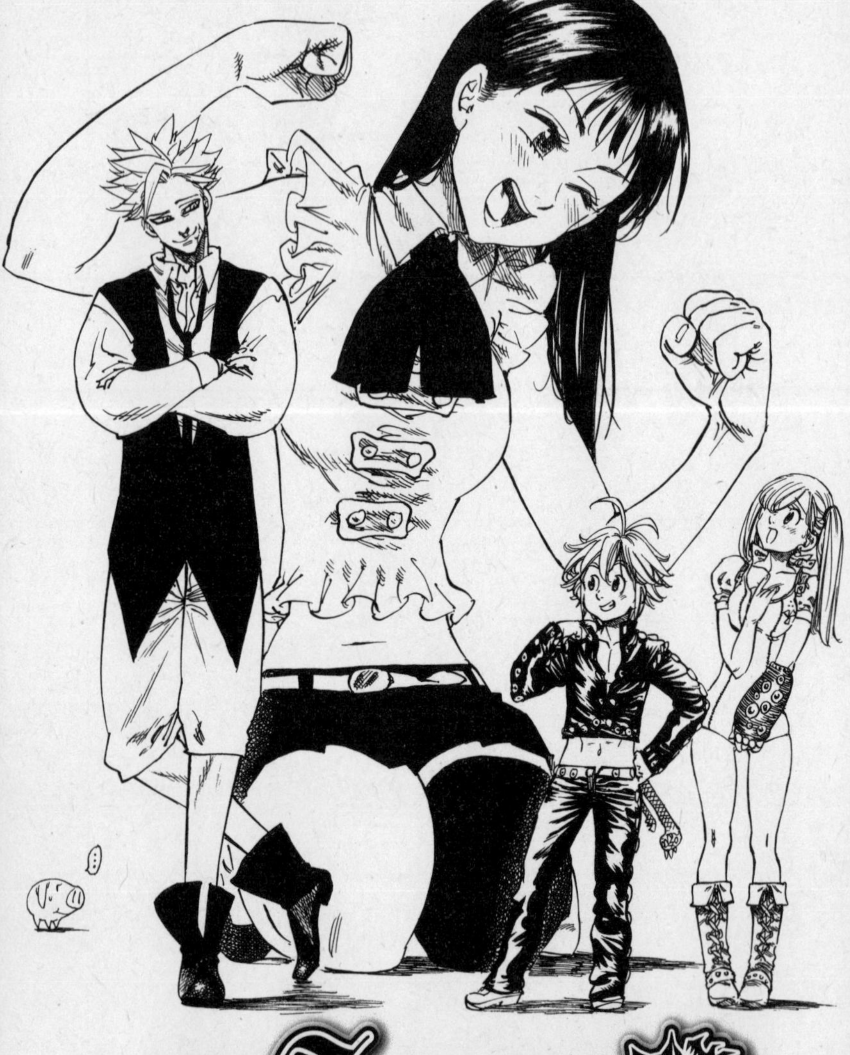

THE SEVEN DEADLY SINS

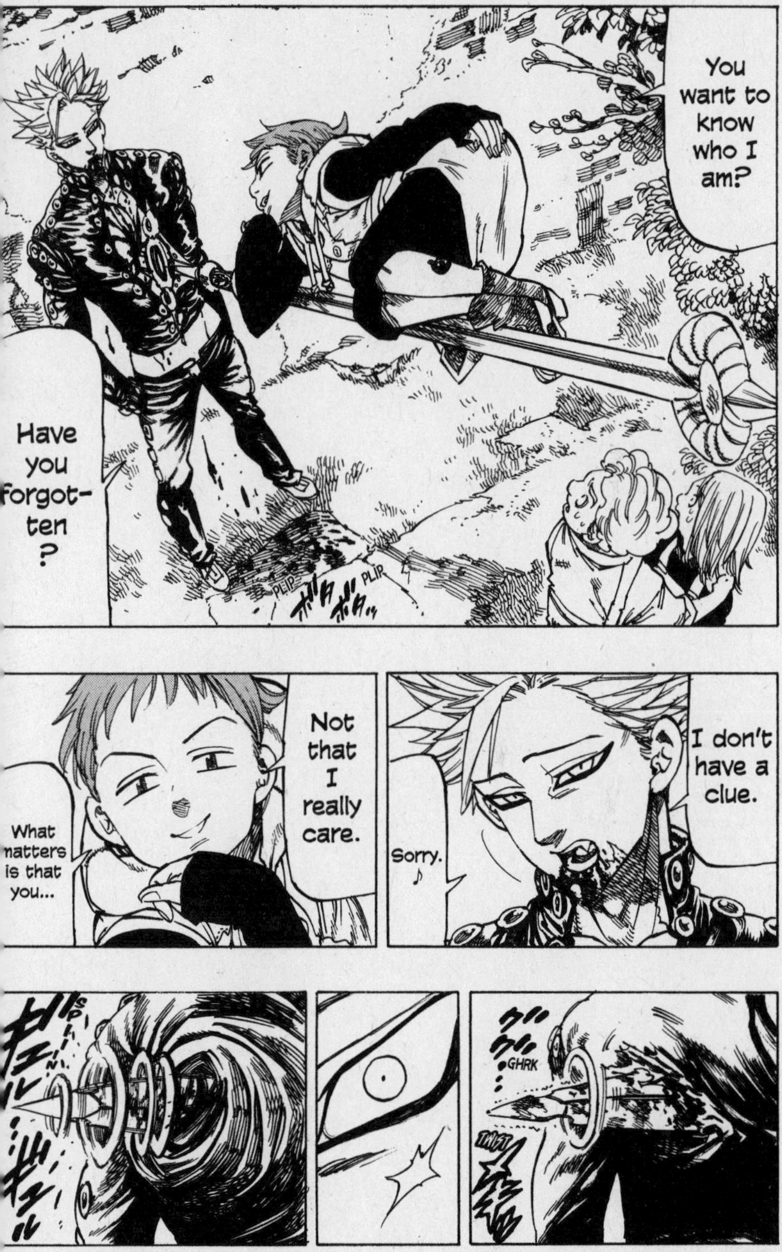
You want to know who I am?
Have you forgotten?
PLIP
PLIP
I don't have a clue.
Sorry. ♪
Not that I really care.
What matters is that you...
GHRK
TWIST
SPI-I-IN

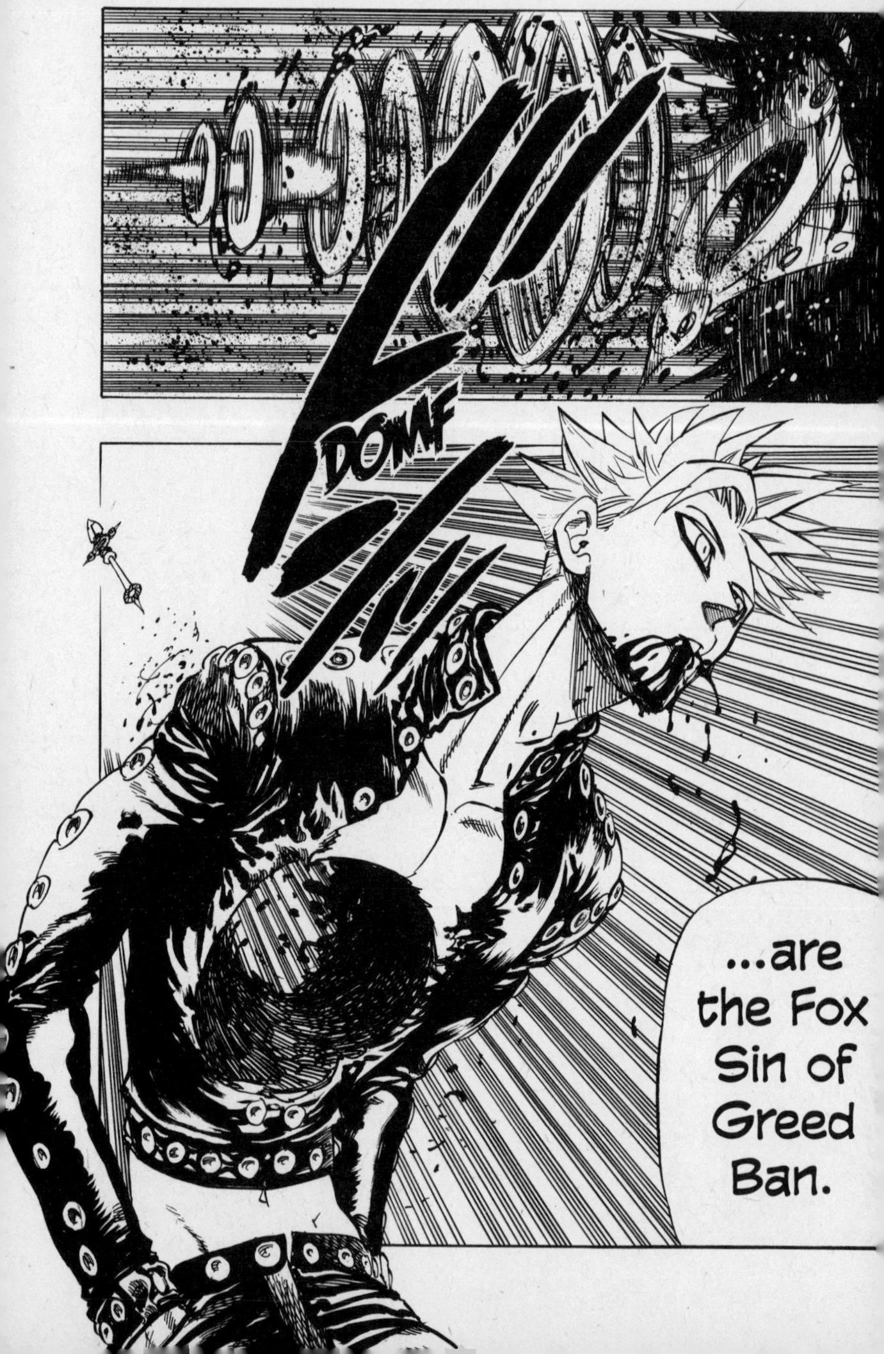
DOMF
...are the Fox Sin of Greed Ban.

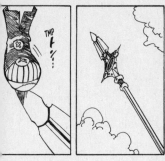

TMP

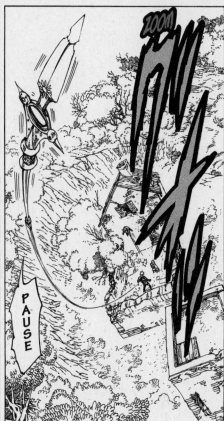

ZOOM

PAUSE

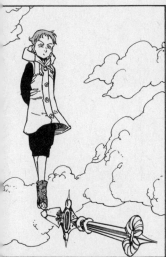

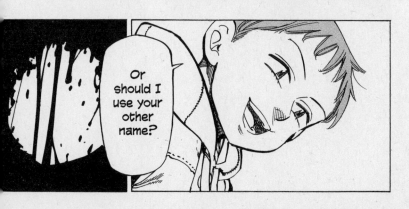

Or should I use your other name?

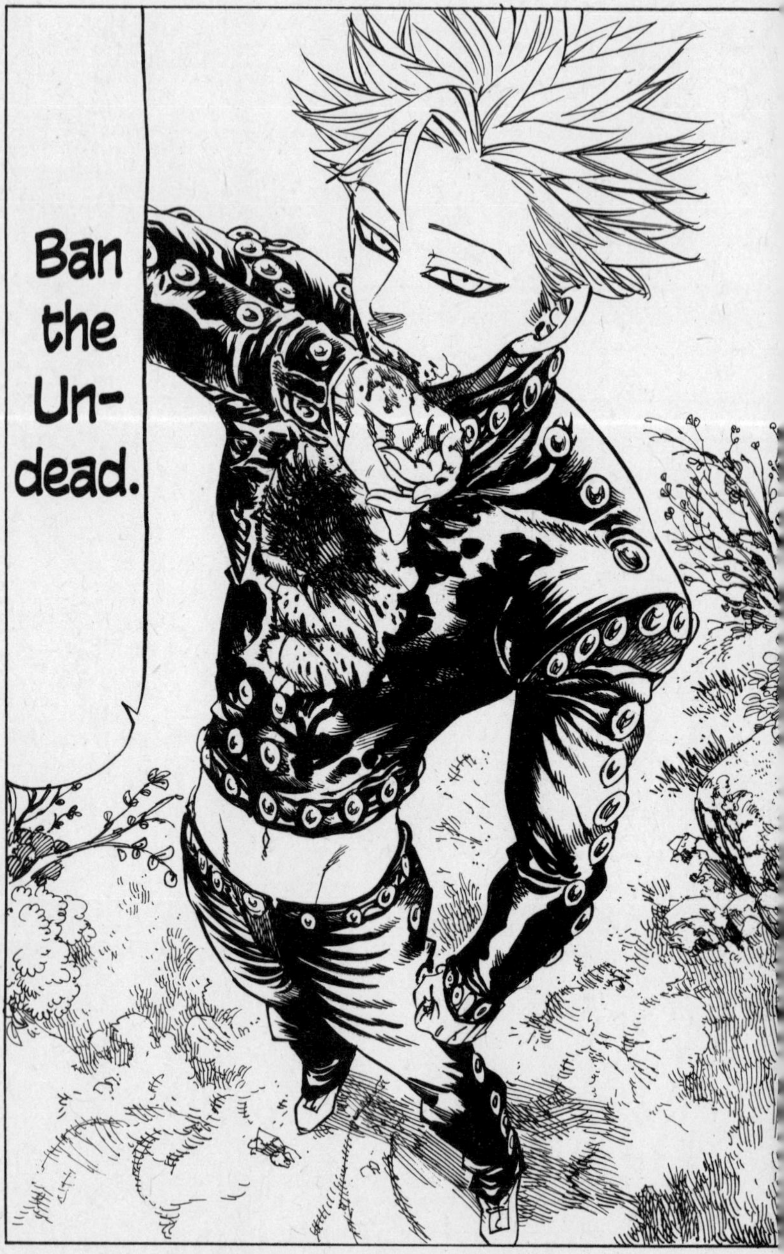
Ban the Un-dead.

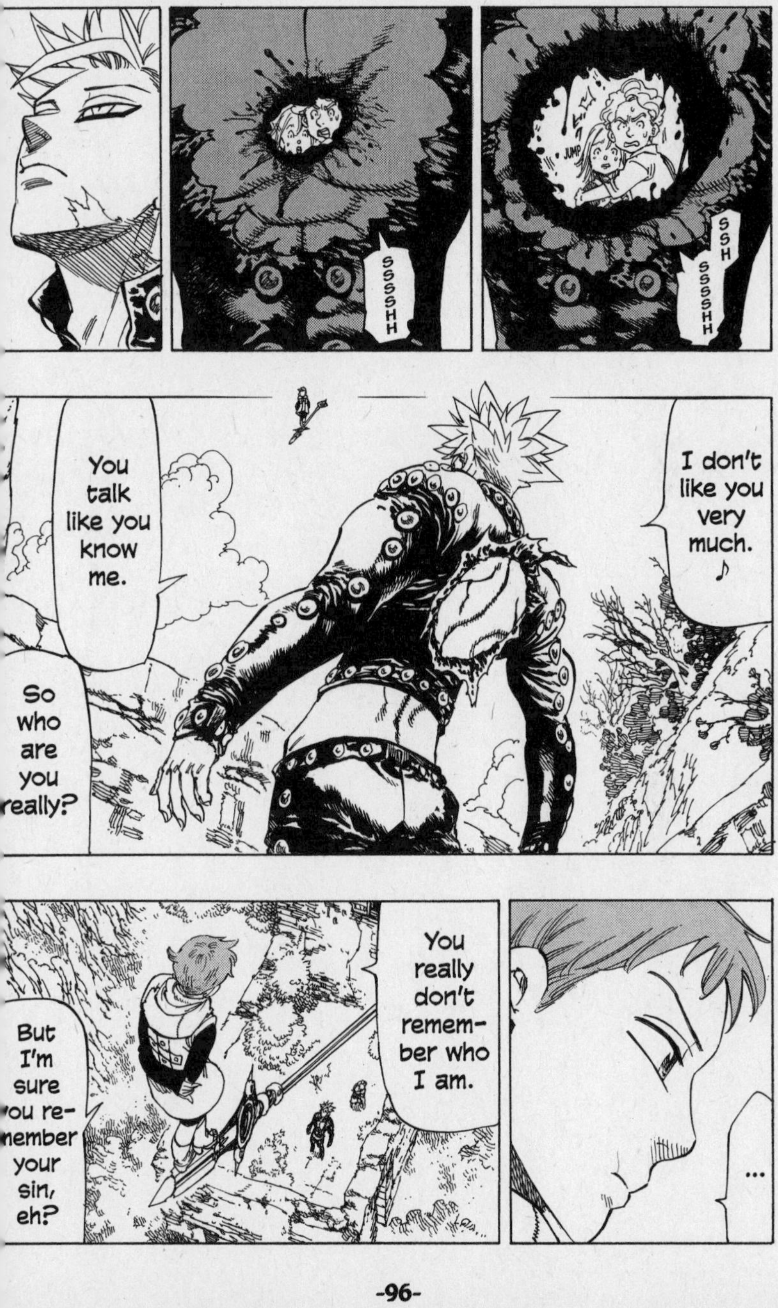
JUMP
SSH
SSSSHH
SSSSHH
I don't like you very much. ♪
You talk like you know me.
So who are you really?
...
You really don't remember who I am.
But I'm sure ou re- nember your sin, eh?

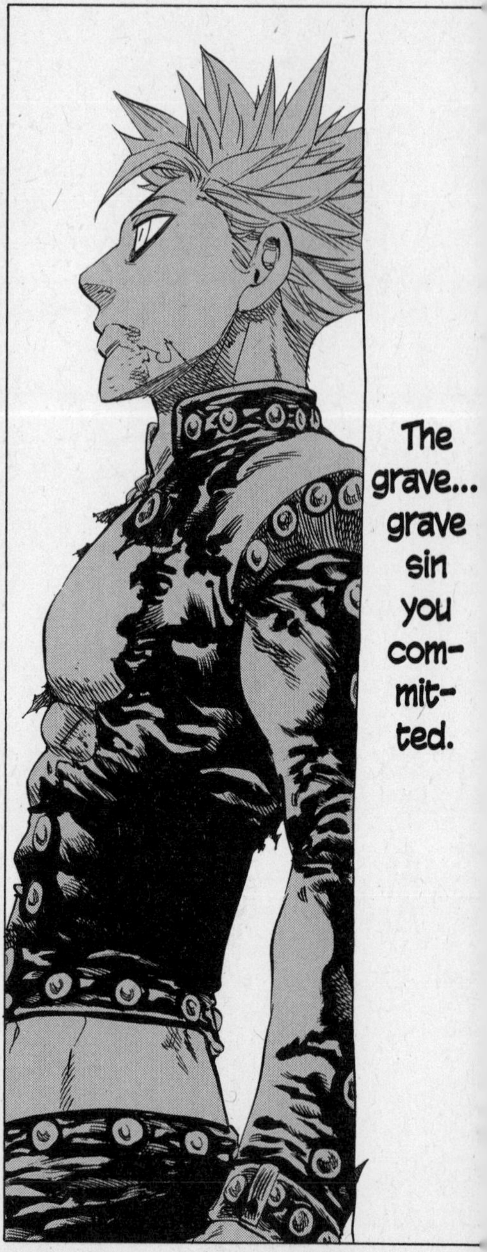
The grave... grave sin you com-mit-ted.

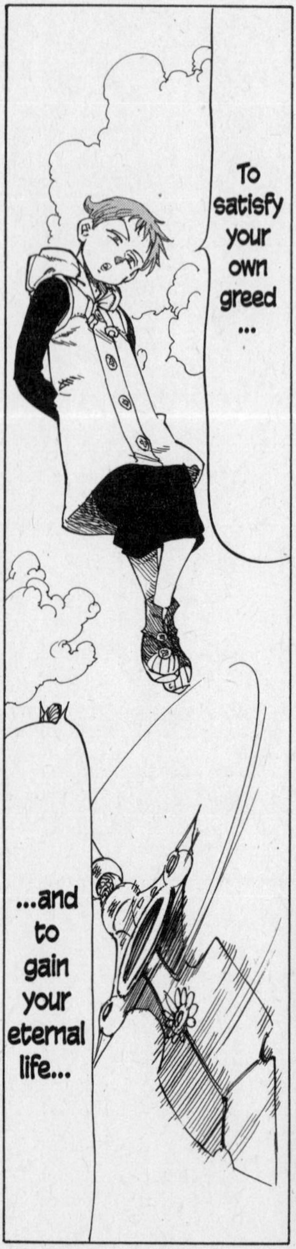
To satisfy your own greed ...
...and to gain your eternal life...

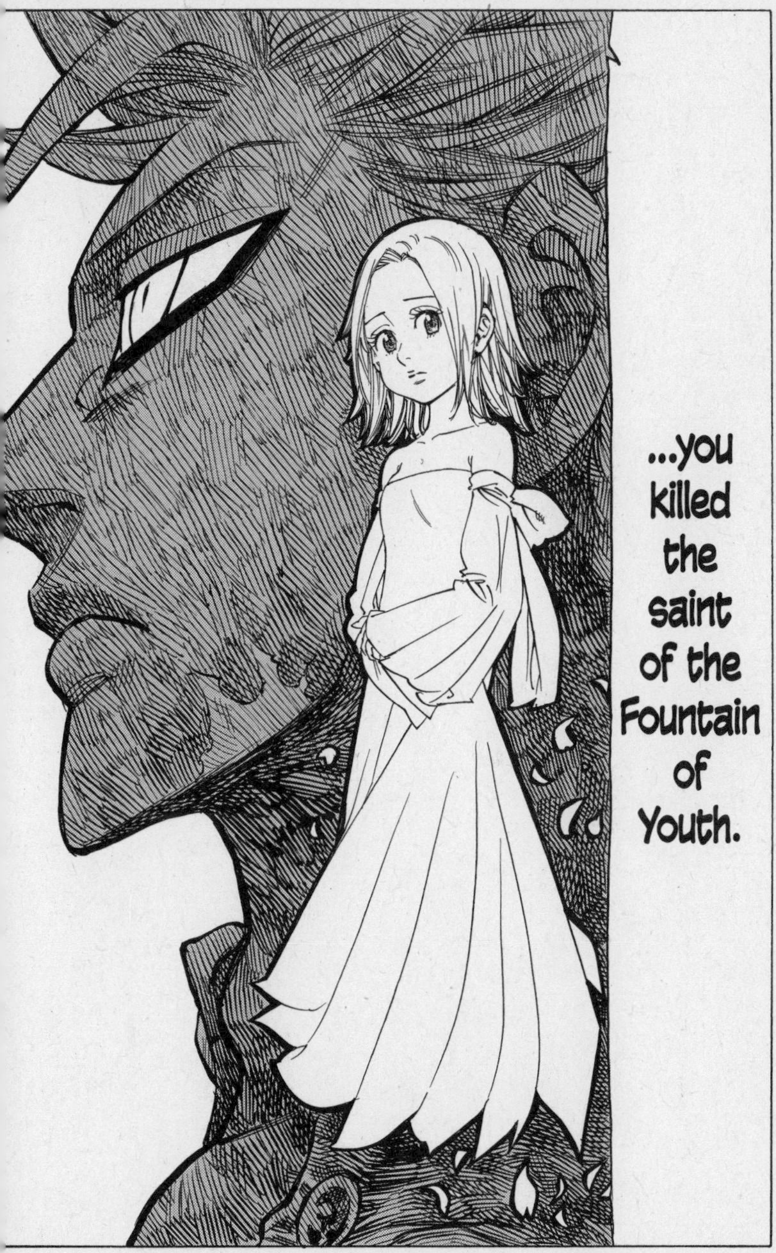
...you killed the saint of the Fountain of Youth.

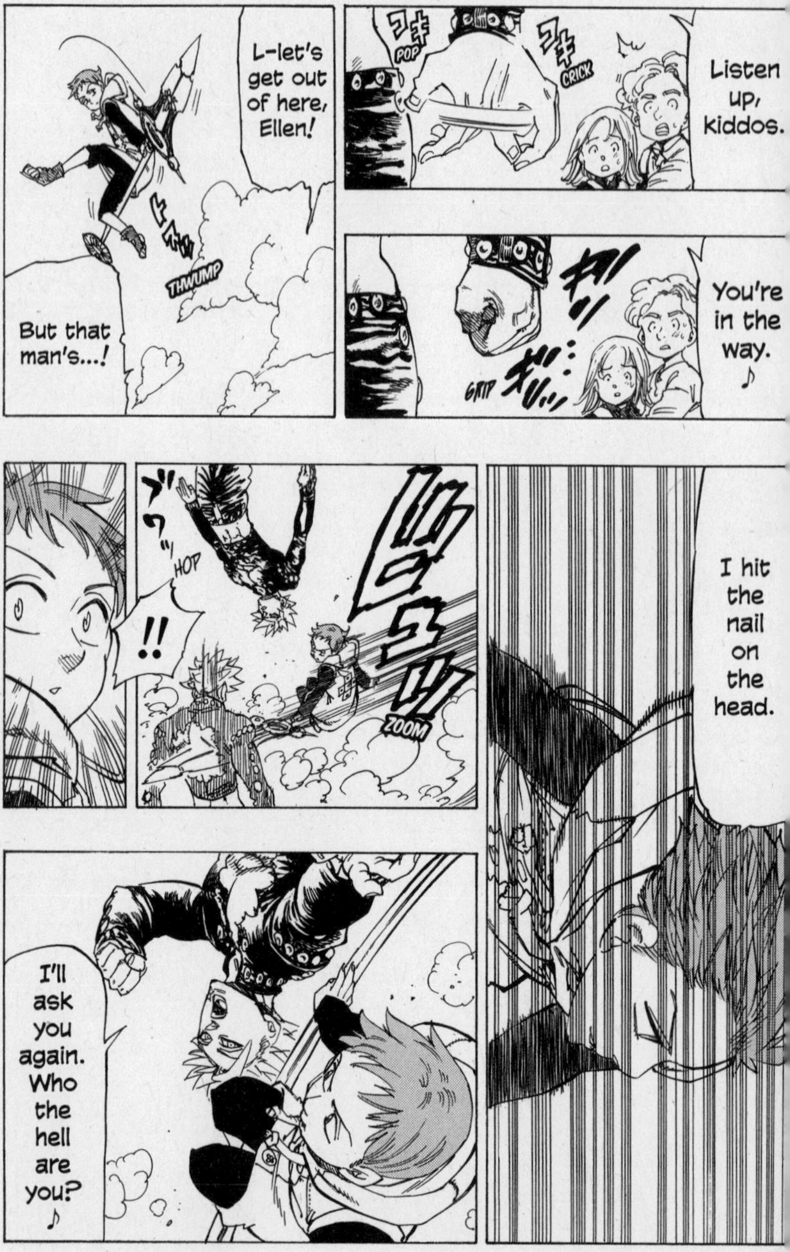

Listen up, kiddos.
POP
CRICK
You're in the way. ♪
GRIP
L-let's get out of here, Ellen!
THWUMP
But that man's...!
I hit the nail on the head.
ZOOM
HOP
!!
I'll ask you again. Who the hell are you? ♪

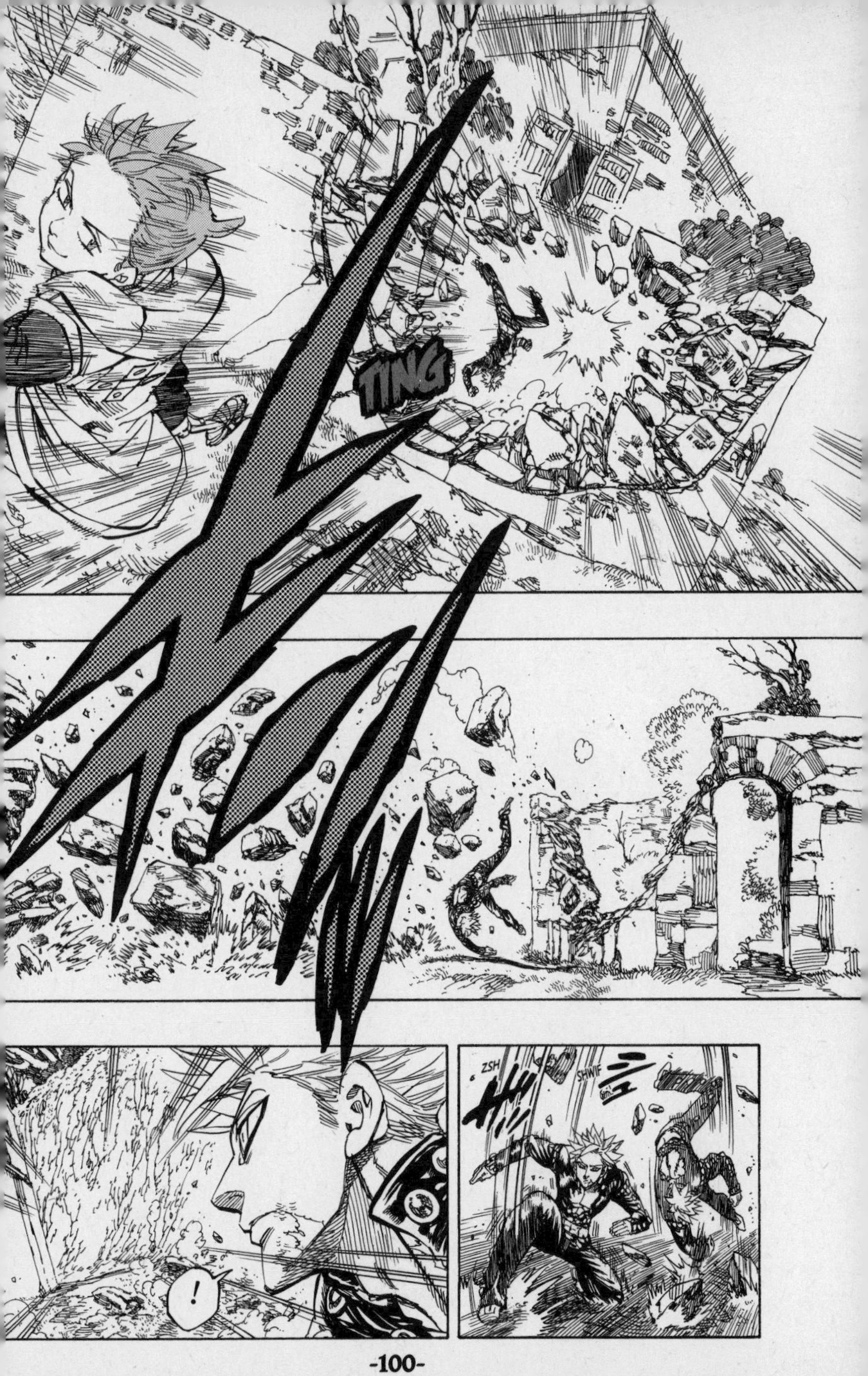
TING
ZSH
SHWIF
!

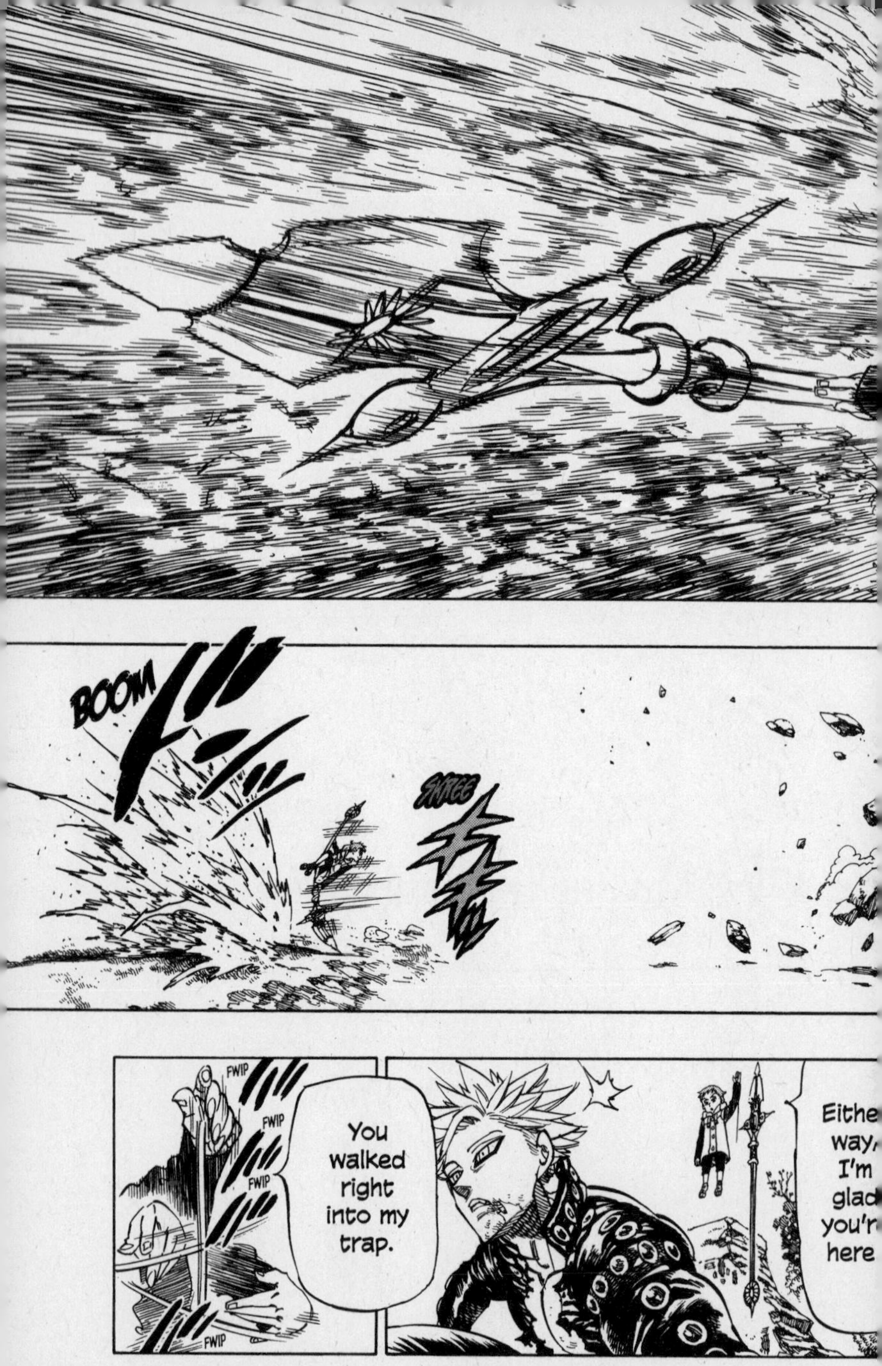
BOOM
SKREE
Eithe way, I'm glad you'r here
FWIP
FWIP
FWIP
You walked right into my trap.
FWIP

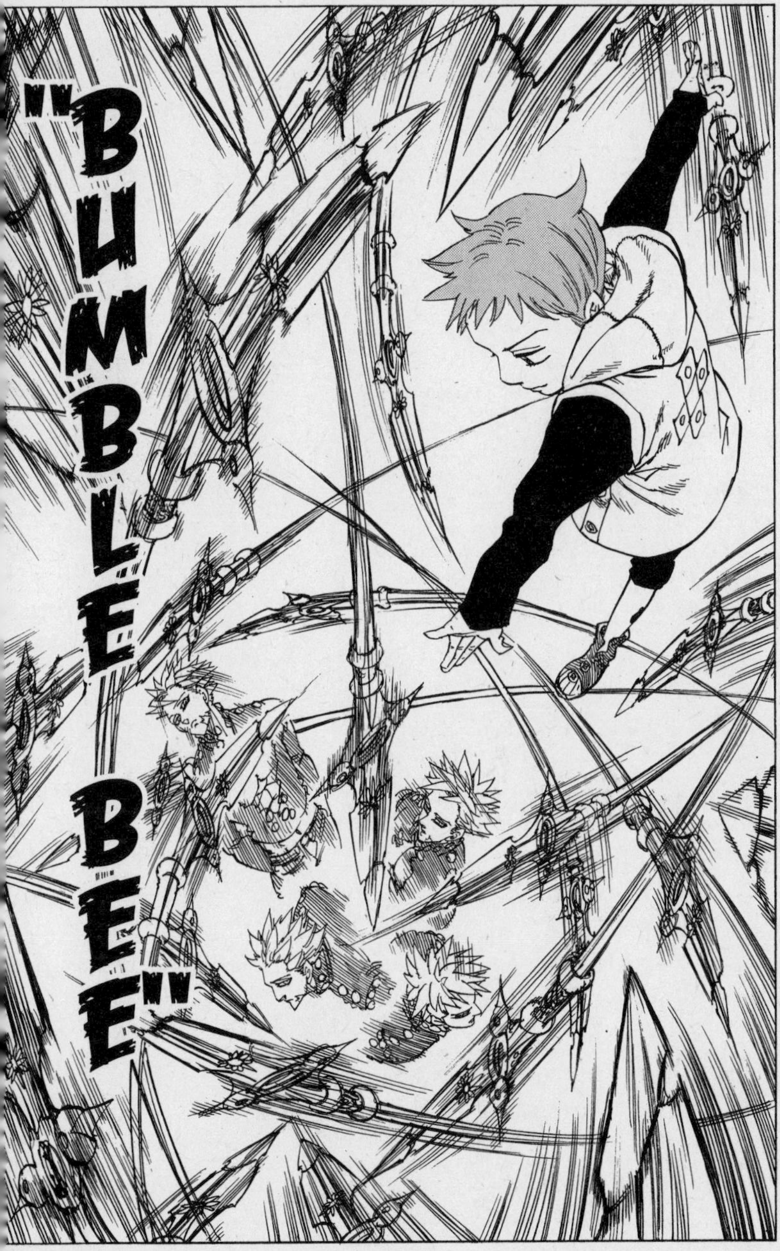
"BUMBLE BEE"

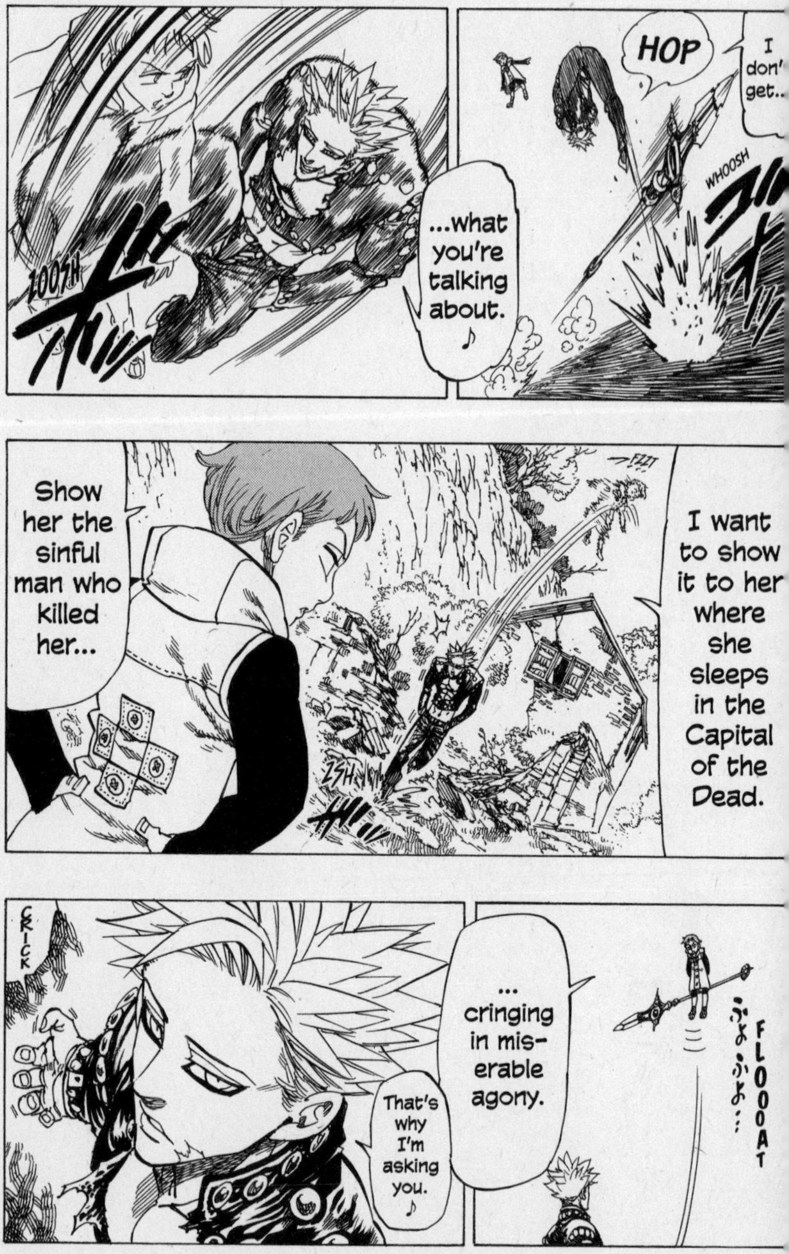
HOP
I don' get..
WHOOSH
...what you're talking about. ♪
ZOOSH
I want to show it to her where she sleeps in the Capital of the Dead.
FZZT
Show her the sinful man who killed her...
ZSH
FLOOOAT
ふよふよ…
... cringing in mis-erable agony.
That's why I'm asking you. ♪
CRICK

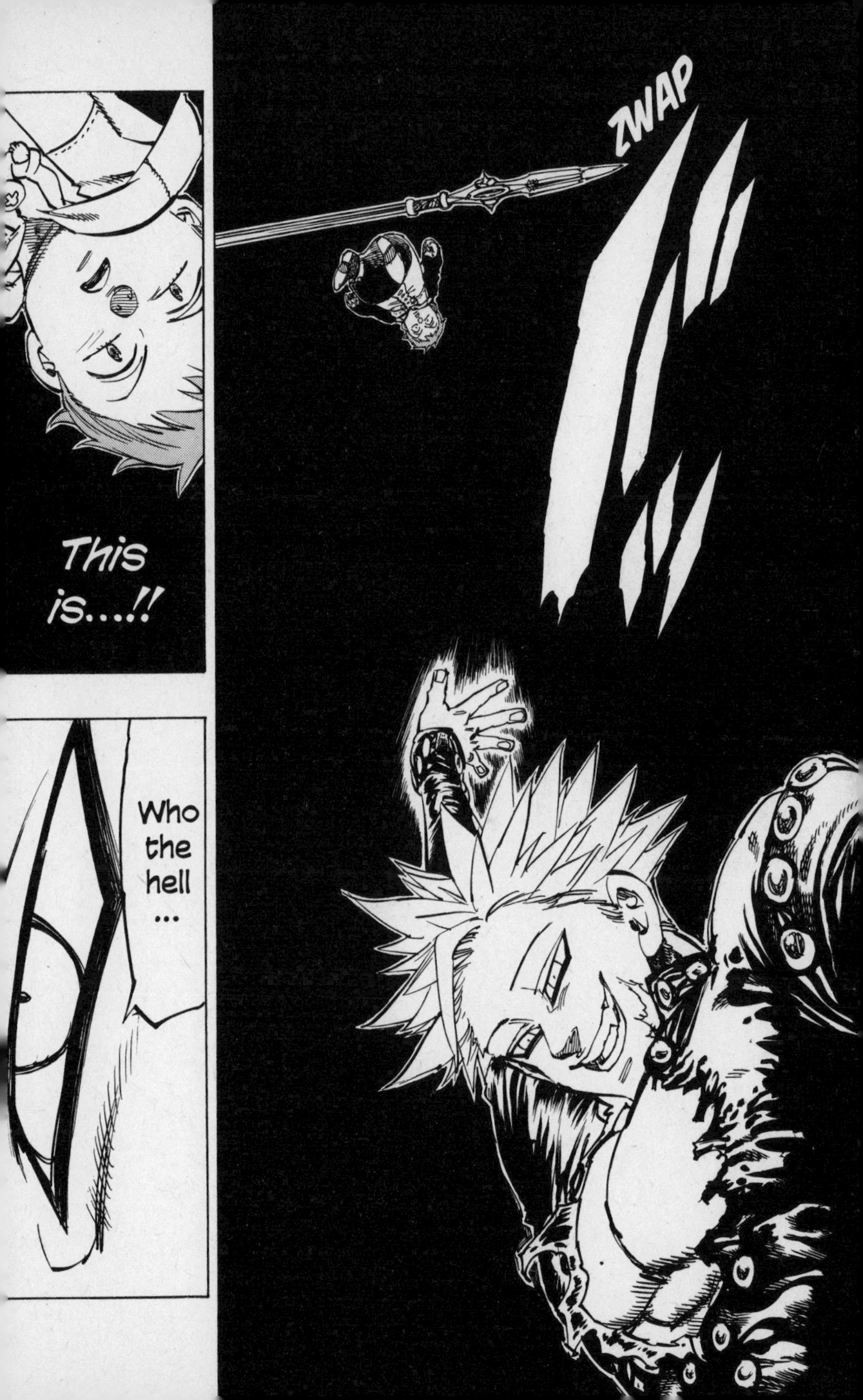
ZWAP
This is....!!
Who the hell ...

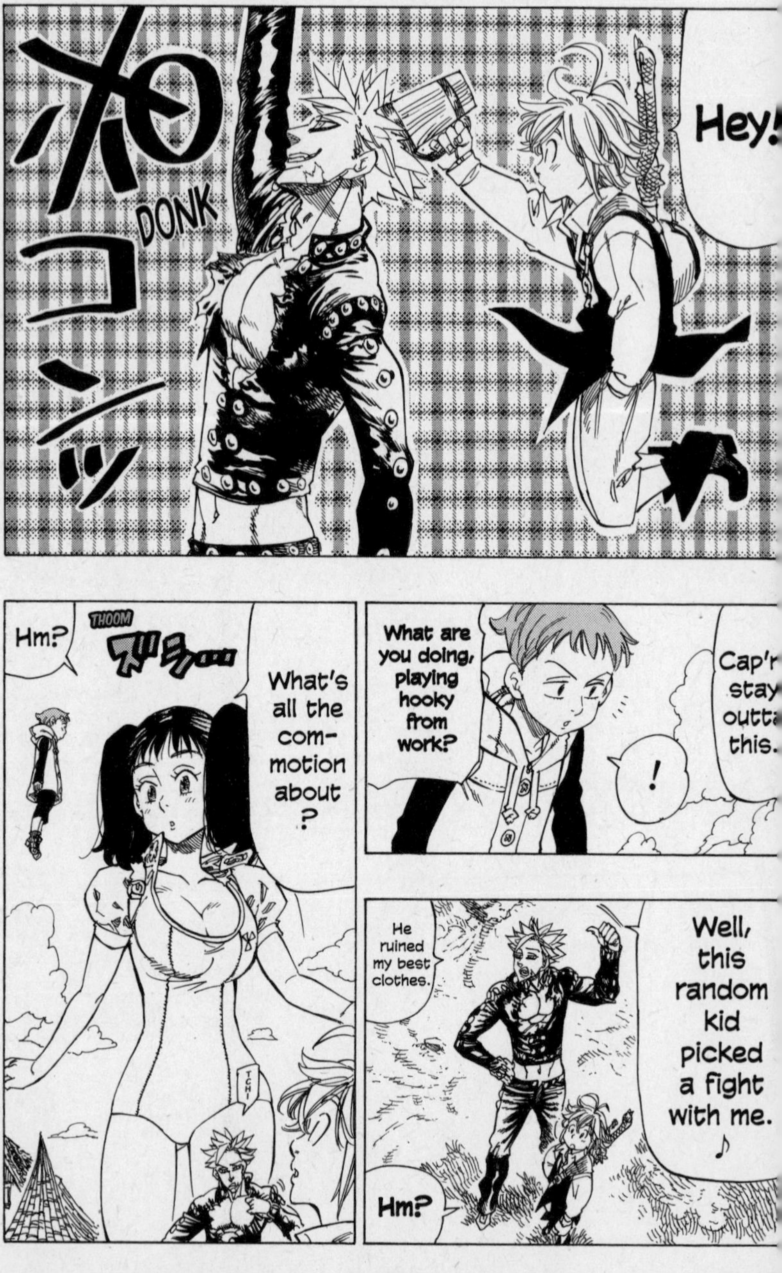
Hey!
DONK
ポコーンッ
Cap'r stay outta this.
!
What are you doing, playing hooky from work?
Well, this random kid picked a fight with me. ♪
He ruined my best clothes.
Hm?
What's all the com-motion about?
THOOM
Hm?
TCH!

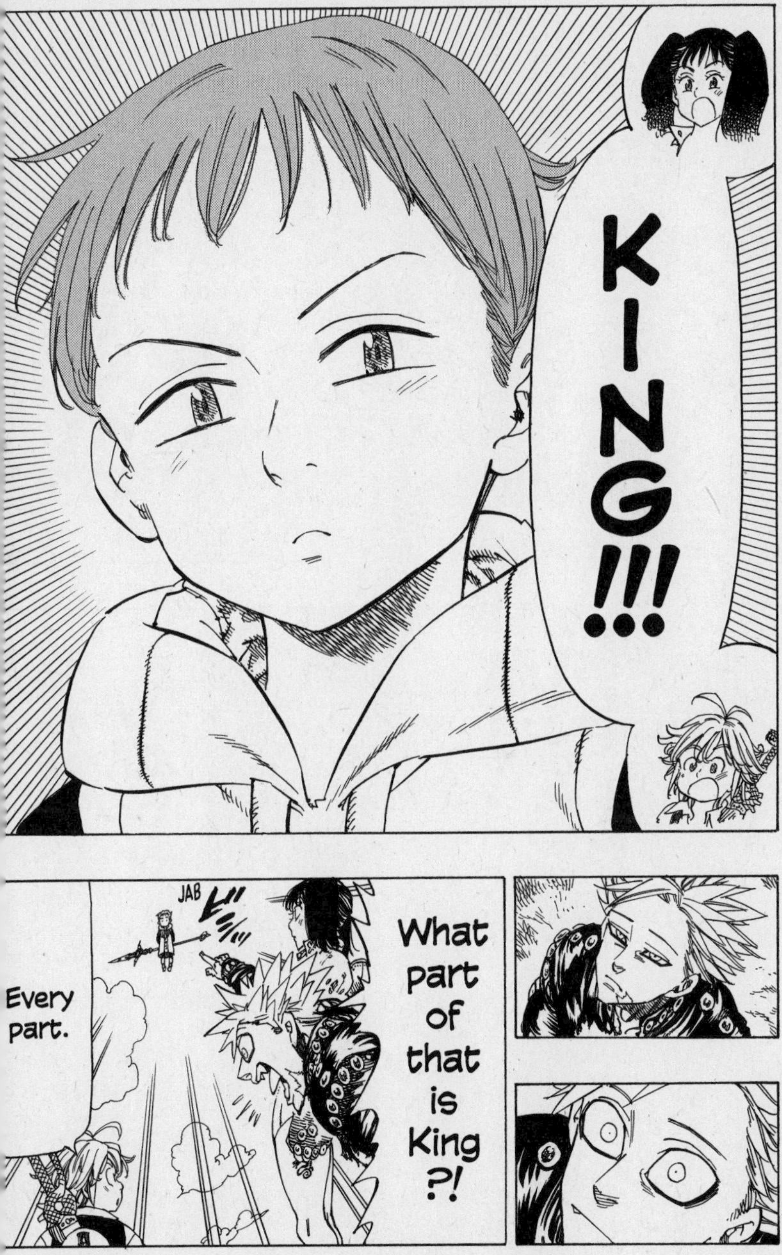
KING!!!
JAB
What part of that is King?!
Every part.

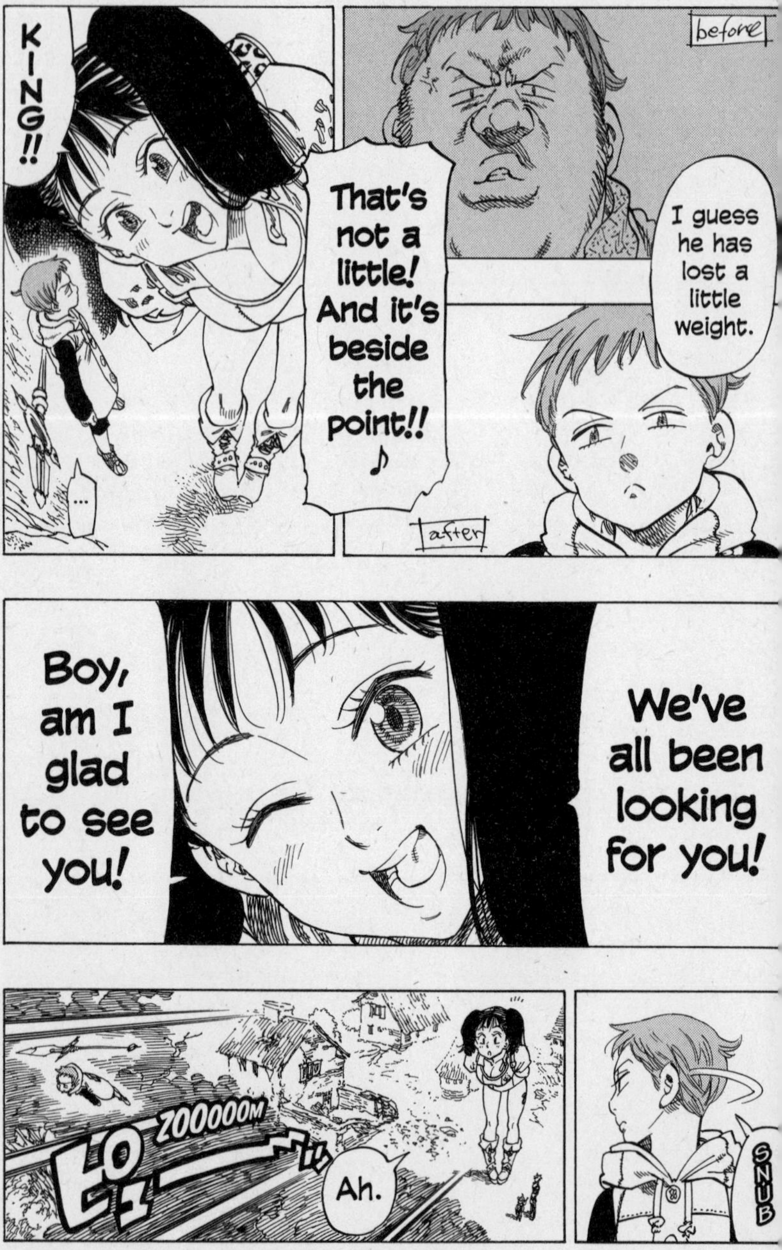
before
I guess he has lost a little weight.
after
KING!!
That's not a little! And it's beside the point!! ♪
...
We've all been looking for you!
Boy, am I glad to see you!
SNUB
ZOOOOOM
Ah.

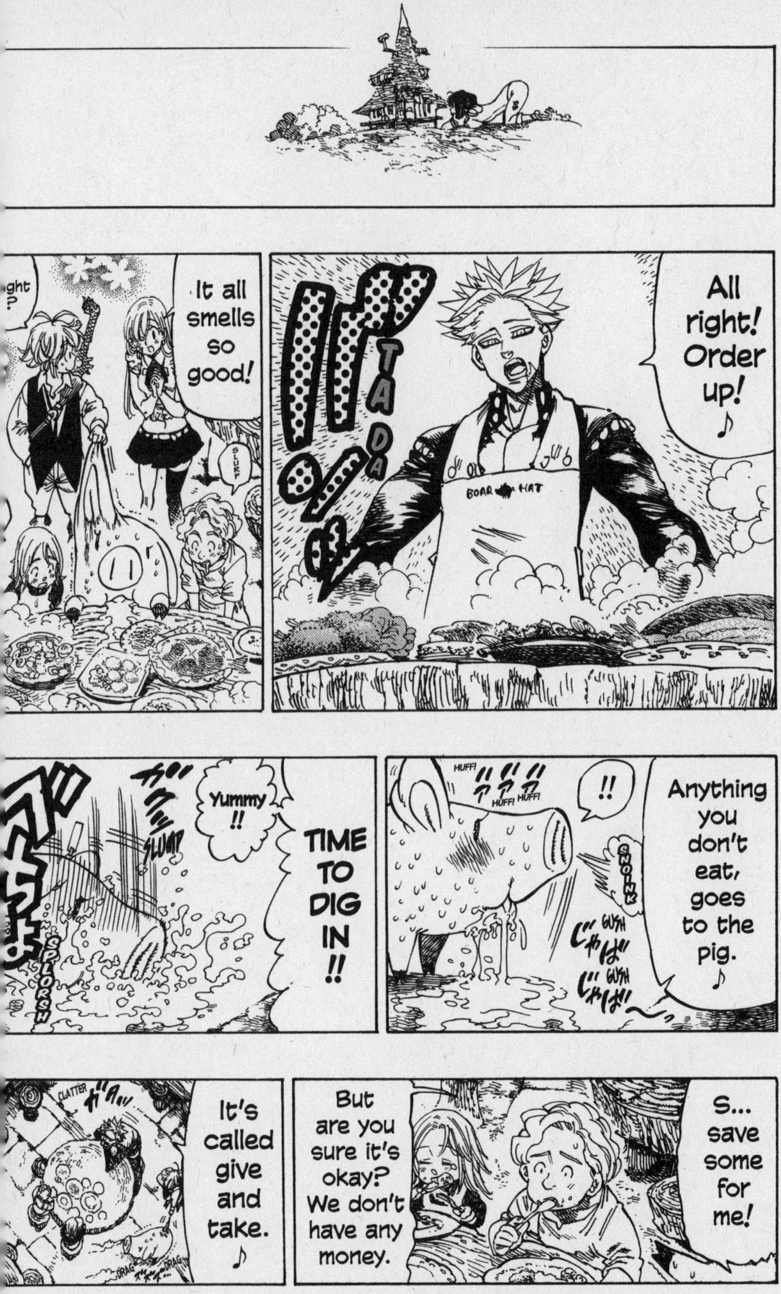
All right! Order up! ♪
TA DA
It all smells so good!
SLURP
Anything you don't eat, goes to the pig. ♪
!!
HUFF! HUFF! HUFF!
SNOINK
GUSH GUSH
TIME TO DIG IN!!
Yummy!!
SLUMP
SPLORSH
S... save some for me!
But are you sure it's okay? We don't have any money.
It's called give and take. ♪
CLATTER
DRAG DRAG

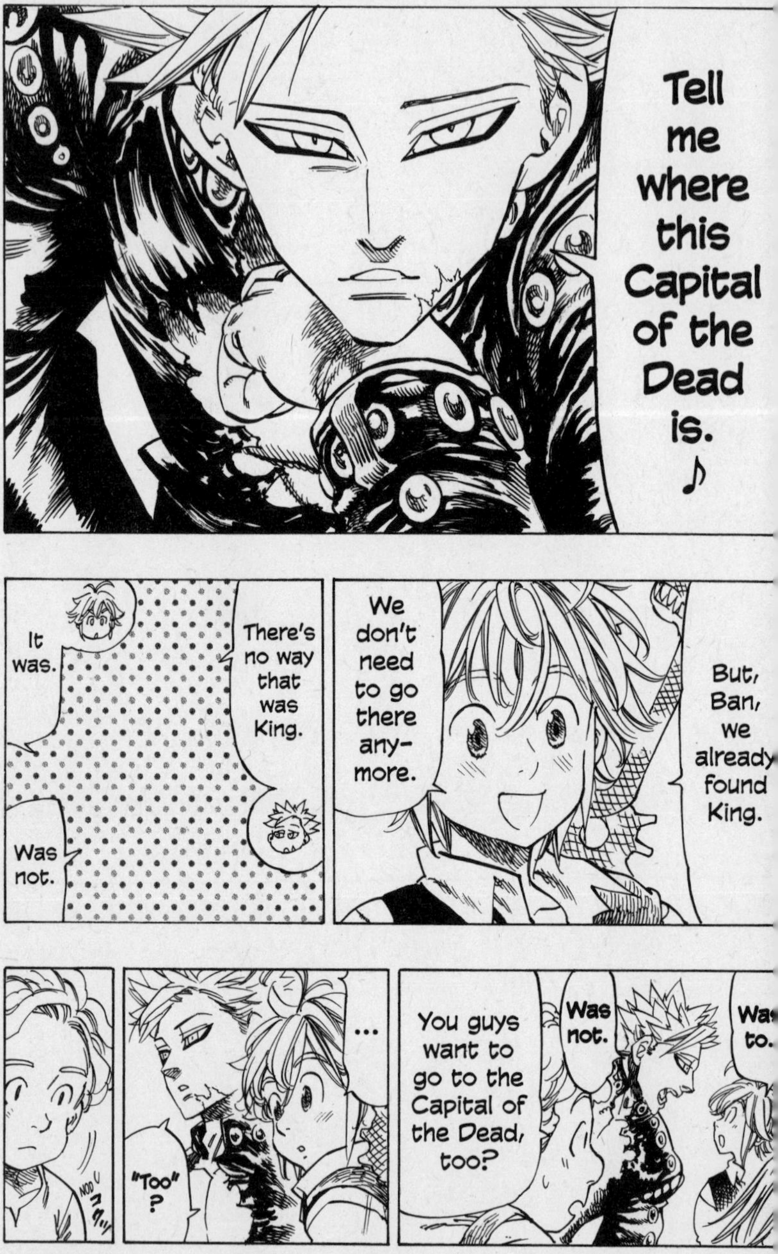
Tell me where this Capital of the Dead is. ♪
But, Ban, we already found King.
We don't need to go there anymore.
There's no way that was King.
It was.
Was not.
Was to.
Was not.
You guys want to go to the Capital of the Dead, too?
...
"Too"?
NOD

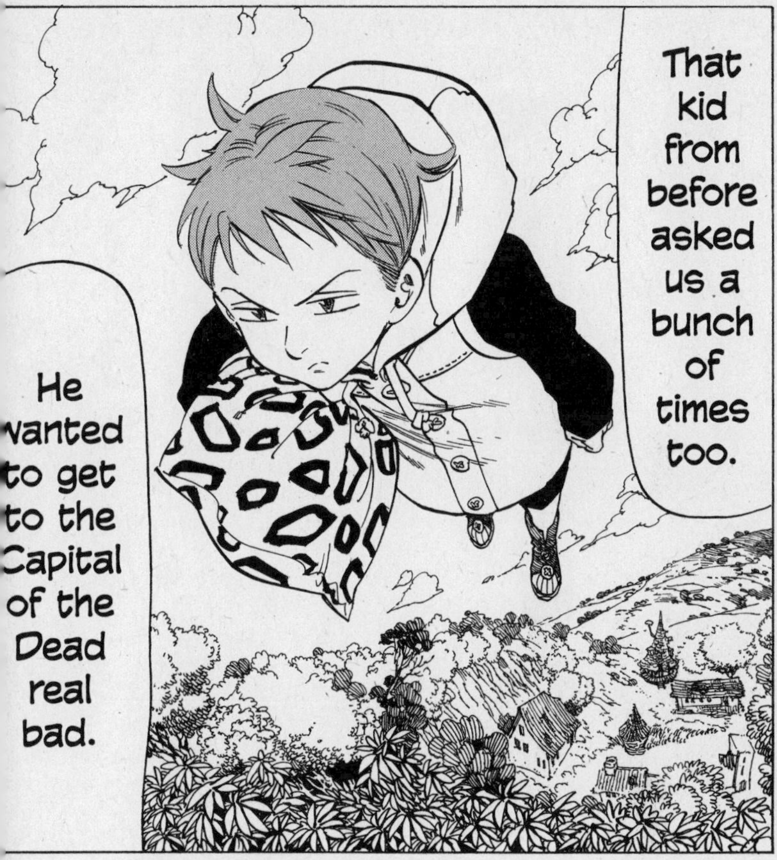
That kid from before asked us a bunch of times too.
He wanted to get to the Capital of the Dead real bad.
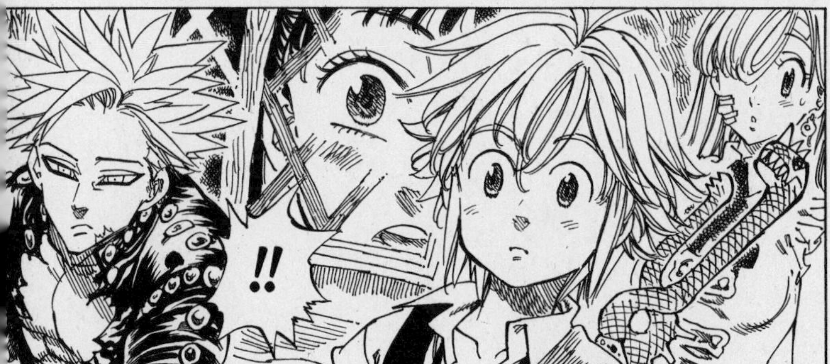
!!

Chapter 20 - Two Paths

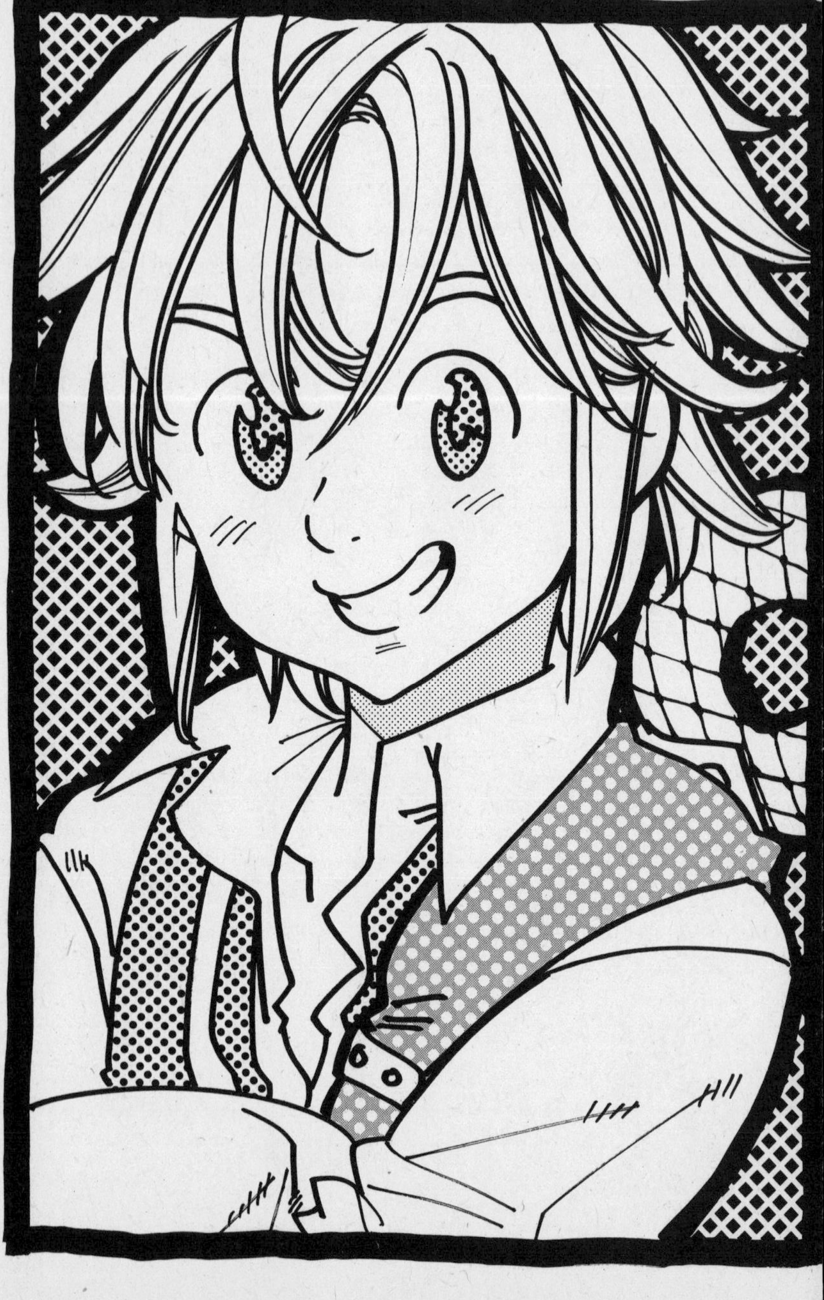

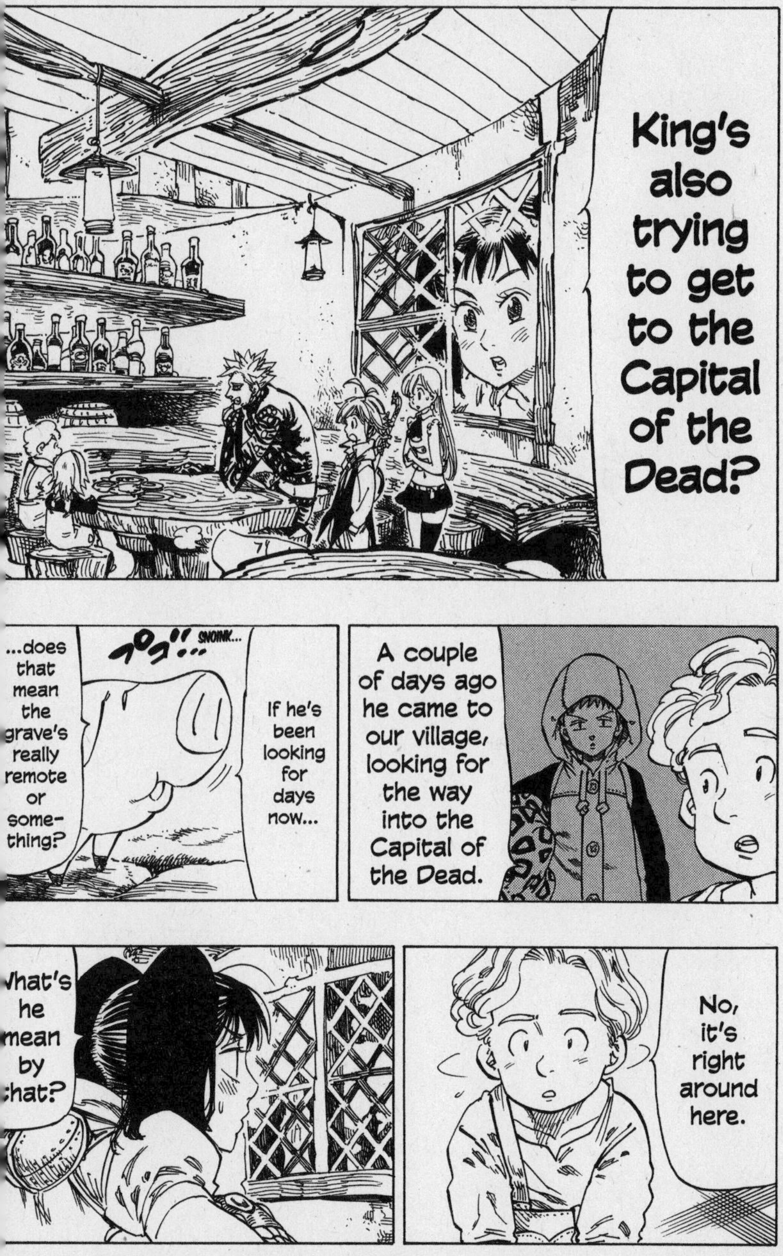
King's also trying to get to the Capital of the Dead?
A couple of days ago he came to our village, looking for the way into the Capital of the Dead.
SNOINK...
If he's been looking for days now...
...does that mean the grave's really remote or something?
No, it's right around here.
What's he mean by that?

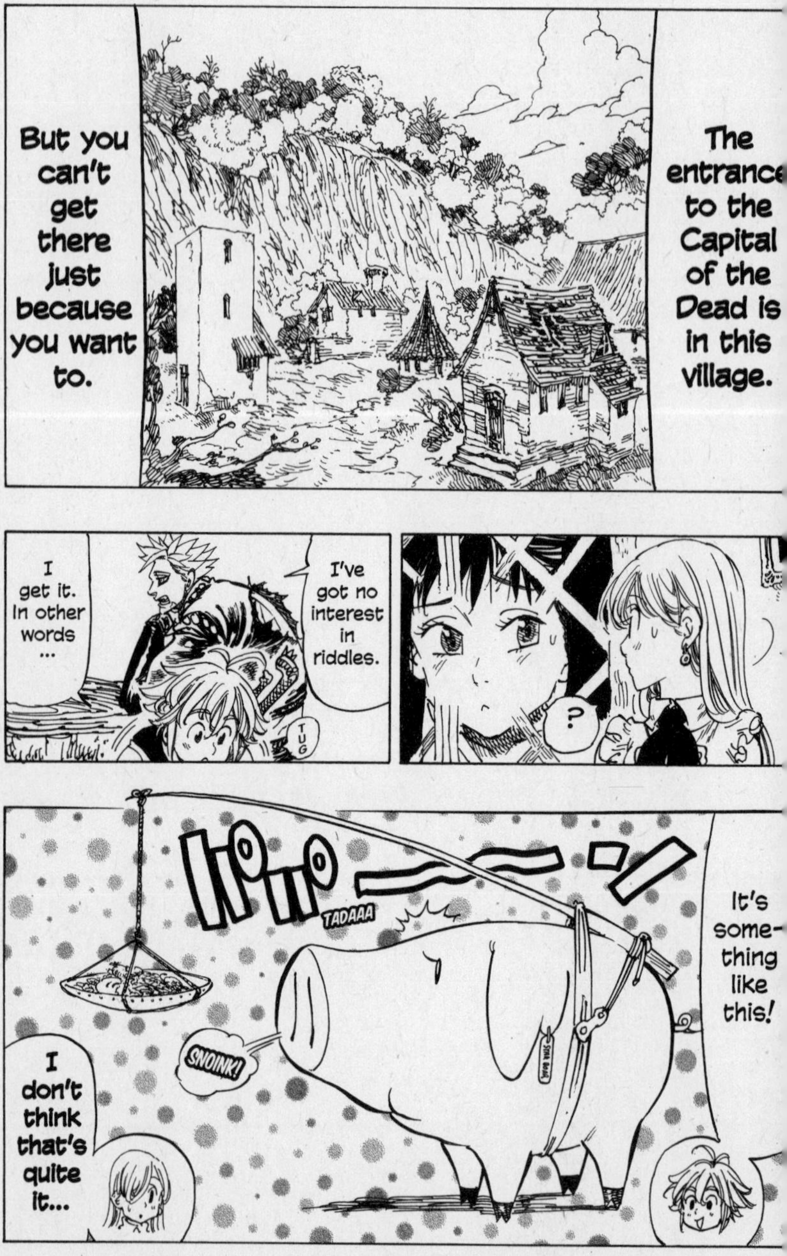
The entrance to the Capital of the Dead is in this village.
But you can't get there just because you want to.
?
I've got no interest in riddles.
TUG
I get it. In other words...
TADAAA
It's something-thing like this!
SNOINK!
I don't think that's quite it...

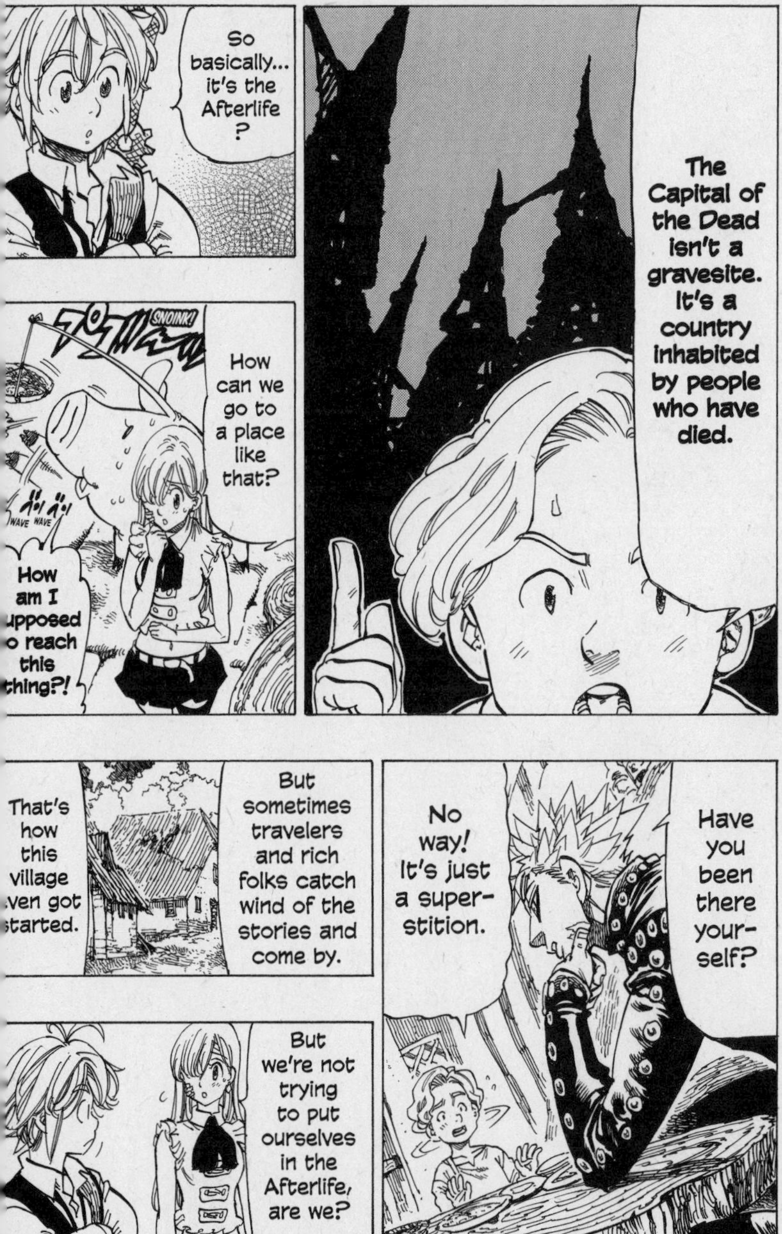
The Capital of the Dead isn't a gravesite. It's a country inhabited by people who have died.
So basically... it's the Afterlife?
How can we go to a place like that?
SNOINK!
WAVE WAVE
How am I upposed o reach this thing?!
Have you been there your-self?
No way! It's just a super-stition.
But sometimes travelers and rich folks catch wind of the stories and come by.
That's how this village ven got started.
But we're not trying to put ourselves in the Afterlife, are we?

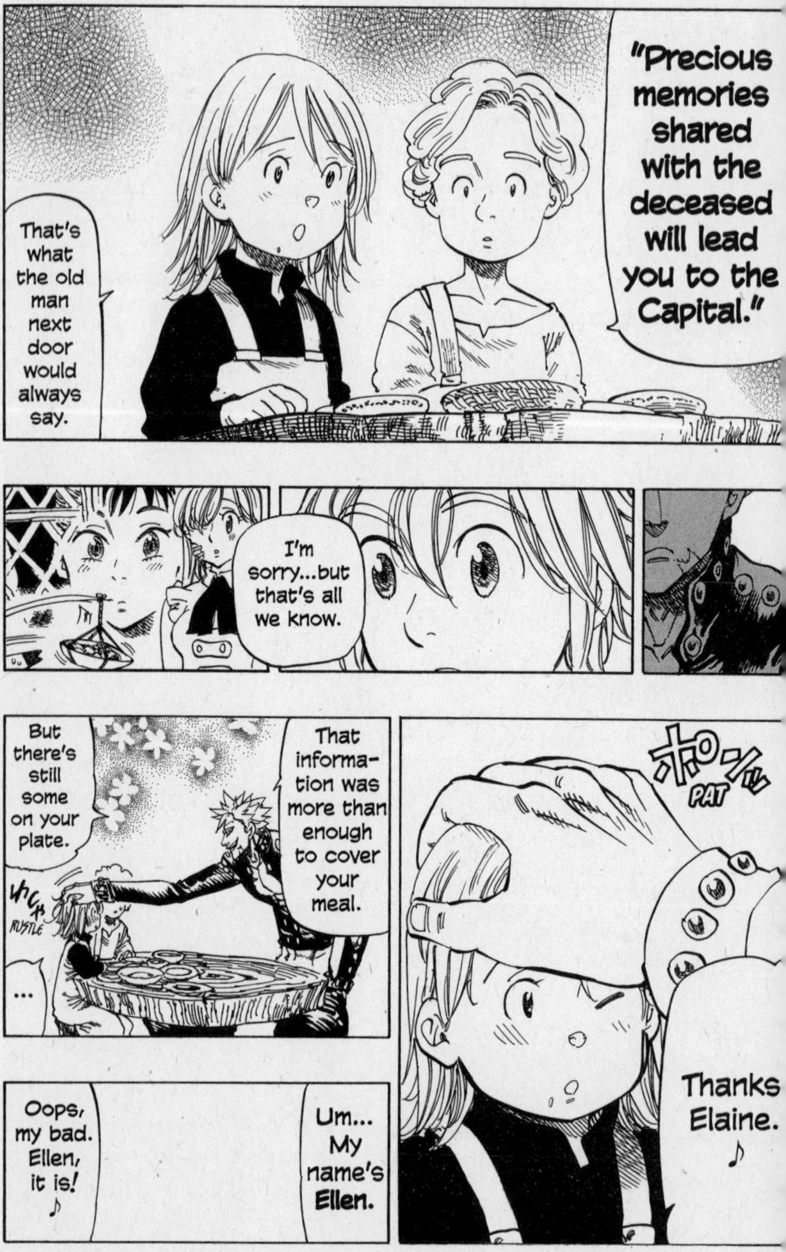
"Precious memories shared with the deceased will lead you to the Capital."
That's what the old man next door would always say.
I'm sorry...but that's all we know.
PAT
Thanks Elaine. ♪
That information was more than enough to cover your meal.
But there's still some on your plate.
RUSTLE
...
Um... My name's Ellen.
Oops, my bad. Ellen, it is! ♪

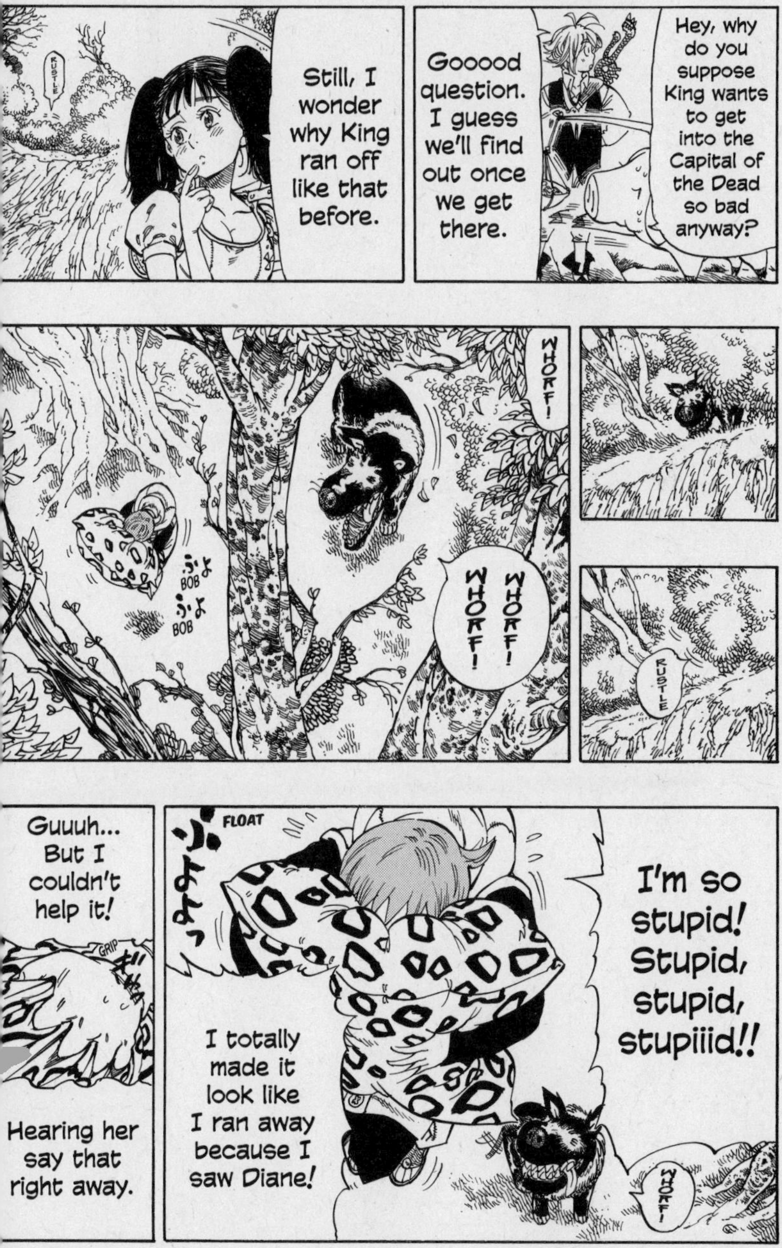

Hey, why do you suppose King wants to get into the Capital of the Dead so bad anyway?
Gooood question. I guess we'll find out once we get there.
Still, I wonder why King ran off like that before.
RUSTLE
RUSTLE
WHORF!
WHORF! WHORF!
ぷよ BOB
ぷよ BOB
ぷよっ FLOAT
I'm so stupid! Stupid, stupid, stupiiid!!
I totally made it look like I ran away because I saw Diane!
WHORF!
Guuuh... But I couldn't help it!
GRIP
Hearing her say that right away.

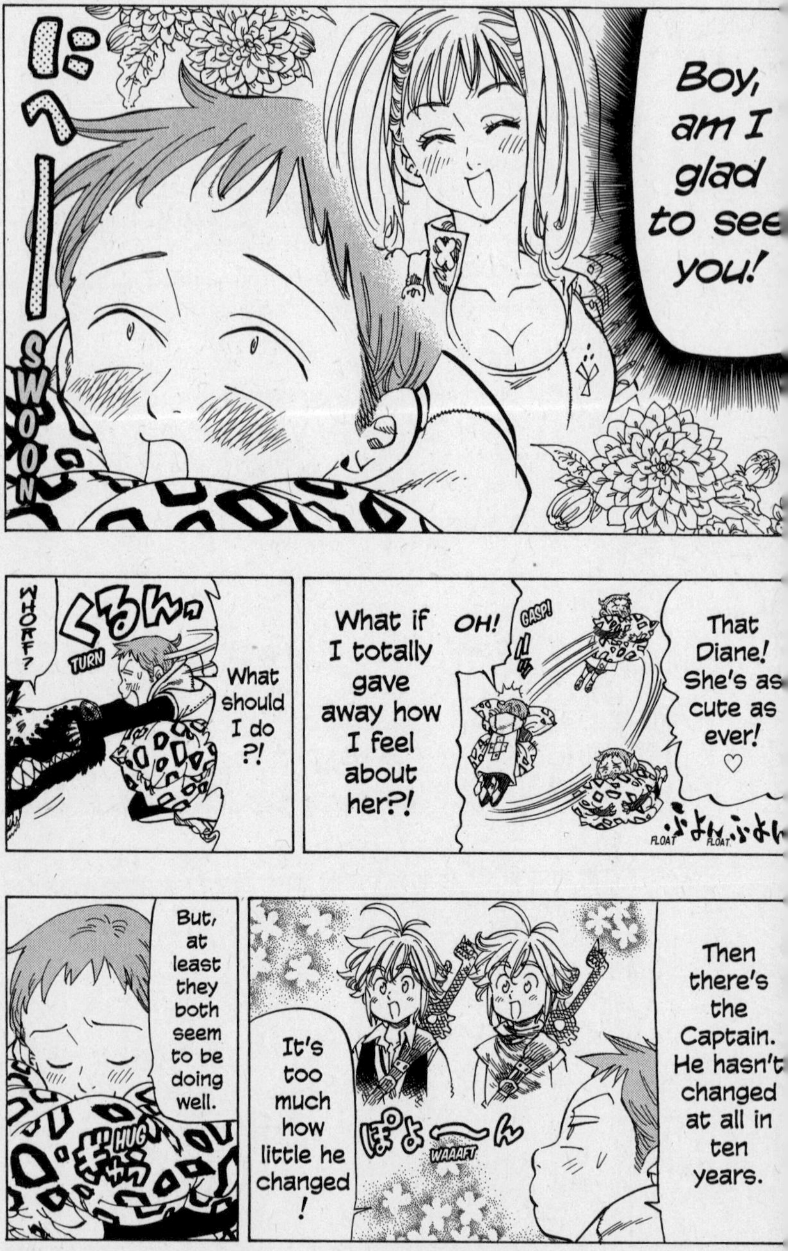
Boy, am I glad to see you!
SWOOON
That Diane! She's as cute as ever! ♡
FLOAT FLOAT
GASP!
OH!
What if I totally gave away how I feel about her?!
What should I do ?!
TURN
WHORF?
Then there's the Captain. He hasn't changed at all in ten years.
WAAAFT
It's too much how little he changed!
But, at least they both seem to be doing well.
HUG

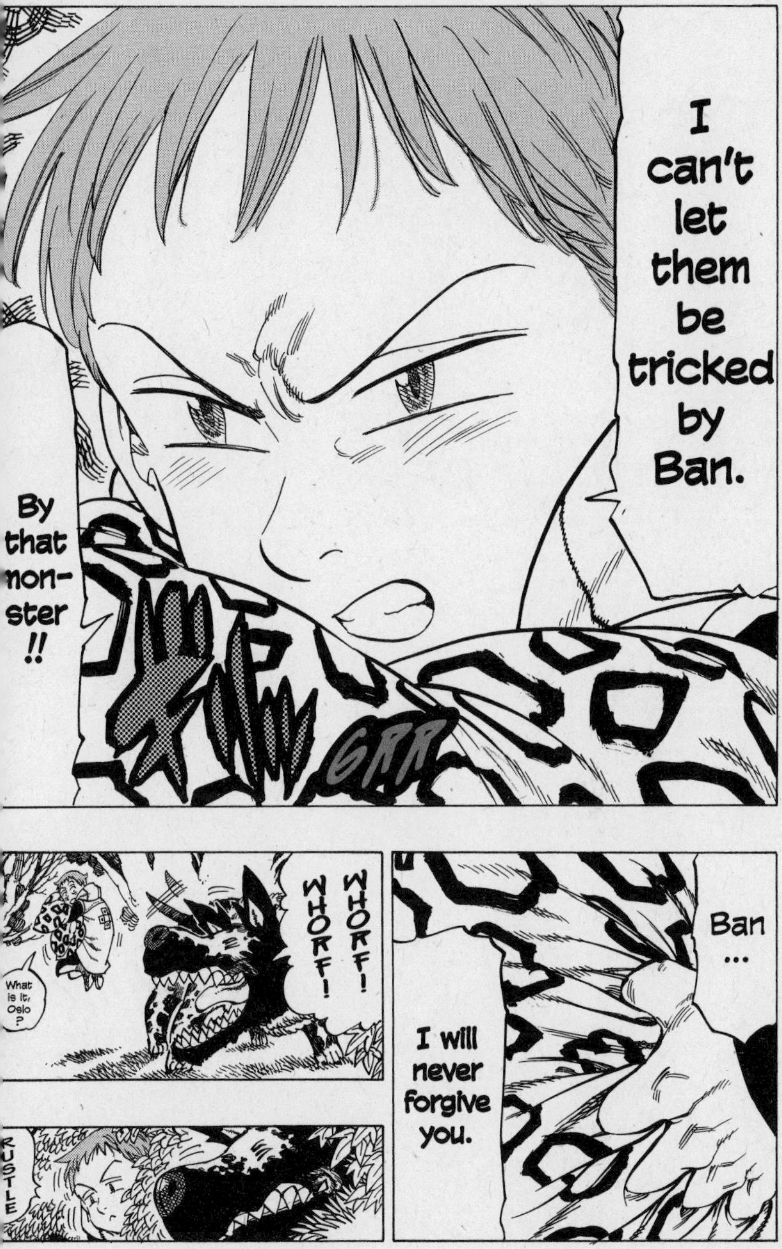
I can't let them be tricked by Ban.
By that monster!!
GRR
Ban...
I will never forgive you.
WHORF! WHORF!
What is it, Oslo?
RUSTLE

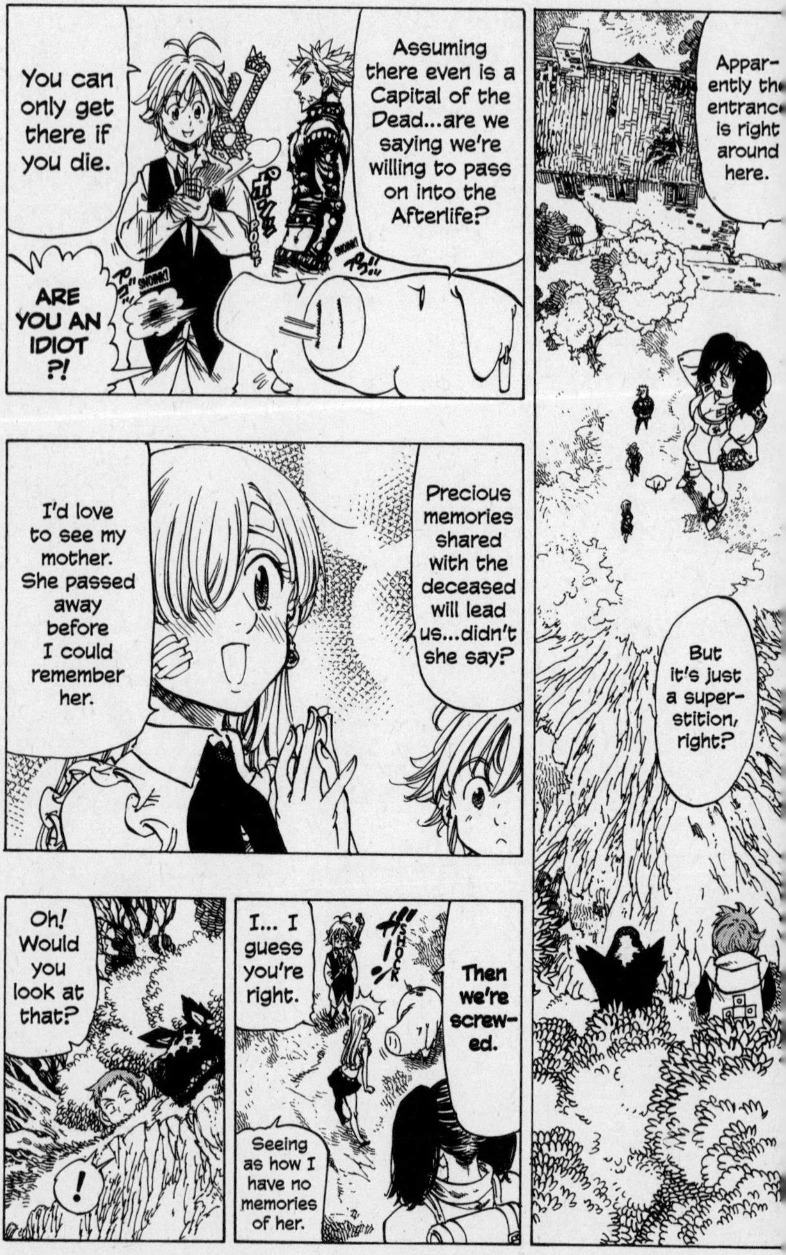
Apparently th
entranc
is right
around
here.
But it's just a superstition, right?
Assuming there even is a Capital of the Dead...are we saying we're willing to pass on into the Afterlife?
POOF
SNONK!
You can only get there if you die.
SNONK!
ARE YOU AN IDIOT?!
Precious memories shared with the deceased will lead us...didn't she say?
I'd love to see my mother. She passed away before I could remember her.
Then we're screwed.
SHOCK
I... I guess you're right.
Seeing as how I have no memories of her.
Oh! Would you look at that?
!

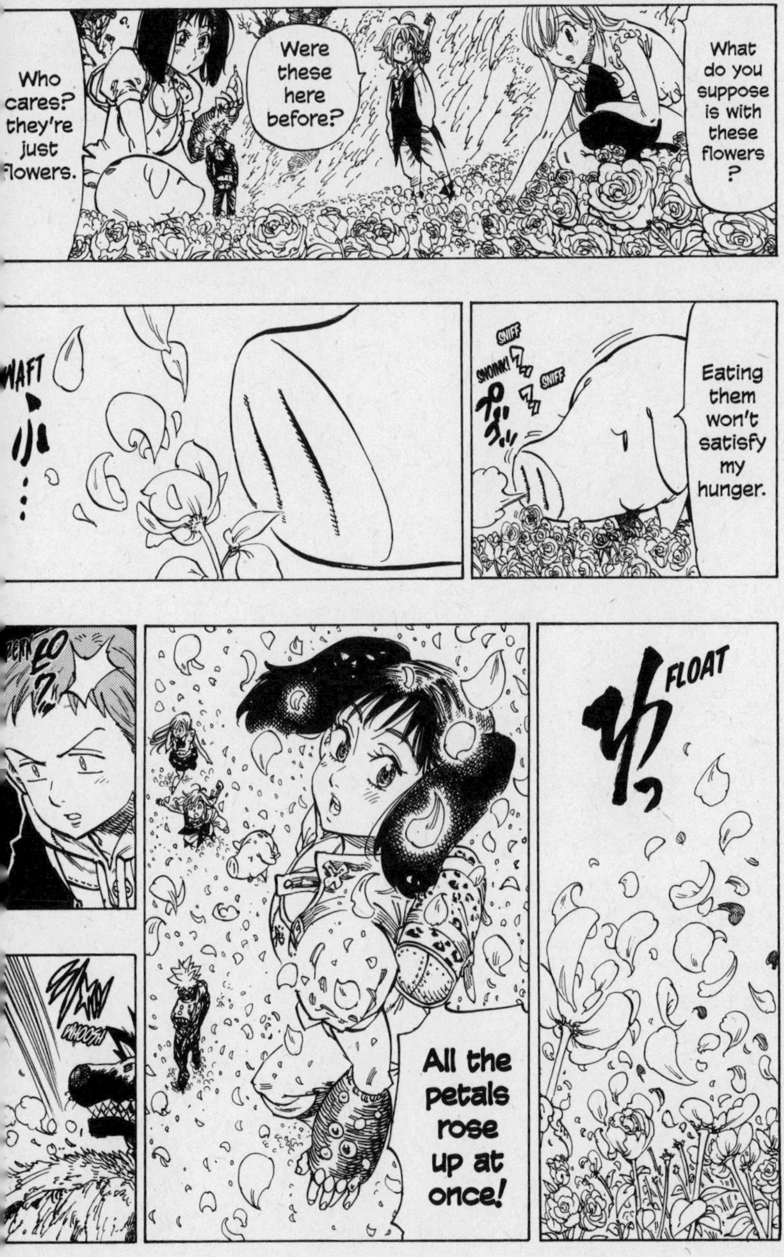
What do you suppose is with these flowers?
Were these here before?
Who cares? they're just flowers.
SNIFF
SNIFF
Eating them won't satisfy my hunger.
FLOAT
All the petals rose up at once!
WHOOSH

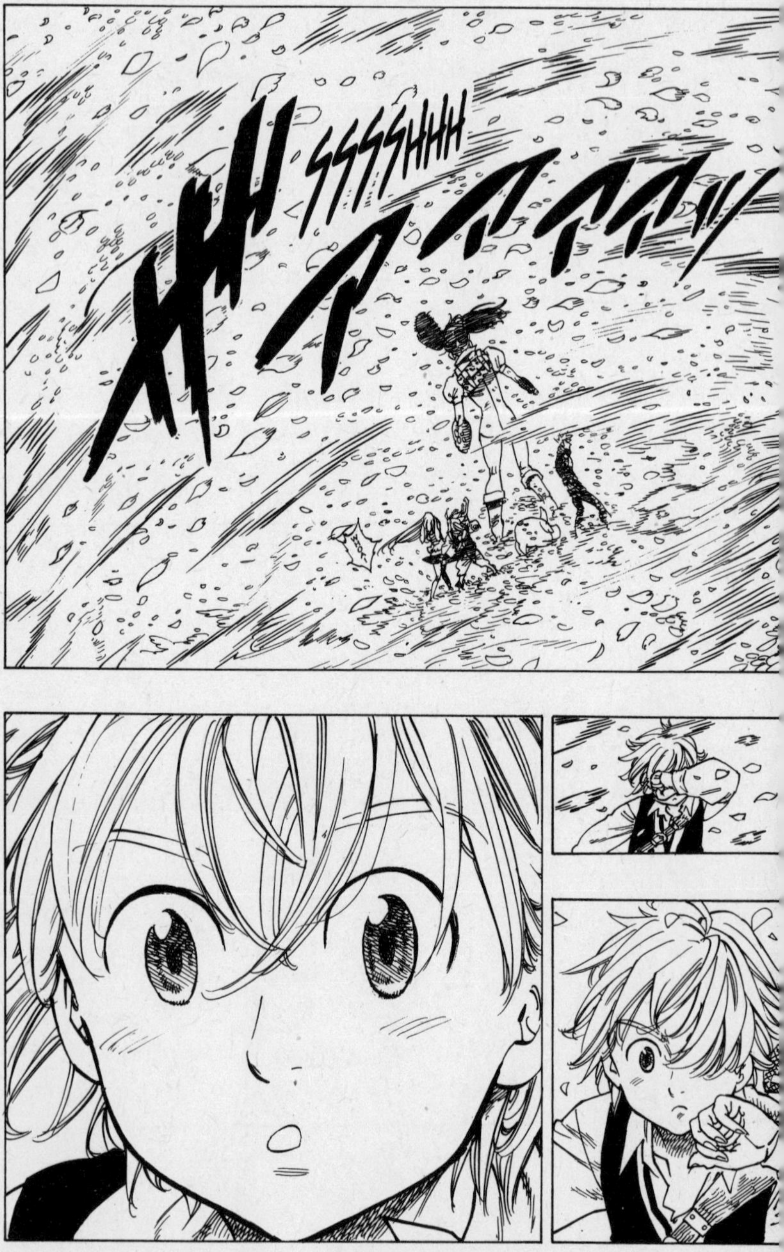
SSSSHHH

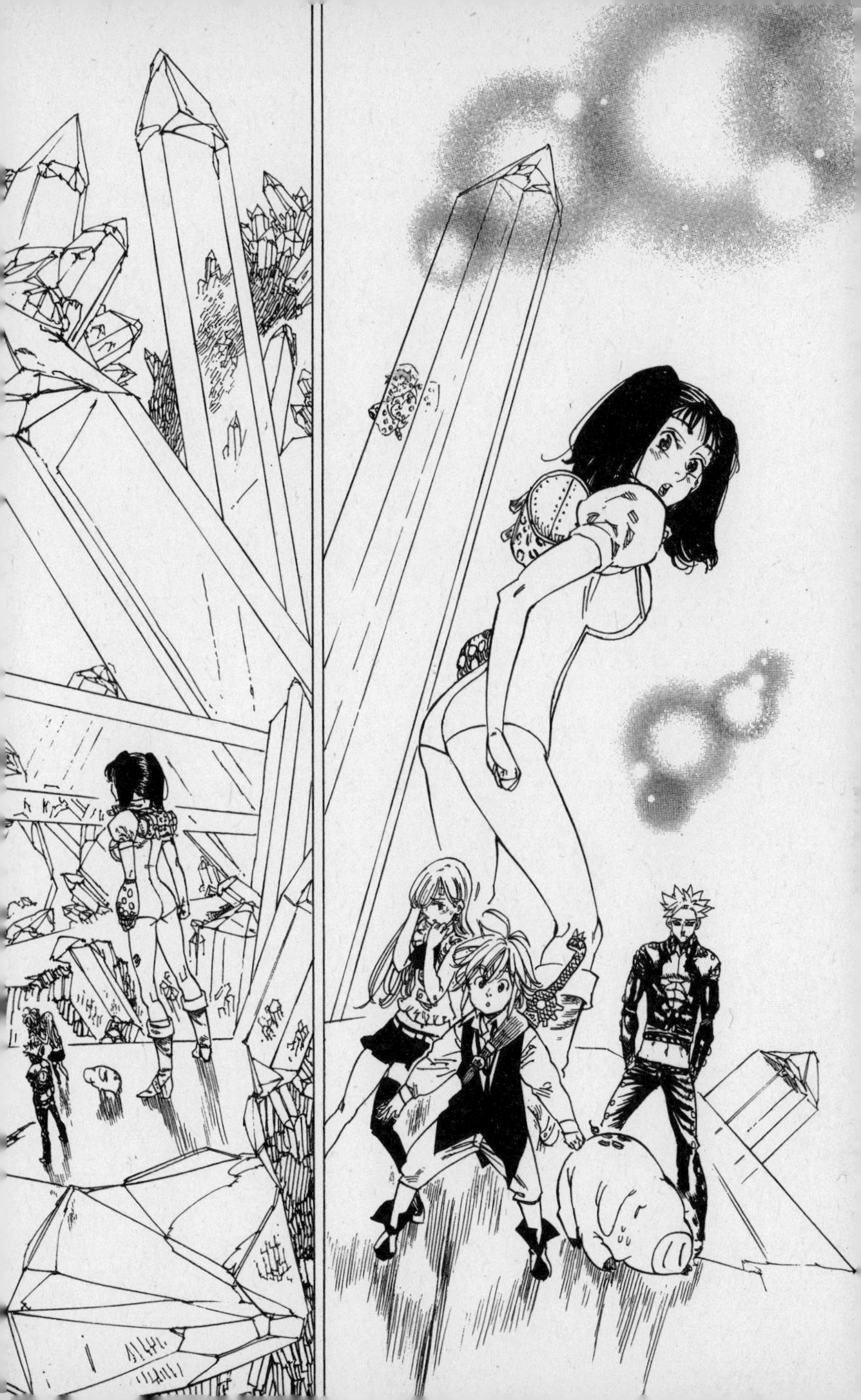

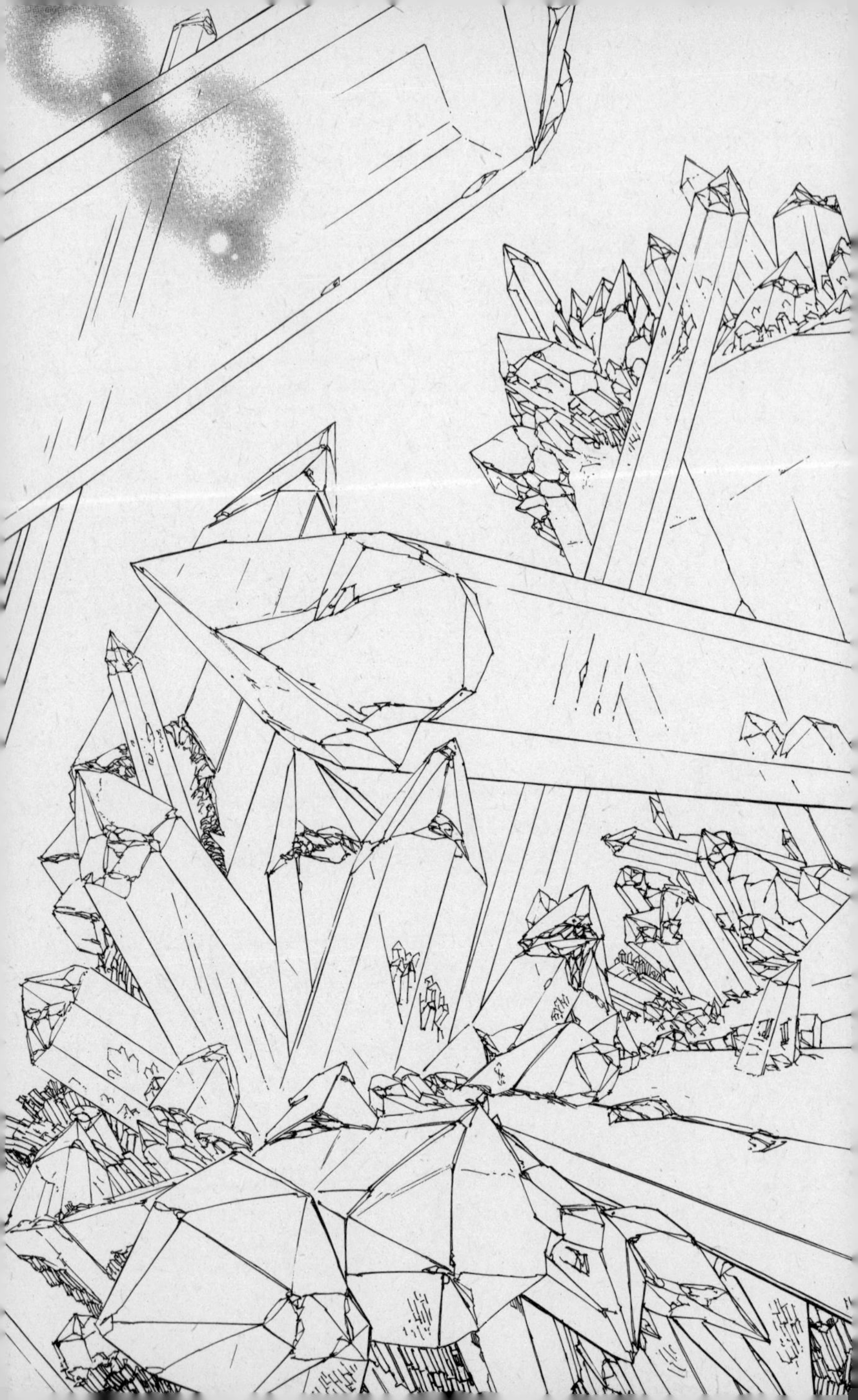

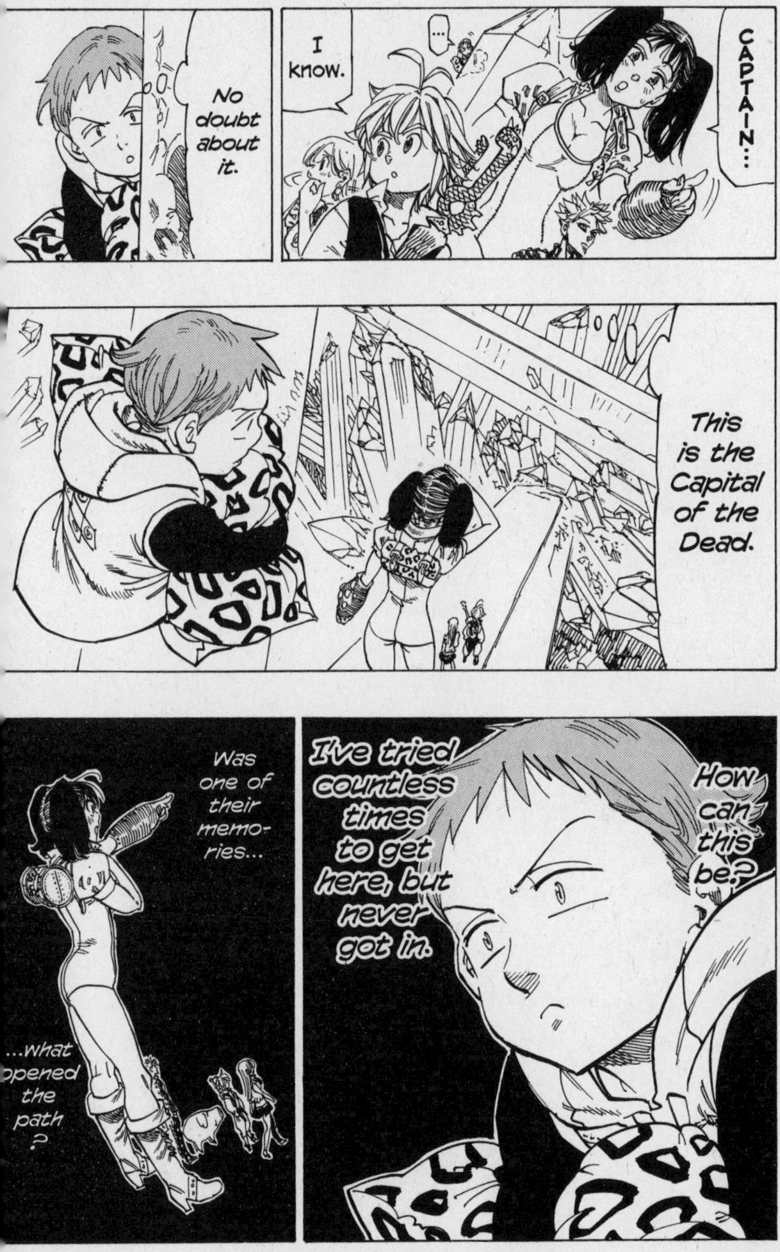
CAPTAIN...
...
I know.
No doubt about it.
This is the Capital of the Dead.
How can this be?
I've tried countless times to get here, but never got in.
Was one of their memories...
...what opened the path ?

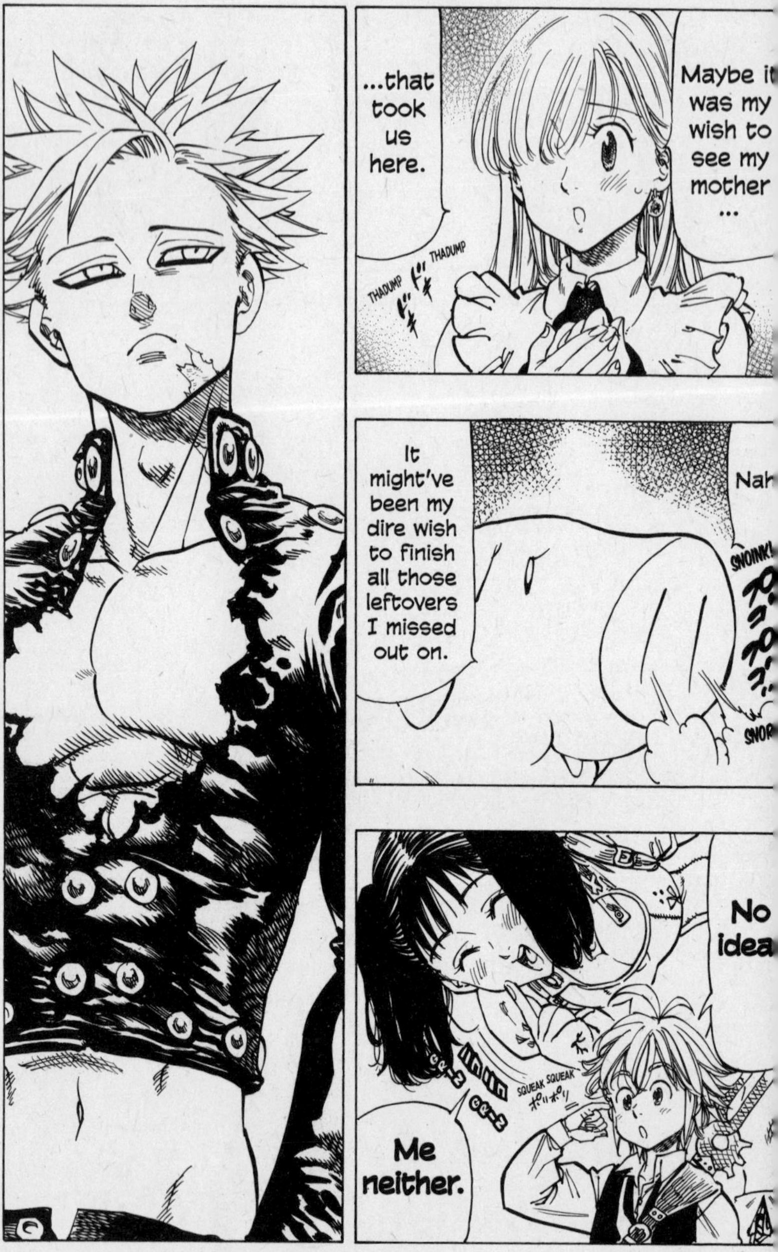
Maybe it was my wish to see my mother ...
...that took us here.
THADUMP
THADUMP
Nah
SNOINK!
SNOR
It might've been my dire wish to finish all those leftovers I missed out on.
No idea
SQUEAK SQUEAK
Me neither.

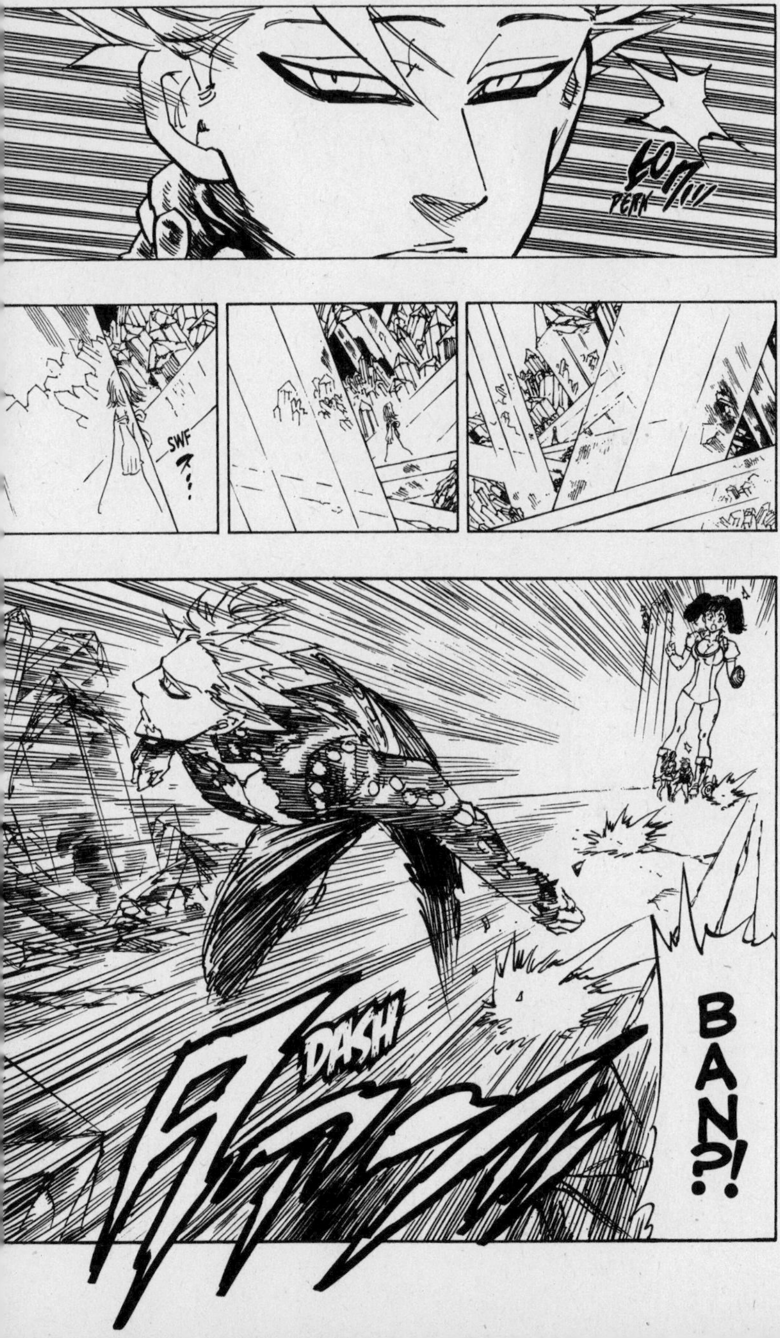
PERK
SWF
BAN?!
DASH

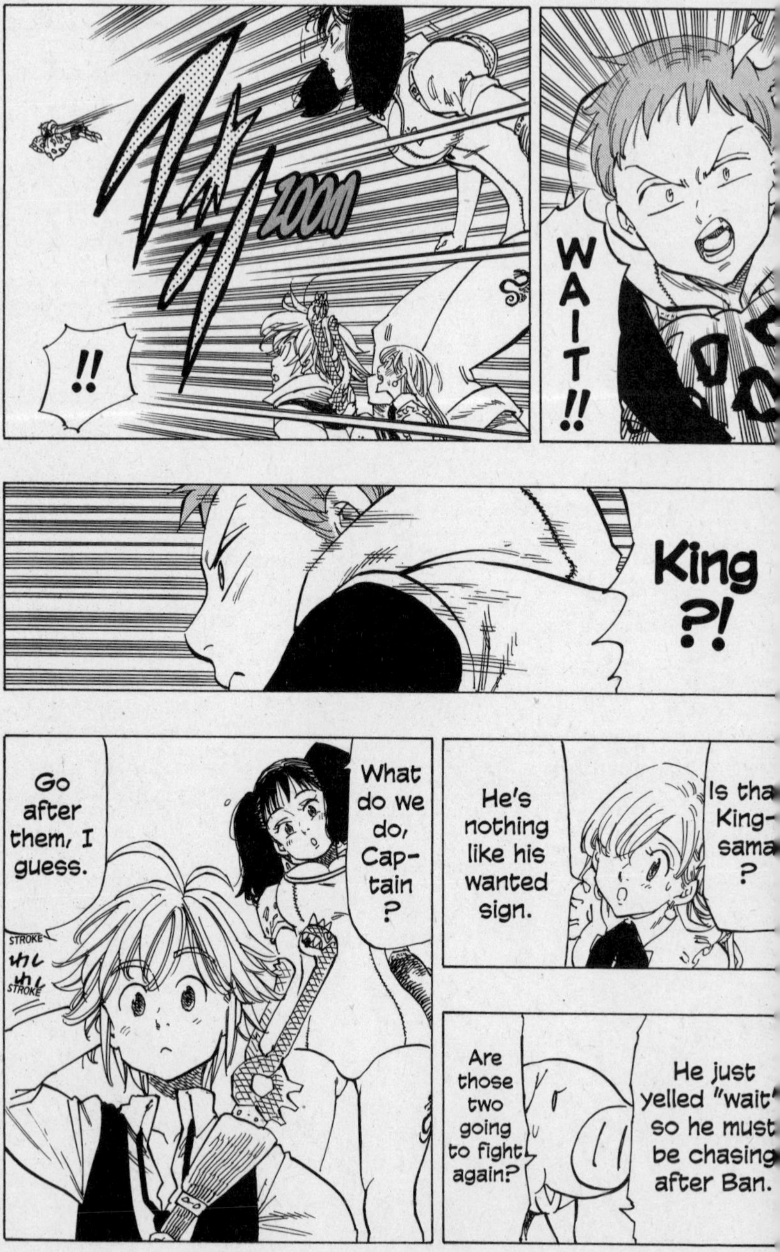
WAIT!!
ZOOM
!!
King?!
Is tha King-sama?
He's nothing like his wanted sign.
He just yelled "wait" so he must be chasing after Ban.
Are those two going to fight again?
What do we do, Captain?
Go after them, I guess.
STROKE
STROKE

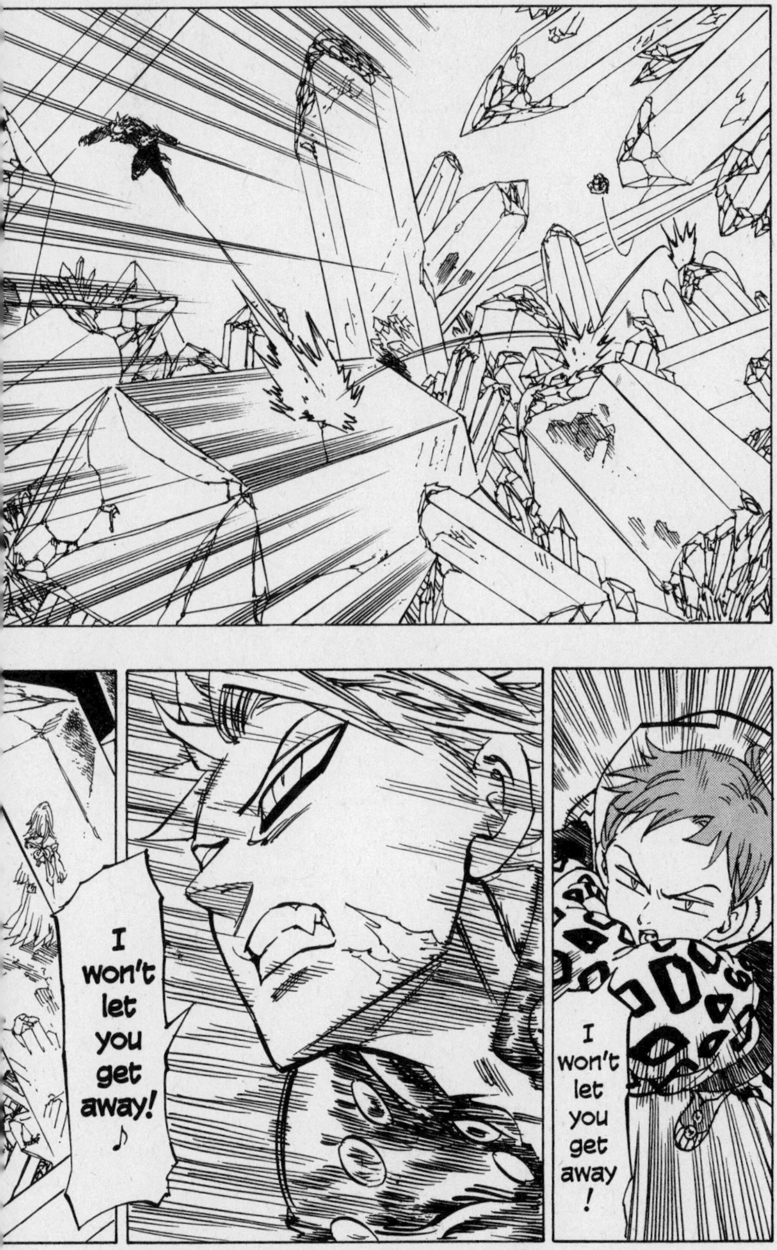
I won't let you get away!
I won't let you get away! ♪

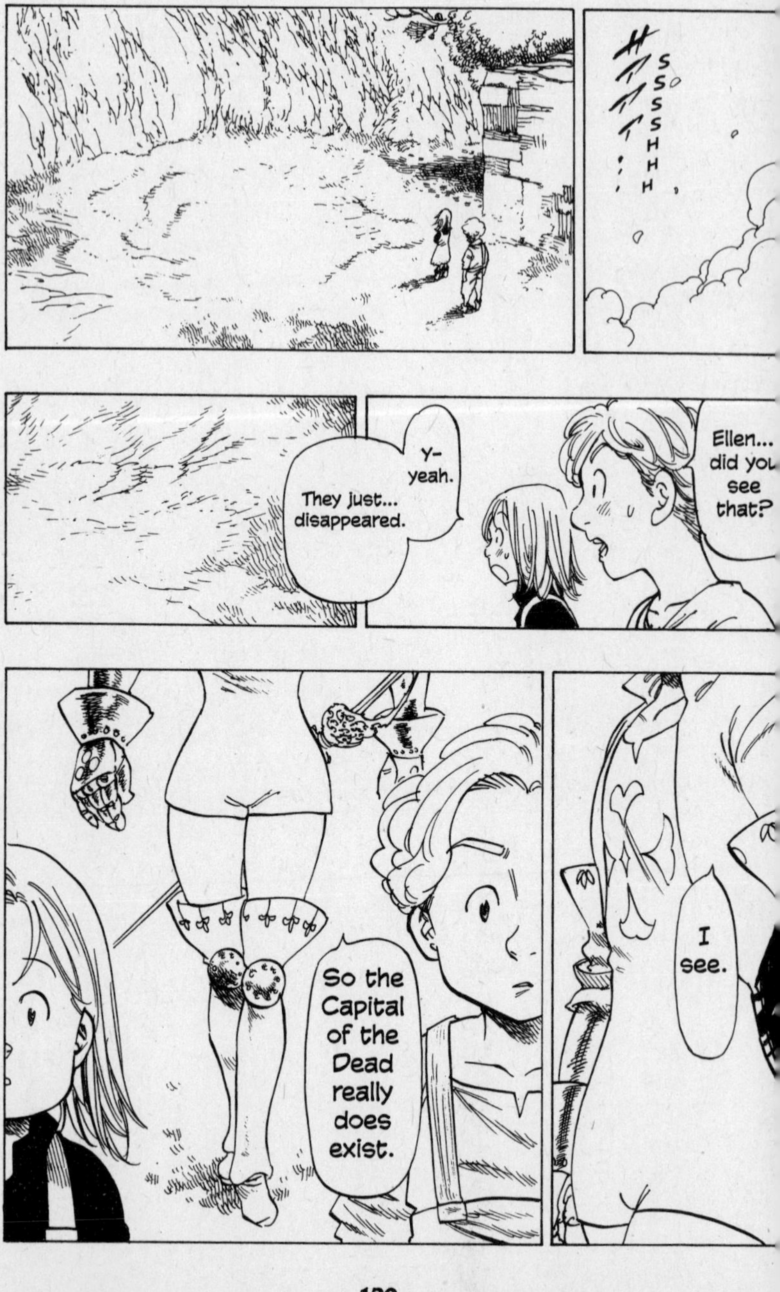
SSSSHHH
Ellen... did you see that?
Y-yeah.
They just... disappeared.
I see.
So the Capital of the Dead really does exist.

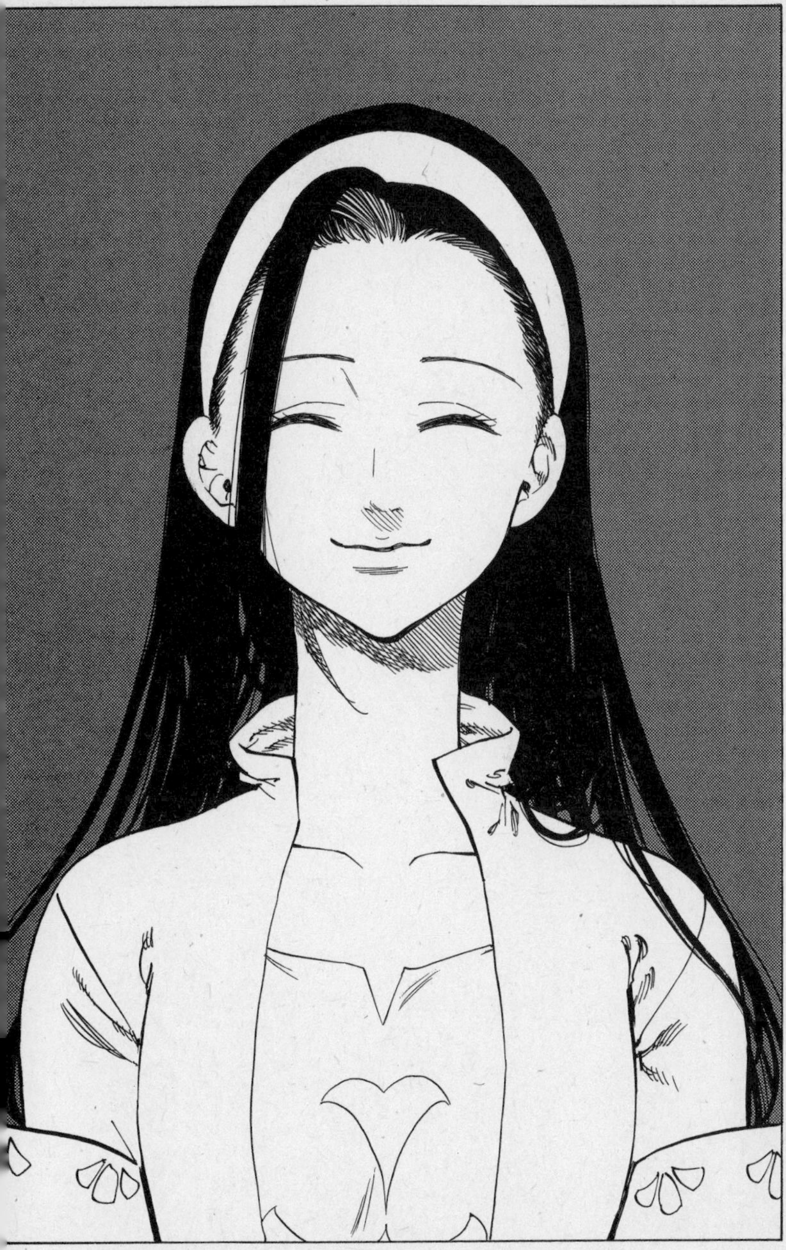

Chapter 21 - Revenge Knight

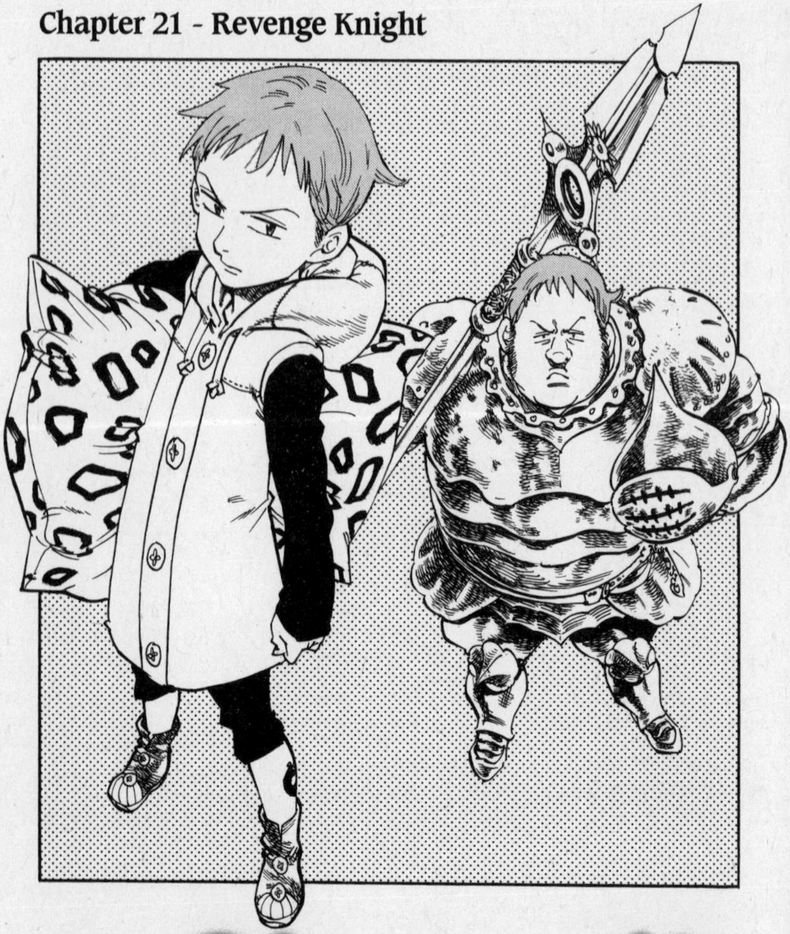

THE SEVEN DEADLY SINS

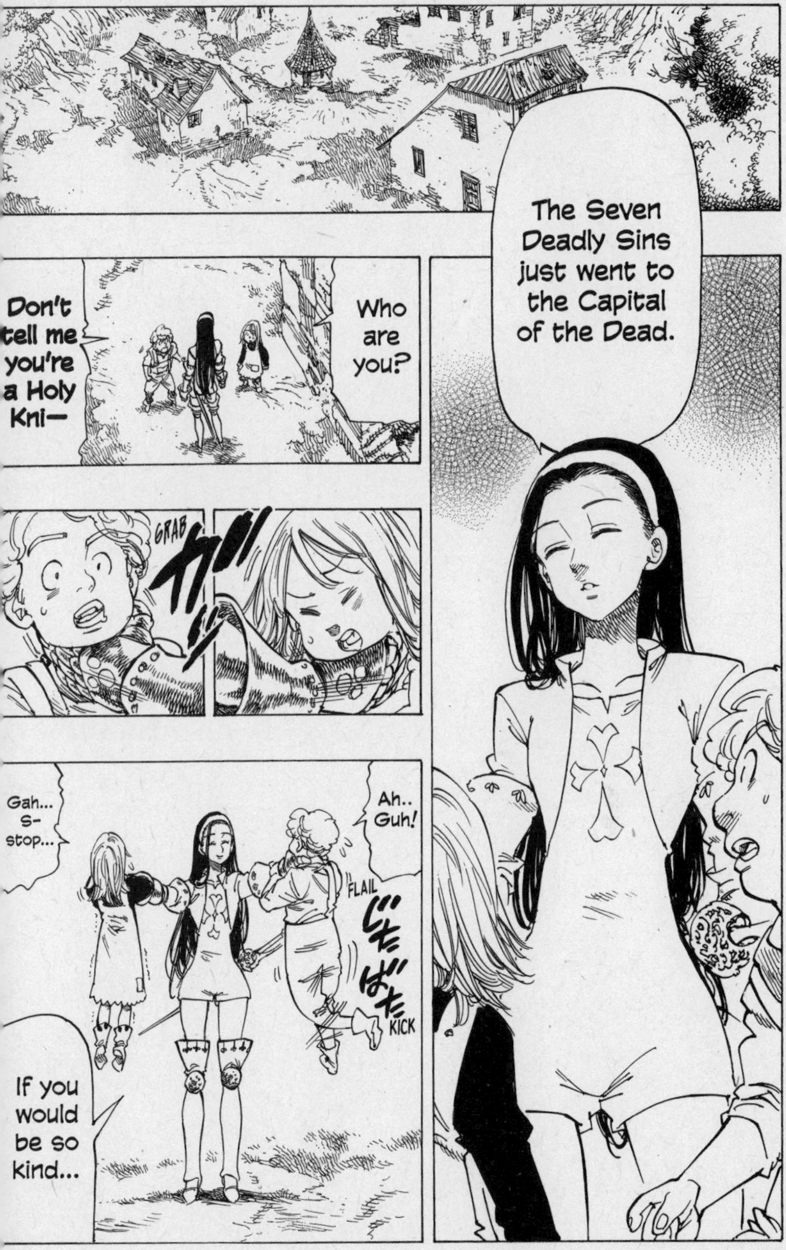

The Seven Deadly Sins just went to the Capital of the Dead.
Who are you?
Don't tell me you're a Holy Kni—
GRAB
Ah.. Guh!
FLAIL
KICK
Gah... S-stop...
If you would be so kind...

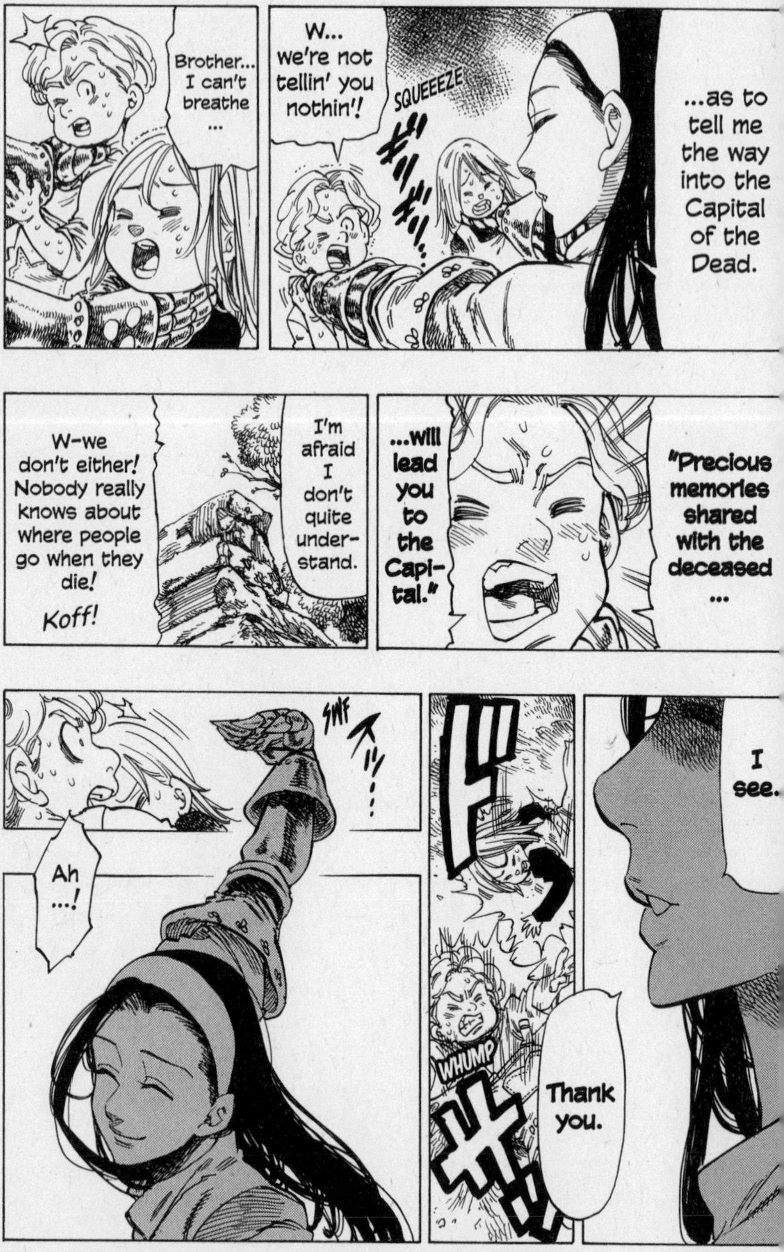
...as to tell me the way into the Capital of the Dead.
SQUEEEZE
W... we're not tellin' you nothin'!
Brother... I can't breathe ...
"Precious memories shared with the deceased ...
...will lead you to the Capital."
I'm afraid I don't quite understand.
W-we don't either! Nobody really knows about where people go when they die!
Koff!
I see.
WHUMP
Thank you.
SWF
Ah ...!

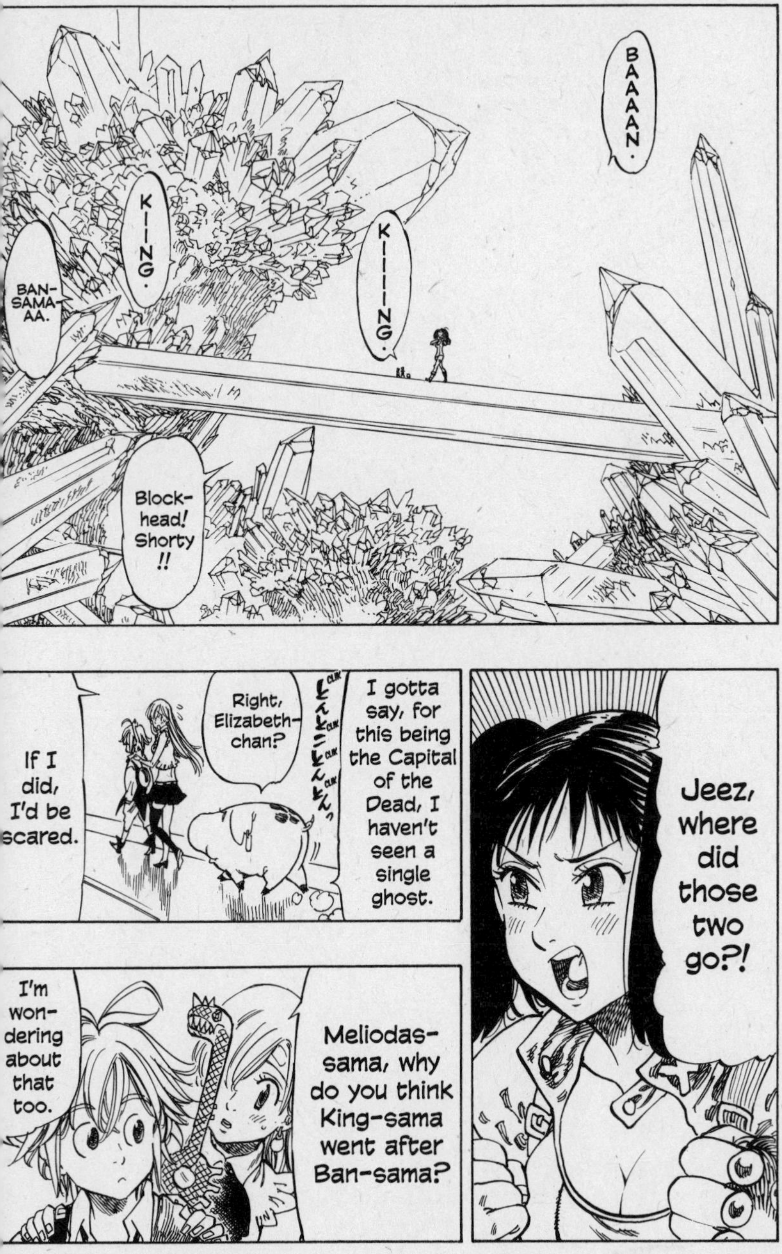
BAAAAN.
KIIIING.
KIING.
BAN-SAMA-AA.
Blockhead! Shorty!!
Jeez, where did those two go?!
I gotta say, for this being the Capital of the Dead, I haven't seen a single ghost.
CLIK CLIK CLIK CLIK
Right, Elizabeth-chan?
If I did, I'd be scared.
Meliodas-sama, why do you think King-sama went after Ban-sama?
I'm wondering about that too.

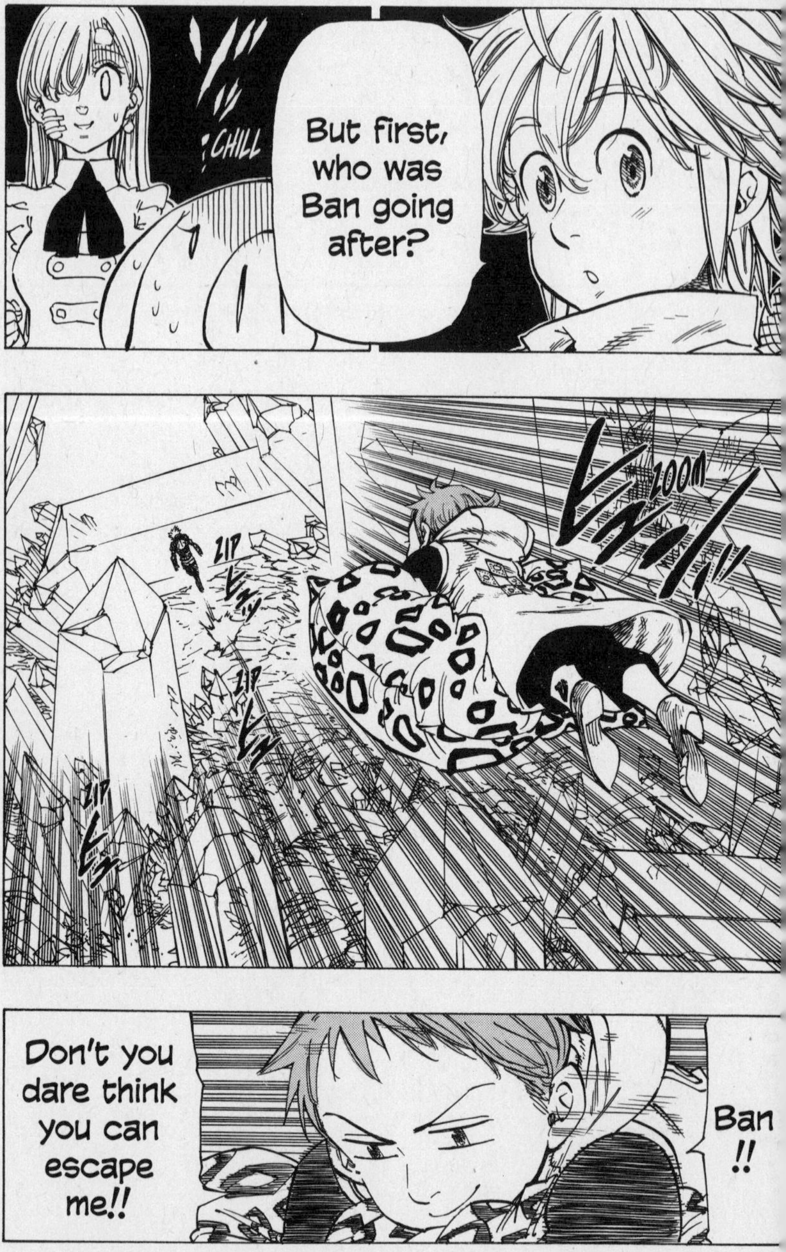
But first, who was Ban going after?
CHILL
ZOOM
ZIP
ZIP
ZIP
Ban !!
Don't you dare think you can escape me!!

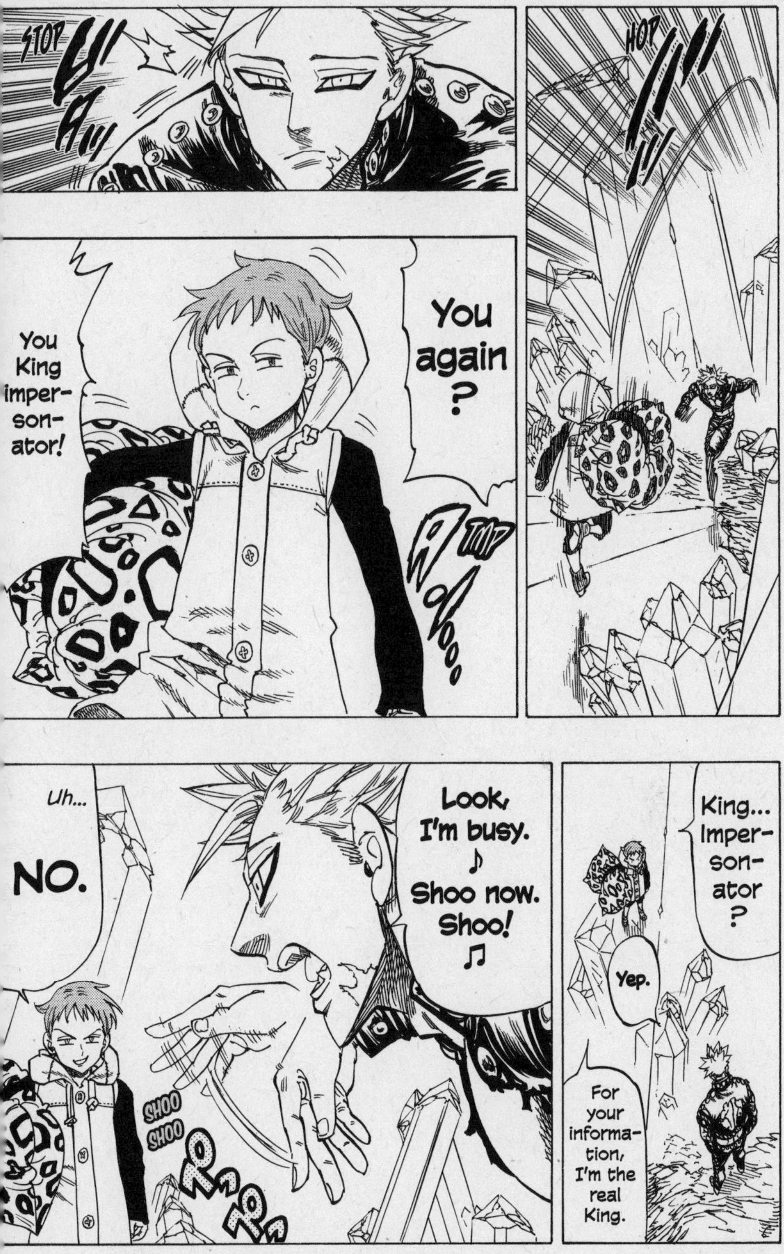
HOP
STOP
You again?
You King impersonator!
TAP
King... Imper-sonator?
Yep.
For your information, I'm the real King.
Look, I'm busy. ♪ Shoo now. Shoo! ♫
Uh...
NO.
SHOO SHOO

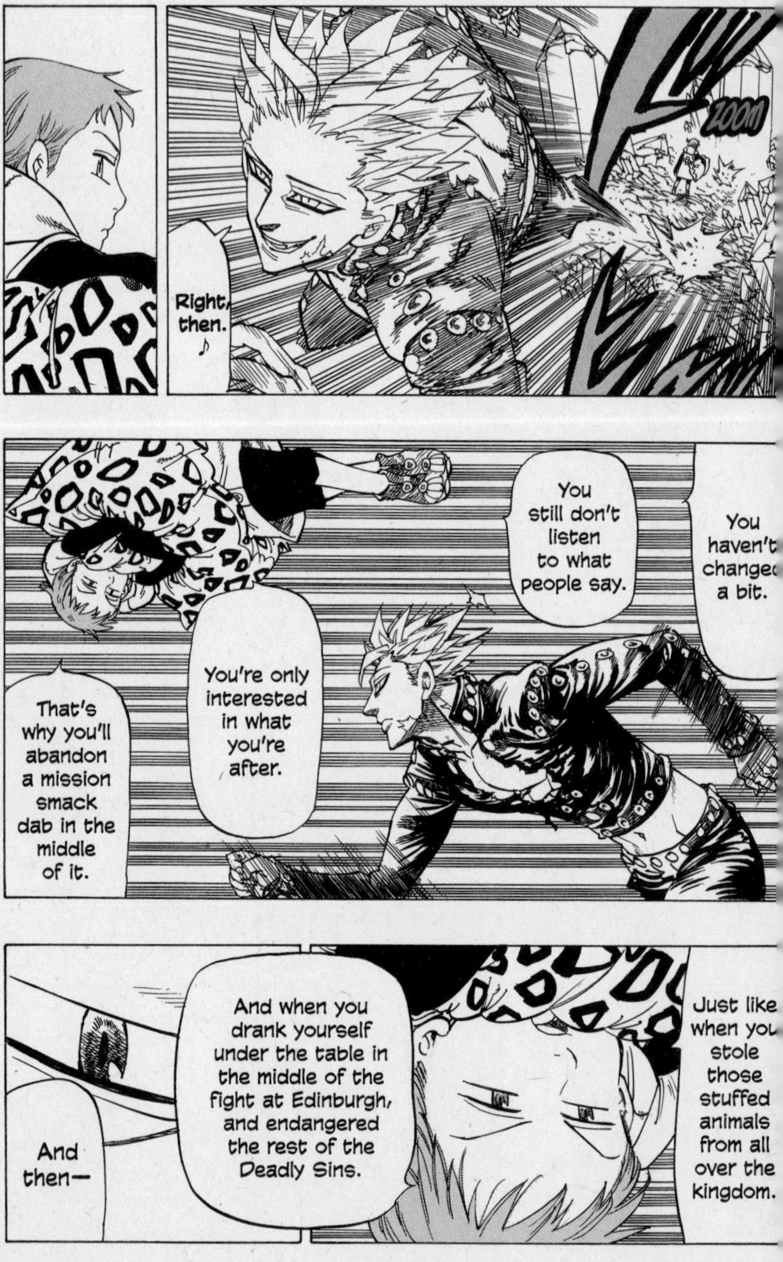
ZOOM
Right, then. ♪
You haven't changed a bit.
You still don't listen to what people say.
You're only interested in what you're after.
That's why you'll abandon a mission smack dab in the middle of it.
Just like when you stole those stuffed animals from all over the kingdom.
And when you drank yourself under the table in the middle of the fight at Edinburgh, and endangered the rest of the Deadly Sins.
And then—

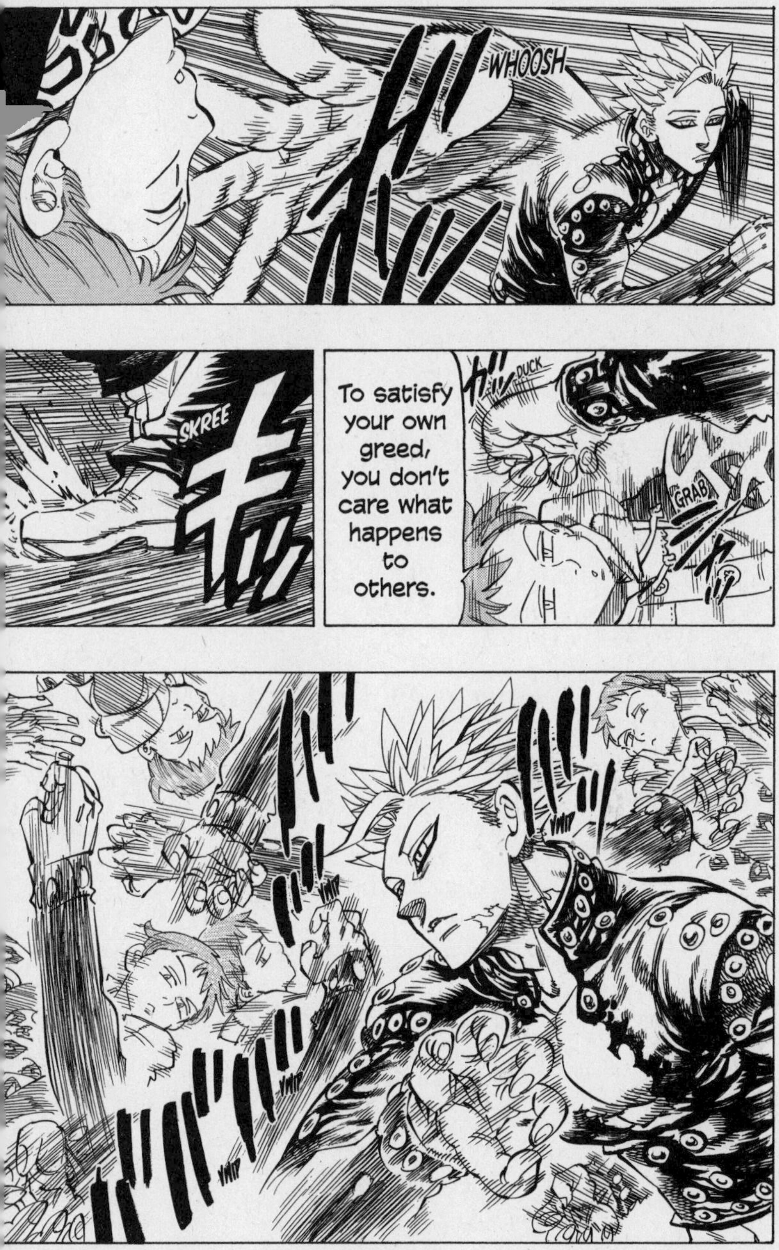
WHOOSH
DUCK
To satisfy your own greed, you don't care what happens to others.
GRAB
SKREE

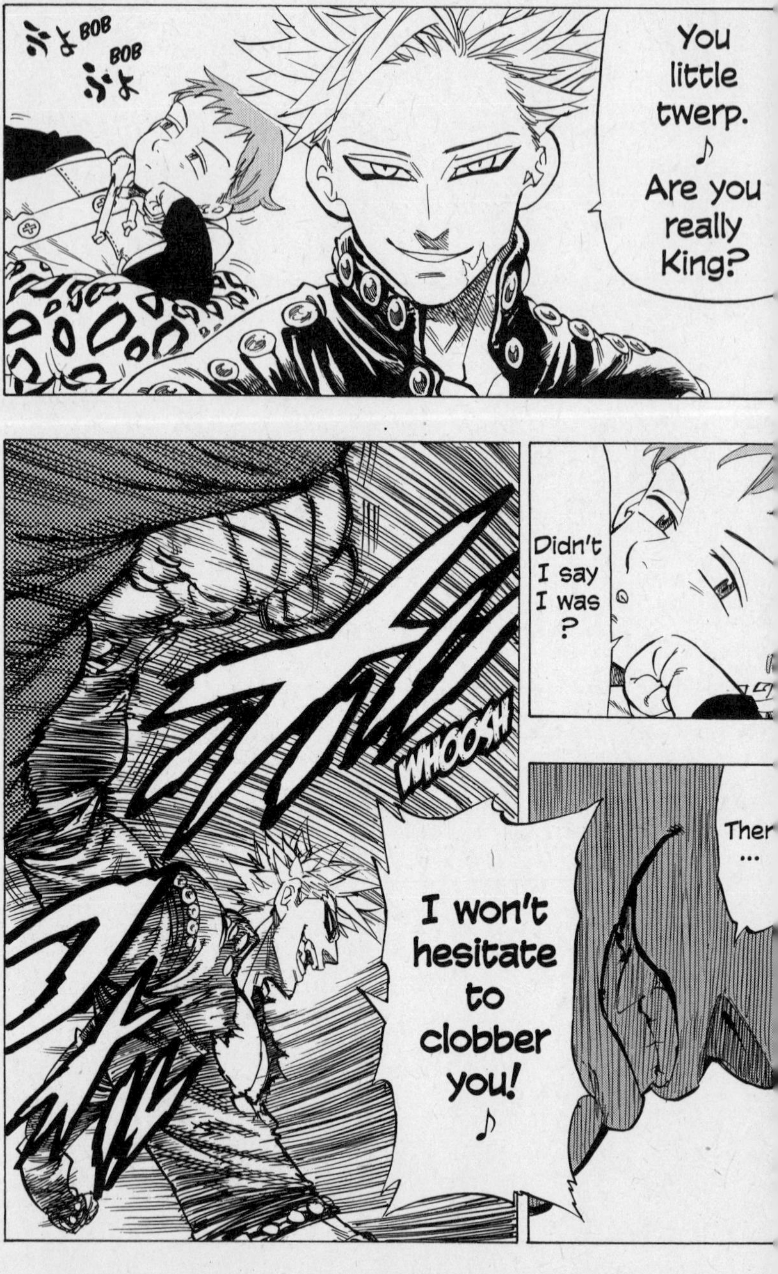
You little twerp. ♪ Are you really King?
ぷよ BOB
ぷよ BOB
Didn't I say I was?
Ther ...
WHOOSH
I won't hesitate to clobber you! ♪

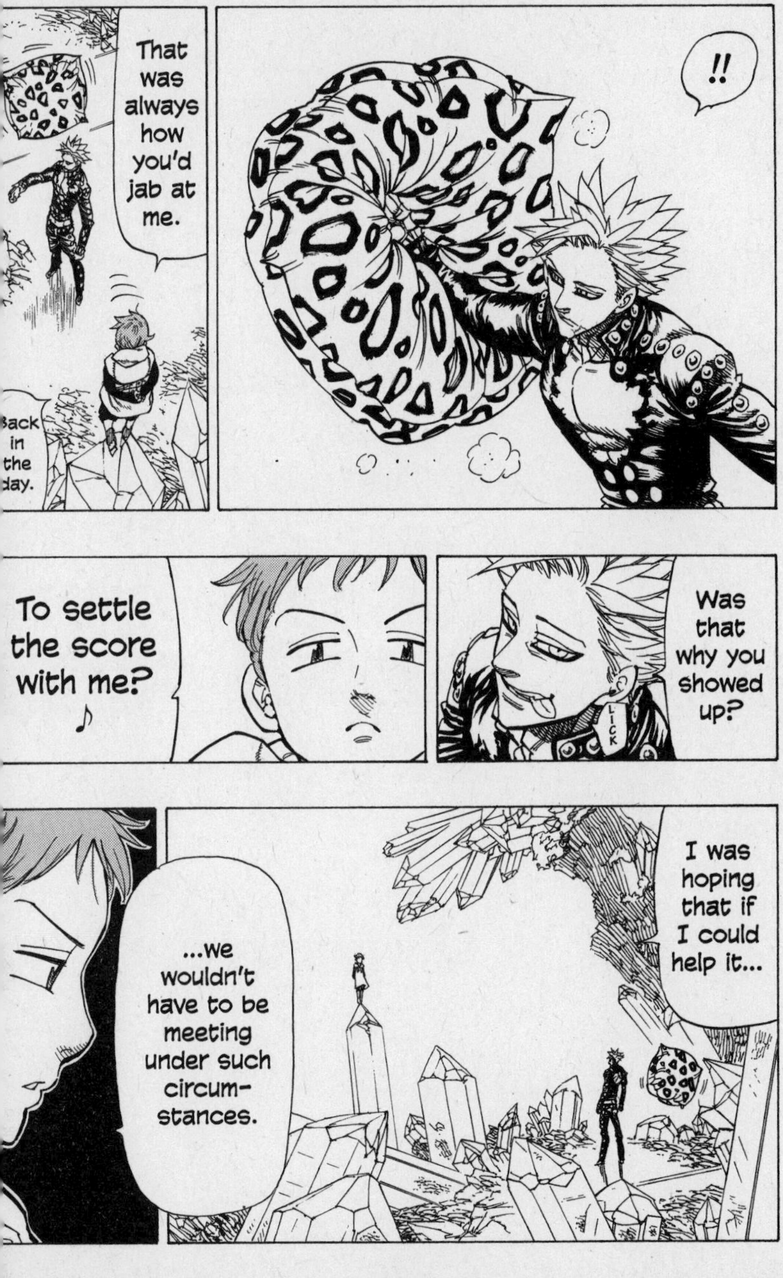
!!
That was always how you'd jab at me.
Back in the day.
Was that why you showed up?
LICK
To settle the score with me? ♪
I was hoping that if I could help it...
...we wouldn't have to be meeting under such circum-stances.

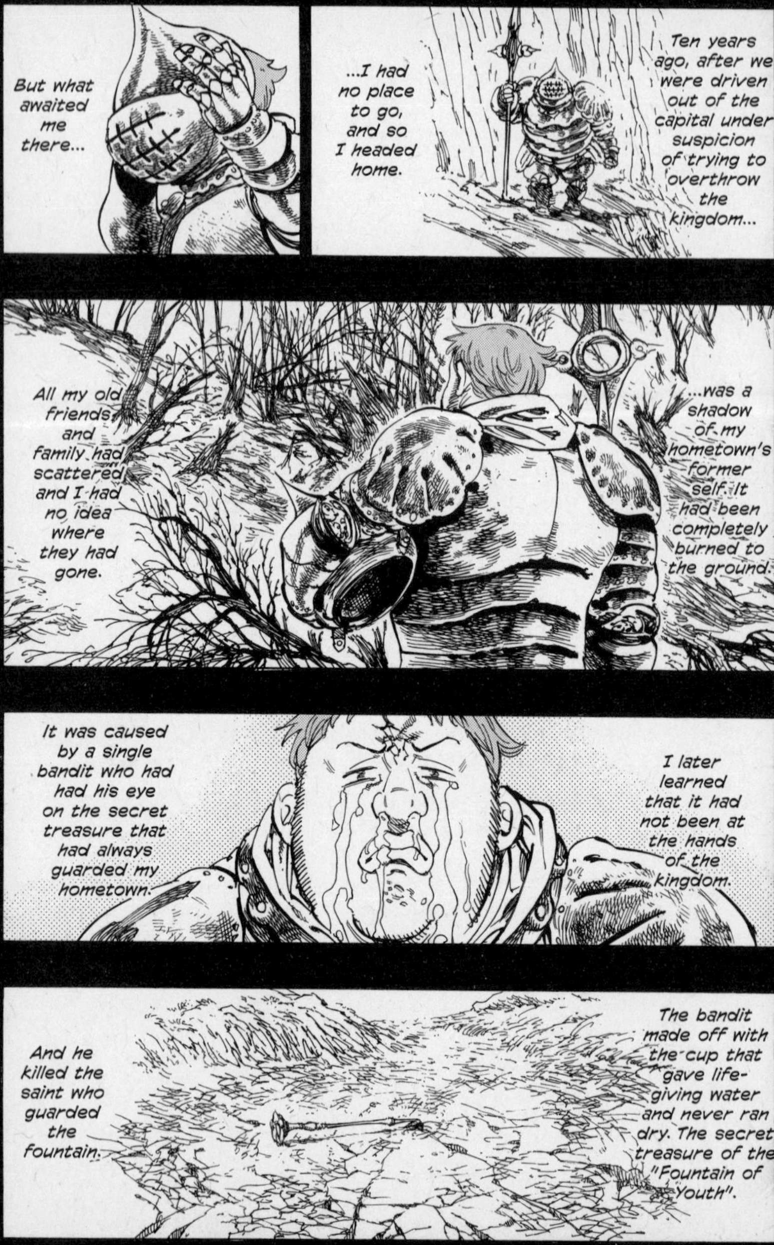
Ten years ago, after we were driven out of the capital under suspicion of trying to overthrow the kingdom...
...I had no place to go, and so I headed home.
But what awaited me there...
...was a shadow of my hometown's former self. It had been completely burned to the ground.
All my old friends and family had scattered and I had no idea where they had gone.
I later learned that it had not been at the hands of the kingdom.
It was caused by a single bandit who had had his eye on the secret treasure that had always guarded my hometown.
The bandit made off with the cup that gave life-giving water and never ran dry. The secret treasure of the "Fountain of Youth".
And he killed the saint who guarded the fountain.

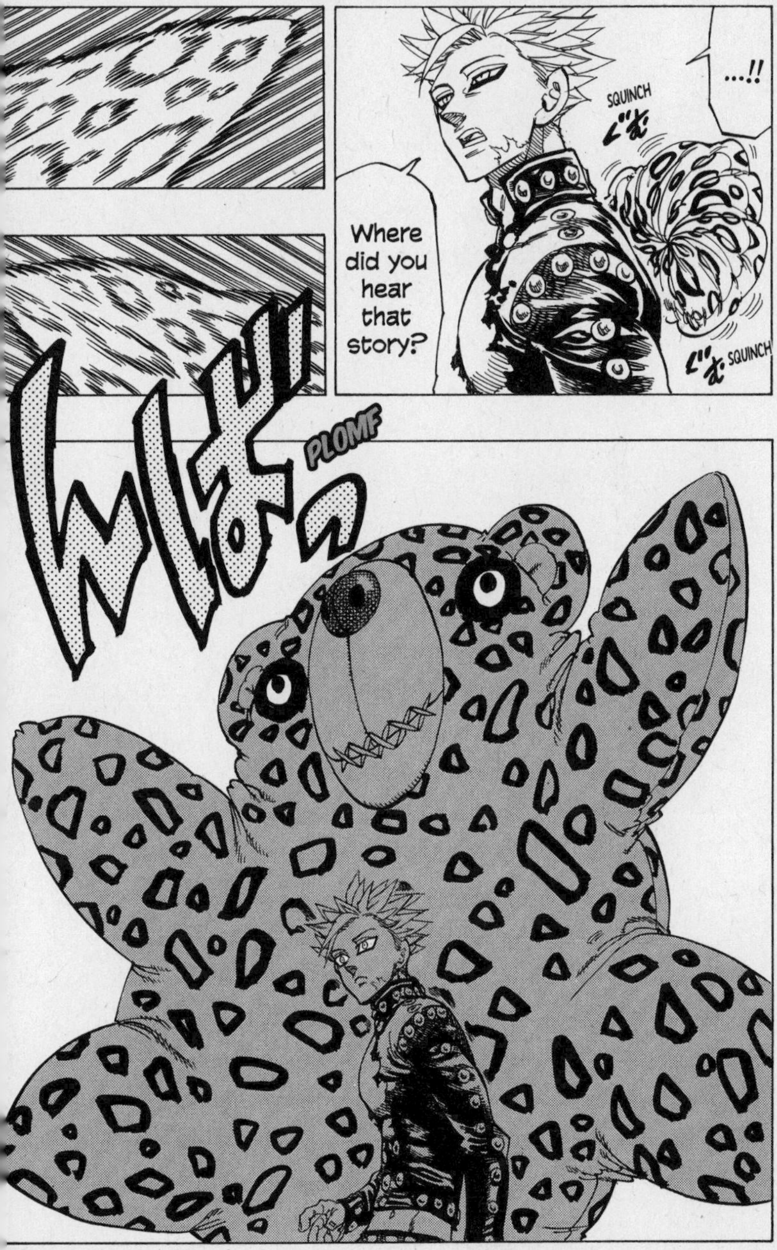
...!!
SQUINCH
SQUINCH
Where did you hear that story?
PLOMF

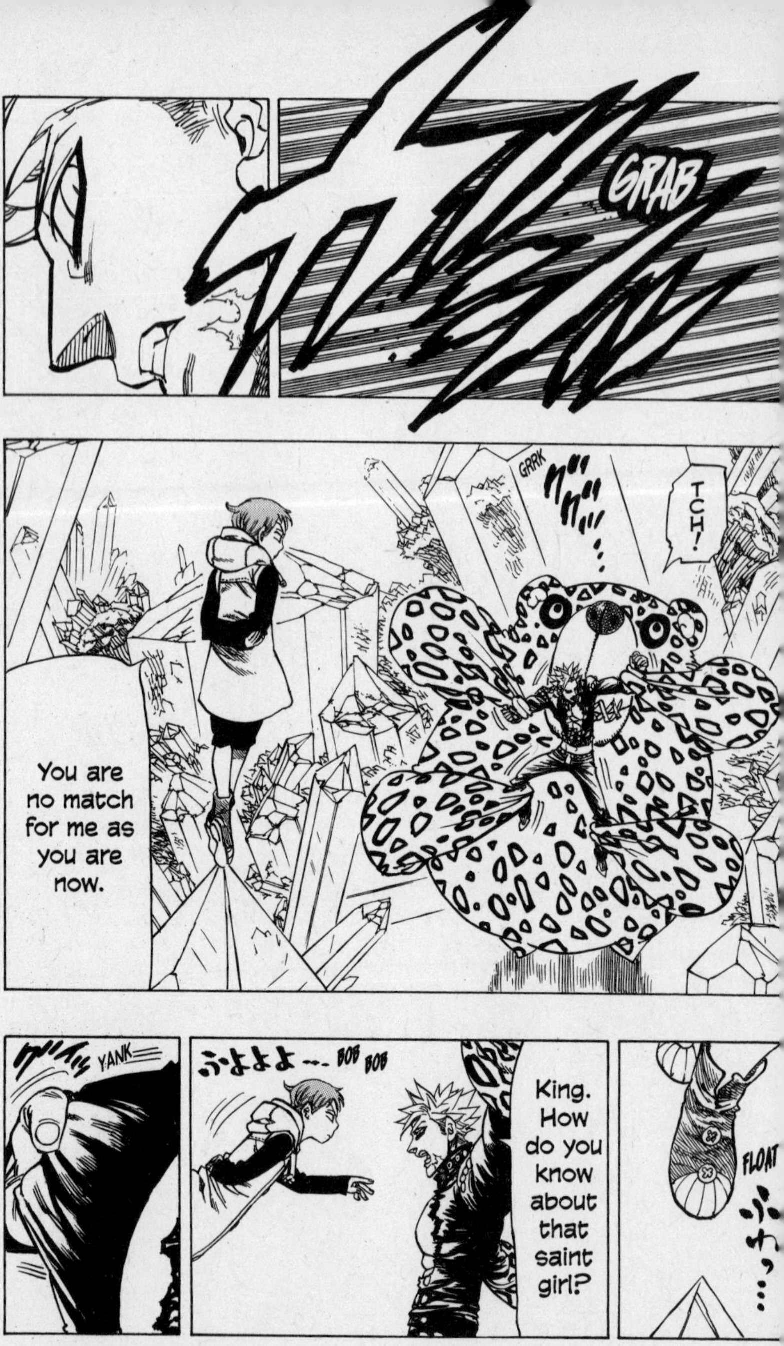
GRAB
TCH!
GRRK
You are no match for me as you are now.
FLOAT
ふわっ…
King. How do you know about that saint girl?
ふよよよ…
BOB BOB
YANK

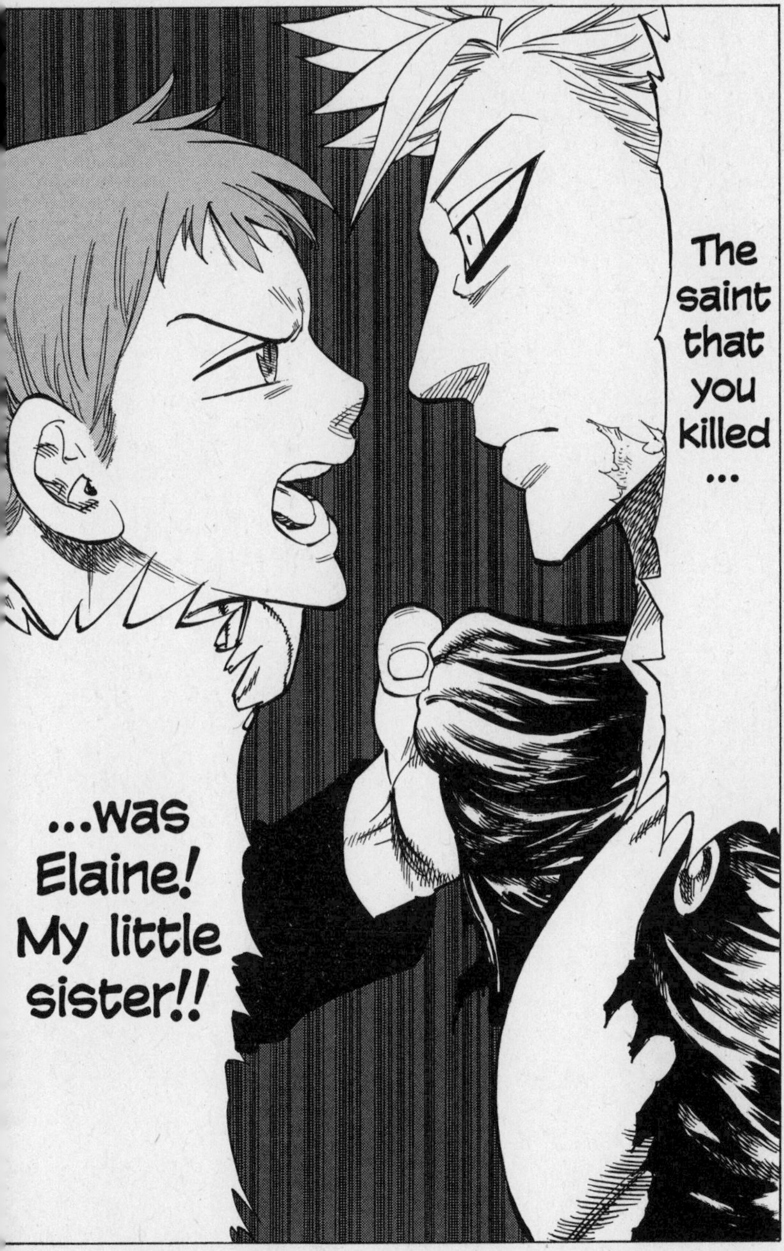
The saint that you killed ...
...was Elaine! My little sister!!

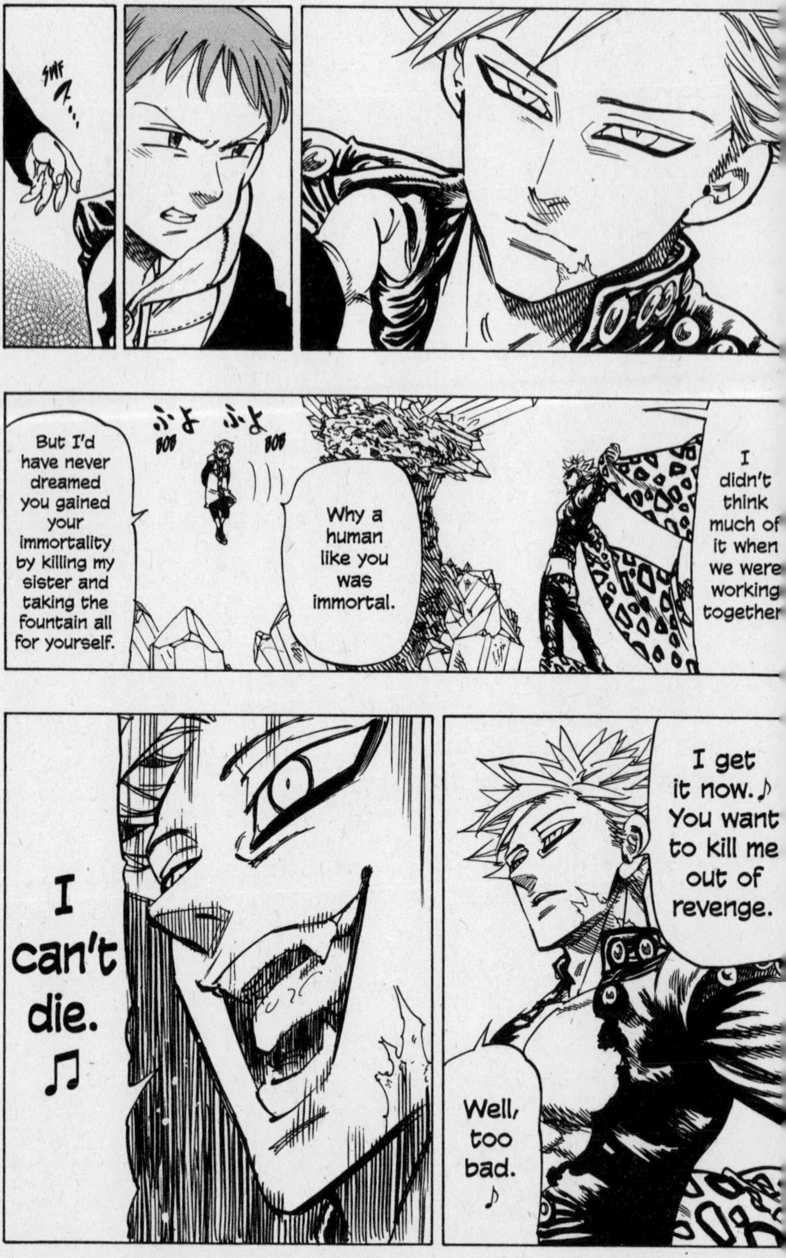
SWF
I didn't think much of it when we were working together
Why a human like you was immortal.
ふよ ふよ
BOB BOB
But I'd have never dreamed you gained your immortality by killing my sister and taking the fountain all for yourself.
I get it now.♪ You want to kill me out of revenge.
Well, too bad. ♪
I can't die. ♫

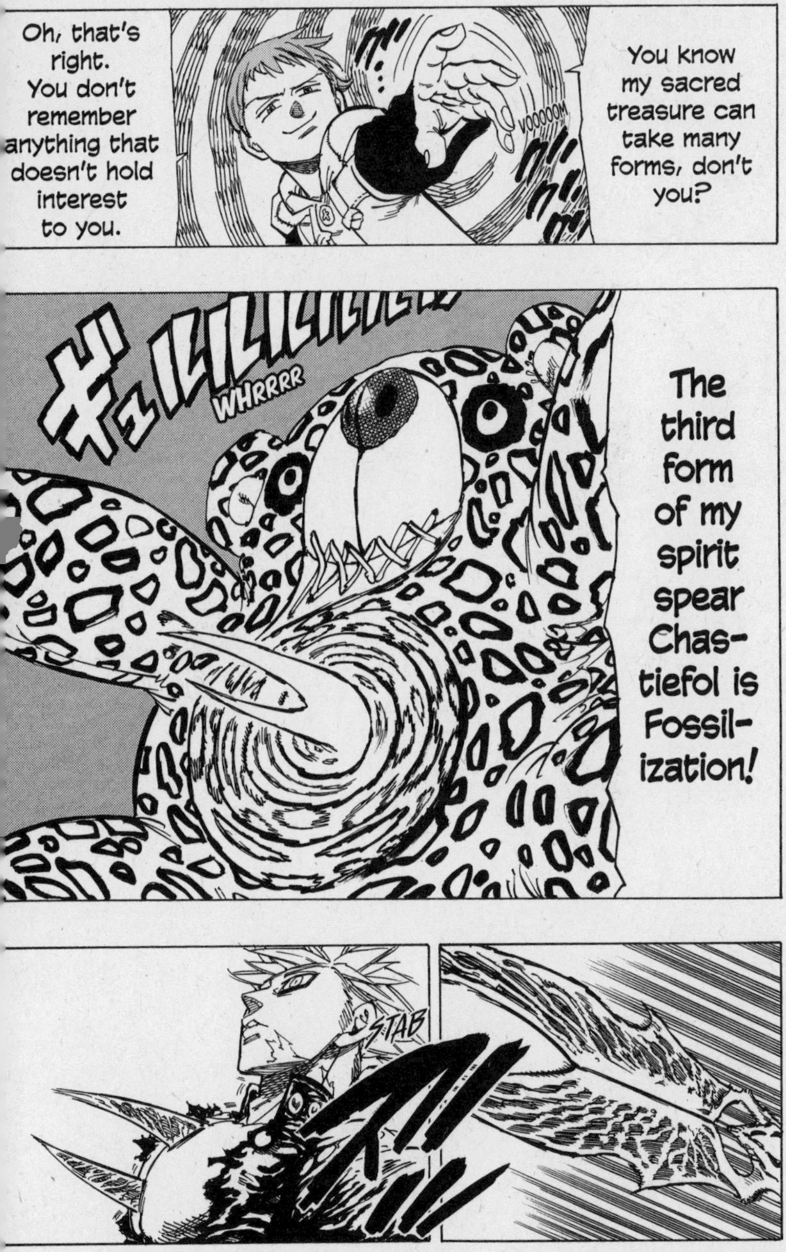

You know my sacred treasure can take many forms, don't you?
VOOOOOM
Oh, that's right. You don't remember anything that doesn't hold interest to you.
The third form of my spirit spear Chastiefol is Fossilization!
WHRRRR
STAB

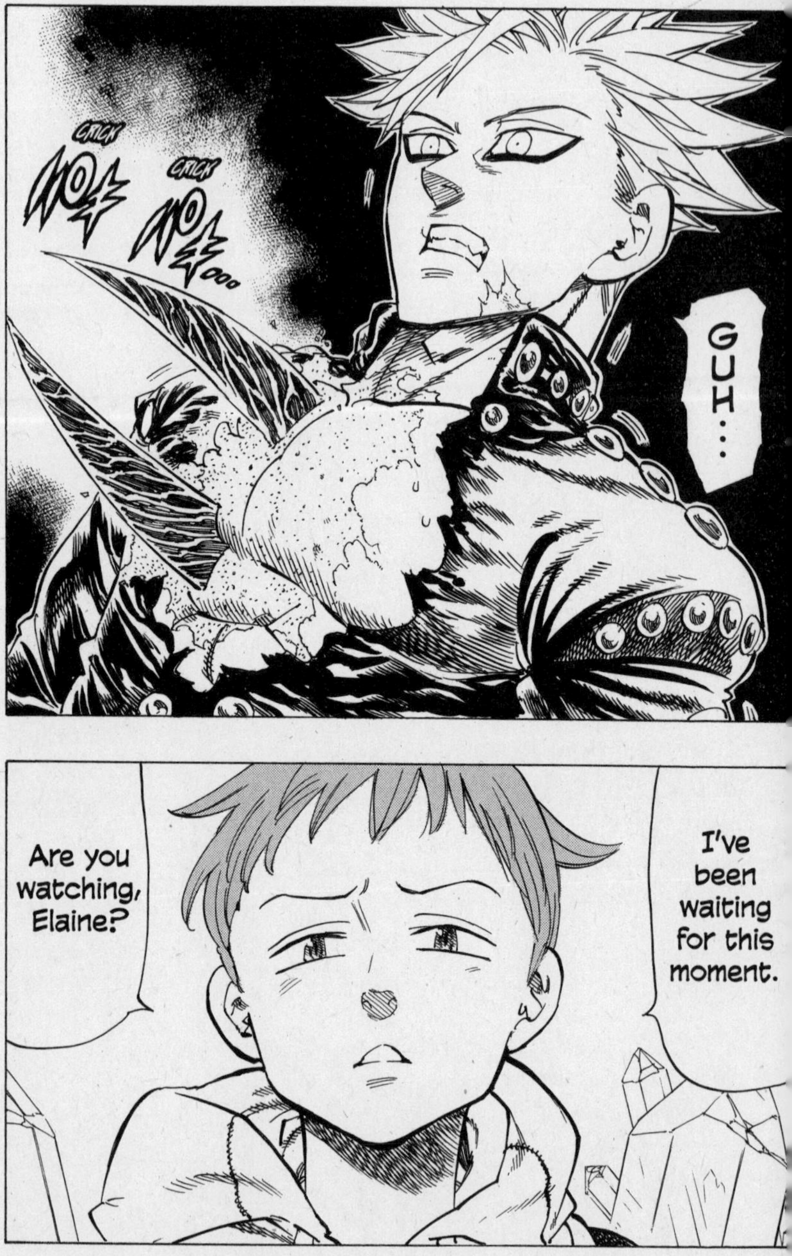
GUH...
CRICK
CRICK
I've been waiting for this moment.
Are you watching, Elaine?

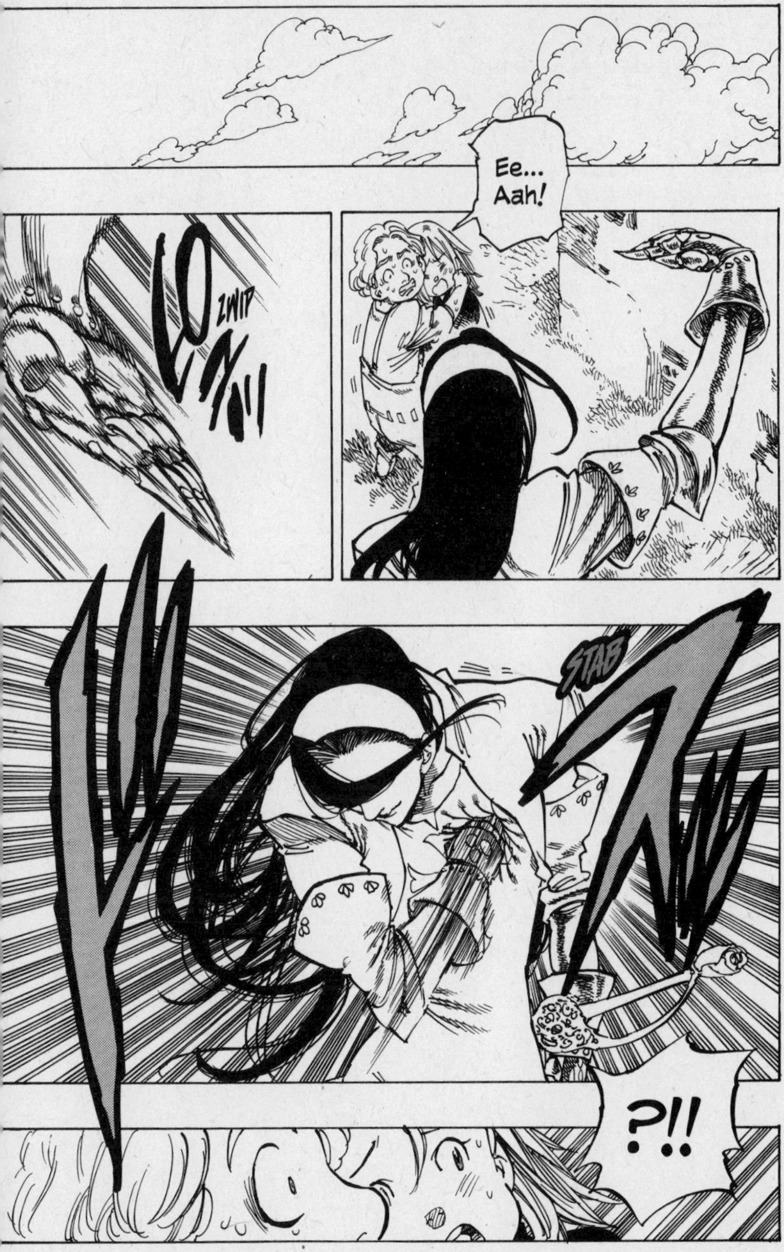
Ee... Aah!
ZWIP
STAB
?!!

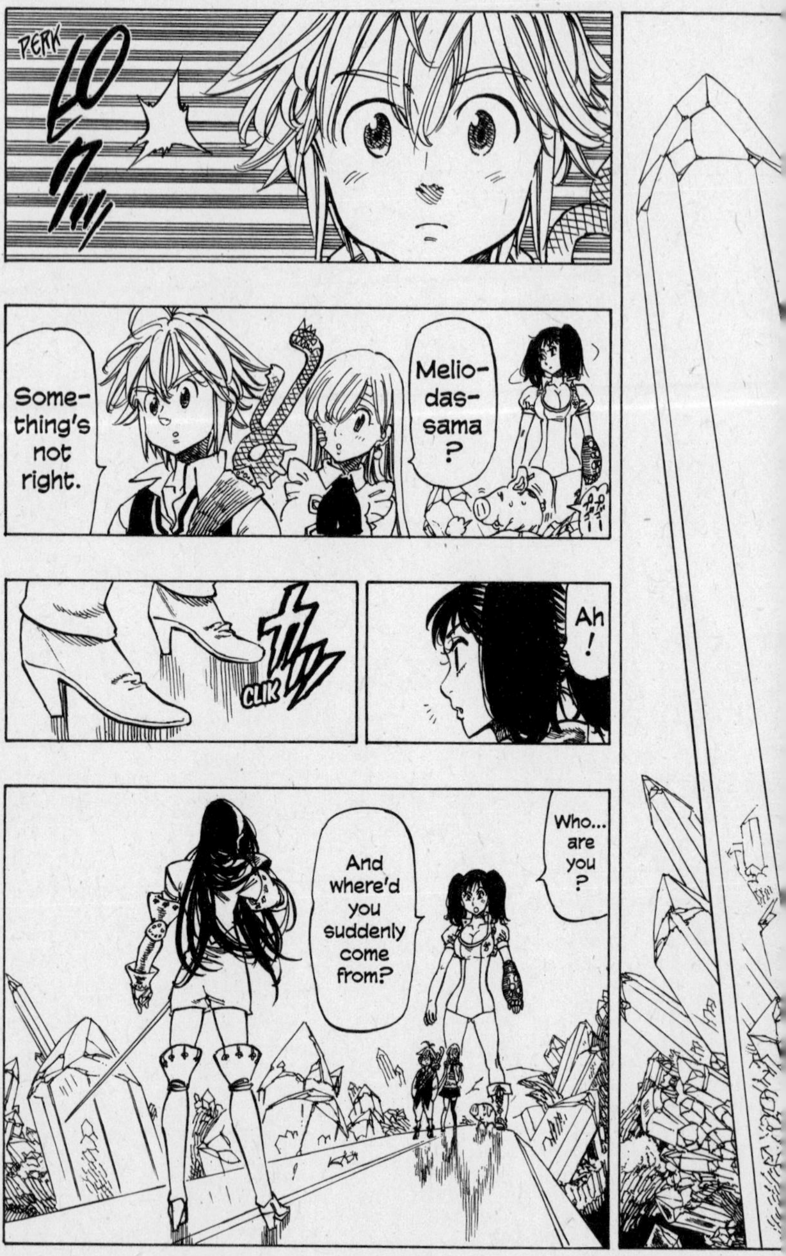
PERK
Melio-das-sama?
Some-thing's not right.
Ah!
CLIK
Who... are you?
And where'd you suddenly come from?

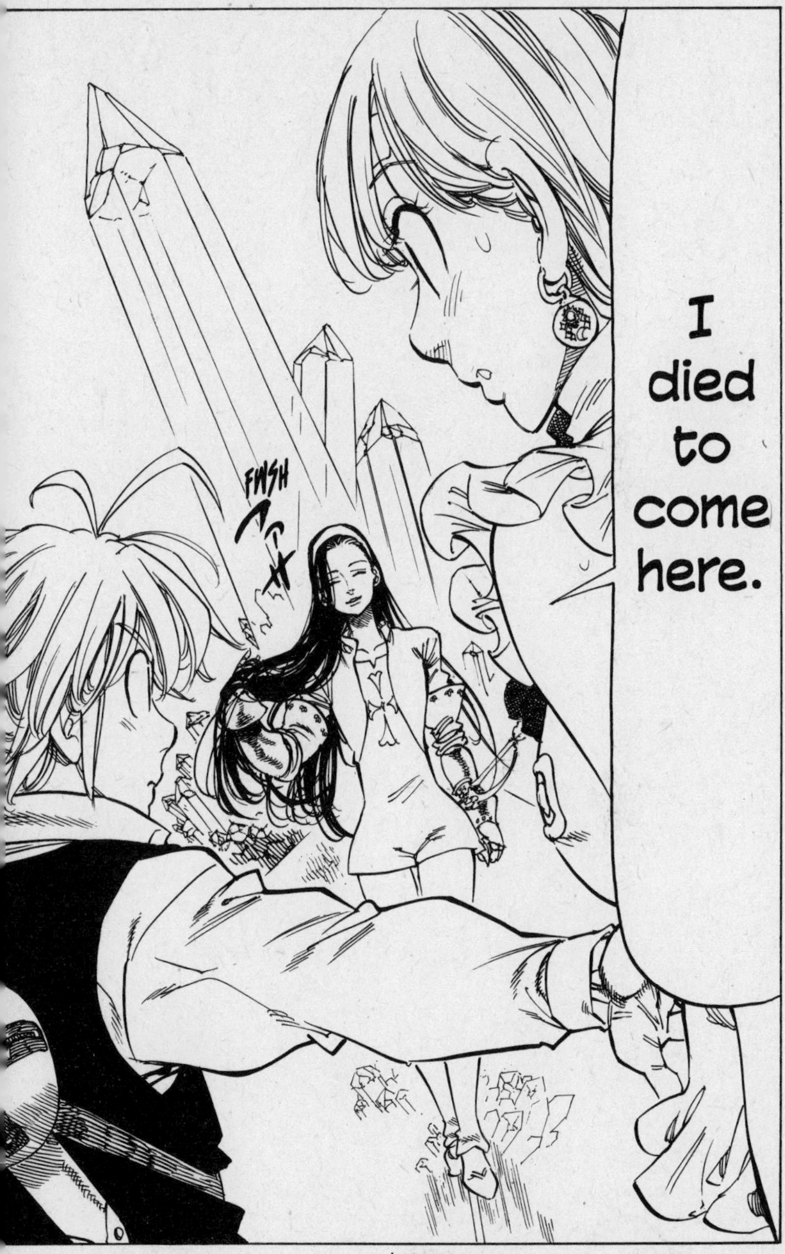
I died to come here.
FWSH

Chapter 22 - A Pursuer to Fear

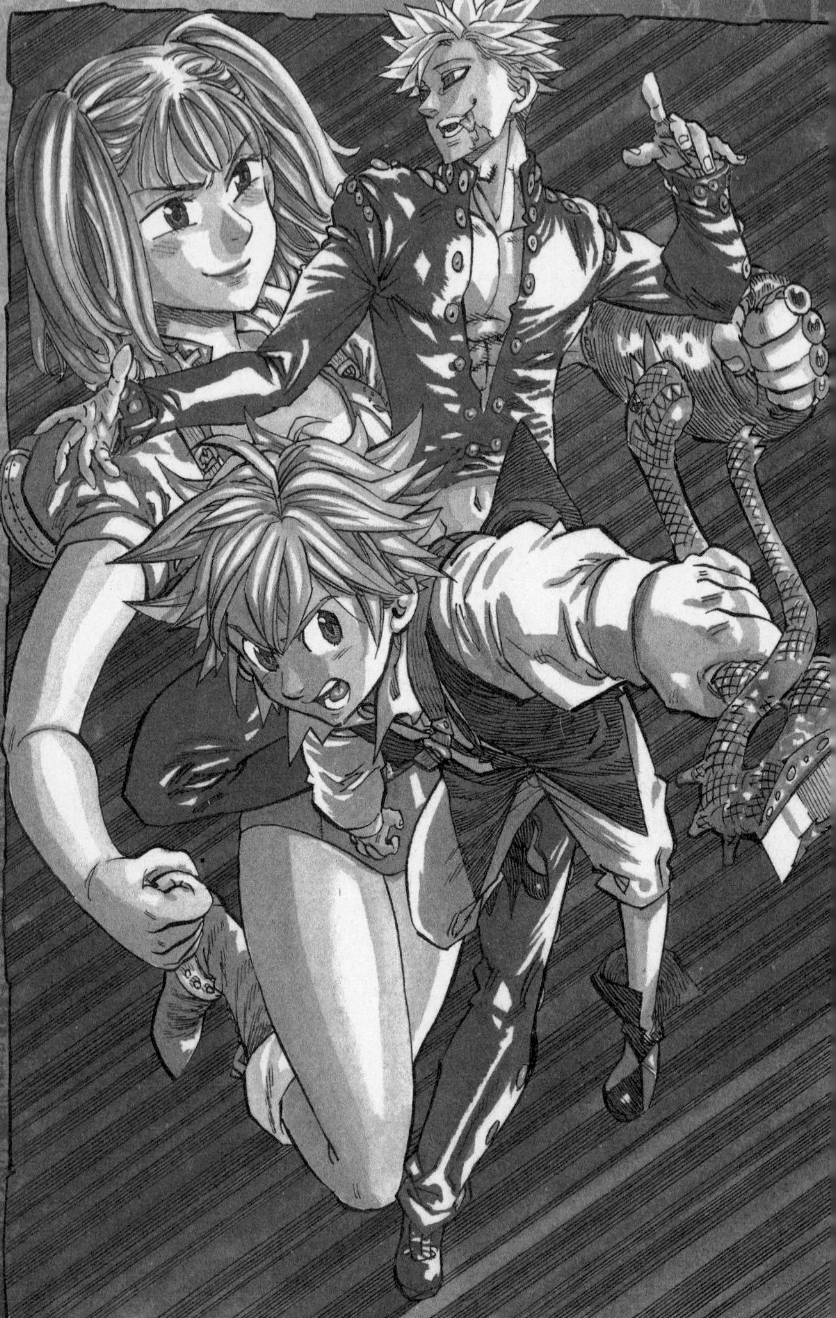

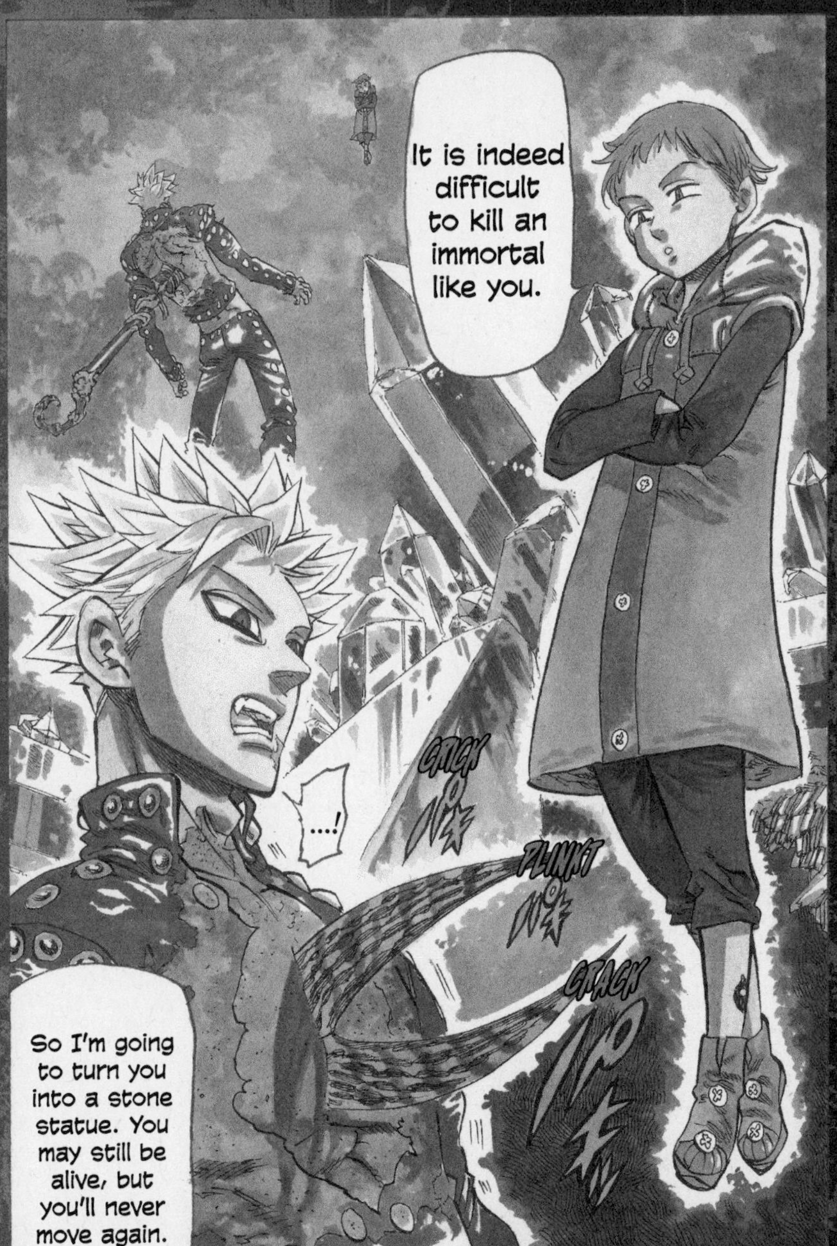
It is indeed difficult to kill an immortal like you.
...!
CRICK
PLINK
CRACK
So I'm going to turn you into a stone statue. You may still be alive, but you'll never move again.

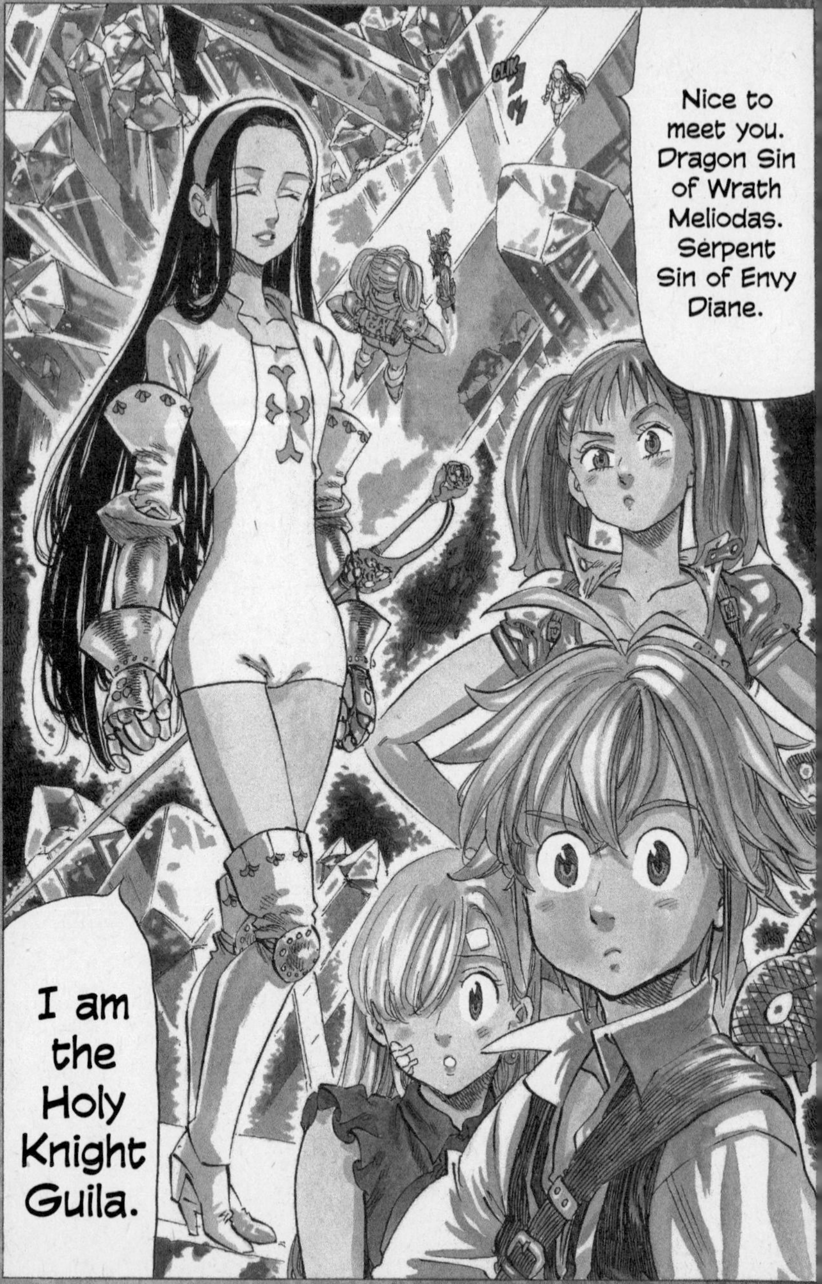
Nice to meet you. Dragon Sin of Wrath Meliodas. Serpent Sin of Envy Diane.
CLIK
I am the Holy Knight Guila.

They wouldn't necessarily sacrifice their lives in the name of leftover scraps, but the more food scraps you promise them, the greater their power. Or so they say.

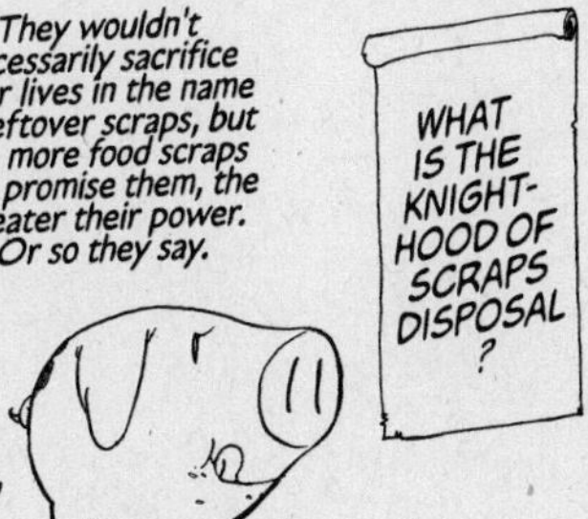
WHAT IS THE KNIGHT-HOOD OF SCRAPS DISPOSAL ?

Apparently, they're always looking for new members.

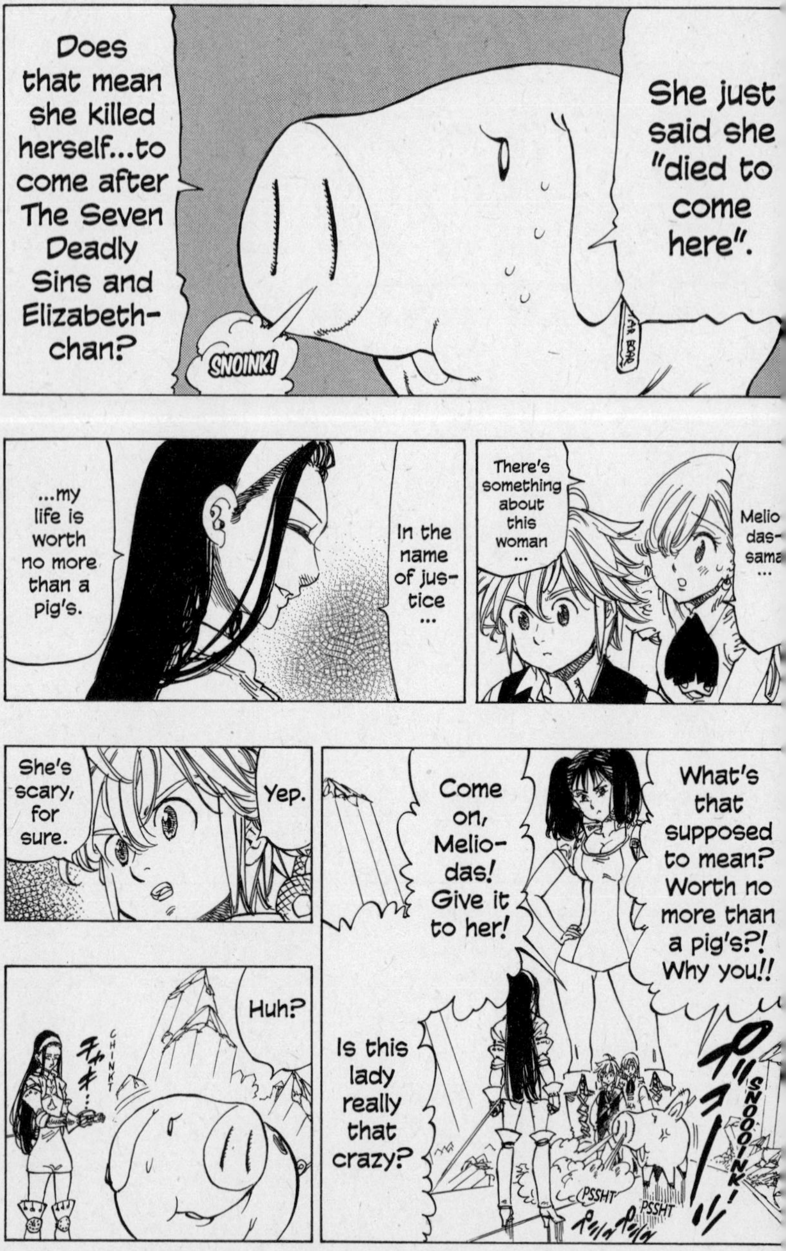
She just said she "died to come here".
Does that mean she killed herself...to come after The Seven Deadly Sins and Elizabeth-chan?
SNOINK!
Melio das-sama...
There's something about this woman...
In the name of justice...
...my life is worth no more than a pig's.
What's that supposed to mean? Worth no more than a pig's?! Why you!!
Come on, Melio-das! Give it to her!
Is this lady really that crazy?
SNOOOINK!!
PSSHT
PSSHT
Yep.
She's scary, for sure.
Huh?
CHINK

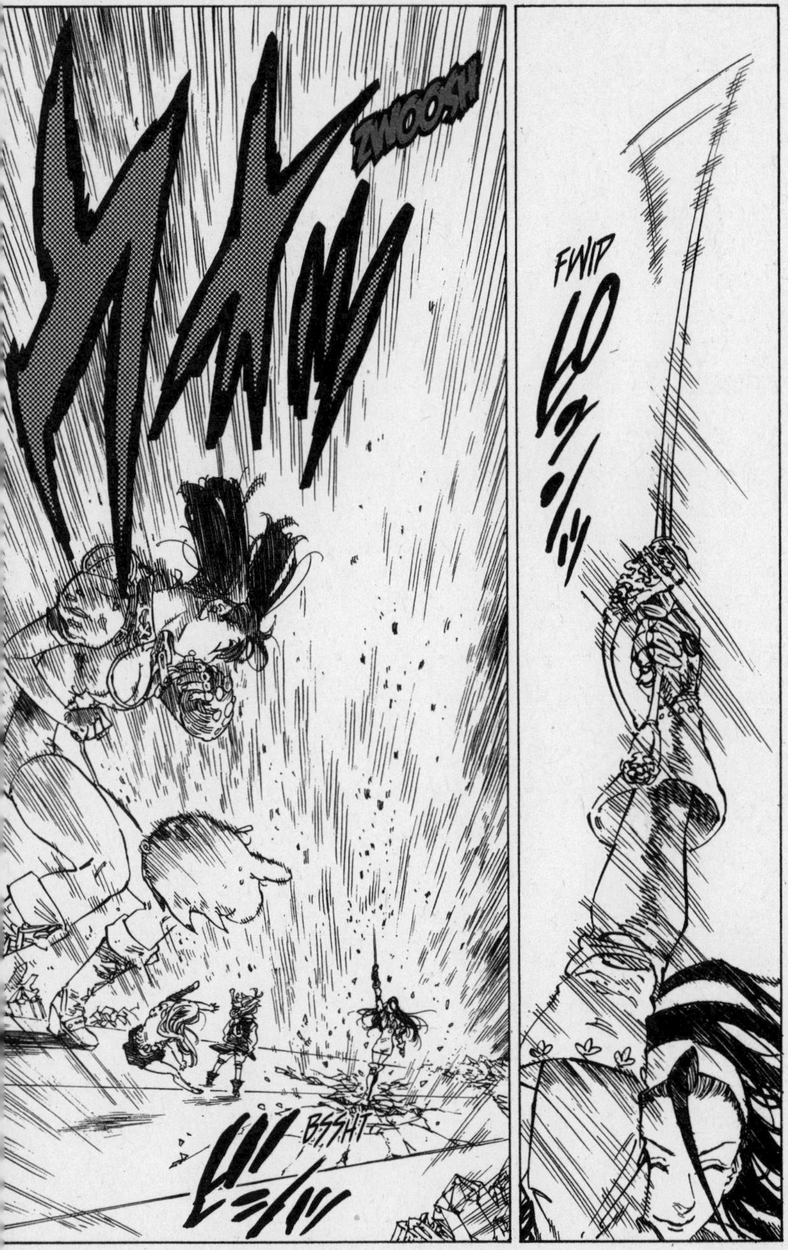
FWIP
ZWOOSH
BSSHT

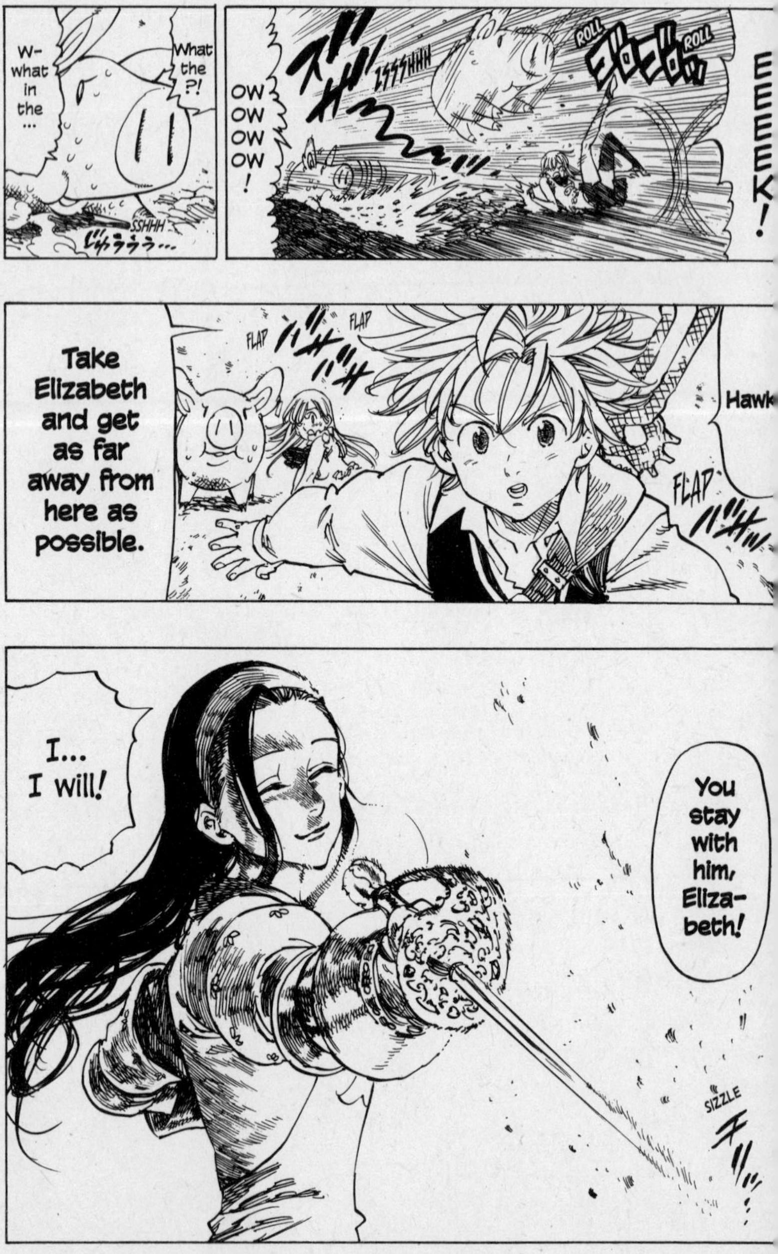
EEEEK!
ROLL
ROLL
OW OW OW OW!
What the ?!
W-what in the ...
SSHHH
Hawk
FLAP
FLAP
FLAP
Take Elizabeth and get as far away from here as possible.
You stay with him, Eliza-beth!
SIZZLE
I... I will!

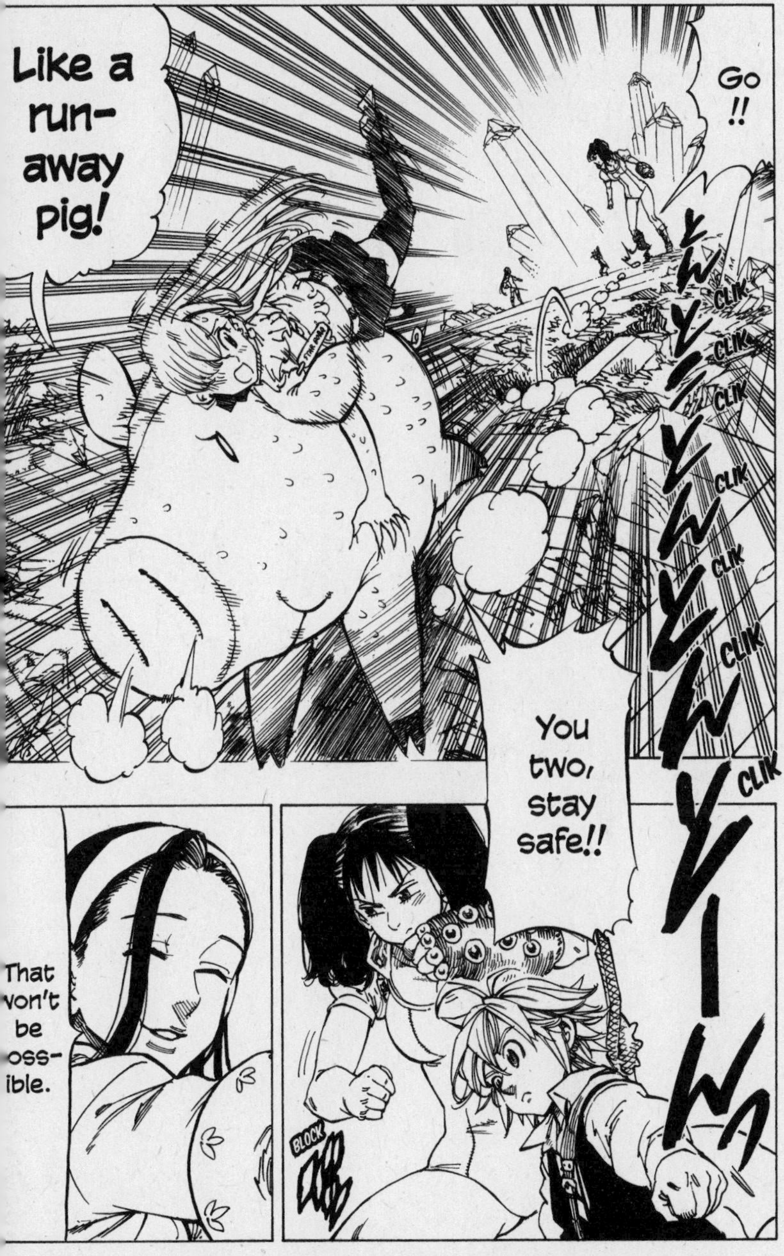

Go!!
CLIK
CLIK
CLIK
CLIK
CLIK
CLIK
CLIK
Like a run-away pig!
You two, stay safe!!
BLOCK
That von't be oss- ible.

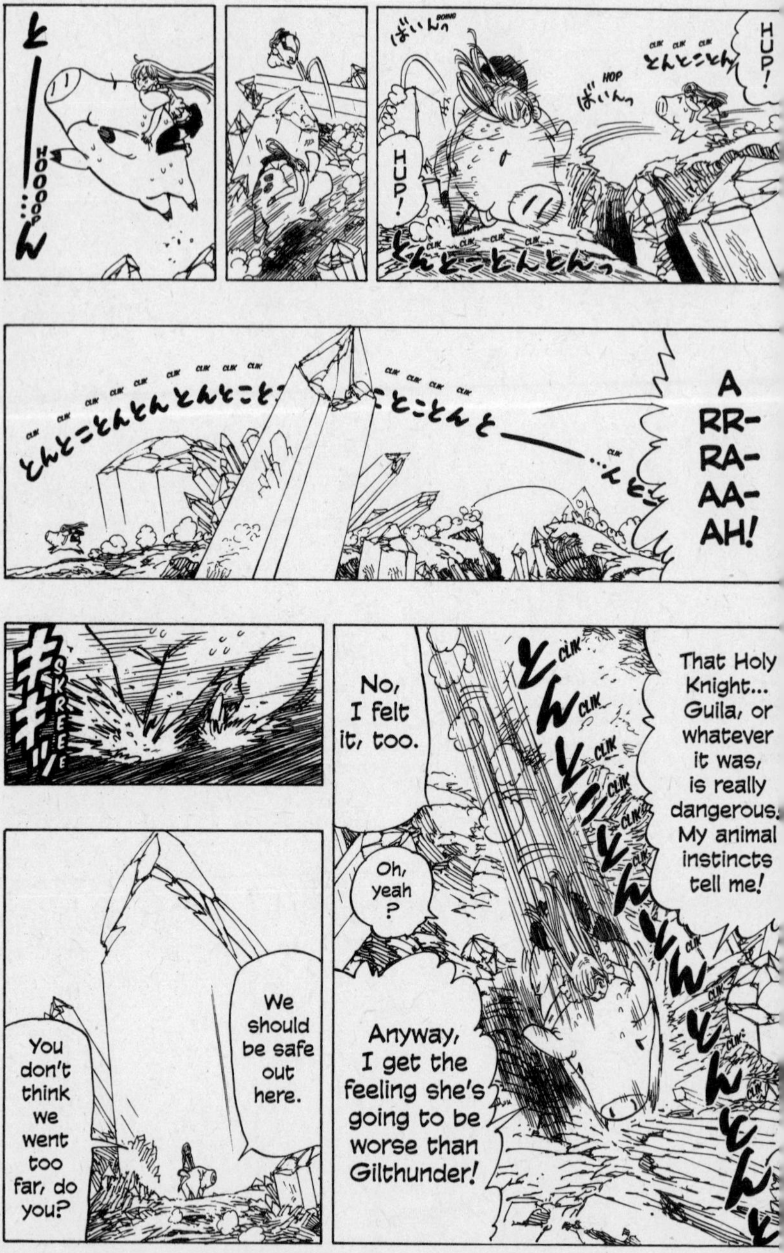
HUP!
CLIK CLIK CLIK
とんとこどん
HOP
ばいんっ
BOING
ばいんっ
HUP!
CLIK CLIK CLIK CLIK
とんとことんとんっ
HOOOOOP
と―――…ん
ARRRAAAAH!
CLIK CLIK CLIK CLIK CLIK CLIK CLIK CLIK CLIK CLIK CLIK CLIK CLIK
とんとことんとん とんとこと…ことことんと―――…とと
That Holy Knight... Guila, or whatever it was, is really dangerous. My animal instincts tell me!
No, I felt it, too.
Oh, yeah?
Anyway, I get the feeling she's going to be worse than Gilthunder!
CLIK CLIK CLIK CLIK CLIK CLIK CLIK CLIK CLIK
キキッ
SKREEE!
We should be safe out here.
You don't think we went too far, do you?

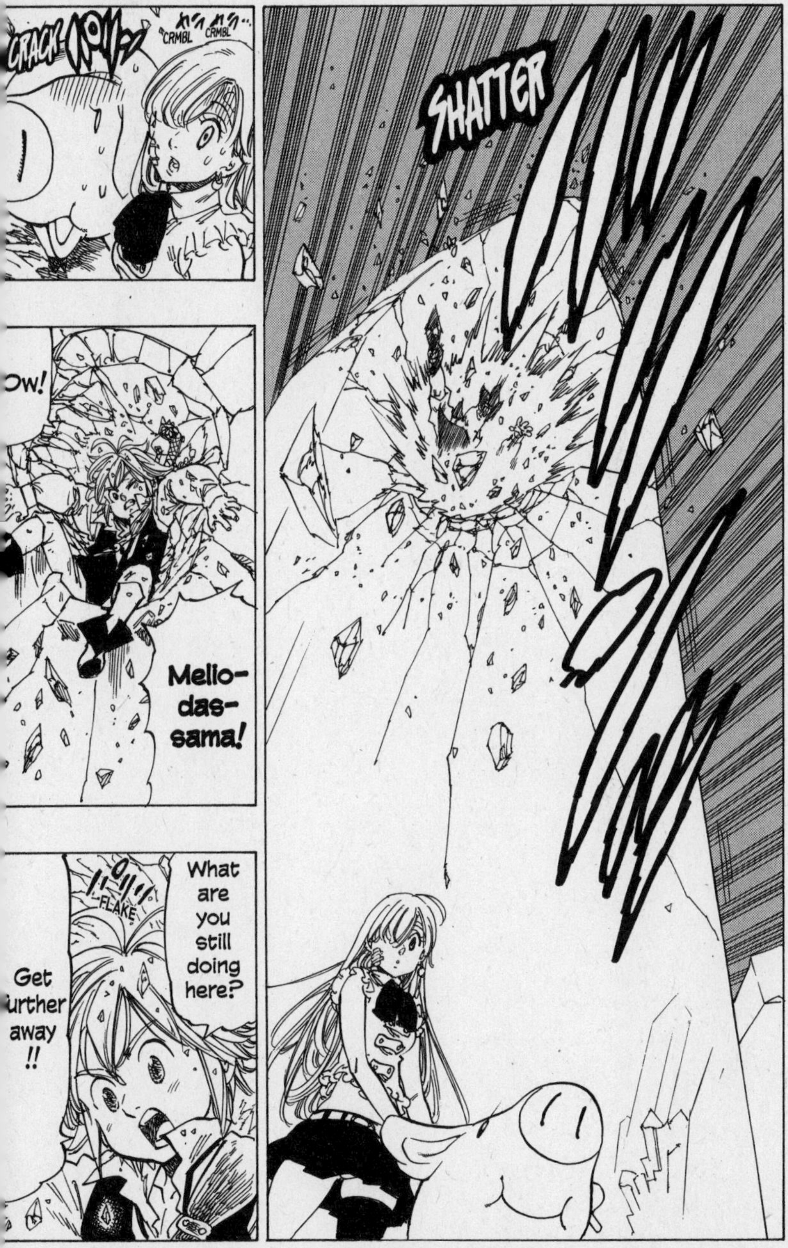
SHATTER
CRACK
CRMBL CRMBL
Ow!
Mellio-das-sama!
FLAKE
What are you still doing here?
Get urther away !!

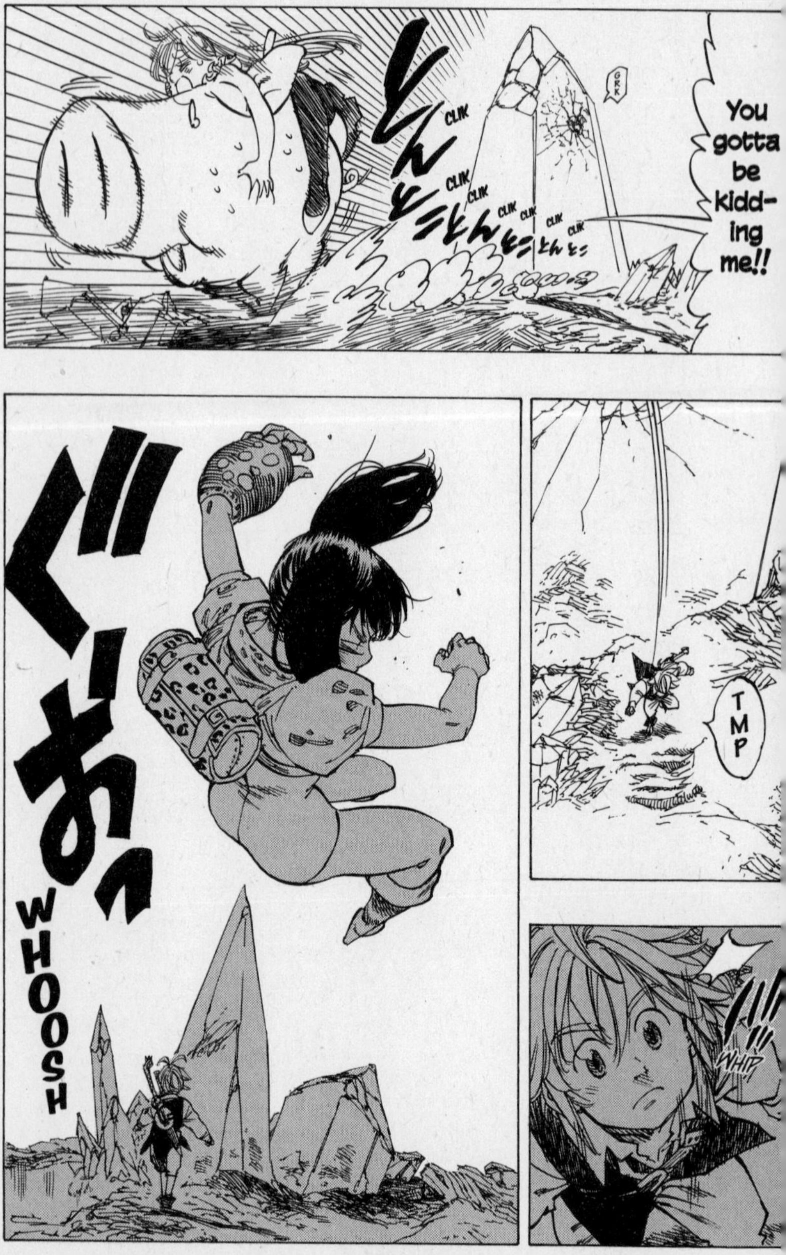

You gotta be kidding me!!
GRK
CLIK
CLIK
CLIK
CLIK
CLIK
CLIK
CLIK
TMP
!!
WHIP
WHOOSH

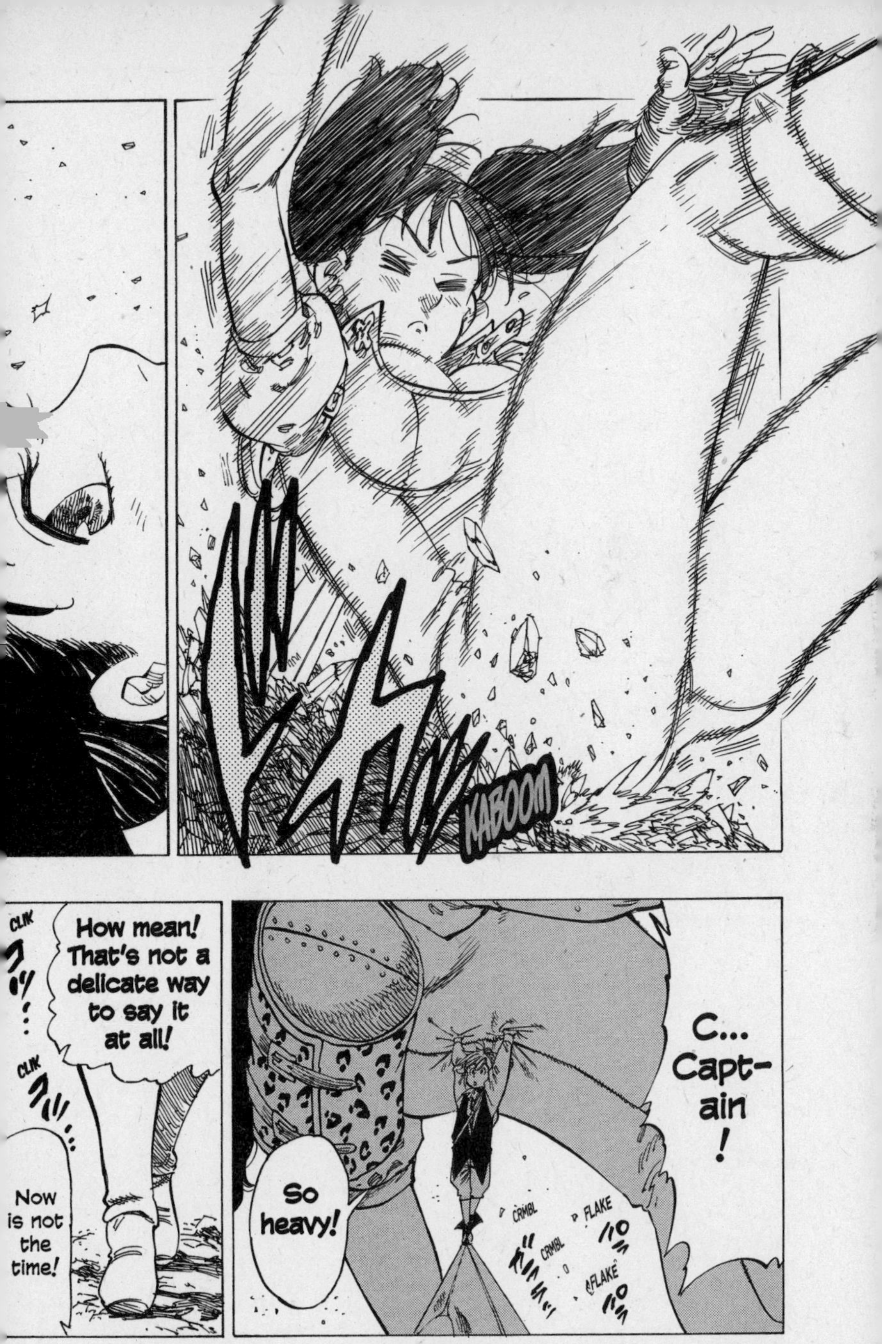
KABOOM
C... Capt-ain!
FLAKE
CRMBL
FLAKE
CRMBL
So heavy!
CLIK
How mean! That's not a delicate way to say it at all!
CLIK
Now is not the time!

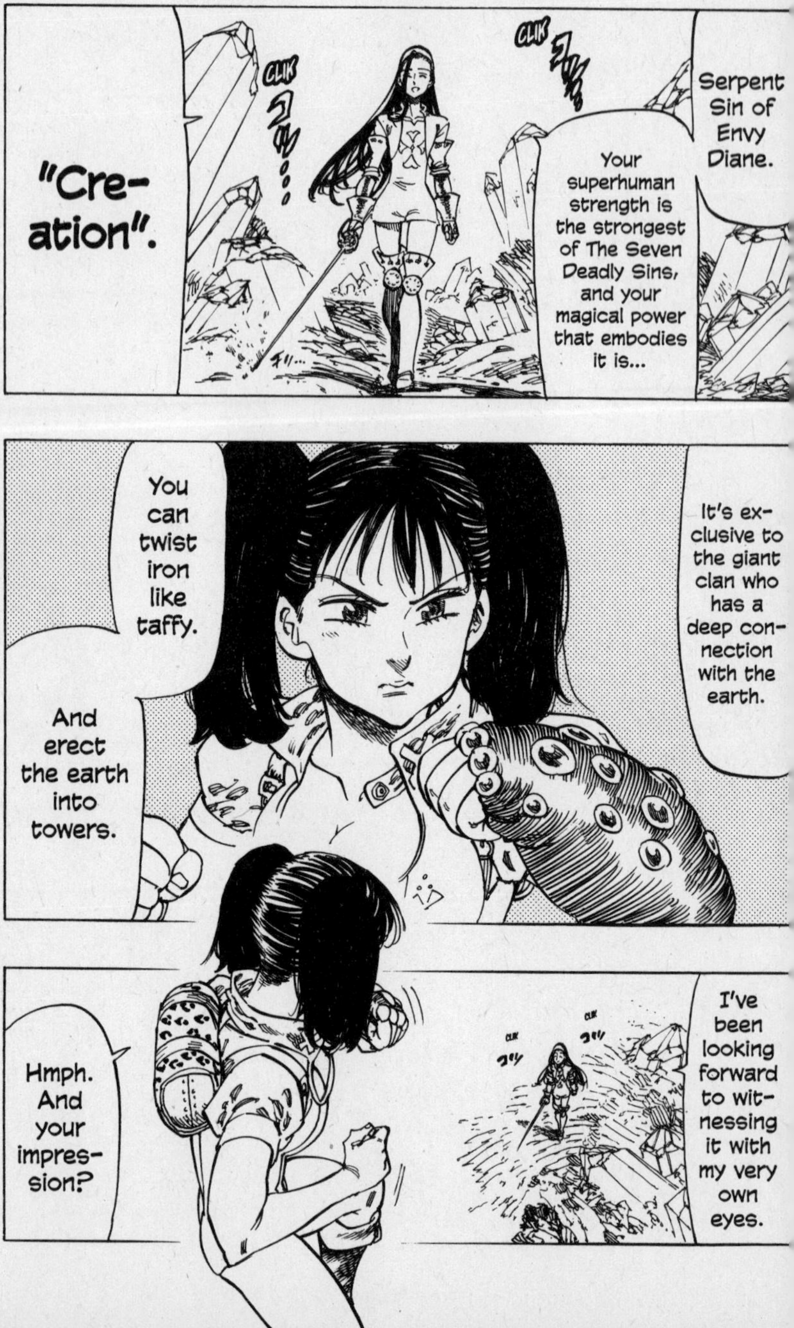
Serpent Sin of Envy Diane.
CLIK
Your superhuman strength is the strongest of The Seven Deadly Sins, and your magical power that embodies it is...
CLIK
"Creation".
It's exclusive to the giant clan who has a deep connection with the earth.
You can twist iron like taffy.
And erect the earth into towers.
I've been looking forward to witnessing it with my very own eyes.
CLIK
CLIK
Hmph. And your impression?

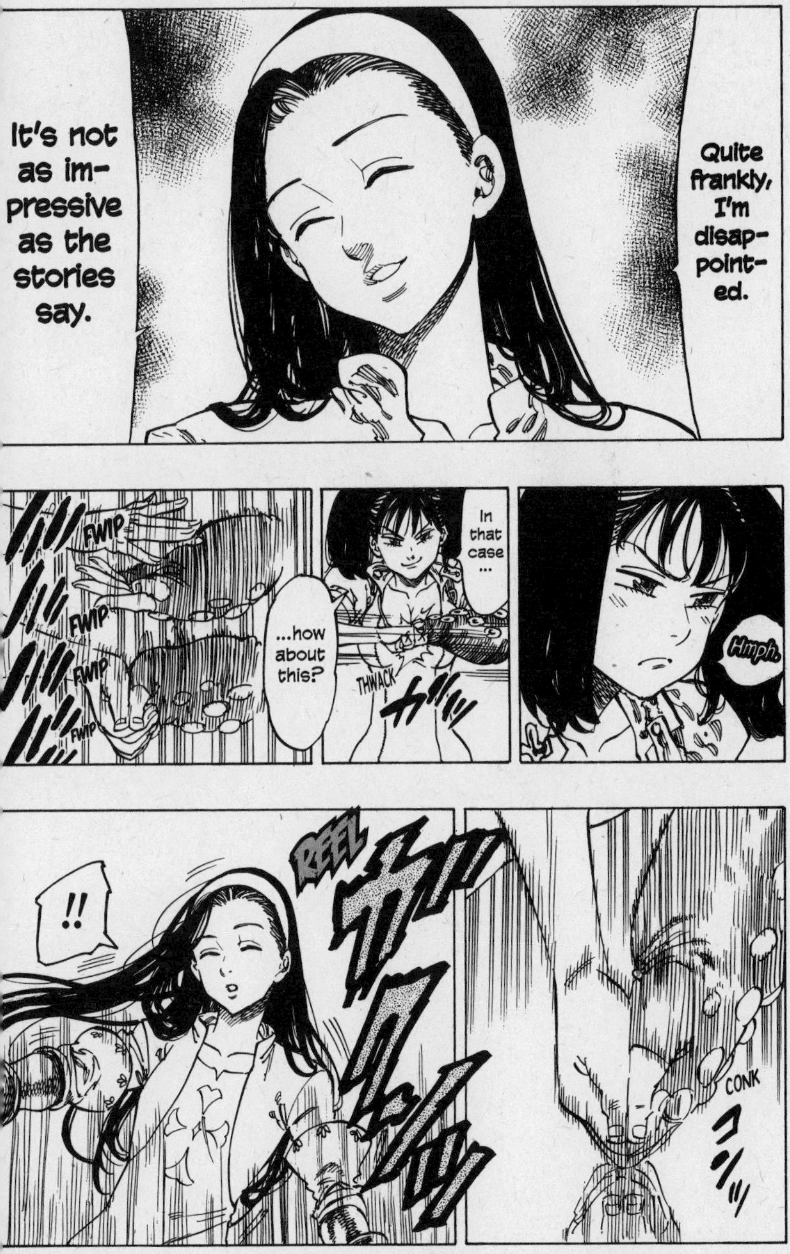
Quite frankly, I'm disappointed.
It's not as impressive as the stories say.
Hmph.
In that case...
...how about this?
THWACK
FWIP
FWIP
FWIP
FWIP
CONK
REEL
!!

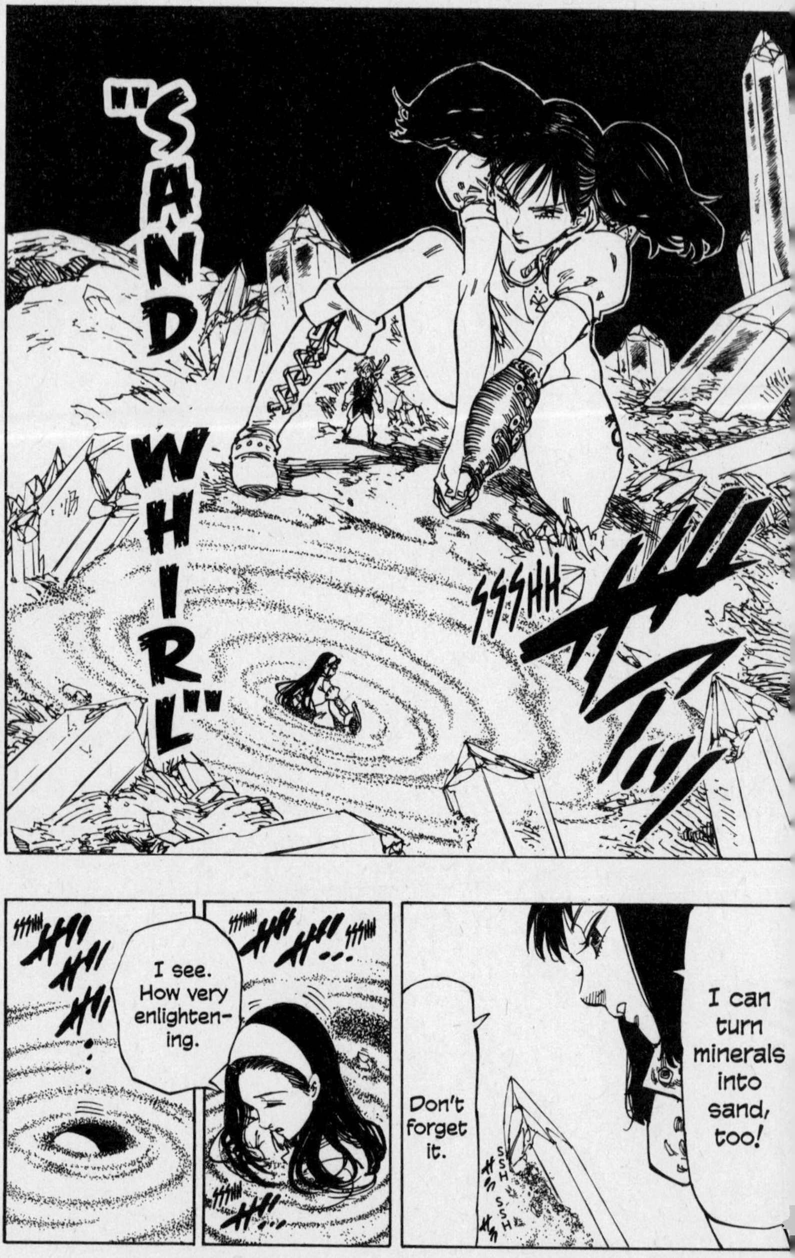
"SAND WHIRL"
SSSHH
I can turn minerals into sand, too!
Don't forget it.
SSH SSH
I see. How very enlightening.

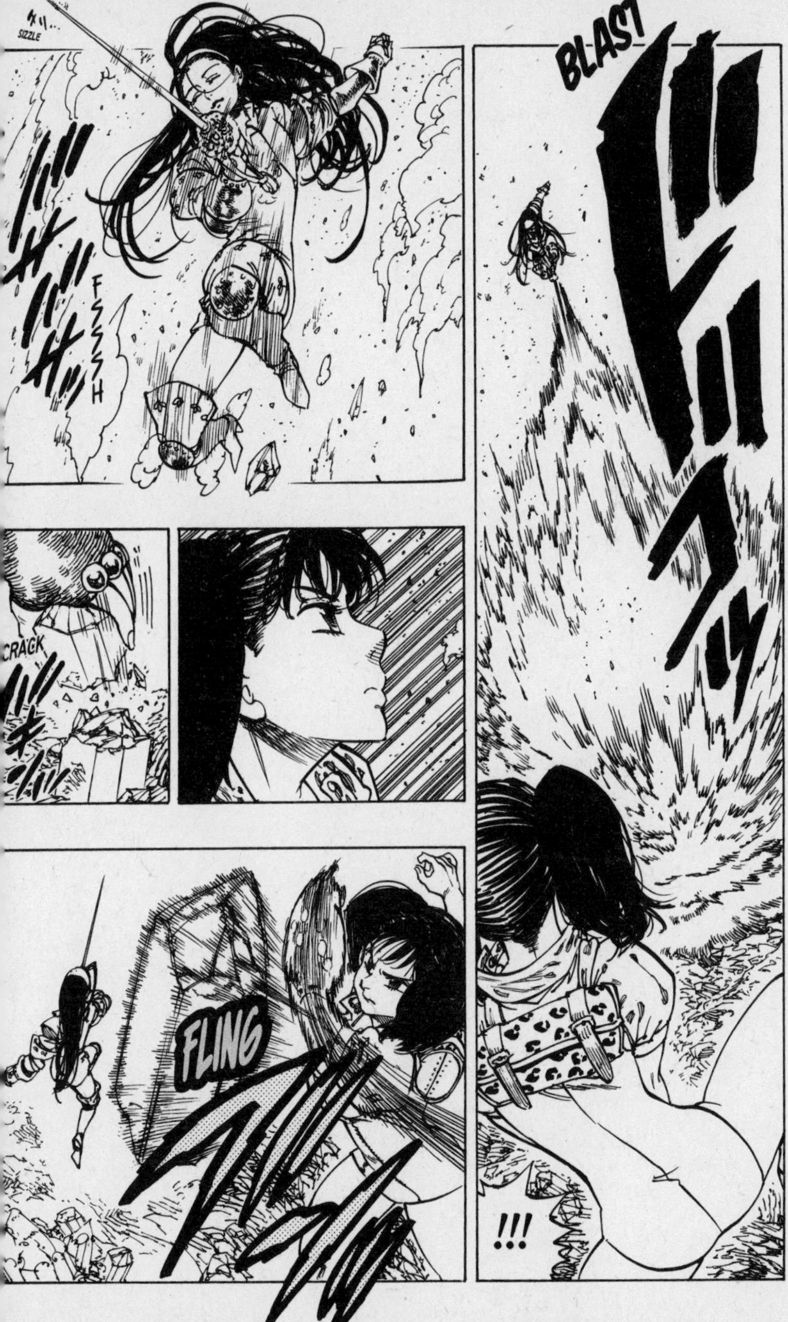
BLAST
!!!
SIZZLE
FSSSSH
CRACK
FLING

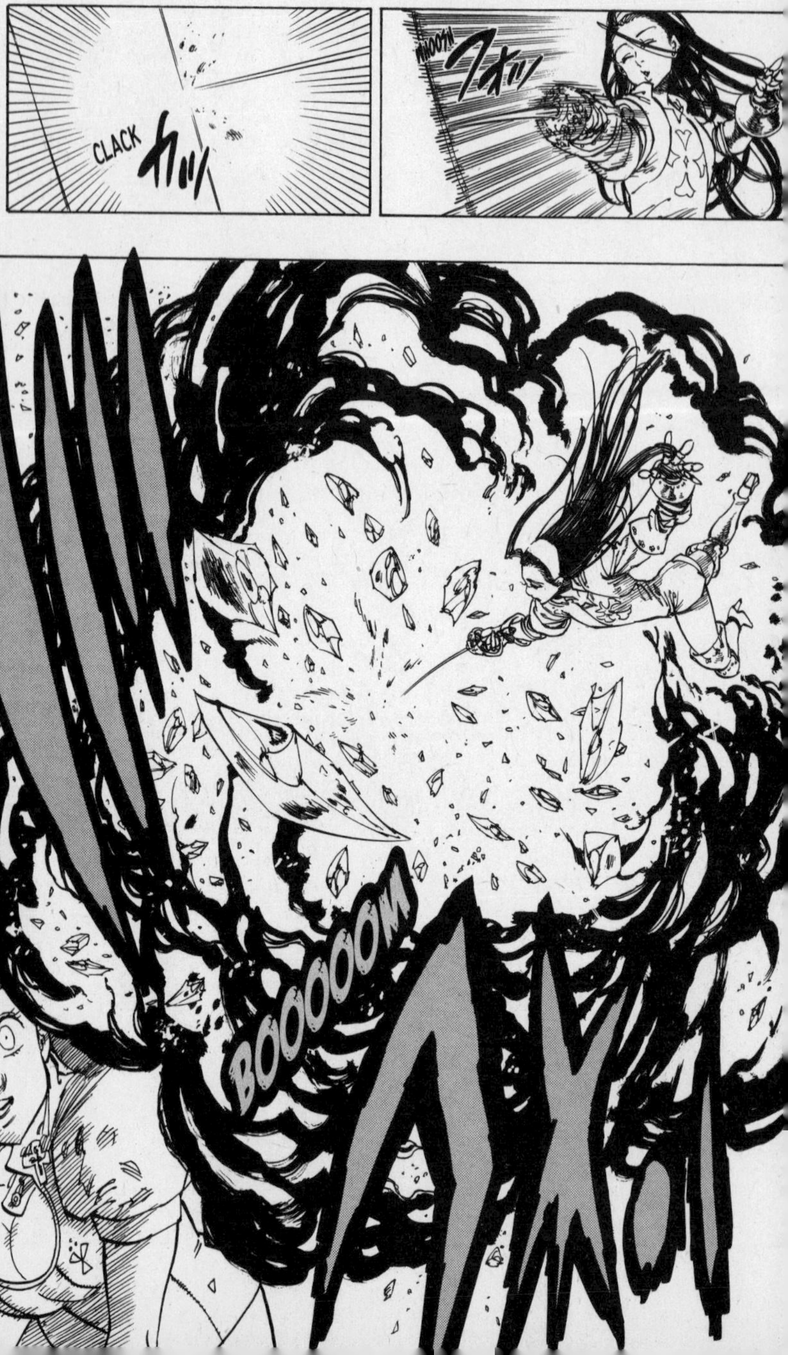
WHOOSH
フォッ
CLACK
カッ
BOOOOOM

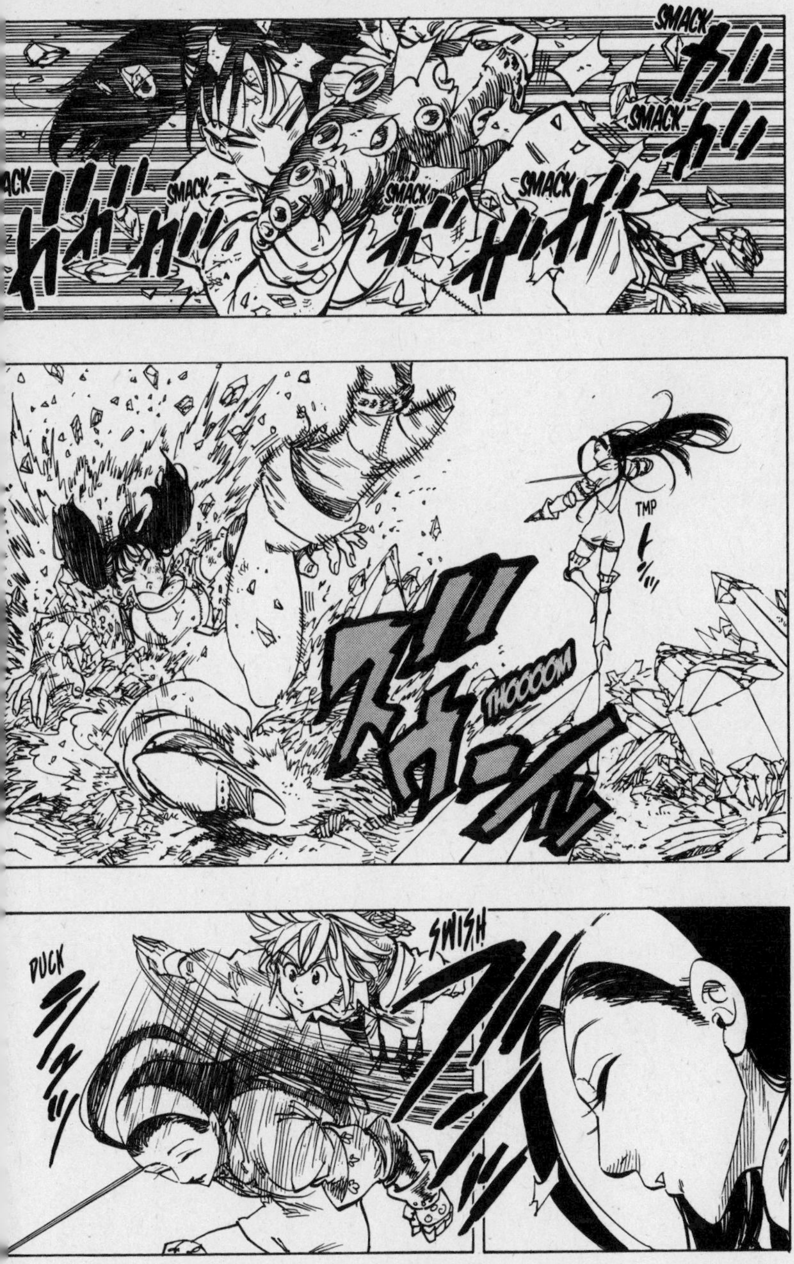
SMACK
SMACK
SMACK
SMACK
SMACK
ACK
TMP
THOOOOM
SWISH
DUCK

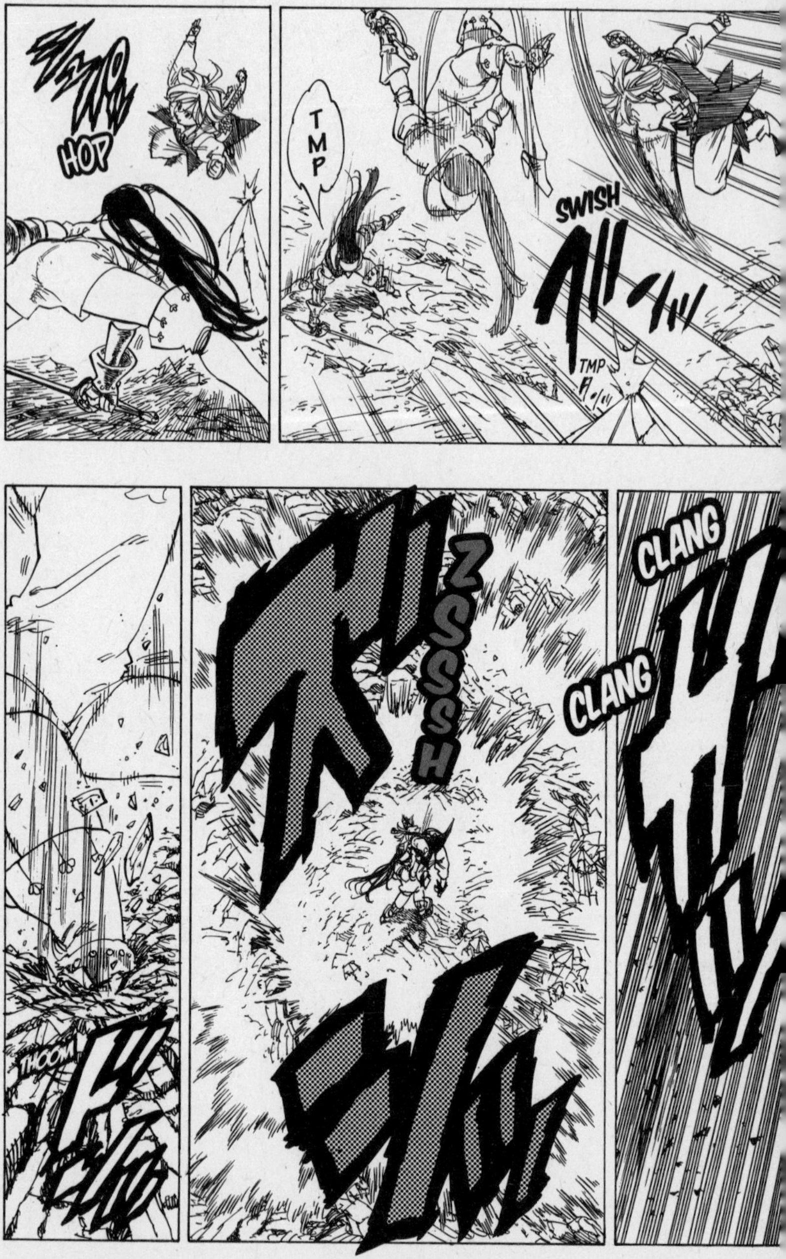
TMP
SWISH
TMP
HOP
CLANG
CLANG
ZSSSH
THOOM

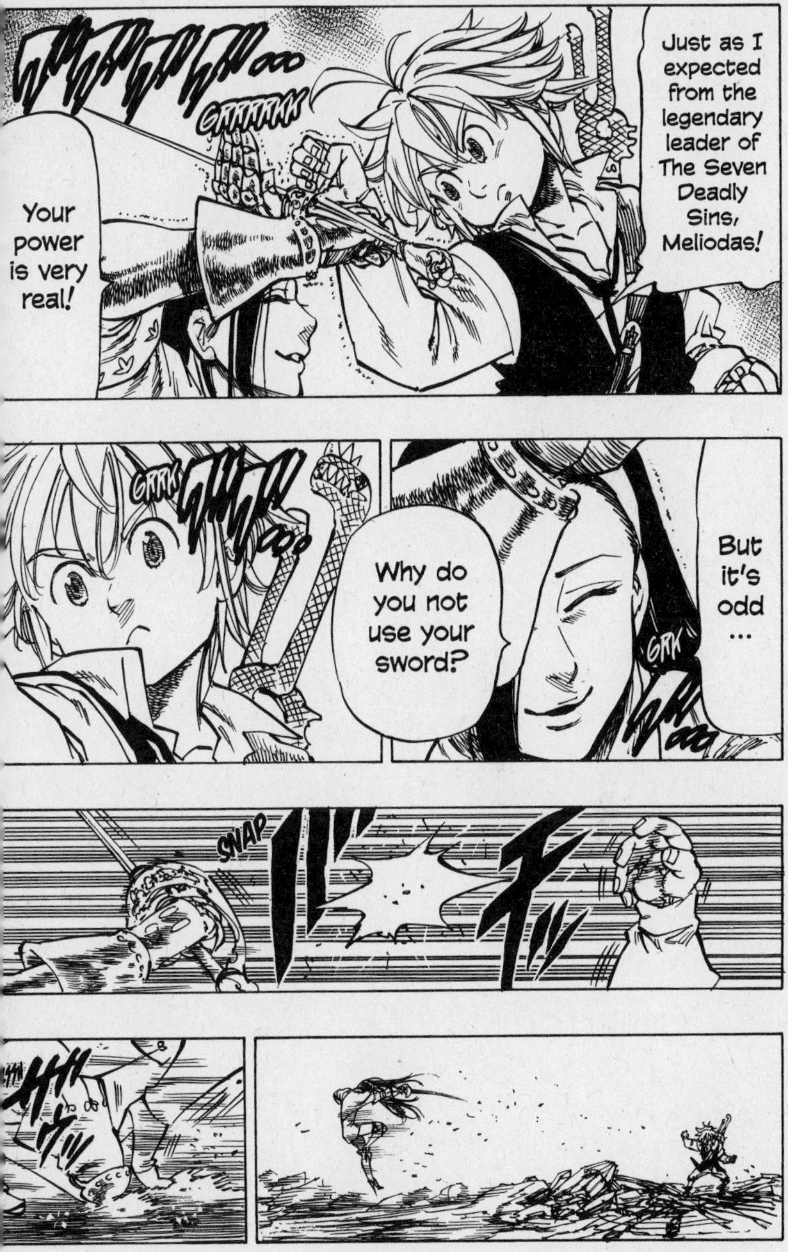
Just as I expected from the legendary leader of The Seven Deadly Sins, Meliodas!
GRRRRRK
Your power is very real!
But it's odd ...
Why do you not use your sword?
GRK
GRRK
SNAP

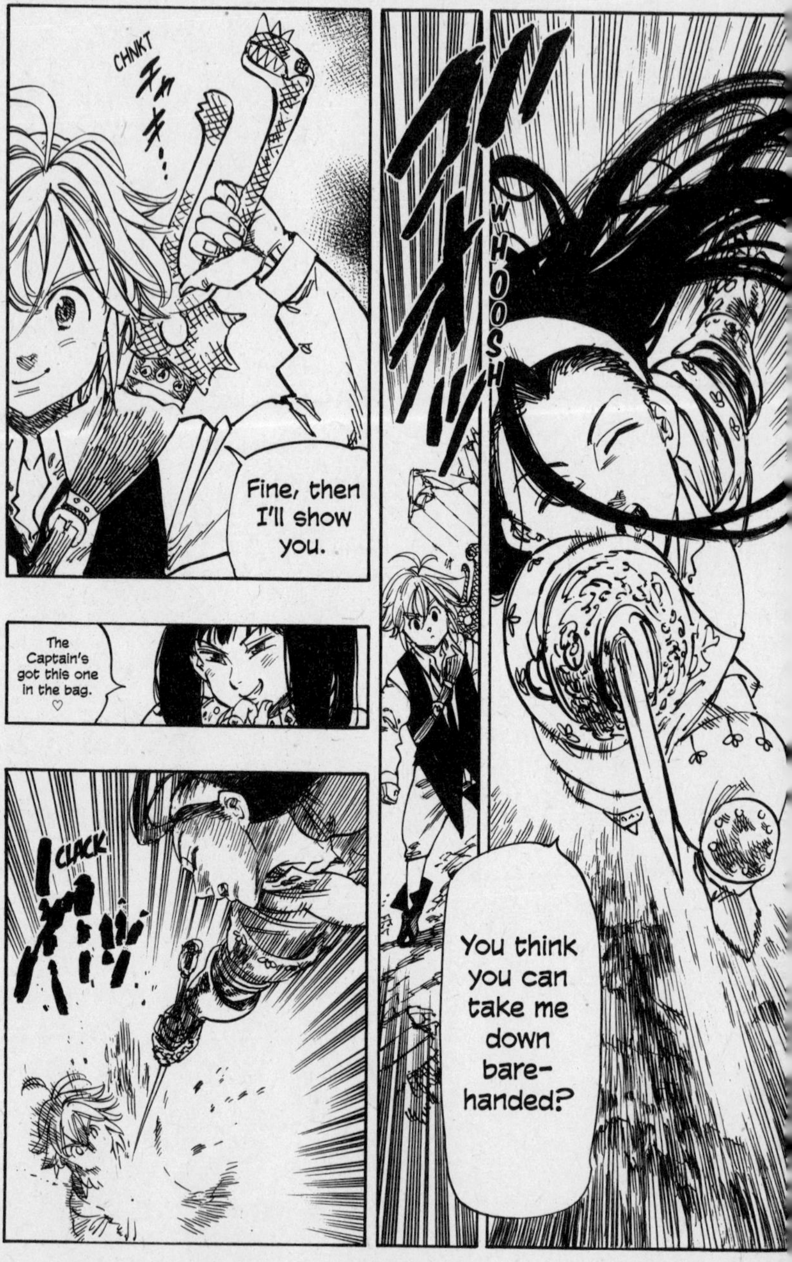
WHOOSH
You think you can take me down bare-handed?
CHNKT
Fine, then I'll show you.
The Captain's got this one in the bag. ♡
CLACK

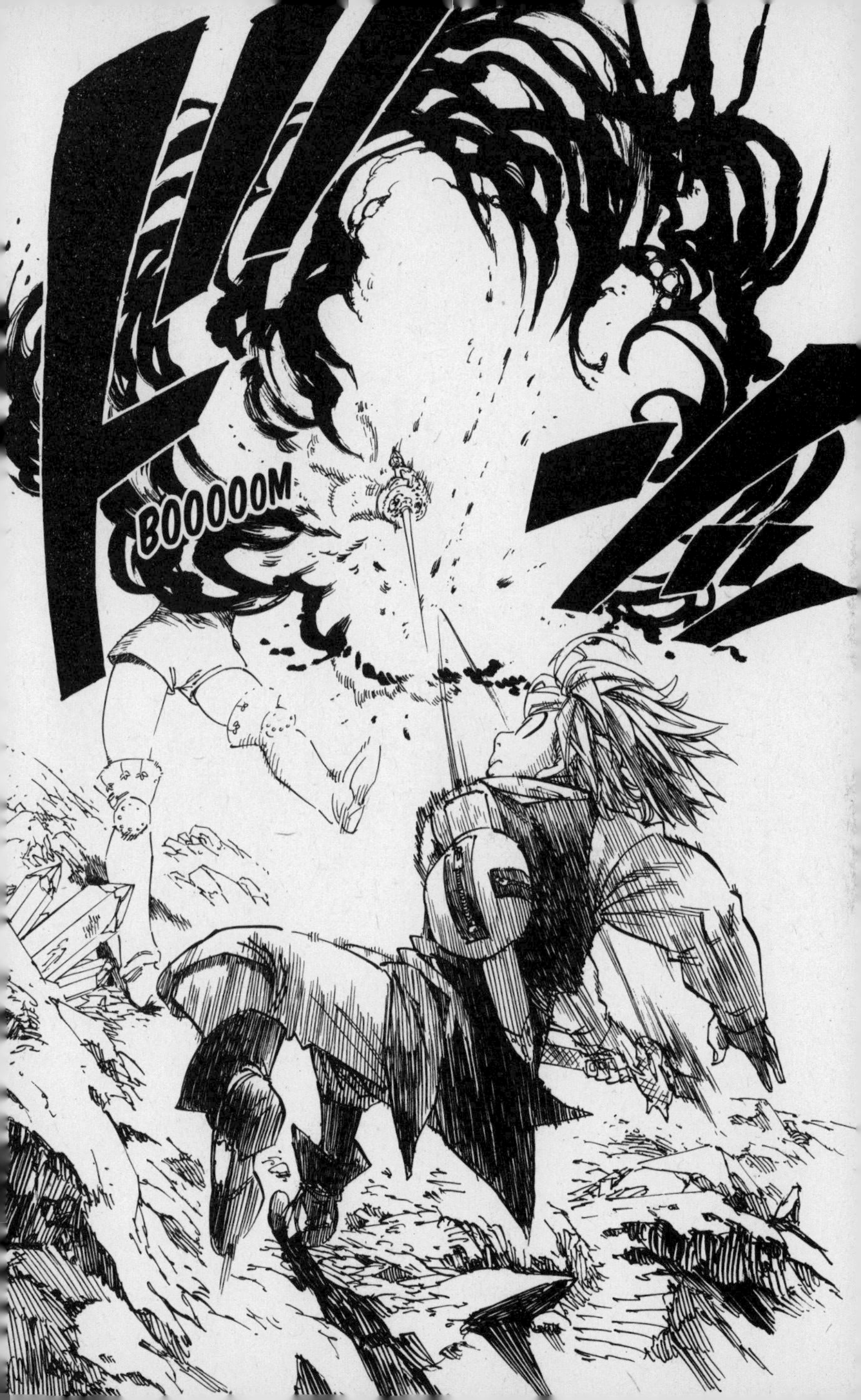
BOOOOOM

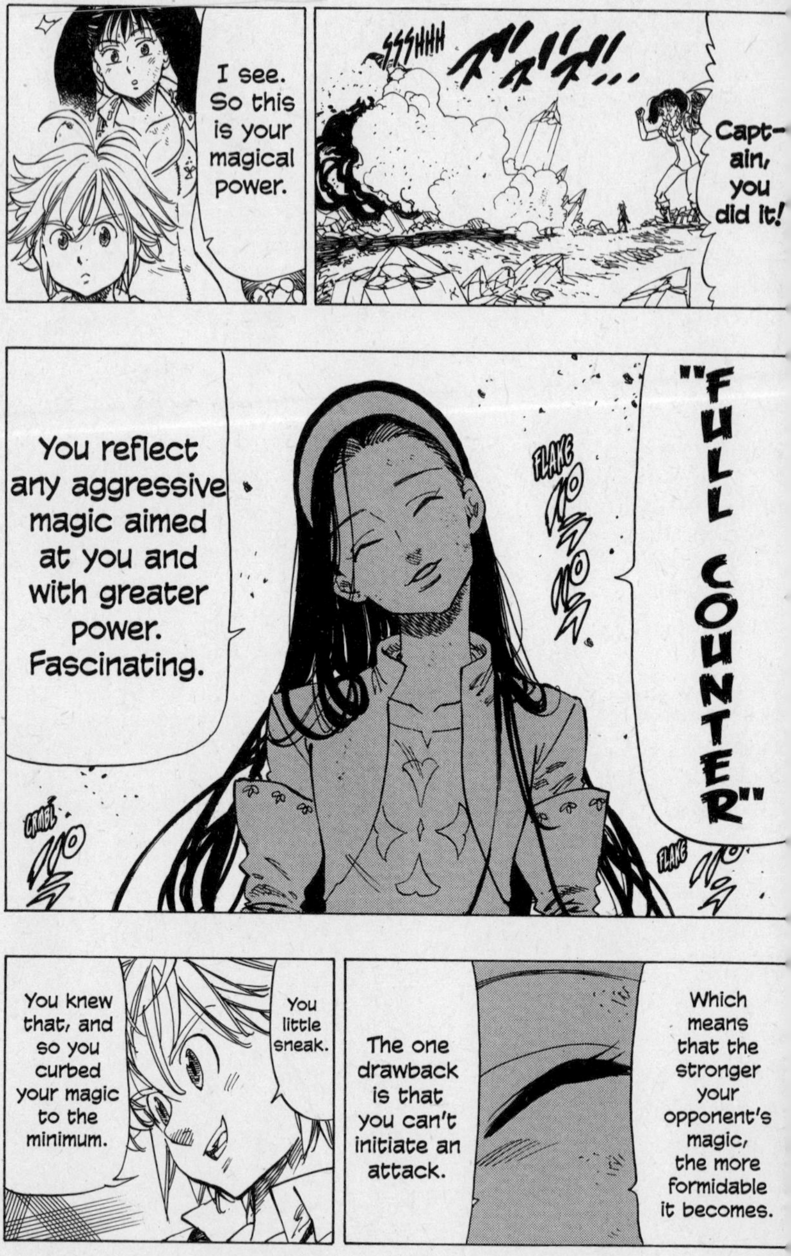
SSSHHH
Capt-ain, you did it!
I see. So this is your magical power.
"FULL COUNTER"
FLAKE
FLAKE
You reflect any aggressive magic aimed at you and with greater power. Fascinating.
CRMBL
Which means that the stronger your opponent's magic, the more formidable it becomes.
The one drawback is that you can't initiate an attack.
You little sneak.
You knew that, and so you curbed your magic to the minimum.

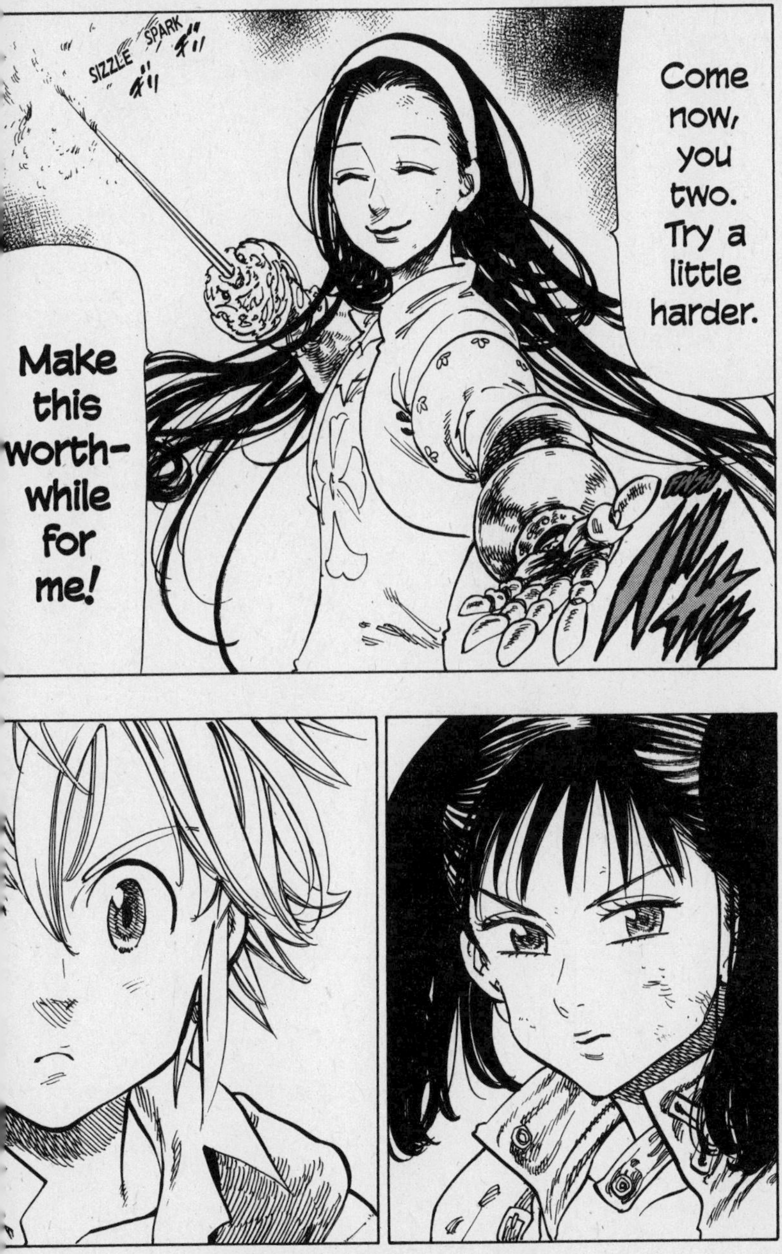
Come now, you two. Try a little harder.
FWSH
SPARK
SIZZLE
Make this worth-while for me!

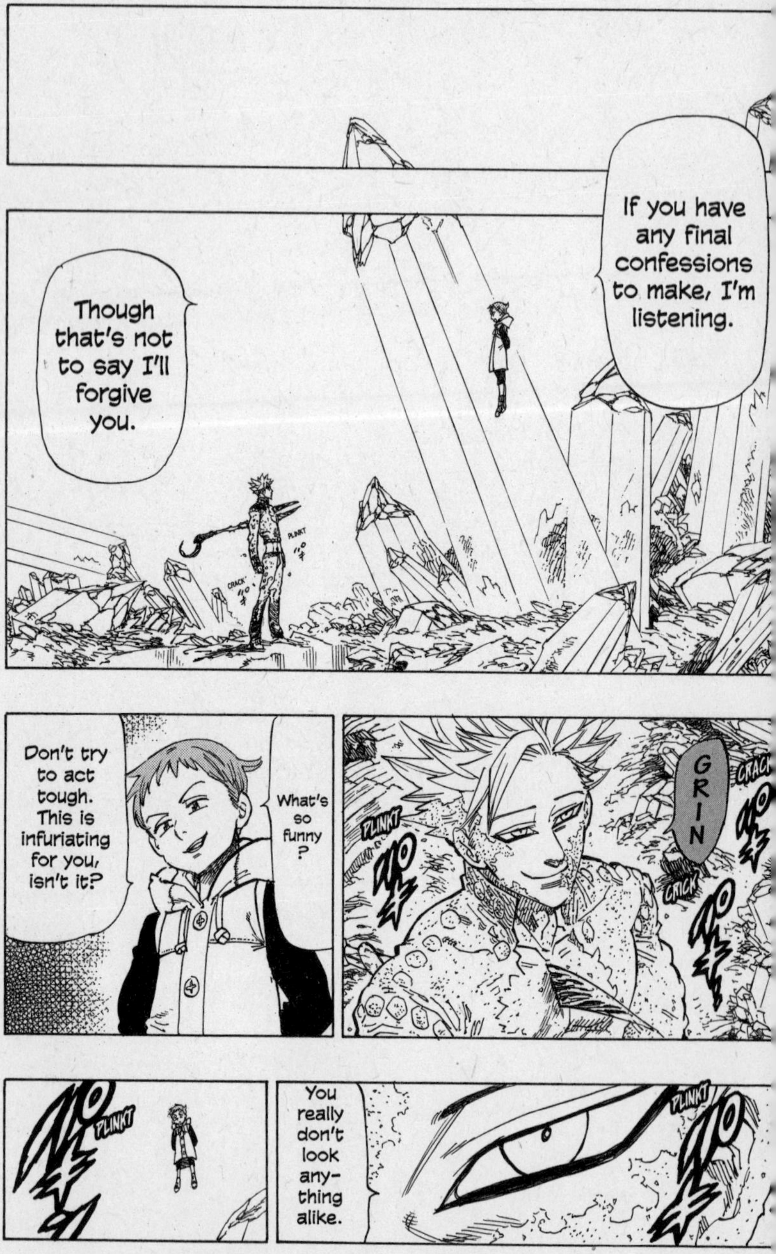
If you have any final confessions to make, I'm listening.
Though that's not to say I'll forgive you.
PLINK!
CRACK
CRACK
GRIN
CRICK
PLINK!
What's so funny?
Don't try to act tough. This is infuriating for you, isn't it?
PLINK!
You really don't look anything alike.
PLINK!

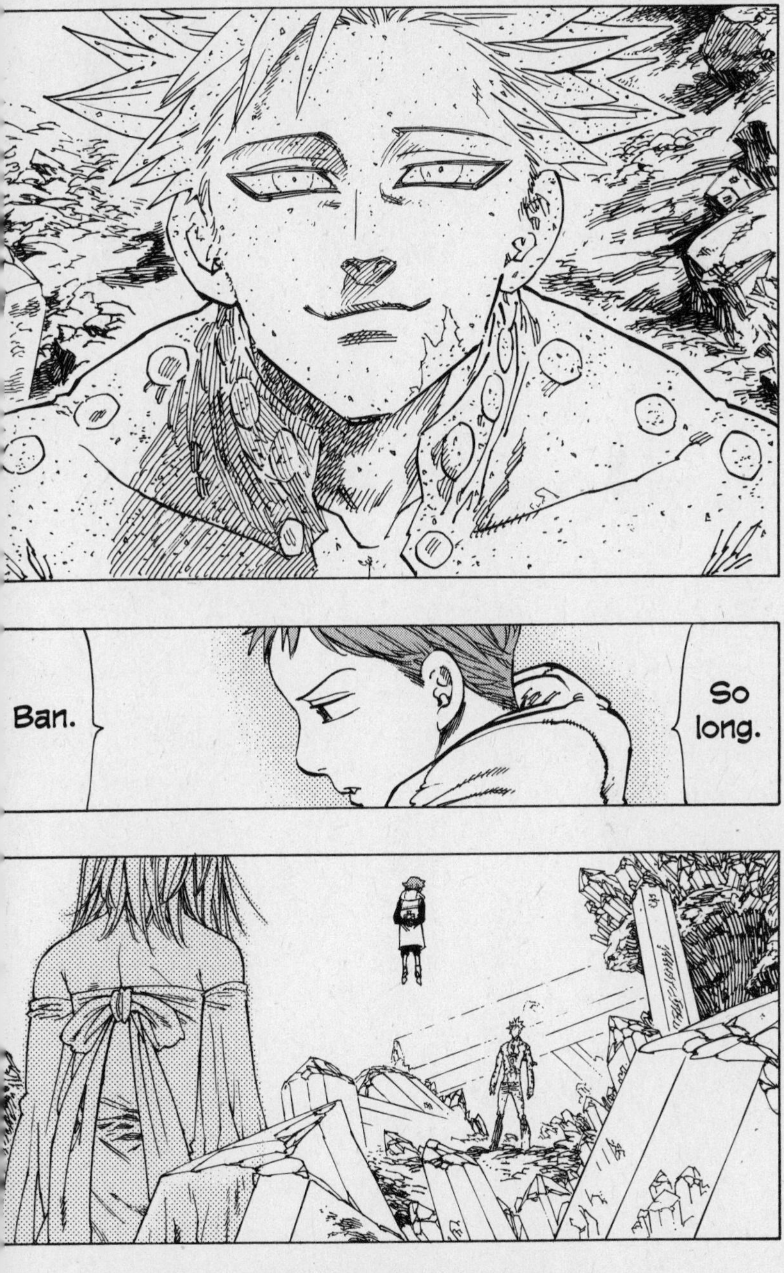
So long.
Ban.

To Be Continued in Volume 4

THE SEVEN DEADLY SINS

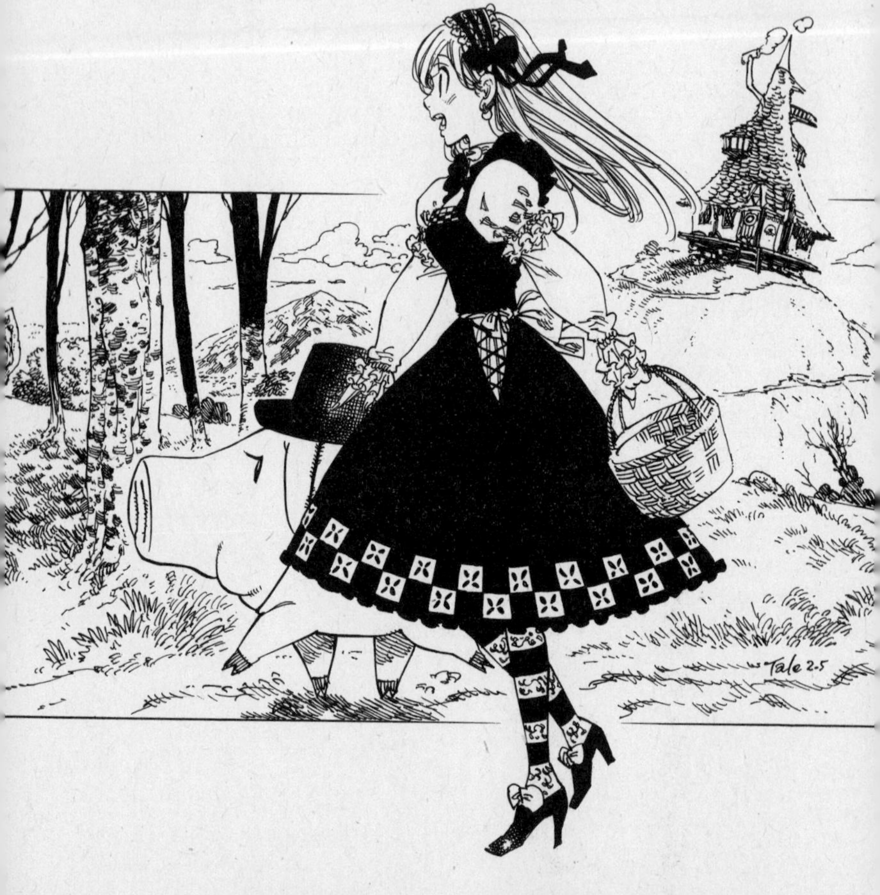
Tale 2.5

Bonus Chapter - Nothing Wasted

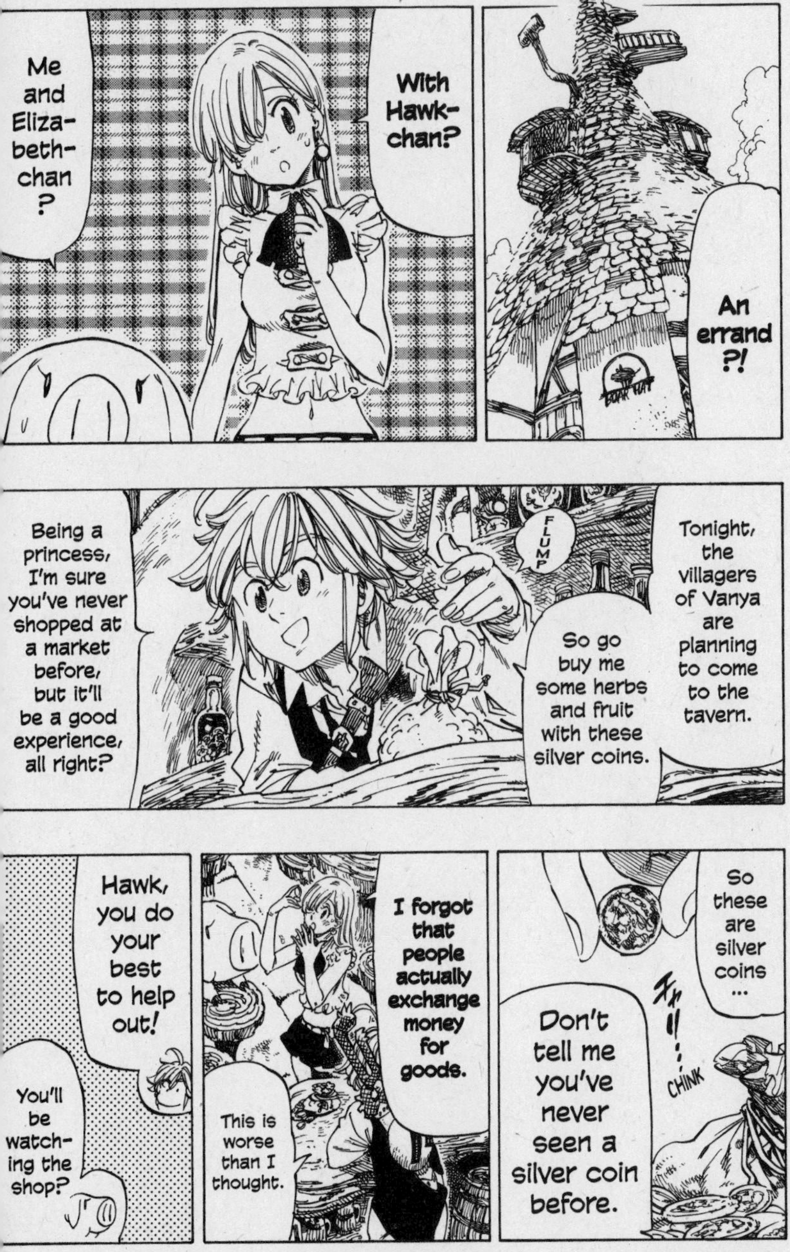

An errand?!
BOAR HAT
With Hawk-chan?
Me and Elizabeth-chan?
Tonight, the villagers of Vanya are planning to come to the tavern.
FLUMP
So go buy me some herbs and fruit with these silver coins.
Being a princess, I'm sure you've never shopped at a market before, but it'll be a good experience, all right?
So these are silver coins...
CHINK
Don't tell me you've never seen a silver coin before.
I forgot that people actually exchange money for goods.
This is worse than I thought.
Hawk, you do your best to help out!
You'll be watching the shop?

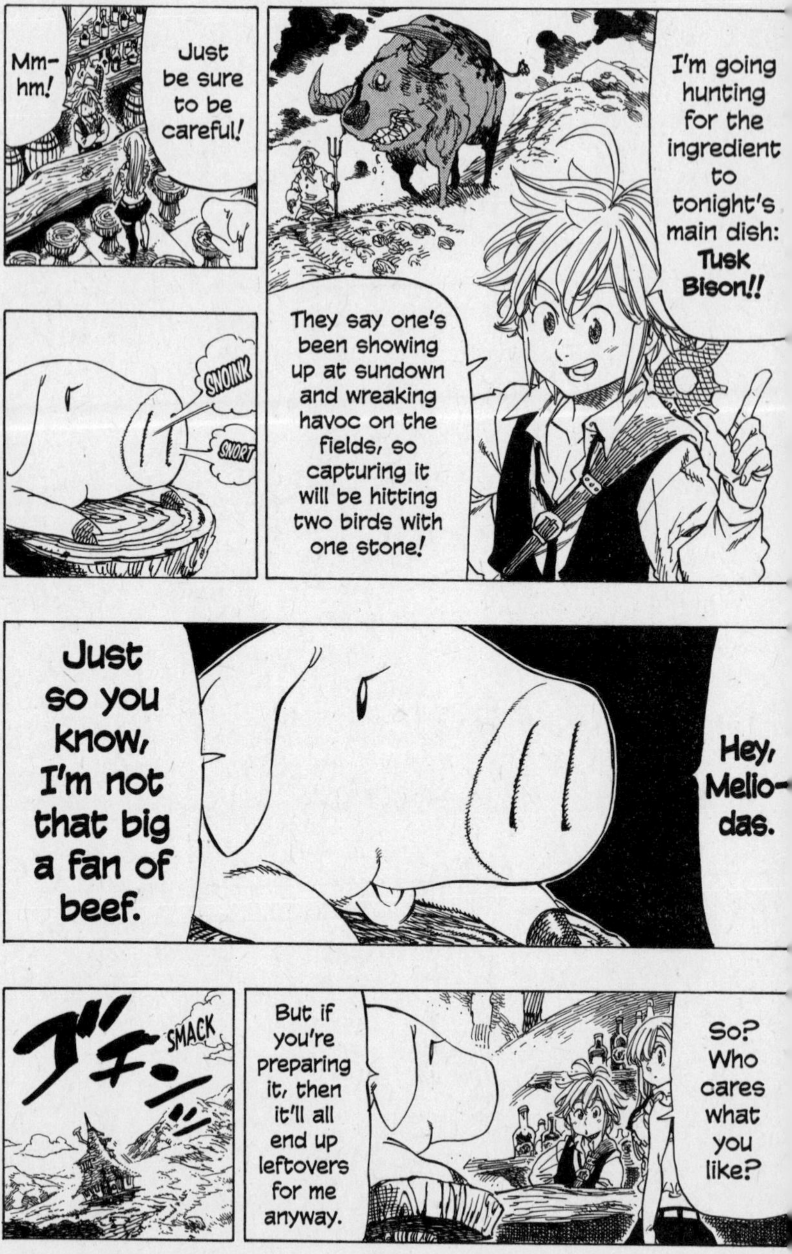
I'm going hunting for the ingredient to tonight's main dish: **Tusk Bison!!**
They say one's been showing up at sundown and wreaking havoc on the fields, so capturing it will be hitting two birds with one stone!
Just be sure to be careful!
Mm-hm!
SNOINK
SNORT
Hey, Meliodas.
Just so you know, I'm not that big a fan of beef.
So? Who cares what you like?
But if you're preparing it, then it'll all end up leftovers for me anyway.
ブチンッ
SMACK

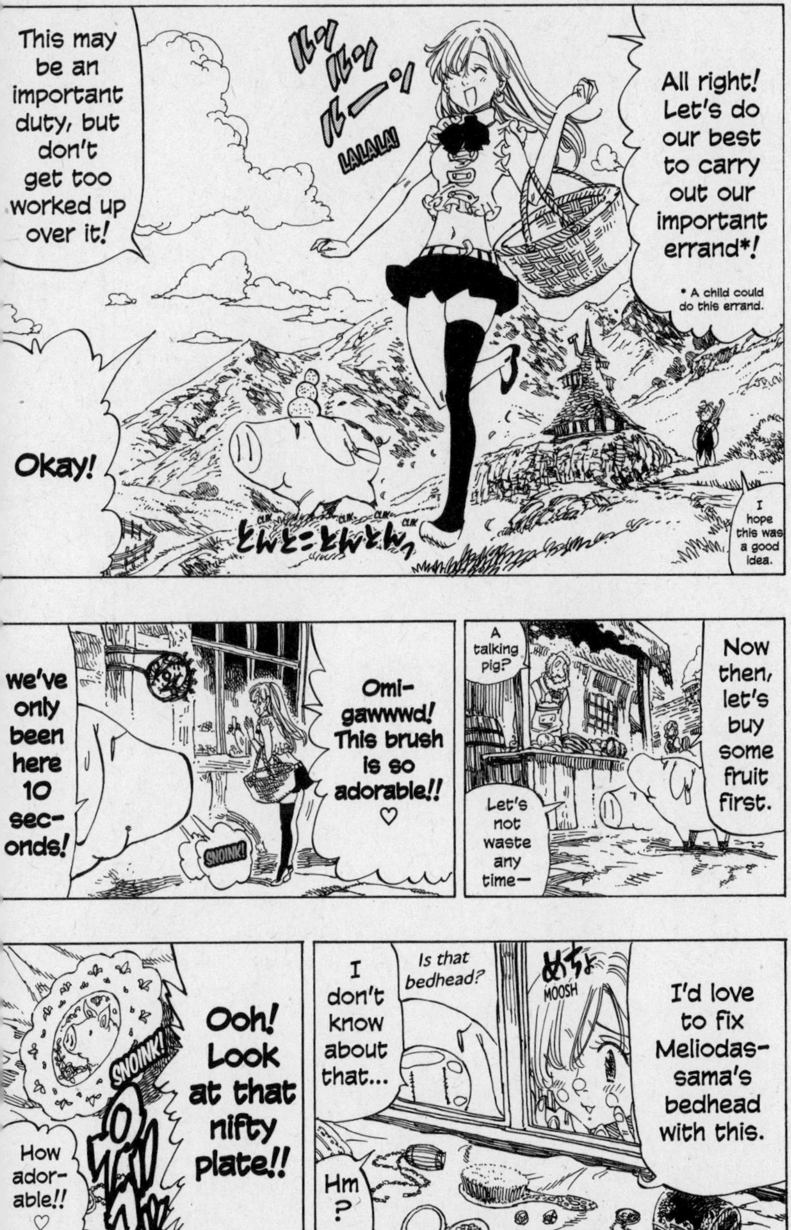
All right! Let's do our best to carry out our important errand*!
* A child could do this errand.
LALALA!
This may be an important duty, but don't get too worked up over it!
I hope this was a good idea.
Okay!
CLIK CLIK CLIK CLIK
Now then, let's buy some fruit first.
A talking pig?
Let's not waste any time—
Omi-gawwwd! This brush is so adorable!! ♡
SNOINK!
we've only been here 10 sec-onds!
I'd love to fix Meliodas-sama's bedhead with this.
MOOSH
Is that bedhead?
I don't know about that...
Hm?
Ooh! Look at that nifty plate!!
SNOINK!
How adorable!! ♡

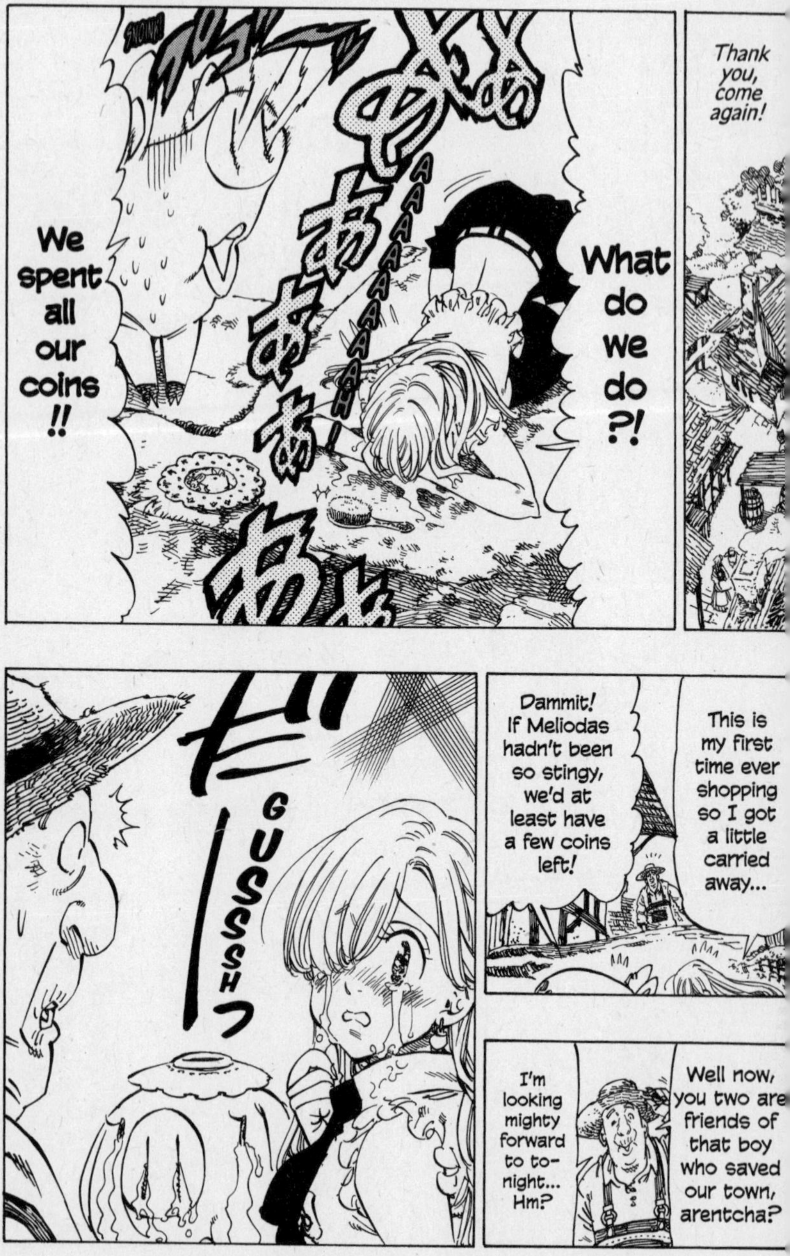
Thank you, come again!
What do we do?!
AAAAAAAAAH!
We spent all our coins!!
This is my first time ever shopping so I got a little carried away...
Dammit! If Meliodas hadn't been so stingy, we'd at least have a few coins left!
Well now, you two are friends of that boy who saved our town, arentcha?
I'm looking mighty forward to to-night... Hm?
GUSSSSH

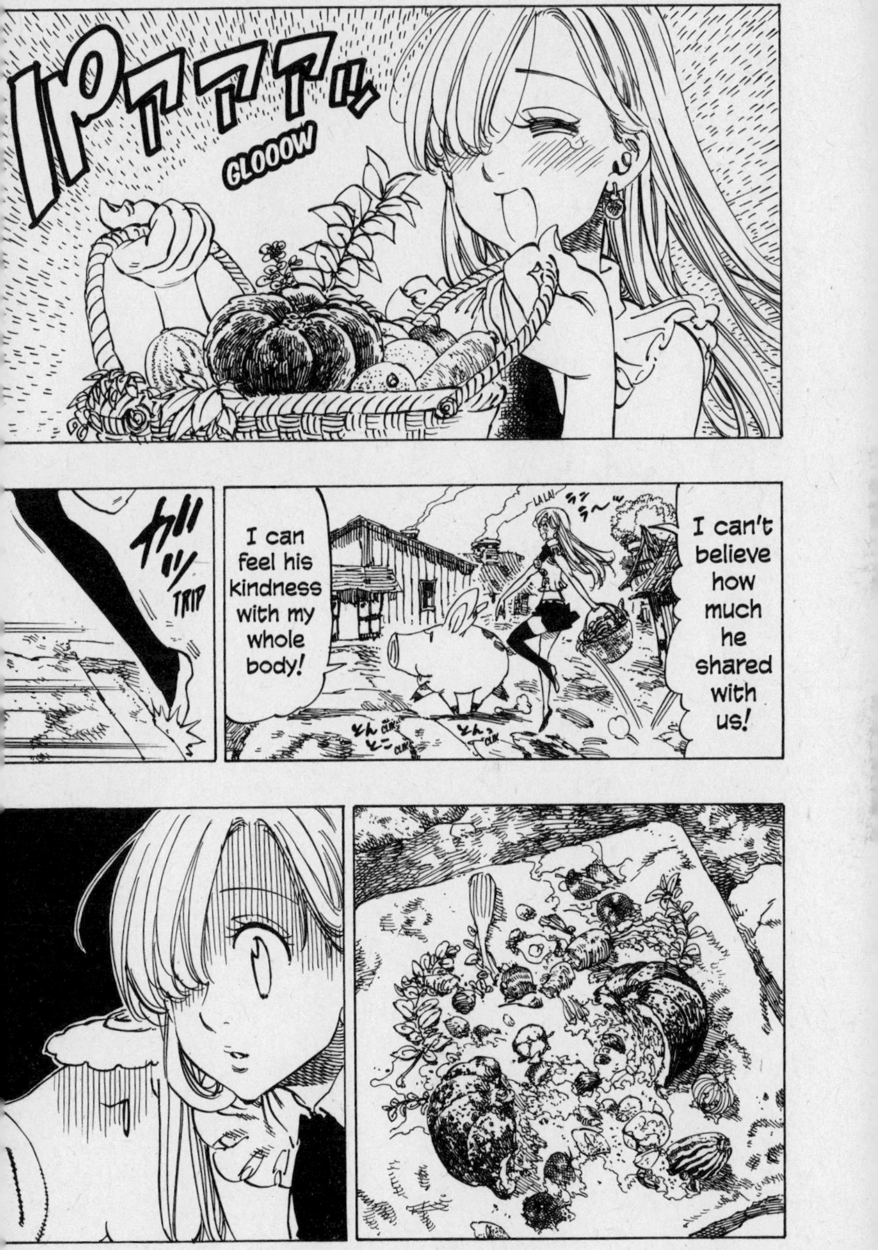
GLOOOW
I can't believe how much he shared with us!
LA LA!
I can feel his kindness with my whole body!
TRIP

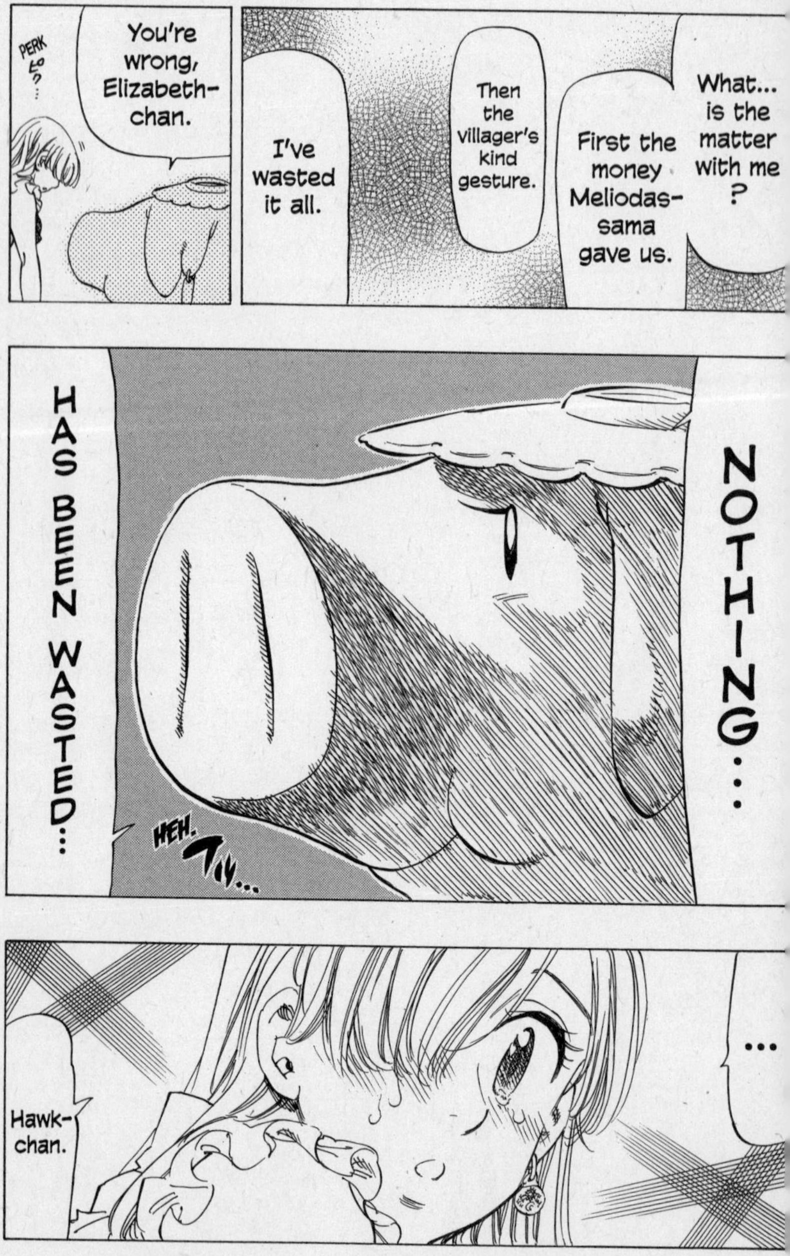
What... is the matter with me?
First the money Meliodas-sama gave us.
Then the villager's kind gesture.
I've wasted it all.
You're wrong, Elizabeth-chan.
PERK ピク...
NOTHING...
HAS BEEN WASTED...
HEH.
...
Hawk-chan.

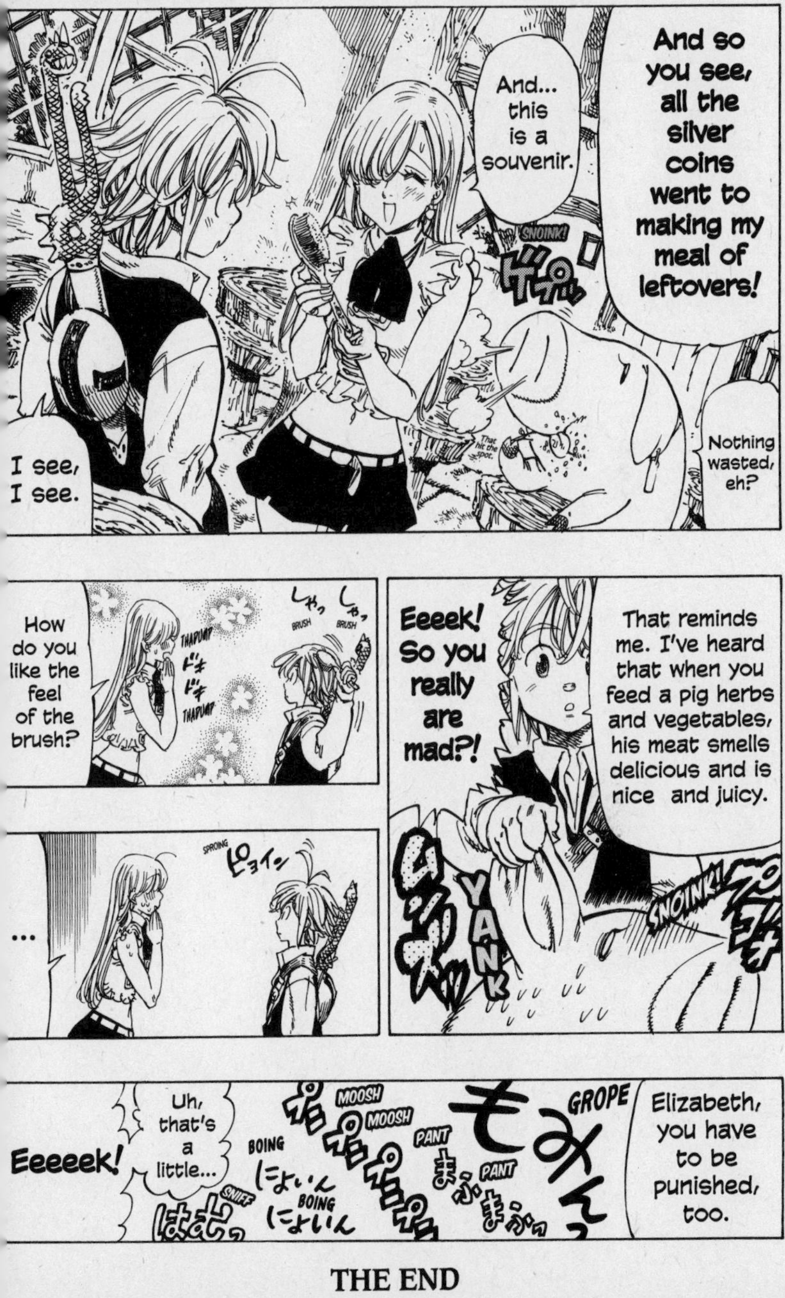
And so you see, all the silver coins went to making my meal of leftovers!
And... this is a souvenir.
SNOINK!
That hit the spot.
Nothing wasted, eh?
I see, I see.
That reminds me. I've heard that when you feed a pig herbs and vegetables, his meat smells delicious and is nice and juicy.
Eeeek! So you really are mad?!
YANK
SNOINK!
BRUSH
BRUSH
THAPUMP
THAPUMP
How do you like the feel of the brush?
SPROING
...
Elizabeth, you have to be punished, too.
GROPE
PANT
PANT
MOOSH
MOOSH
BOING
BOING
SNIFF
Uh, that's a little...
Eeeeek!

THE END

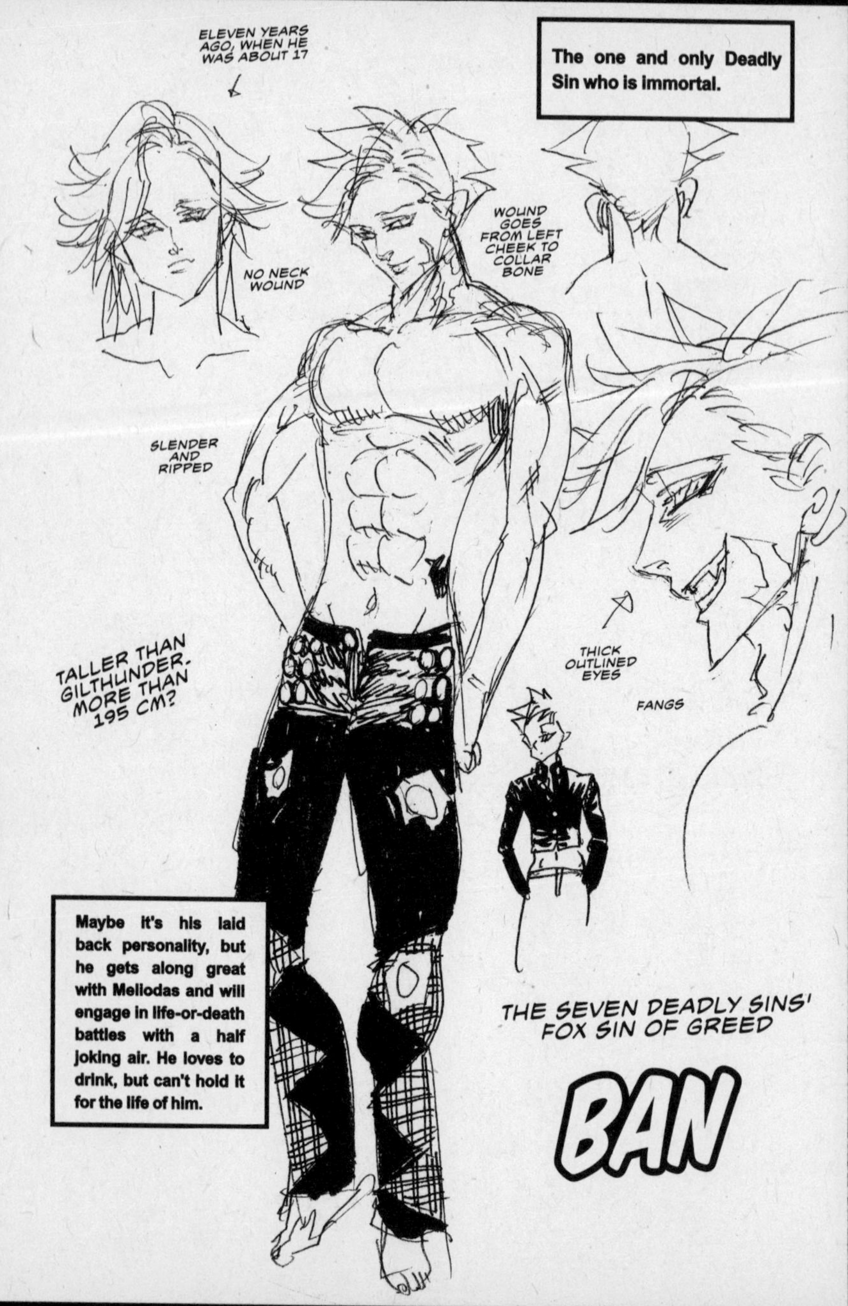
The one and only Deadly Sin who is immortal.
ELEVEN YEARS AGO, WHEN HE WAS ABOUT 17
NO NECK WOUND
WOUND GOES FROM LEFT CHEEK TO COLLAR BONE
SLENDER AND RIPPED
THICK OUTLINED EYES
FANGS
TALLER THAN GILTHUNDER. MORE THAN 195 CM?
Maybe it's his laid back personality, but he gets along great with Meliodas and will engage in life-or-death battles with a half joking air. He loves to drink, but can't hold it for the life of him.
THE SEVEN DEADLY SINS' FOX SIN OF GREED
BAN

なな"THE SEVEN DEADLY SINS"
ILLUSTRATION CORNER

"THE DRAWING KNIGHTHOOD" SPACE

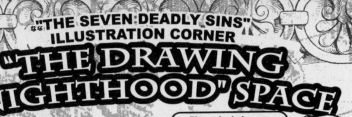

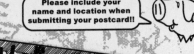

Please include your name and location when submitting your postcard!!

M =
H =
E =
D =
B =

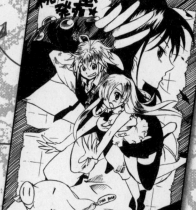

IWATE PREFECTURE, RION-SAN

祝1巻発売★
STAR BEAR
これからも応援してます♥

SPECIAL PRIZE

Not only is there a lot of attention to detail, but it's very dynamic. Wonderful!

And of course, I'm the coolest looking one!

Nah-uh, it's me. See?

Both of you, calm down! Say what you like, it's obviously me!

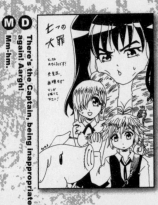

OSAKA, MAYU KURAHA-SAN

七つの大罪

D There's the Captain, being inappropriate again! Aargh!

M Mm-hm.

H Could you care any less?!

KANAGAWA PREFECTURE, AIO OBARA-SAN

the Seven deadly sins
Fox Sin BAN

H Nice body!! ...Though not as nice as mine.

ALL ....

H Why're you all looking at me like that?!

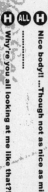

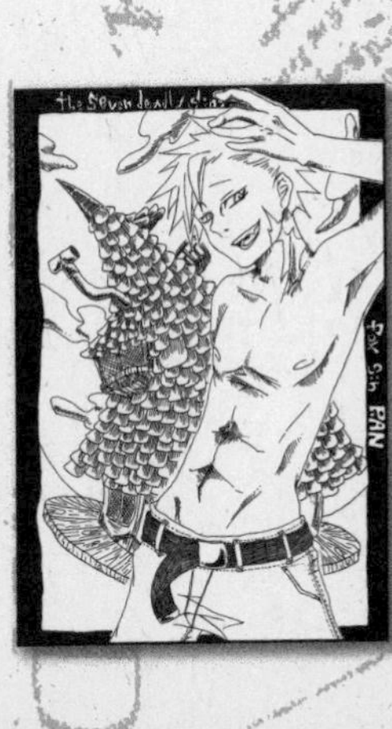

Ooh, collage work!

Does that mean they love me most?!

Don't think too highly of yourself.

MIE PREFECTURE, HEAD-IN-THE-SAND-SAN

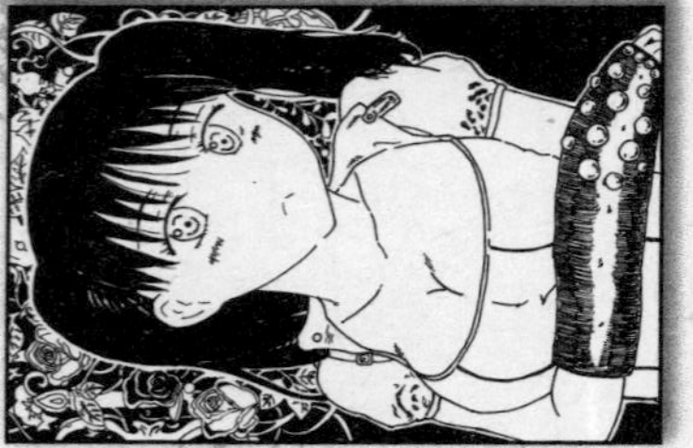

H: Just how big is your bust measurement?

D: You never ask a girl that!

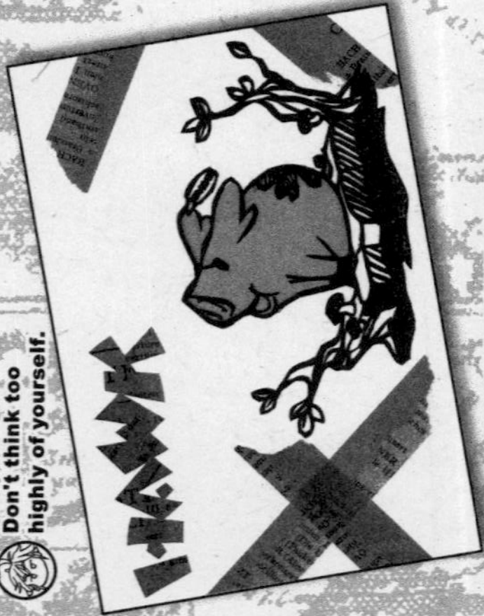

HAWK

AICHI PREFECTURE, ARATA ITOU-SAN

OSAKA, KOROMARU-SAN

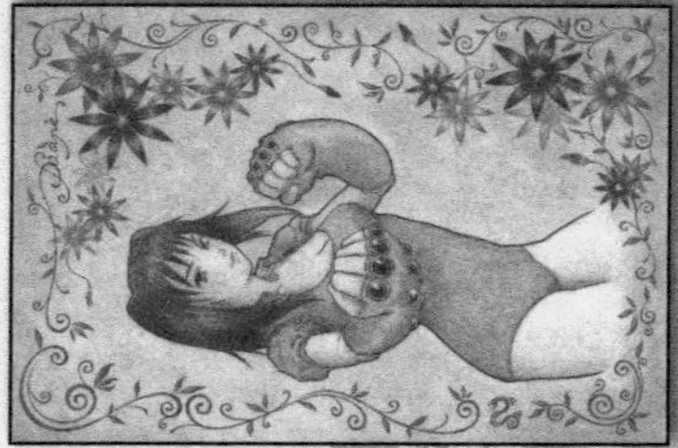

E: It's a shame that we can't show the color version of this one!

D: Wow, even the flowers were done by hand!

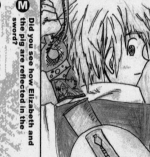

SAITAMA PREFECTURE, RIKU TAKENOYA-SAN

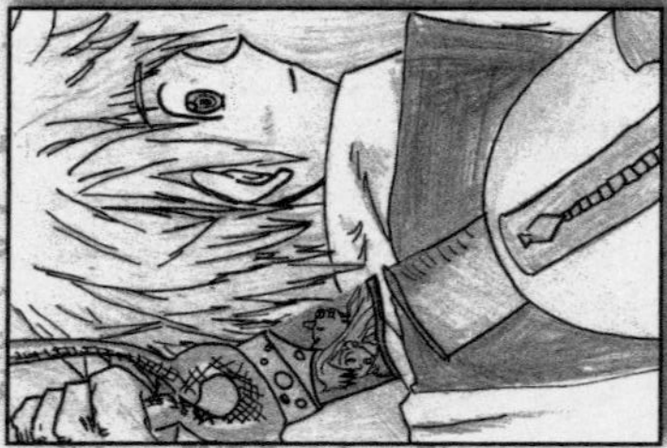

M: Did you see how Elizabeth and the pig are reflected in the sword?

H: ..."the pig"?

KANAGAWA PREFECTURE, TATSURIN-SAN

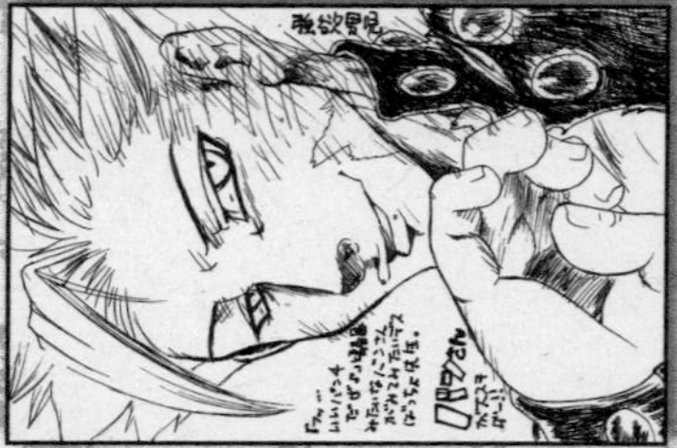

M: It's got the smug look you always have on.

B: Well, Cap'n ♪ Maybe if you tried hitting puberty for once...

IBARAKI PREFECTURE, KAYOGAYO-SAN

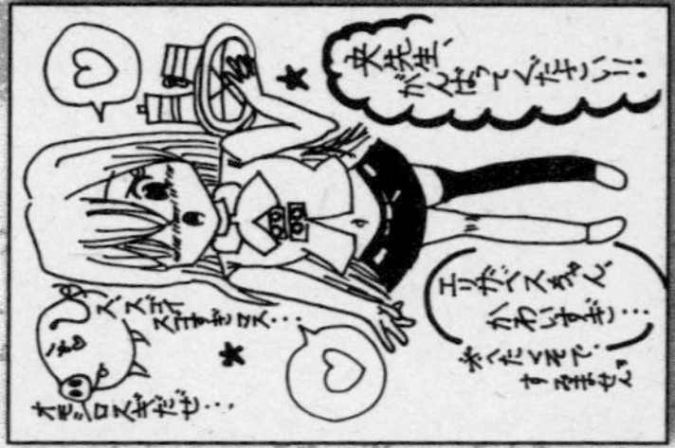

央先生、がんばってください!!

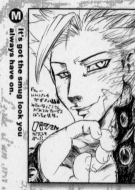

H: Times like this I'm so happy we've got such a great drawing card.

M: And the uniform I chose for her has been quite a hit, don't you think?

OSAKA, AACHI SAKI-SAN

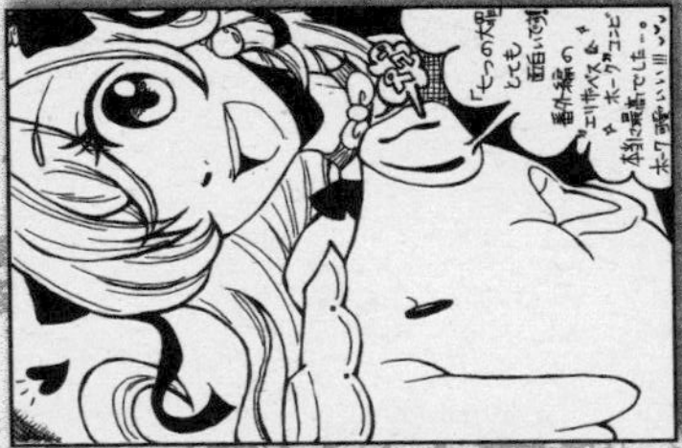

M You two really make a good team.

E Aaw...

M Why do you look so put out?

AICHI PREFECTURE, MADOKA KANEKO-SAN

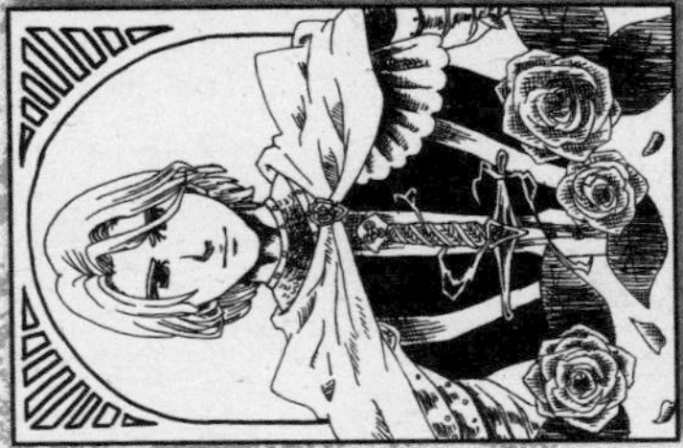

H Darn this pig jerk!! I'll pummel him next time I see him!

M ...You're only chance of winning would be if you attacked him in his sleep.

TOKYO, KEIKO KUROZAWA-SAN

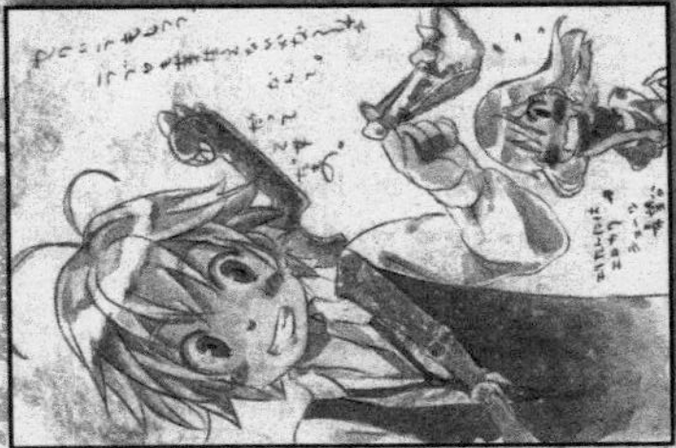

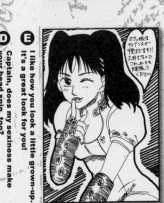

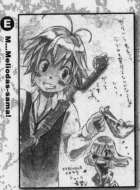

E M...Meliodas-sama!

M Meh.

H You perverted shopkeeper!

TOCHIGI PREFECTURE, RIRIKA YAMANAKA

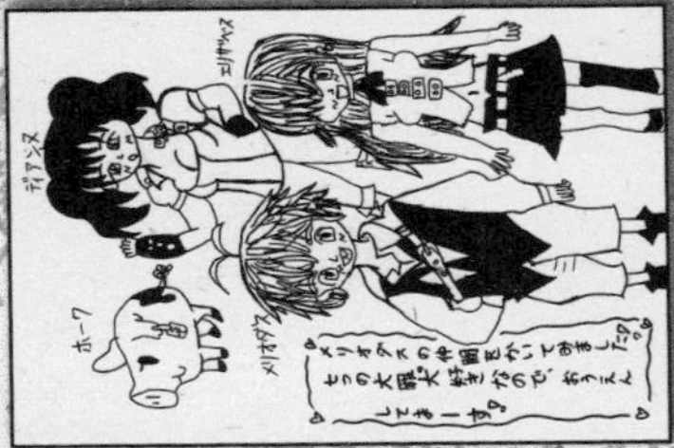
ディアンヌ
エリザベス
ホーク
メリオダス

M We've got to find the other Deadly Sins and fast.

D I wouldn't mind if it was just you and me.

NAGASAKI PREFECTURE, HIIKO-SAN

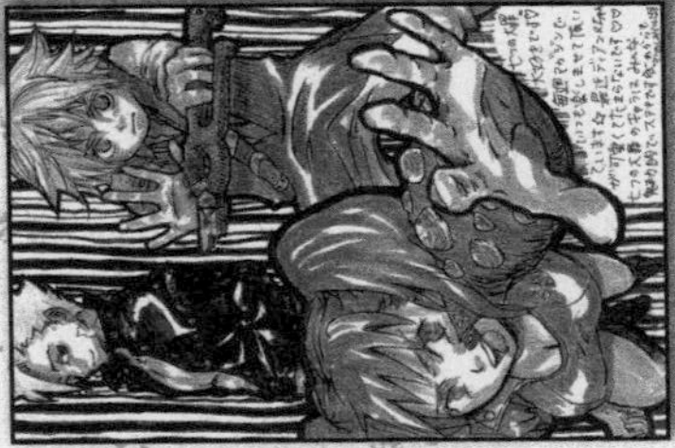

E This has a cool feel to it, like it's saying "the battle begins!"

H I wonder which of these three is the strongest.

FUKUOKA PREFECTURE, MINAKO MATSUO-SAN

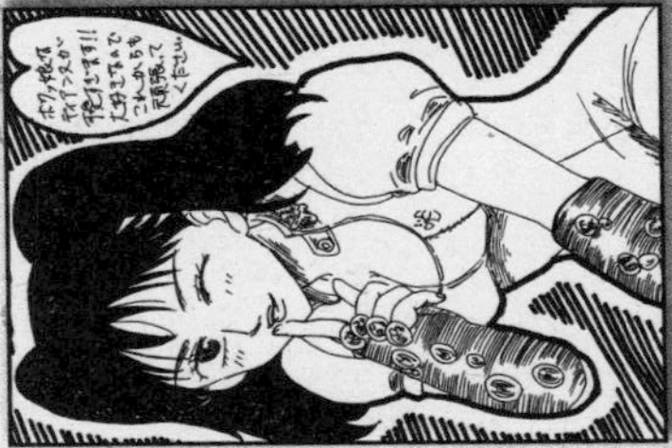

E I like how you look a little grown-up. It's a great look for you!

D Captain, does my sexiness make your head spin, too?

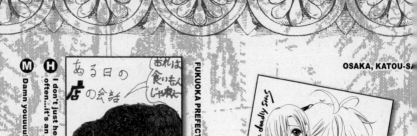

OSAKA, KATOU-SA

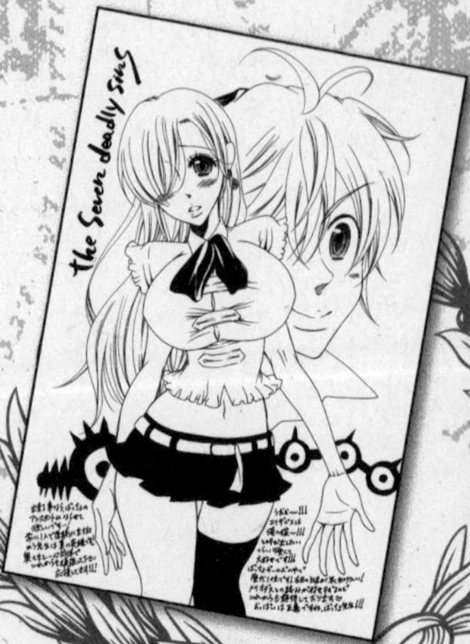
The Seven deadly Sins

Wait a second, Captain...Where are yo looking? At her breasts, aren't you?!

Mm-hm.

....

FUKUOKA PREFECTURE, IORI SUENAGA-SAN

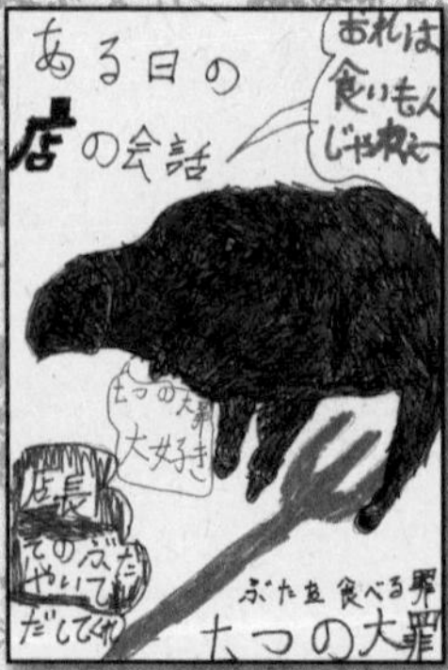
ある日の
店の会話
七つの大罪

H I don't just hear that just every so often...it's an everyday conversation!

M Damn youuuu!

YAMAGUCHI PREFECTURE, HARUNA HARADA

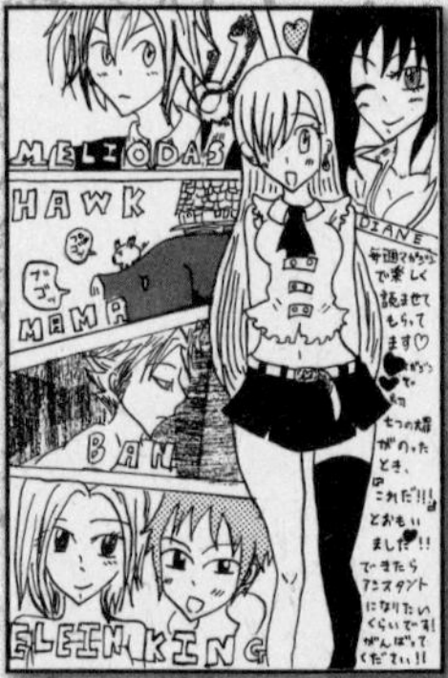
MELIODAS
HAWK
MAMA
DIANE
BAN
ELEIN KING

M Ban, what on earth did you do?

B Kah kah! ♪ You wanna know? It's a secret. ♪

Now Accepting Applicants for the Drawing Knighthood!

- Draw your picture on a postcard, or paper no larger than a postcard, and send it in!
- Don't forget to write your name and location on the back of your picture!
- You can include comments or not. And colored illustrations will still only be displayed in black and white!
- The Drawing Knights whose pictures are particularly noteworthy and run in the print edition will be gifted with a signed specially made pencil board! And the best overall will be granted the special prize of a signed shikishi!!

Kodansha Weekly Shonen Magazine
Re: The Seven Deadly Sins Drawing Knighthood
2-12-21 Otowa Bukyo-ku, Tokyo 112-8001

* Submitted letters and postcards will be given to the artist. Please be aware that your name, address and other personal information included will be given as well.

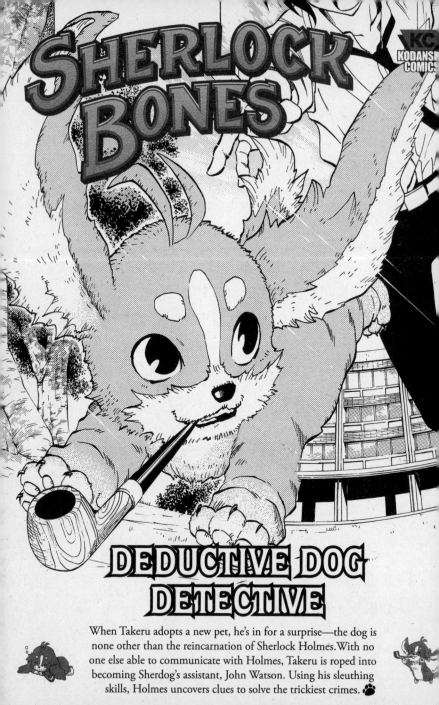

SHERLOCK BONES

KC KODANSHA COMICS

DEDUCTIVE DOG DETECTIVE

When Takeru adopts a new pet, he's in for a surprise—the dog is none other than the reincarnation of Sherlock Holmes. With no one else able to communicate with Holmes, Takeru is roped into becoming Sherdog's assistant, John Watson. Using his sleuthing skills, Holmes uncovers clues to solve the trickiest crimes.

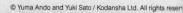

P9-ELW-142

The Seven Deadly Sins volume 3 is a work of fiction. Names, characters, places, and incidents are the products of the author's imagination or are used fictitiously. Any resemblance to actual events, locales, or persons, living or dead, is entirely coincidental.

A Kodansha Comics Trade Paperback Original.

The Seven Deadly Sins volume 3 copyright © 2013 Nakaba Suzuki
English translation copyright © 2014 Nakaba Suzuki

All rights reserved.

Published in the United States by Kodansha Comics, an imprint of Kodansha USA Publishing, LLC, New York.

Publication rights for this English edition arranged through Kodansha Ltd., Tokyo.

First published in Japan in 2013 by Kodansha Ltd., Tokyo.

ISBN 978-1-61262-925-4

Printed in the United States of America.

www.kodanshacomics.com

9 8 7 6 5 4 3 2 1

Translator: Christine Dashiell
Lettering: James Dashiell